The Asiar
on Hol.
Action

The Asian Influence on Hollywood Action Films

BARNA WILLIAM DONOVAN

McFarland & Company, Inc., Publishers
Jefferson, North Carolina, and London

LIBRARY OF CONGRESS CATALOGUING-IN-PUBLICATION DATA

Donovan, Barna William, 1970–
    The Asian influence on Hollywood action films /
Barna William Donovan.
      p.   cm.
    Includes bibliographical references and index.

    ISBN 978-0-7864-3403-9

    softcover : 50# alkaline paper ∞

    1. Adventure films — United States — History and criticism.
2. Adventure films — Asia — History and criticism.   I. Title.
PN1995.9.A3D66   2008
791.43'6582 — dc22   2008026489

British Library cataloguing data are available

On the cover: Chow Yun-Fat in the 1998 film *The Replacement Killers*
(Columbia Pictures/Photofest)

Manufactured in the United States of America

McFarland & Company, Inc., Publishers
  Box 611, Jefferson, North Carolina 28640
   www.mcfarlandpub.com

Table of Contents

Preface

This book is a study of action films. It's a study of high-adrenaline, double-barreled, martial arts–using, sword-fighting, vengeance-seeking action films. It takes a look at a genre of entertainment that is often overlooked by media and film scholars, but one that is the most popular in movie houses and video rental establishments the world over. Action films are also Hollywood's main export to the world. However, films like this are also the most prominent and successful genre of a number of Asian countries, and in several key moments in cinematic history, Asian action films have given Hollywood a serious challenge in the competition for the world's moviegoing audiences.

How can the world's most powerful and wealthiest filmmaking industry be challenged so easily by foreign media? More precisely, how can Hollywood be challenged so easily by a handful of low-budget film companies in places like Hong Kong and Thailand? What can we conclude about the nature of globalization, cultural influences, and the power of audiences when in less than a decade's time we have seen what film scholar David Bordwell calls the "Hong Kongification of American cinema"?[1]

This book hopes to probe the issue by looking at how Asian films, specifically action-oriented films, have not only become the most popular and influential in the world, but had a serious impact on the look, the sound, the feel, the aesthetics of Hollywood filmmaking. Several times over the last four decades, and most recently in the 1990s, Asian action/adventure films have prompted Hollywood to virtually rewrite its rules on story-telling. This book will try and examine how such sea-change events can come about so suddenly in a film industry that has been dominating the world entertainment market for nearly a century.

Furthermore, understanding the relationship between global audiences and action films is crucial because action/adventure is also an extremely controversial genre — or it has the power to ignite heated controversy in the U.S.

at least with predictable regularity. Since action films are founded mainly on the depictions of violent behavior, they are often vilified and used as a convenient scapegoat for most of society's ills. Ironically, as the U.S. has seen a steady, decades-long decline in its crime rates, stoking anti-media moral panics and censorious paranoia has been the favorite pastime of a surprisingly diverse coalition of activists. From the liberal left to the conservative right, hating the media is fashionable and worrying about the "destructive" effects of "all that sex and violence" is a mark of the virtuous person in modern America. By looking at the global traffic in violent action films, this book will try and bring a new perspective to this contentious issue as well.

This book, therefore, is a study of the most prominent and influential personalities in Asian action cinema and the relationship they had with Hollywood. It will look at the process that brought about their films, how they came to the attention of American audiences, and why they were able to influence Hollywood filmmaking to the degree they did.

There is much more, of course, to Asian cinema than action films. I wholeheartedly urge readers to take advantage of every opportunity to immerse themselves in the rich and vibrant cinema, art and culture of Japan, China, Taiwan, Korea, Thailand and all the nations of the Pacific Rim. However, the fact remains that most of the exchange between the East and West has been through the action film genre. The most significant impact on Hollywood has come from Asian action directors and stars. Studying the cultural exchange between the U.S. and Asia could lead to the compilation of a library-full of material, so this book will try and do a thorough job in focusing on one specific area of the East-West connection.

A note on the identification of Japanese and Chinese individuals throughout the book: Since the Japanese may write their names with the family name either first or last, Japanese personalities are all identified with the surname placed after the given name. Most of the famous filmmakers and actors discussed herein are already known that way to Americans. For example, most are familiar with Akira Kurosawa and not Kurosawa Akira.

In the case of Chinese names, however, the surname will always be put first because that is how the Chinese *always* identify themselves. The only exception to that rule is when they adopt a Western name. For example, Chan Kong-sang's family name is Chan and it will always be listed first. However, once he takes the name Jackie, he is identified only as Jackie Chan.

1

Why Asian Action Matters

Film students can be a tough audience to please, especially when it comes to genre entertainment. They will usually expect a film to test the edges of the genre. They will be looking for the director to bring a certain personal flair to the film. Will that director be able to rise above mere hack-work? this audience will ask, as well as they should. Can the director make the genre his own?

In 1993, Hong Kong action film director John Woo went to screen his film *Hard Boiled* at the University of Miami film school. *Hard Boiled* was the last film he made in Hong Kong before relocating to Hollywood. At the time of his appearance in Miami, Woo had just helmed Jean-Claude Van Damme's *Hard Target*.

There was curiosity in the audience before *Hard Boiled* screened. There was also some skepticism. The skepticism wasn't so much about the fact that they were about to be shown a crime film. The audience wasn't a group of elitist art snobs looking down upon a pedestrian genre like cop action films. But word had gotten around that Woo had a reputation for making the action in his films look extreme. *This* was what set expectations very high. Filmmakers testing the limits of screen violence had already gone far in the U.S. A generation ago, filmmakers like George Romero and Wes Craven and Tobe Hooper had already gone the distance with blood and gore in their independent horror films. Not to mention that in the early '90s, Quentin Tarantino had just become the darling of independent filmmakers with his anarchic, ultra-violent movies. The film students, as a matter of fact, were already doing their best to imitate him in their screenwriting classes. The concern before Woo's film started to roll was whether or not the Hong Kong filmmaker had what it took to surprise a jaded American group already used to far-out spectacle.

By the time the film was over, the film students were in awe. One might have expected a rowdy, loud, over-stimulated crowd, considering what had just unfolded in the theater. Instead, there was quiet all across the auditorium. Then a question broke the silence. "Why would you want to come and work in Hollywood when in Hong Kong you can make films like this?"

It was a good question. It was something I thought of myself since I too was in the audience, one of the film students. I, too, had wandered into the screening with a critical eye, after all. As an action film fan, I was skeptical about whether or not this foreign effort would live up to the very high American standards. After all, I had usually haunted the action film aisles of the local video stores and seen all installments of the *Rambo* (1983, 1985, 1988), *Terminator* (1984, 1991, 2003) and *Die Hard* (1988, 1990, 1995, 2007) series available up until that point a countless number of times.

But sitting through this screening, I experienced a bloody, apocalyptic epiphany. I had seen the new yardstick against which all other action films would be measured.

Hard Boiled distilled the essence of the action genre and overwhelmed the viewer with two hours of destruction elevated to art form like no other film had ever done. The essence of an action film is *action*—meaning *violence*—the *Time* magazine movie critic, Richard Schickel, writes.[1] But no American director had understood that as well as John Woo. Or maybe others just never had the guts to film violence as well as John Woo. "Well" in the sense that viewing fast paced, savage, destructive ultra violence can be *fun*. As much as we—or many of us, at least—like to put forth a façade of gentility, pretend to frown on and condemn aggression in film, it can be excellent, anarchic, exhilarating *fun*. Viewing violence when we know that it is not real can be enjoyable. This is what John Woo had the gumption to admit with *Hard Boiled*. If an audience comes to see stylized violence in an action film, *Hard Boiled* delivers exactly that. Chow Yun Fat had often said in interviews that the film is about 30 percent story and 70 percent action.[2]

Hard Boiled, in fact, is *about* action in its purest sense. It examines every possible way, every possible angle and speed destruction can be filmed. The picture ruminates on the ways holes can be blasted in walls, furniture, cars, and people. It dwells on the way splashing gouts of blood can be photographed spraying from writhing, spasming bodies. *Hard Boiled* revels in the art of anarchy for two hours, pausing on occasion, very briefly, very economically, to show a pair of conflicted heroes grappling with identity, honor and brotherhood.

Needless to say, I rushed to see *Hard Target* (1993) as soon as I could afterward, getting just about what I was expecting. Filmed in Hollywood, *Hard Target* appeared to be a pale imitation of the style that lit up the screen in *Hard Boiled*. Like a photocopy that is not quite as sharp as the original, *Hard Target* was more like an eager fan paying homage to Woo than a true

John Woo original. Re-edited a countless number of times to please the MPAA ratings board and avoid an NC-17 mark, the film has violence aplenty, yet appears sluggish, just lacking passion. In other words, it's very American.

The 1990s' migration of Asian filmmakers and stars, particularly from Hong Kong, created one of the biggest stylistic overhauls of American cinema since the Spaghetti Westerns shook up the venerable horse operas in the 1960s and the film school-trained Baby Boomers rose to power in the late '60s and '70s. Just like the '60s brought forth a generation of filmmakers around the world who had an impact on film style that's felt to this day, from Sergio Leone and the Italian Westerns and Akira Kurosawa's samurai films to such international art house favorites as Antonioni, Bergman, Fellini, Godard, and Truffaut, films from the East are now putting an indelible mark on Hollywood, starting with the action/adventure genre.

Anyone taking even a passing glance at the latest Hollywood action adventure films will quickly recognize them as an art form of highly stylized violence that gladly abandons most semblances to reality in favor of sheer, exhilarating spectacle.[3] Reality is ignored now, in fact, even more than it had ever been in such genre classics as the *Rambo* or *Die Hard* action extravaganzas in the 1980s. Action heroes today routinely perform physical feats that are beyond the abilities of mere mortals. They outrun explosions and face off against overwhelming numbers of opponents while defying the laws of gravity. They routinely soar through the air, shooting two guns at a time. From the slow motion showdowns of *Mission: Impossible 2* (2000) to the computerized martial arts of the *Matrix* films, today's top action movies are all borrowing their visual hyperbole, their choreography of mayhem, from Hong Kong, Taiwanese and Japanese cinema. In the East, where surreal filmmaking sought to recreate a colorful, fantastic version of the world rather than present lifelike reality, radically over-the-top action movies have been filmed for decades. By the 1990s, however, Hollywood had begun to take notice. To fully understand why American audiences were now able to embrace such offbeat renderings of one of their favorite genres, we should return to John Woo's two *Hard* films for another moment.

Hard Target appears to be a homogenized, half-hearted exercise. Most of all, looking at the film's individual parts, its scenes, its moments of action, editing and overall *feel*, *Hard Target* appears to be inconsistent. It looks as if someone at the helm of the vehicle had badly lost his way. The film's action sequences are blunted by what appears to be a schizophrenic attitude toward violence, an incomprehensible Puritanical hypocrisy. Many of the cuts made just don't seem to make any sense. For example, the MPAA censors allowed plenty of scenes of characters firing guns, yet they forced the removal of a scene where a villain walks through a wall of flames while firing his gun.

Characters getting shot and killed are depicted many times, yet one scene where a wounded character pulls an arrow from his shoulder had to be left on the cutting room floor.[4]

The objection over the arrow scene is odd, especially when action film aficionados recall the classic wound-treatment scene in *Rambo III* back in 1988. There, not only is a bullet gouged out of a gushing wound in Sylvester Stallone's side, but gunpowder is inserted into the flesh and lit to cauterize the wound. This gruesome scene of self-administered surgery is filmed in a series of very tight close-ups, pushing the audience's face right into the blood and gore. *Rambo III* had no problem getting the R-rating, however.

But other examples of the MPAA's peculiar attitude toward *Hard Target* include green-lighting a scene of a man getting shot and falling into a river, yet the forced removal of a follow-up scene where the man's corpse is seen floating face down in the water. One character is allowed to be shot, yet he cannot be shown getting kicked after the shooting. Another villain is shot by Van Damme, but a follow-up scene where he delivers a Schwarzeneggeresque one-liner, "Give it up, pal," had to be excised.[5]

As the *Variety* (1993) review summed up, "Ultimately, *Hard Target* is a compromised work, a stylistic hybrid of the American and Hong Kong action pics. But Woo's distinctiveness is still in evidence. He is a virtuoso at staging and editing intricate set pieces with precision, visual inventiveness, and humor."[6]

Universal, the studio releasing *Hard Target*, dutifully went through with the film's mauling according to the MPAA's bizarre instructions because of very basic economic reasons. The NC-17 rating would have hurt the film's box office. Many newspapers don't advertise NC-17 films.[7] The major theater chains don't carry such films, nor do the large video store chains. Nevertheless, these economic pressures created a dulled, watered-down version of a unique vision of an action film. These same pressures, however, have always had the tendency to dull and homogenize all Hollywood films, so much so that American audiences, at various moments, will hunger for a truly unique vision, something coming from outside the proverbial box.

It is during those moments that foreign filmmakers have always established themselves in the U.S. Moments like that have always profoundly affected Hollywood art.

Hard Target, for all its compromises, was still a successful film and American audiences and critics quickly recognized a truly special talent in John Woo. As Georgia Brown wrote in the *Village Voice*, "still, mercifully, it has his signature, even if smudged with some letters erased.... Even so, *Hard Target* has real style as well as terrific kinetic sequences, and I'll take it over all other summer pix any humid day."[8]

John Woo's version of action, displayed in *Hard Target*, was that first important outside-the-box vision, to be followed up by *Broken Arrow* (1996) and *Face/Off* (1997), that captured audiences' imaginations by feeding the desire for something that breaks the safe, expected, oft-repeated Hollywood formulas. The very look and feel of American suspense and action films were transformed remarkably in the wake of John Woo's first move into the Hollywood system.

While the advent of Woo and the Asian influence is similar to the European influence of the Spaghetti Westerns, it is also different in a key way. Unlike the producers of the Spaghetti Westerns, this time the overseas filmmakers have actually relocated to Hollywood. This was not so in the '60s. Rather, as in the case of the Baby Boomer–directors, the relocation of Woo, along with other directors like Ang Lee and stars like Jackie Chan and Jet Li, Hollywood's co-opting of the Asian action style seems to have permanently altered the Hollywood approach to its most lucrative genre.

Looking at the Asian influence on American films, one can learn some interesting lessons about how the Hollywood machinery functions, when it thrives and when it falters both creatively and financially. The exercise paints a vivid picture of global media today and over the past century. The history of Asian cinematic impact will reveal a long process of cross-cultural artistic influence. The typical Hollywood style, after all, was shaped by immigrants, like Ernst Lubitsch, Joseph Von Sternberg, Charlie Chaplin and Alfred Hitchcock in the classic era, as well as John Schlesinger, John Boorman, Ken Russell, Nicholas Roeg, Milos Forman and Roman Polanski in the '60s and '70s.[9] It is the '90s, however, the post–Cold War world of fading borders and global media, when not only was the world being flooded with more American media, but the door was opened for more foreigners to be noticed by Hollywood and be invited in to practice their craft.

How the Revolution Was Born

Connoisseurs of the action/adventure film might look back at the early 1990s as both the best of times and the worst of times. It was the beginning of the digital era, the days of *Terminator 2* and *Jurassic Park* (1993). Unfortunately, it was also the era of *Last Action Hero* (1993) ... and the problems of *Hard Target*.

A genre built on spectacle and stunts, action/adventure films are supposed to thrive on special effects innovations. Nevertheless, the innovations that would make films like the *Jurassic Park* series, or the *Matrix* (1999, 2003) films at the turn of the millennium, record-setting blockbusters also marked a stagnation in the genre, if not an artistic stagnation in the film industry itself. By the 1990s, spectacle and technology had, surprisingly, drained action films of a lot of the energy, wit or impact delivered by many of the 1970s and '80s standard-setters like the *Dirty Harry* (1971, 1973, 1976, 1983, 1988), *Lethal Weapon* (1987, 1989, 1992, 1998), *Rambo* and *Die Hard* franchises.

Hollywood filmmaking, not unlike other creative media, is a highly precarious, volatile and often unpredictable interplay of financial pressures, artistic temperament, societal trends and the ever unpredictable tastes and whims of audiences. But major evolutions in Hollywood product eventually come about when the so-called dark side of the industry, the financial obligations and pressures, first overwhelms the artistic temperament. As Mandalay Pictures chief Peter Guber has enthusiastically remarked, quite often, Hollywood *must* be understood by all the critics and scholars and analysts and cultural commentators as show *business*. "It's not show *show*," Guber likes to say, "it's show *business*."[10] Thus, show *business* will always attempt to function the same way any other business functions. It will attempt to create a conveyor belt assembly system where a steady stream of product, of uniform quality and predictability, will be turned out at a fast and nearly endless pace. But there the seeds of the system's major problems are sown.

Unfortunately — or maybe fortunately, for those with very deep artistic inclinations and impulses —filmmaking, cultural production, is *not* exactly like all other businesses. A cultural, artistic product can not be treated like any other assembly line creation. However, the business side of the show/business balance will always try and quantify the unquantifiable. The early "studio system," in fact, was created as this sort of assembly line approach to filmmaking.[11] In time, however, the conveyor belt will begin unloading vapid, formulaic, irrelevant cultural product. Quantifying an unquantifiable like a film, an idea, a story, will create rigid, soulless formulas artists will ache to break out of. In the right moments in history, they will do just that. It happened in the 1960s and it has been happening since the early '90s.

In the 1960s, the conveyor belt began falling apart, setting up a radical change in the way Hollywood films looked. The competition the major studios had been facing from television since the '50s was reaching a dangerous level, and the kinds of films Hollywood produced failed to stand up to the challenge. The studios' response to the TV threat was to spend more money. Garish, wide-screen color spectacles with expensive stars, expensive sets, stunts, special effects and "casts of thousands" were supposed to be the "event" pictures that enticed audiences out of their living rooms and into the movie theater. Movies like *The Bible* (1966), *The Greatest Story Ever Told* (1965), *Hawaii* (1966), *Krakatoa, East of Java* (1969), *Camelot* (1967), *Dr. Dolittle* (1967), and *Song of Norway* (1970) lumbered onto the big screens in displays of overpriced excess.[12]

But the solution didn't entirely solve the problem, because the studio bosses in the '60s no longer understood the problem. Simply, the safe, expensive, traditional Hollywood entertainment, the massive "event" pictures, at their core, were out of touch with the audiences. Precisely, they were out of touch with an enormous audience segment coming into its own as a very powerful economic force. The youth market, the Baby Boomers in their teens and twenties who were chafing from the rigid cultural conservatism of American society, was not spending its money on the over-hyped event films. They were not even interested in the stars their parents had been fans of. As discussed by Peter Biskind in his seminal work on the entry of the Baby Boom generation into the film business, *Easy Riders, Raging Bulls: How the Sex, Drugs and Rock 'n' Roll Generation Saved Hollywood*, as the Vietnam War escalated and degenerated into a chaotic quagmire, the young revolted against their parents' world and politics not only through free love, drugs and protest, but by rejecting their films and the conservative values they represented. While young people burned draft cards, marched on Washington and experimented with LSD and pot, Hollywood insisted on turning out cute bedroom comedies starring Rock Hudson and Doris Day, Biblical epics, musicals, old-fashioned Westerns, and rousing World War II sagas revolting to the young radicals. In the '60s, the aging moguls who had founded the studio system were still in power and they simply didn't get it. As Biskind recalls the impact on the film business, the late '60s saw Hollywood's box-office profits decimated by the studios' cultural cluelessness. Quoting *Variety* editor Peter Bart, "the movie industry was more on its ass than in any time in its history, literally about to be wiped off the face of the earth."[13]

What saved the industry were films that discarded the traditional formulas or showed outright disdain for them. Warren Beatty's *Bonnie and Clyde* (1967) and Dennis Hopper's *Easy Rider* (1969) were among these films. *Easy Rider* glorified the drug culture and rebellion while co-opting Western imagery and archetypes like the loners and outlaws running from a stifling, corrupt civilization. *Bonnie and Clyde* subverted the classical gangster genre. It used its criminal antiheroes as stand-ins for the '60s' rebellious youth and shocked viewers with its brutal ending.

As far back as 1960, producers Walter Mirisch and star Yul Brynner had sensed that Westerns, in their formulaic, strict and moralistic execution, as seen in the John Wayne and Gary Cooper films, were becoming passé. They bought the rights to and adapted Japanese director Akira Kurosawa's *Seven Samurai* (*Shichinin no Samurai*, 1954) to the Old West.[14] *The Magnificent Seven*'s (1960) protagonists often doubted themselves and their brutal profession. They watched with a great deal of disdain as the wild frontier was turning into something unpleasant and hypocritical with the advent of civilization.

There was never any self doubt, nor doubt about the progress and growth of American culture, in a John Wayne Western.

Sergio Leone's Spaghetti Western "Man with No Name" trilogy (1964, 1965, 1966) found American distribution because it starred Clint Eastwood. Since Eastwood played the popular heartthrob character in the TV Western *Rawhide*, and the Leone films were already smash hit successes in Europe, United Artists distributed them in the U.S.[15] The American success of the Leone trilogy, in turn, would help alter the look and feel of Westerns while Hollywood was in the midst of seeing the youth culture wresting power from the aging founders. Most importantly, the Leone films were also breaking the rules of the traditional Western as they set Eastwood up as both John Wayne's successor and antithesis. The Eastwood protagonist of the Leone Westerns was morally ambiguous, greedy and cynical, whereas the Western heroes of the previous age were America's gallant knights in spurs and chaps. As Wayne had always insisted, a Western hero always had to stand for all *The Values That Made America Great*. The Eastwood heroes, on the other hand, were cold, self-interested and ruthless. They were out for themselves, not to help carve a glorious nation out of the savage wilderness.

By the 1990s, filmmaking, especially action filmmaking, had come to reflect a lot of the '60s rather uncannily. Making movies became a process of giant budgets and tiny ideas, astounding special effects and stunt innovations coupled with a craven lack of artistic daring and vision. Film historians will often want to go further back in time, to the mid– to late 1970s, and point an accusing finger at the original blockbuster movement. They will quarrel with the first *Jaws* (1975), *Star Wars* (1977), *Superman* (1978), or *Close Encounters of the Third Kind* (1977) and lay the blame for the stifling of vision and originality in Hollywood in the '90s on the unprecedented profits generated by these films. These historians, like Biskind in *Easy Riders*, point to the '70s blockbusters as the moment the Baby Boomers lost their innocence — or, perhaps, the moment they sold their souls. The mid– to late '70s were the time when youth-generation geniuses like Steven Spielberg and George Lucas were no longer the rebels challenging the system but *became* the system. The critics are partly right in this assessment. Once the studios' appetites — or, rather, the appetites of the corporations taking over the studios — had been whetted by the *Jaws* and *Star Wars*–sized box office receipts, there was a demand for more of the same to attempt to replicate the profits. Quantifying the unquantifiable. If special effects and big budgets made for big returns in the case of *Jaws*, *Superman* or *Close Encounters*, then the formula was clear and it needed to be used. Make more movies with big budgets and big special effects, and expect big profits. Then make sequels with even bigger budgets, even more dazzling, noisy special effects, and expect even bigger profits than before. In time, the formula will have eliminated all the character development, wit, surprise or creativity that might have ever existed in the original. In time, even the Baby Boom visionaries gave their corporate bosses the exact blockbusters they were looking for.[16]

This is the point where I part ways with many film critics and historians, as they would scoff at the claim of wit, character development or creativity in the original blockbusters. The fact is that the original *Jaws*, *Superman*, *Close Encounters*, *Star Wars*, along with other '70s era super successes like the first *Rocky* (1976) or *Saturday Night Fever* (1977), were *good* movies. When any of these films turn up on TV or in a new, "deluxe," "special," "never before seen," or "director's cut" edition on DVD, audiences will tune in or buy them in droves. Young people who were not even alive in the '70s are still discovering *Rocky* and *Close Encounters* and *Jaws* even as new films with flashier computer generated image (CGI) special effects and young, hip stars appear. Many of these young filmgoers are even admitting that the first three *Star Wars* films were superior to the current line of CGI-overloaded prequels (1999, 2002, 2005). The original blockbusters were good films made by talented filmmakers with a passion for the art. Even '80s action epics like the original *Rambo*, the original *Die Hard*, *Terminator* and the first *Lethal Weapon* were excellent films. They broke new ground, they went to new places audiences had never been taken. By the 1990s, however, the corporate process, the quantification of the unquantifiable, the reduction of all major studio films to predictable, repetitive, derivative formulas, had been taken to nearly unwatchable extremes.

The ultimate example of the folly of the quantification mindset was 1993's *Last Action Hero*. This was the film that became the *Camelot*, *Hawaii*, or *The Greatest Story Ever Told* of its day: corporate, bloated with excesses, ego, greed, special effects and a cynical lack of regard for the taste and intelligence of audiences.

Released the same summer as *Hard Target*, *Last Action Hero* is a grotesquely overblown mutation of story elements and tones that do not fit together, that should never be combined in any film. As *Variety*'s film critic Todd McCarthy wrote, the picture is "a joyless, soulless machine of a movie."[17] As Nancy Griffin and Kim Masters detail in their book *Hit and Run*, about the Sony takeover of Columbia Pictures and Peter Guber's co-stewardship of the studio with Jon Peters, at the core of *Hero*'s failure lies the fact that it was conceived by studio executives as a giant equation. Combining Arnold Schwarzenegger with action and a fantastic, supernatural plot, putting in a cute, precocious kid, adding comedy, and a PG-13 rating would be the perfect formula to attract action fans, fantasy fans, comedy fans and kids too young to see R-rated films. The equation, in turn, should all add up to massive box-office receipts. Furthermore, the vehicle would be ideal for video game, action figure, clothing and fast food merchandise tie-ins. As Masters and Griffin document, the Sony mantra under the Guber/Peters regime was "synergy." Of course, the film is now in the league of legendary megaton bombs, in the company of *Ishtar* (1987), *Waterworld* (1995), *Dune* (1984), *Hudson Hawk* (1991) and *Howard the Duck* (1986) precisely because of its formula. Radically different elements brought together to please radically different audiences wound up alienating all of them.

Although not all of the '90s megabudget, CGI-enhanced epics were commercial failures, too many of them, by even the most generous artistic standards, were creative failures. For example, the noise and CGI behemoths by the Centropolis production company run by Roland Emmerich and Dean Devlin, the "event" films like *Stargate* (1994), *Independence Day* (1996), *Godzilla* (1998), and 2004's *The Day After Tomorrow* were successful. But they were exactly the same type of soulless, joyless machineries as *Last Action Hero*. Director Stephen Sommers' CGI fests like the *Mummy* (1999, 2001, 2008) films, along with their spin-off, *The Scorpion King* (2002), were likewise successful, but *Good Morning America* critic Joel Siegel said that the films represented everything that is wrong with Hollywood: too much money, too many special effects, and a mindless story. Many of the '90s sequels to some of the most profitable films of the last two decades, including *Jurassic Park*, *Batman* (1989) and *Lethal Weapon*, steadily degenerated into witless repetition, noise and/or moronic, sophomoric humor.

However, just as in the '60s, the past decade has been witness to outsiders filtering into the Hollywood system through sheer originality. The '90s saw the rise of the independent film movement, the Sundance film festival and Miramax Pictures ascending as a major Hollywood power broker by specializing in independent films.

The independent film festival circuits had become the entry point of the latest wave of Asian films. In the U.S., it was actually the art house crowd that first saw John Woo's films.[18] They were the ones who first saw Ang Lee's work, who followed Jackie Chan's films as they put most American action films to shame with the audacity of their stunts. It was this audience that recognized the vision and energy the Asian film community could bring to Hollywood. It was through this independent circuit that Hollywood's own stars and producers took note of the vibrant and rich Asian cinema and invited John Woo and the latest wave of Asian filmmakers and stars into the American market.

Hollywood has long been well aware of Asian cinema, but it was only in the '90s that artists from Japan, Hong Kong, mainland China and Taiwan crossed over in such numbers and changed the look and style of American films. There had been temporary, limited incursions in the past, just as filmmakers in the late '50s and '60s took note of the power of Akira Kurosawa's films. When new waves and new generations of filmmakers shook up Hollywood in its moments of stagnation, there had also been an interest in Asian films. Bruce Lee, for example, caught the attention of American action fans in the early '70s, just as the Baby Boomer filmmakers were taking over. From there on, through the rest of the '70s and '80s, the Asian martial arts had been present in Hollywood. They have often thrived at the B-movie level and sometimes attained A-list visibility and popularity through the fleeting moments of Jean-Claude Van Damme and Steven Seagal in the superstar spotlight, during the ninja craze of the '80s, or during Chuck Norris' tenure as an A-list martial artist action star. But the most substantial impact Asian film art made on American movies came in the '90s. Not only were Asian filmmakers here to stay, but Hollywood was now following their lead in making more exciting, innovative and original action/adventure and fantasy films.

2

The Master: Akira Kurosawa and the Art of Warriors

Not only were a small handful of movies by legendary Japanese director Akira Kurosawa the first Asian films to have a serious influence on Hollywood, but they reveal a complex, two-way relationship between the filmmakers from the East and the West. Kurosawa made a major impression on American directors — on *world* cinema, in effect — with his groundbreaking film *Rashomon*, in 1950, but he would always readily speak of his love for Hollywood films. American movies, American culture, in part, helped shape Kurosawa's storytelling sensibilities, while his movies, in turn, helped establish some of the bedrock conventions of modern American film. More than anything, much of the thematic and stylistic conventions of action filmmaking owe an incredible debt to Akira Kurosawa.

The truth is that the relationship between Asian and Hollywood filmmaking is remarkably cyclical. Today, much of the stylized gun-battles and CGI–enhanced martial arts in the latest Hollywood action/adventure epics borrow their look, feel, sound, and pacing from Hong Kong and Japanese gangster, science fiction and crime thrillers. But the Asian directors, at the same time, sing the praises and reference the works of such Hollywood legends as John Ford, Howard Hawks and, especially, Sam Peckinpah. For example, while the signature style of Hong Kong action might be the slow-motion, two-gunned style of balletic bloodletting, John Woo, the modern king of Hong Kong–style action films, readily credits Peckinpah as his chief inspiration. In truth, Eastern and Western filmmaking has been entwined a lot longer than many realize. The ironic fact is that the real credit for this oft-used staple of action directing, the slow-motion effect, originated in the East, not in the West. Akira Kurosawa had discovered the effectiveness of manipulating the pacing of an action scene by intercutting slow-motion with high-speed violence in his first film, *Sanshiro Sugata* (1943). Peckinpah himself had often readily confessed his admiration for Kurosawa. Analysts of the similarities between the films of Kurosawa and Peckinpah have called the latter an informal student of the Japanese director.[1]

Kurosawa's career, in fact, can be read as a series of highs and lows, moments of glowing critical acclaim — in both Japan and the rest of the world — as well as stinging derision — mostly in Japan — because of his ties to, influence on, and reflections of the West. Most film historians write Akira Kurosawa's epitaph as a filmmaker who, perhaps more than any other, helped the world discover Japanese cinema and Japanese culture, yet at the same time, a filmmaker who was often regarded with cold, critical hostility by many of his own countrymen. His earliest moments of international acclaim had almost immediately drawn condemnation by the Japanese intelligentsia. Near the end of his career, Kurosawa had also been rejected as an irrelevant, reactionary, rear-guard director by young Japanese filmmakers. He became the very symbol of all that modern Japanese film had to overthrow.[2] By the last three decades of his career, he had found it nearly impossible to get a film made through Japanese financing alone. Nevertheless, in the United States filmmakers like George Lucas, Steven Spielberg, Martin Scorsese, and Francis Ford Coppola have hailed him as one of the greatest directors ever to work in the medium. They all confessed to having taken inspiration from Kurosawa's films. In fact, when in the last three decades of his career Kurosawa found it impossible to get financing for his films in Japan alone, Lucas, Coppola, and Spielberg used their clout with American studios to raise funds for *Kagemusa* (1980), *Ran* (1985) and *Dreams* (*Yume*, 1990).[3]

"The term 'giant' is used too often to describe artists," Martin Scorsese said after Kurosawa's death in 1998, "but in the case of Akira Kurosawa, we have one of the rare instances where the term fits."[4] Steven Spielberg called him "the pictorial Shakespeare of our time."[5]

Akira Kurosawa helmed thirty-two films in a career that spanned over five decades, but despite the fact that he is regarded in greater esteem outside of Japan, much of the international movie-going lay public might only be able to name three, perhaps four, films from this extensive body of work. Nevertheless, these films have had an impact whose ripples are still felt in the world of film, ripples that have shaped the foundations of some of the most popular Hollywood genres of all time.

These four films have such a long-standing impact because they have been imitated, borrowed from, and remade so many times. Some of the films they inspired have, in turn, set a standard that subsequent filmmakers would aspire mightily to meet. Yet it is remarkable that film-going audiences still know where the original source material comes from. Kurosawa has never been eclipsed by anyone imitating his work. *Rashomon*, the film that catapulted him to virtually overnight international fame, is an intricate — but not confusing — rumination on the power of subjective experiences and the nature of reality. Although never exactly remade, its basic plot of an event told from several points of view has been imitated by various films, television shows, and even satirical cartoons.[6]

Seven Samurai, Kurosawa's most famous film, was not only remade in 1960 by John Sturges as the iconic American Western, *The Magnificent Seven*, but has been praised by film critics, directors, and action/adventure fans as the inspiration for the "team of specialists on a mission" action subgenre that has thrived through hundreds of films and television programs.[7]

The Hidden Fortress (*Kakushi Toride no San Akunin*), released in 1958, is still referenced as a partial inspiration for *Star Wars*, and *Yojimbo* (1961), much like *Seven Samurai*, was faithfully remade by Italian director Sergio Leone as a Western and superstar-making vehicle for Clint Eastwood.

While Eastwood is now among the ranks of the most accomplished and influential filmmakers of all time, and a film like *Star Wars* is credited for revolutionizing everything from film technology to marketing and merchandising, Kurosawa's original works are not forgotten. New generations of fans of the movies he inspired are rediscovering Kurosawa's elemental stories of warriors and their struggles with duty and codes of honor, and, at a more basic level, the filmmaker's very personal and poignant take on the struggles to live a fulfilling life.

Such a track record begs an understanding of why Kurosawa's work has proven to be so universal. His films are true classics because they deal with elemental issues, questions about life and death, about existence, that transcend culture, that are beyond Eastern or Western sensibilities. They are human stories about life and survival during desperately trying situations. As Kurosawa himself had written in *Something Like an Autobiography* (1982), all of his films, in some way, have attempted to examine what it takes to live a virtuous life in difficult times.

Perhaps these concerns are also the reason why Kurosawa is mainly remembered for his samurai, action, and combat-oriented films and why his influence has so shaped the action/adventure and Western genres, or the high-adrenaline, shoot-'em-up space operatics of the *Star Wars* films. Certainly, films about violence, showdowns, confrontation — *action* — have always traveled easily from culture to culture. Fights for one's life, a fight against tyranny or overwhelming odds, are universal subjects easily translated into any language — or, rather, a scenario of opponents facing off against each other, on the verge of violent confrontation, weapons drawn or fists about to fly, does not need translation at all. However, the enduring appeal of Kurosawa's films goes beyond these universals. War and combat are the most extreme trials people have ever faced. War, brutality, and violence are also the times when virtue and morality face their strongest challenge. Whereas countless thousands of films about war, killing, crime, and violence of every sort have been made in various film industries around the world, a filmmaker like Kurosawa stands out because his rousing adventures transcend the use of violence for the sake of simple action stories. At their conclusion, Kurosawa's action stories ask questions about humanity. They acknowledge the dark consequences of violence and ask what people need to do to remain human beings of virtue when violence has taken over their lives. "I keep saying the same thing in different ways," Kurosawa has remarked, "If I look at the pictures I've made, I think they ask, 'Why is it that human beings aren't happy?'"[8] When the violent, uncontrollable forces of the world, of society, or even our own darker, violent urges keep buffeting us, Kurosawa's films like to explore the question, what can we do to stay moral human beings, to find our own happiness?

These themes, however, came out of a life that often posed the same questions to Akira Kurosawa. From personal turmoil to living through war and abrupt, disorienting social upheaval, Kurosawa's films can be seen as the ruminations of an artist coping with the sudden, often violent reordering of the world all around him. In fact, Kurosawa has always insisted that if anyone wanted to understand him, all they needed to do was watch his films. Even the tongue-in-cheek title of his autobiography suggests the same thing. His words on paper are but a perfunctory attempt at approximating his life's story. His films are closer to the mark. "It is hard to be dishonest when pretending to be other people," he writes. [9] In creating fiction, he explains, an artist can succeed only if he turns to the facts of his own life to inform the story. More pointedly, he writes that "more important is my conviction that if I were to write anything at all, it would turn out to be nothing but talk about movies. In other words, take 'myself,' subtract 'movies,' and the result is 'zero.'"[10] Understanding Akira Kurosawa's films thoroughly, therefore, can help in understanding the filmmaker, but understanding the entirety of his career can also give an enlightening glimpse of how Japanese culture and Japanese artists have always struggled to make sense of how a foreign medium like film had a place in their tradition- and history-bound society.

Artist and Culture

Born in Tokyo in 1910, the last of eight children, Akira Kurosawa traced his lineage to the Japanese warrior class he would become so famous for exploring on film. Kurosawa's father, Isamu, came from samurai ancestry, still proud of and actively preserving the martial traditions in his life and career. Sometimes described as a "severe" man, even by his son, Isamu was a graduate of the Toyama School for army officer training and later he was a physical education teacher at the Ebara Middle School. Although he often appeared to be very much the image of the Spartan samurai warrior, Isamu was, nevertheless, quite progressive in other respects, especially in his support of the arts and a life-long supporter of Kurosawa's interests in art, literature, and eventually film. During Kurosawa's childhood, academic consensus in Japan argued that watching films was bad for children's development, yet Isamu regularly took his family to watch the European silent films that started appearing in Tokyo's theaters. Even as reactionary political currents would overtake Japanese society, condemning foreign films — when not all of filmmaking as a whole — Isamu would remain a steadfast supporter of film as an important art form.[11]

The years of Kurosawa's childhood afforded Japanese audiences an extremely rich period for watching films. The Taisho Period, or the reign of Emperor Yoshihito Taisho from 1912 until 1926, was an era of both political and cultural liberalization, opening Japan to an influx of Western art, film and literature. It was also a period when Japanese film made its most significant advance in adapting European and American editing and story-telling techniques. At last, Japanese filmmakers began advancing past several decades' worth of theoretical struggle over how such a foreign art form could find its place in traditional Japanese drama.

To appreciate how controversy could often flare around Japanese film's relationship with the West and Japanese filmmakers' borrowing too much from the West or being too influential in the West, one must understand the turbulent time in which film technology first appeared in Japan.

The first motion pictures were exhibited in Japan in 1897, showing a flickering scenery of the Nihonbashi bridge in Tokyo. A year later, the first commercial film showed several minutes of three dancing Geisha.[12] This, however, took place a mere three decades after the country's return to imperial rule, after the end of a feudal order and a political system where a shogun dynasty ruled Japan for nearly three centuries. With the removal of the Tokugawa shogunate in 1867 and imposition of the 15-year-old Emperor Mutsuhito — to be thereafter known as the Meiji Emperor and his era the "Meiji Restoration" or the "Enlightened Rule" — Japan began its sudden transformation from a thoroughly isolated society to an industrialized, militarized world power. The Meiji period became one of jarring upheaval for Japanese culture, not merely because of an embrace of foreign contact and industrialization, but from the sudden abolition of centuries-old customs, dearly-held traditions and an entire structure of social hierarchies. The Meiji period saw first the dramatic curtailing of the powers and privileges of the samurai class, then the abolition of the samurai altogether. Under the Meiji rule, Japanese were encouraged to abandon traditional dress for Western clothing and adopt Western meat-eating dietary practices; they saw the abolition of the topknot hairstyle of the samurai, were forced to adopt the Western calendar, and saw the establishment of a public school system, universal conscription, a nationwide telephone system and a postal system.[13]

Japanese society, founded on centuries of reverence for tradition and a very powerful sense of cultural identity, would now begin to struggle with the question of how modernization, industrial development, foreign contact, and the need to attain the status of a global power could, at the same time, remain compatible with their insular, traditional Japaneseness. In any society, what serves as the primary tool for the codification and preservation of a cultural identity, a set of cultural values and traditions, is art. In Japan, the Kabuki, Noh, and Kyogen theatrical traditions and the Bunraku puppet theaters were imbued with that same sense of cultural identity, that inherent Japaneseness.[14] The staging and performance of such theater has always been governed by iron-clad rules, which existed as a statement of reverence for tradition in and of themselves. Therefore, if Japanese story-telling was governed by such strict rules, where did a new technology like film fit in? For decades, the question Japanese film artists had to ask was how, if at all, film could be subjugated to the traditional requirements of Japanese theater.

In fact, early Japanese films were essentially filmed stage performances. Although a lot of early Western narrative story-telling on film amounted to little else — a basic continuous filming of the action on the theatrical stage — the development of a distinct grammar of film advanced much faster in the West. The use of cuts, close-ups, montage editing, location filming and camera movements showed up in early twentieth-century American film in particular, as well as European film. For Japanese artists, with Japanese culture in the throes of jarring, startling upheaval, the theatrical format would not leave film as easily. For example, early Japanese films were still cast according to the Tokugawa-era theater regulations forbidding women from acting. Male actors specializing in female roles, the *oyama*, remained in film until 1922. Furthermore, the theatrical role of the *benshi* was likewise retained in Japanese film until the mid–1930s.[15] In traditional theatrical presentations, the *benshi* performance, or off-screen narration, was as much a highly regarded art form as acting. Since the first films were silent, using the *benshi* was actually a very reasonable approach to filmic story telling. The strength of tradition, however, became apparent even after the introduction of sound. Even as films started talking, the *benshi* would still not leave Japanese films easily. Off-screen *benshi* narrators would comment on the action, describe scenery and add insight to character motivation even as the audiences were fully surrounded by the sounds of music, sound effects and speaking actors on screen.

While talking films grew to dominate Japanese cinema, just as they did throughout the rest of the world, sometimes the celebrity status of a particularly skilled *benshi* would be a bigger audience draw than a star actor, a famous director or the film's subject matter. Aside from the *benshi* being such an ingrained part of Japanese drama, their very powerful union also helped their anachronistic role remain a part of early cinema.[16]

One of Kurosawa's older brothers, Heigo, worked as a successful *benshi*, helping cement the would-be director's interest in drama during his teenage years. In his biography, Kurosawa recalls tours Heigo would take him on through Tokyo's sprawling Asakusa entertainment district. They would see and discuss everything from films to the *yose* vaudeville-style theaters and the *kodan* plays about samurai. "I learned a very great deal from him," Kurosawa explains, "particularly about literature."[17] For many of his films, in fact, Kurosawa would turn to literature as a source of inspiration. To be able to make great films, he would later advise, directors should be well versed in the classics of literature. Shakespeare and Dostoevsky are among the source materials Kurosawa himself used as templates.

Film, however, remained a primary battle ground for Japan's struggle in its definition of cultural identity for decades to come. Throughout the Meiji period, filmmakers continued the trend of adapting Western techniques. Their society had to modernize to compete globally, their nation argued, and Japanese film had to be able to match the standards of Western films to be able to stand a chance of competing with American and European artists. But by the 1930s, reactionary and ultra-nationalistic military powers were taking over Japan. As would be the case in numerous other societies in the grip of totalitarian regimes, film would become an extension of official political dogma. With the outbreak of World War II, Japanese film had to support the war effort and writers and directors needed to tell stories glorifying the nation's cause in the struggle. Celebrating the superiority of Japanese culture, the greatness of its history and traditions, had become the officially sanctioned and expected theme in films. It would be the post-war period, however, that once again set the stage for filmmakers to grapple with the meaning of "Japaneseness." They had to try and come to terms with how much of their traditions and history they had a right to glorify and the extent to which they needed to critique and bring to task their countrymen for supporting the government's aggressive military expansionism, its role in starting a war, and the atrocities Japan committed in the lands it occupied.[18]

Kurosawa's career began during this tumultuous period. He worked through years of government control and censorship, the devastation of a lost war, then more official control and censorship imposed by the Allied Occupation Forces. Finally, he made a mark on the world film scene as a vibrant new Japanese cinema emerged, a period where the most accomplished film-makers tackled the issues of national identity, culture and the conflicted feelings they had toward that question of how exactly "Japaneseness" can be defined, understood and celebrated.

Kurosawa's career in film began in 1936 when he answered a newspaper ad requesting applications for assistant director positions at Photo Chemical Laboratory (PCL) Studios. His general interest in film and particular artistic inclinations motivated him to try out for the position. By then, Kurosawa had studied both painting and literature and was a good enough painter to have been selected for two major painting exhibitions. Although he had confessed that even after years of watching films, inspired both by his father's interest in the art and his brother Heigo's work, he was still not possessed by a particular passion to become a filmmaker, the PCL position promised a more lucrative income than he could earn as a painter. "My family was poor," he writes, "I couldn't really study because I had to work so hard; even a tube of red paint was usually too expensive for me, there was no question of my going abroad to study.... What I mainly felt was that I could not be dependent on my parents. I had to make my own living and this seemed to offer a way."[19]

Plus, at that time Kurosawa was also grappling with personal turmoil. Heigo, who had lived a troubled life and had a turbulent, conflicted relationship with their father, had committed suicide shortly before. Film was the strongest bond Kurosawa had with his brother.[20]

At PCL (later to become Toho Studios) Kurosawa embarked on an extensive training and apprenticeship program. It was something akin to the Hollywood studio system where promising performers and technicians were discovered and polished for work in a factory-like production facility. Eventually Kurosawa became part of a repertory group of writers, production and assistant directors working with director Kajiro Yamamoto. Although up until that point Kurosawa had his doubts about a career in film, often actually considering quitting, working with Yamamoto finally ignited his passion for staying at PCL and completing the training program.[21] Kurosawa always readily explained that Yamamoto was his one true teacher in film and the force behind his success and career.

Yamamoto, in turn, often recalled Kurosawa's natural aptitude for film production and, particularly, scriptwriting. Although Kurosawa had the same strenuous work schedule as most assistant directors, Yamamoto would be impressed by the amount of work he was able to put into writing original stories as well as his skills for reworking and saving other writers' flawed scripts. "Everyone began to realize how enormously talented he was," Yamamoto would later explain when discussing how quickly he grew to trust his apprentice's judgment and input on films. "People began to talk about him and his brilliant future."[22]

In a number of Yamamoto's films Kurosawa worked on before getting his solo directorial opportunity in 1943, he actually shot more of the film than any assistant director usually would. "When we were making *Horses* (*Uma*, 1941)," recalls Yamamoto, "he was still called my assistant, but he was much more than that, he was more like my other self. He took responsibility for the second unit work in this semi-documentary about farmers in the Tohoku district. I could come down to Tokyo and work on a musical comedy knowing that things were going fine up in the country."[23]

Sanshiro Sugata, Kurosawa's first film, is often analyzed by his fans and film historians for hints of how much of the future filmmaking giant's style, themes, and distinctive touches were already in evidence in his rookie effort. This is usually how an accomplished director's first films are revisited. In the case of *Sanshiro Sugata*, the consensus is that it's uncanny how much of the later Kurosawa style is already evident. According to Donald Richie's assessment in his seminal study, *The Films of Akira Kurosawa*, how mature Kurosawa's handling of the film appears to be is nothing less than "astonishing." "Besides ... fondness for a certain kind of story," Richie writes, "a certain kind of hero, for cyclic form, for theory and practice in parallel scenes, for the resultant implications of illusion and reality; and besides his liking for such punctuation marks as the wipe — there are many other elements of the Kurosawa style which are visible in *Sugata*."[24] *Sanshiro Sugata* is not only a remarkable preview of all that will come from Kurosawa, but a valuable assessment of why the filmmaker was destined to leave such a mark on world cinema — particularly American cinema — and the controversies and travails that would continue haunting him in Japan for most of his career.

Like Kurosawa's most famous films, *Sanshiro Sugata* is an action story. It focuses on a martial arts student's training in judo. With a passing resemblance to what would become a cliché in so many martial arts films and sports films, the story's eponymous hero not only perfects his fighting skills but develops his character and grows as a human being as result of his judo training. When the reigning martial art style is jujitsu, a curious Sanshiro Sugata (Susumu Fujita) joins a judo teacher (Denjiro Okoohi) and embarks on what will be a long and strenuous quest not only to understand a strange, often dismissed and ridiculed fighting form, but to understand himself. Once his martial skills are perfected, Sugata's character and his soul have been perfected. A callow youth, by the end of the story, has grown into an enlightened adult. The film's story arc follows Sugata's tutelage under Shogoro Yano, the judo master. Sugata's skills and fighting moves, at first, develop faster than his wisdom and ethical core. But, after an initial rebuke and rejection by his disapproving teacher, he trains further and eventually becomes not just a great fighter but a great man.

Kurosawa heard of the *Sugata* story before it was published in novel form by Tsuneo Tomita. Persuading his bosses at Toho to buy the rights to the book, he was finally successful in his long-fought effort to be given the opportunity to actually direct an entire script he had written. A number of scripts Kurosawa had written prior to *Sugata*, like *Horses, Currents of Youth* (*Seishun no Kiryu*, 1942) and *A Triumph of Wings* (*Tsubasa no Gaika*, 1942) were eventually given to directors like Yamamoto, Osamu Fushimizi and Satsuo Yamamoto, respectively, to shoot.[25] But other scripts, despite Kurosawa's growing reputation as a superb scenarist, were quickly rejected for their subject matter and themes. Studio censors often deemed his stories too "Western."[26] Already a fan of American films, Kurosawa gravitated to stories that apotheosized individual effort, free will and achievement. A superior strength of character, will power, and personal responsibility interested Kurosawa above all else in a story. His individualist orientation was at odds with Japanese values to begin with — and would continue to be after the war and throughout his career, forming the chief argument against his work by his Japanese detractors — and his views certainly could not be allowed to make it onto the screen when all of the nation's media were forced to glorify the subjugation of the individual will to the greater cause of winning a war.

In such an atmosphere, it was remarkable that a film like *Sugata* was green-lighted by the Toho leadership at all. The central theme of the film, after all, is the growth and development of the individual. Sugata defies tradition in his martial arts training, choosing to learn the strange new art of judo instead of the established jujitsu all other fighters pursue.

What saved the film, however, was its overall plot of martial training and Kurosawa's argument that it was a simple adventure story with no political implications that might antagonize the government. "It was wartime and you weren't allowed to say anything worth saying," Kurosawa later wrote in his autobiography. "The information bureau was being extremely troublesome, saying you can't film this and you can't shoot that.... Back then everyone was saying that the real Japanese-style film should be as simple as possible."[27] But, in the final analysis, Sugata quests and becomes a superb warrior. That theme was enough for the censors to let Kurosawa make the film. Moreover, they liked the apparent message that the creation of a superb fighter meant the creation of a superior man.

Characters like Sugata would continue appearing in Kurosawa's films throughout his career. Strong individualists and people on a quest to complete a seemingly overwhelming task, they are, more than anything, as Donald Richie argues, really students who are attempting to grow. To Kurosawa, fully realized, fully formed individuals who had accomplished all they could, who were already "enlightened" and knew who they were, are of no interest. If anything, complete self-mastery might often turn out to be a mark of villainy in a Kurosawa film. As Richie makes the case in his analysis of *Sanshiro Sugata*, the most striking characteristic of Sugata's main opponent, the villain he needs to vanquish in the film's final fight scene, is the fact that he has learned all that he could about the martial arts. The villain can no longer grow, he can no longer improve himself. Kurosawa protagonists are most often callow or unfulfilled, unrealized individuals who know well enough that they must become something better. While they might find themselves in difficult circumstances they did not create — as do Sanada (Takashi Shimura), the alcoholic doctor in *Drunken Angel* (*Yoidore Tenshi*, 1948), or Watanabe (Takashi Shimura again, who, aside from Toshiro Mifune, is one of Kurosawa's favorite actors), the dying bureaucrat of *Ikiru* (1952) — they are not merely fighting back against their ill fortune, not just trying to survive. They take on one last, epic, desperate effort to become better human beings. Sugata, in search of discipline and training, might as well be Kikuchiyo (Toshiro Mifune), the erratic, impetuous young peasant attempting to remake himself as a samurai in *Seven Samurai*; or Yasumoto (Yuzo Kayama), the immature and arrogant young doctor of *Red Beard* (*Akahige*, 1965) who learns compassion for his impoverished patients; or any of the group of young samurai needing guidance in maneuvering through bureaucratic and political treachery in *Sanjuro* (1962).

A look at Kurosawa's other wartime films reveals a similar ability to buck the system in favor of glorifying individualism the way he did in *Sugata*. These are films that, upon a cursory, surface glance — the sort of simpleminded understanding of art totalitarian regimes are usually capable of— function as chapter-and-verse propaganda vehicles. Nevertheless, they still retain Kurosawa's subversive endorsement of individuality. The most artful of these films is *The Most Beautiful* (*Ichiban Utsukushiku*, 1944), about a group of women working in a lens factory. Through the course of the story, they all face various personal crises, from a sick mother who should be looked after to illnesses and accidents that should preclude them from putting up with the spartan daily work regimen of the factory. But they all forsake personal comfort and safety for their duty to the war effort. They know the lenses they make will be used in binoculars, eyeglasses and precision optical equipment used by soldiers. Their jobs are as crucial to winning the war as those of the men in battle. A crisis point occurs when the leader of the workers (Yoko Yaguchi) accidentally misplaces a defective lens, allowing it to be packed away in a shipping container among thousands of others. Racked with guilt, she spends an entire night unpacking all of the boxes, pushing herself to the limits of exhaustion, to inspect each lens and find the faulty one. Although it is but one lens, she knows that a single bad one could cost a soldier his life in battle and risk the war for all of Japan. While the film does work effectively as pure wartime propaganda, glorifying the patriot who willingly forsakes all personal needs and comfort for the good of the country, Kurosawa's excruciating montage sequence showing the passage of time through the search quietly suggests something else. More than anything else in the film, the girl's endurance of exhaustion and excruciating headaches as she inspects lens after lens in a microscope helps the viewer appreciate the indomitable will and strength of the individual to overcome a crisis alone.

The most interesting comment on Kurosawa's wartime films comes from Stuart Galbraith in his exhaustive work on the parallel lives and careers of Kurosawa and his favorite leading man, Toshiro Mifune. Galbraith argues that Kurosawa could have been a much more "dangerous" filmmaker had he been more devoted to the government propaganda machine and the nation's cause in the war. He could have been a Japanese version of Leni Riefenstahl had his sympathies been more in tune with the government and his required glorification of the martial life not been undercut by his devotion to and romanticizing of the strong individual.[28]

According to Richie's assessment of much of Japanese propaganda filmmaking as a whole, there are really no "outstanding" propaganda films to be found. Japan is a society that did not need propaganda films at that time. It was a world where the reverence for authority, the emperor, and the government were a natural part of the culture. Browbeaten filmmakers did not really need to force messages about why the people needed to support the war down the throats of their audiences. Whether in film or in any other form of Japanese drama, there did not exist a tradition of the bellicose pro-war propaganda story. Japan had a tradition of historical martial drama, what would emerge as the *jidai-geki* film, about the glories of the samurai past, but that art form was hardly on par with the usual saber-rattling wartime propaganda film. In a turn of almost darkly comic irony, several filmmakers, like Fumio Kamei, director of *Fighting Soldier* (*Tatakau Heitai*, 1939), were jailed when their war films — sincere attempts at toeing the party line and giving the government the wartime propaganda films it asked for — turned out to be so grim and depressing as to have an opposite, *anti-war* effect on their audiences.[29]

After the war, Kurosawa himself had never laid claim to inserting subversive, anti-government, anti-propaganda messages of fierce individuality into his films. Mostly he had been apologetic for his films made during the war, saying that he was ashamed of not taking a stand against the government. It was either taking a stand and facing the harsh consequences, Kurosawa would readily admit, or doing as he was told and making a living.[30]

The film industry Kurosawa found himself a part of after the war, however, hardly afforded a completely free and uncensored environment for Japanese filmmakers. Censorship by one government had been replaced by censorship by another. Furthermore, pressures from within the turmoil-ridden Japanese political culture still exerted a very powerful influence on artists. But it was a period that further cemented Kurosawa's devotion to telling stories of individuals fighting the odds and braving tremendous obstacles to stay true to themselves. It was a theme, after all, that echoed the experience of so many Japanese after the war. It was also a theme that, in a few years, would make Kurosawa one of the most famous and influential Japanese directors the world over.

After the war, the Allied Occupation attempted to remake Japan from a militaristic, authoritarian society into a modern democratic one. Once again, much like during the Meji Restoration and the Taisho period, Japanese culture needed to force itself to discard its own traditions and, virtually overnight, become something new. The Occupation government quickly decided that steering an entire nation in the proper direction required the control of its art and popular culture. Filmmakers and their work would now be scrutinized by American censors. Reverence and glorification of Japan's feudal past, the samurai, the war lords, was outlawed until 1952, the year the Allied Occupation withdrew. Japanese militarism, the aggression that prompted it to attack America and start a war, was seen as rooted in its past, rooted in a history enamored of warriors and fighters, codes of combat and loyalty to clans and supreme leaders.

Kurosawa's own *They Who Step on the Tiger's Tail* (*Tora no O o Fumu Otokotachi*, 1945) was banned by the American censors. It would not appear on movie screens until 1953. Although hardly a propaganda film — dealing with a medieval general and his retainers trying to evade his brother's forces during a feud — it was based on the famous Noh drama *Ataka* and the Kabuki play *Kanjincho*. For the American censors, new Japanese films had to abandon the past. Films had to be set in the present and they were encouraged to criticize the militaristic past. New Japanese films had to point to an optimistic future and critique the flaws, the iniquities and problems of traditional modes of behavior and thinking — traditional Japaneseness, in effect.[31]

One of Kurosawa's films perfectly reflecting this enforced period of optimism was *One Wonderful Sunday* (*Subarashiki Nichiyobi*, 1947). Its whimsical storyline involves an impoverished pair of lovers trying to have a romantic evening in a typically blighted, burned out city and the series of complications — mainly stemming from their poverty — that almost ruin their good time. In the course of their Sunday afternoon together, they try to go to a concert but find they can't afford the tickets, go and have coffee but can't pay the bill, try to go to a zoo but can't pay the admission price, and eventually wind up at an empty park band shell pretending to listen to a concert. Although not considered among Kurosawa's notable works — and even he often said that it was certainly not his own favorite film — *One Wonderful Sunday* is noteworthy because it displays so much of the American influences evident in Kurosawa's style. By 1947, American films were shown in Japan in greater numbers than ever before, just as Hollywood product was flooding so much of the world movie market even in places where an occupation government was not helping its proliferation, and Kurosawa became a fan of several American directors. The very core idea of the film, for example, comes from D. W. Griffith's *Isn't Life Wonderful* (1924). The goofball optimism of the film, the characters' sense of humor about their bad situation, and their love that nevertheless carries them through it all, their belief that they are whatever they imagine themselves to be — happy, fortunate, hopeful — all appear to be borrowed directly from Frank Capra. Critics usually remark that Kurosawa's film unmistakably bears the marks of *It Happened One Night* (1934), *Mr. Deeds Goes to Town* (1936) and *Lady for a Day* (1933). The ending of the film, in turn, is an exact remake of the ending of Henry Koster's *One Hundred Men and a Girl* (1937). As Richie writes in *The Films of Akira Kurosawa*, in time it would almost become standard for Kurosawa to list John Ford, William Wyler and Frank Capra as his chief influences whenever interviewed about his favorite filmmakers and inspirations.

Censorship and coercion during this period did not come only from the Allied Occupation, however. The American approach to reordering a dictatorial, militaristic society had some unintended consequences, and they served to further interfere with artistic freedom in the film industry.

The Occupation's efforts at changing a right wing dictatorship in Japan included backing various left wing social initiatives. Leftist trade unions, for example, were supported by the Occupation. In the film industry, many of the unions were quickly taken over by Japanese Communist Party members. Organizations like the Japan Motion Picture and Drama Employees Union had, for a while, the power over what scripts were put in production and what directors were helming projects, and they strictly regulated the content and messages of the films. Many filmmakers were quite overtly pressured into crafting movies that espoused specifically anti-business and anti-capitalist messages.[32]

Of course, at the core of this wave of leftist film control were the original decrees of the Occupation censors. The new Japanese film, after all, had to be critical of the system, had to encourage a complete shakeup of all that was traditional, and had to point to positive, utopian futures of a new society working together to rebuild, reorganize everything, and reeducate. Themes of a drastic reorganization of society were quickly co-opted by the Japanese socialist, Marxist far left. Many of these renewal pictures quickly turned into leftist polemics about the unfair, exploitive old-style system's being a capitalist system brutalizing helpless workers. Bosses, big business owners, factory owners and the like were the forces of evil in these films. They were all ultimately overthrown and the victorious, liberated working masses marched forward into a brave new future, establishing a new workers' paradise.

Ultimately, the censorship exercised over scripts and films by the far left turned out to be as unyielding as the censorship from the far right or the Allied Occupation.

Kurosawa's own philosophical reaction to this period was an even fiercer devotion to individualism. "I believed that the only way for Japan to make a new start was to begin by respecting the 'self,'" he said when discussing his film *No Regrets for Our Youth* (*Waga Seishun ni Kuinashi*, 1946).[33] This is a film that has as much duality and subtle criticism of the post-war left as a wartime propaganda film like *The Most Beautiful* that undermined the spirit of the military censors. Although *No Regrets for Our Youth* critiques the military government of the war and glorifies a young girl who falls in love with a leftist student, it also roundly dispenses condemnation onto the far left. The film attacks the proletarian fantasies of the Communist films and their romanticizing of the working classes. Kurosawa and Japanese artists had not been given freedom to express themselves under any fringe political system, and his films, even his message films about the hardships of life and the problems of the system, refuse to endorse any one political philosophy. In Richie's analysis of Kurosawa's incredible staying power and the influence of his films on so much of world cinema, Kurosawa's strength and appeal lie in the fact that he makes films about the human condition and not narrow "political films." "Because he wants to see a social problem whole and in all of its parts," Richie writes, "Kurosawa has rarely lent himself to politics since this presumes a choosing of sides, and this is just what he is unwilling to do.... He finds it impossible to be partisan."[34] Kurosawa chronicles the hardships and challenges of the human condition and social problems in their entirety. He does not manipulate and filter these issues through left wing or right wing biases.

For film scholars familiar with the breadth and depth of Kurosawa's body of work, an entire oeuvre beyond the adventure films, his primary place is among Japan's most impassioned social-issue filmmakers. Kurosawa's rise to prominence in the Japanese film industry, before his emergence on the world film scene, was as a member of the post-war wave of "realist" directors. Although he might have shunned the dogma of the Marxist left, Kurosawa very much aimed to address the problems, pains and struggles of everyday life. Much like the neorealist movement of post-war Italy and the French New Wave, post-war Japanese films, leftist polemics and all, found their audiences as they addressed the struggles of a war-battered society attempting to rebuild itself as it came to terms with, and repudiated, the darker sides of its militarist past and tried to find what part of its inherent Japaneseness it could still celebrate.

Urban blight, crime, the aftermath of the war on the psyche of the Japanese, the chaos and turmoil brought by a quickly liberalizing society, all are issues that turn up in Kurosawa's films from 1947 to 1950. Much like social commentators and artists who have seen their countries change from an oppressive dictatorship to a liberal democracy, like intellectuals reacting to the dizzying upheavals in the formerly Communist countries after the collapse of the Soviet Union, for example, so Kurosawa reflects in his films the wariness and concern of a country that was glad for its newly attained freedoms and afraid of the chaos too much freedom could bring. Films like *Drunken Angel, Quiet Duel* (1949), *Stray Dog* (1949) and *Scandal* (1950) reflect these concerns.

Japan might have committed itself to moving toward a better future, but *Drunken Angel* shows the spiritual and moral decay that festers in the rubble of a post-war city. People may dream of a better future, but in the present they are mired in poverty, disease, crime and all manner of self-destructive urban vices which they slowly kill themselves with in the name of freedom.

In *Quiet Duel*, only the stoic willpower of a committed doctor (Toshiro Mifune) who puts the needs of his patients above all else can save him from the grief of lost love once he realizes that he had been infected by a syphilitic patient. When all seems hopeless, the film argues, the stubborn commitment to healing others, healing a broken nation, in effect, can give hope to a man who seems to have lost everything else.

In the crime-riddled world of *Stray Dog*, a young cop (Toshiro Mifune) sees so much of himself in the criminality he is committed to fighting. There is no clear good and evil in that film — as they are rarely defined in such black and white terms in any Kurosawa film — only a world of chaos and hurt that has touched all of Japan equally.

In *Scandal*, a film that is still eerily resonant in today's world of tabloids, celebrity gossip, reality TV and paparazzi, Kurosawa lashes out at Japan's early tabloid culture. Here an artist (Toshiro Mifune) and a lowly, shabby lawyer (Takashi Shimura) attempt to fight a tabloid that printed a picture suggesting an illicit affair between the artist and a famous singer. The salacious tabloid culture is portrayed as yet another unwanted byproduct of Japan's new freedoms. Dressed up in the rhetoric of "free speech" and "free expression," it's merely sleazy voyeurism. Tabloids cater to people's baser desires, their tawdry curiosity, once the strict, enforced moralism of the old dictatorial system had been stripped away. "This was not freedom of expression, I felt," Kurosawa argued, "it was violence against a person on the part of those who possess the weapon of publicity. I felt that this new tendency had to be stamped out before it could spread."[35]

Thus, well grounded in the social problems of their times, these films placed Kurosawa among the most notable of the post-war Japanese filmmakers. In 1950, however, he would be noticed by film critics, scholars, fans and film connoisseurs around the world. Once noticed by Western filmmakers, he would turn out to be one of the most imitated, influential and celebrated Japanese directors of all time.

Rashomon

The reasons for Kurosawa's indelible, and seemingly instant, impression on Western filmmakers have been debated and analyzed almost from the moment *Rashomon* won the Grand Prize at the twelfth annual Venice International Film Festival. Perhaps nowhere was this a more pressing issue than among Japanese critics and intellectuals. Although achieving parity with the rest of the world's influential filmmakers had been a Japanese concern since the first influx of motion pictures in the early part of the century — just as the country had been concerned with making a mark on the world stage since the Meiji restoration — easy acceptance by foreigners was just as much of a troubling concern now. Was Kurosawa doing something wrong, something somehow un–Japanese, that he was being embraced so enthusiastically by the West? Certainly, winning a major international film prize by a Japanese director was good, but there was also enough cause for alarm. Japanese culture also needed to be inscrutable, tradition dictated, and Kurosawa's success with *Rashomon* might have been a sign that he had abandoned his cultural identity.

The idea that Kurosawa is the most Western of all Japanese filmmakers had often been used as a simple argument for his world success. The Westerners, the Americans, "get" Kurosawa because he was essentially telling Western stories, this argument states. But, again, the argument had always been forwarded by Japanese critics with the greatest force. The focus on the individualism, the self-sacrifice and personal responsibility was the major root of all the "Western Kurosawa" critiques. Although even a passing understanding of post-war Japanese social issues reveals the undeniable fact that Kurosawa's films were well-rooted in the most pressing concerns of the day and in Japanese culture, the "too Western" stigma was something Kurosawa could never shake.

Peter Biskind's analysis of the 1960s Baby Boomer, or "film school brat," impact on Hollywood suggests something more complex about the appeal of certain foreign directors in the eyes of Hollywood. Kurosawa's appeal, perhaps, lies in Biskind's assessment. The foreign movies watched by all the aspiring young American filmmakers or the rookies making their first films or toiling on TV shows, the film students in college in the '60s or the established insiders unhappy with the status quo, had a heartfelt, personal importance. Those films had a passion a lot of American artists felt but were unable to express in a stifling, formula-driven studio system. Just like a Kurosawa or a Fellini or an Antonioni or a Truffaut or a Goddard made statements about the state of their own worlds, so too were a lot of American filmmakers eager to make passionate and personal movies. "Although these films were 'foreign,'" Biskind argues, "they seemed more immediate, more 'American' than anything Hollywood was turning out. They hit home with a shock of recognition."[36] These were films by artists who wanted to speak out, who wanted to criticize things, protest, make arguments and effect change. These films were doing things a lot of American artists in the '60s, or even as early as the '50s, already wanted to do but couldn't.

Indeed, Kurosawa's influence is so lasting because he was seen by a generation of young filmmakers who eventually established themselves in and took over the Hollywood system. The foreign films they were so enthralled by in their youth would be the ones they repeatedly paid homage to, imitated in their own blockbusters and, in turn, used as new standards for action and science fiction archetypes.

When audiences first saw *Rashomon* at the Venice Film Festival, they were stunned by the experience because it was so unlike anything they had ever seen on film before. The film had an unusual narrative, a story-telling style that completely demolished all previous expectations of structure. Essentially, Kurosawa discards the idea that a film must be a strictly linear narrative, a story where a problem is presented, its repercussions follow and, in turn, protagonists take action to deal with the problem. *Rashomon*, instead, is a masterful execution of the most difficult filmic devices one can ever incorporate into a story: flashbacks and completely subjective framing narratives. While *Rashomon* certainly presents a very compelling and immediate problem, its solution is arrived at through a series of subjective vignettes, a story told from various perspectives.

The basic story of *Rashomon* involves the murder of a man in a forest and attempts at figuring out who killed him and how. In essence, it's a murder mystery. In any such classic story, the detection of the truth might involve the presentation of various conflicting points of view, perhaps a brilliant detective trying to ferret out the truth and uncover the lies of a murderer. But in

Kurosawa's hands, this formula is quickly deconstructed, turned inside out and even accused of being nothing but a tool for a self-deluding fantasy. Mysteries are always a search for a clear, undeniable, objective truth. In *Rashomon*, however, Kurosawa wonders whether such a thing exists at all.

The film is structured in such a way as to present a series of flashbacks within a flashback. It begins as a traditional "frame" story, one where the entire film is someone's recollection told to a group of listeners. Here, the film opens in a rain storm, finding three men taking shelter under the Rashomon Gate. One of them is a woodcutter who was witness to a shocking crime and its trial. To pass the time until the rain lets up, he tells his companions, a young priest and a commoner, what happened. Thus begins the mystery story and the flashback into the film's central narrative.

The mystery, in turn, is what happened in a desolate stretch of forest where a traveling samurai, his wife, and a bandit crossed paths. What the woodcutter himself discovered was the dead body of the husband. What occurred between these people, who killed the husband and for what reason, is up to the authorities to figure out. Once the bandit was caught, however, and an official inquest begun, the woodcutter recounts, several confoundingly different versions of the events emerge. Each of them sounds much more complicated than what the evidence might suggest.

The inquest starts by listening to the bandit's version of the events. This is a man who must obviously have tried to rob the couple and wound up killing the husband out of avarice and simple-minded cruelty when resistance was offered. The bandit, though, confesses to only wanting to rob the samurai and his wife, then rape the wife. He would have gotten away with that, too, had the wife not asked the two men to fight over her. A simple rape would shame her immensely, the wife pleaded. At least the men should fight over her. When the men fight, the bandit winds up killing the husband.

The wife's version of the events is much different, though. She confesses to killing her husband accidentally. In her version of the events, the bandit is also successful in his robbery and rape. Her husband, though, is so repulsed by his wife's defilement — and the suspicion that she did not do enough to resist — that he can do nothing but stare at her with a simmering, disgusted hate. As she pleads with him to kill her, the wife passes out with a knife in her hands and stabs her husband to death.

Afterward, the inquest takes an audacious turn. A medium is ordered to help call up the spirit of the husband so his side of the story can be heard. According to the ghost's version of the crime — if he is indeed communicating through the medium and it's not the frightened woman making up the story to please the court — the wife, indeed, did nothing to resist the rape. She willingly gave herself to the bandit, then begged him to kill her husband.

Finally, the woodcutter himself recounts his version of what happened. In his tale, the bandit only wants to rob and rape. The wife willingly has sex with him, but the bandit won't kill the husband as the woman demands. Repulsed by the betrayal, the husband then asks the bandit to kill his wife. The bandit refuses. The woman then goads the two men until they fight. What ensues, though, is a clumsy, reluctant flailing of swords and a couple of hysterical charges through the woods. It is by sheer accident that the husband gets killed.

But which version of the story is real? Is any of it real at all? The commoner raises this question as a final twist to the events under the Rashomon Gate presents itself. The men discover an abandoned baby in a corner. The commoner attempts to steal the baby's clothes, but the woodcutter quickly chastises him. How could he steal from a helpless infant abandoned in the pouring rain? The commoner, though, wants no part of the woodcutter's moralizing. Isn't it true, the commoner guesses, that the only reason the woodcutter got involved in the incident between the samurai and the bandit was to steal the valuable ceremonial dagger used as the murder weapon? (The commoner's guess, of course, is correct.) Can we even trust the woodcutter's story as the truth, or isn't it just another self-serving lie?

Finally, to redeem himself and redeem the young priest's faith in humanity, the woodcutter decides to take the baby home, save him and raise him as his own.

Critics, including a lot of Japanese ones, interpreted *Rashomon*'s success as nothing more than Westerners' desire to see something exotic. Perhaps they longed for a diversion to the proverbial mysterious Orient. The film's power, however, especially for future filmmakers who would become Biskind's "generation that saved Hollywood," lies in the fact that *Rashomon* was a vivid example of all that could be done with film, with its visual narrative possibilities, and a bright symbol of everything that a more and more rigid studio system was not brave enough to do. *Rashomon* was willing to trust its audiences to think about a film like no other film had done before. It challenged them to understand something beyond simple linear narratives that usually told them what to think about, how to read a film's message, what to *think*.

Perhaps in more abstract terms, *Rashomon* was an early cinematic example of the postmodernist thought that would enthrall that generation soon enough.[37] *Rashomon* questioned reality, questioned objective truths and declared that all was suspect beyond individual perception and experience.

In the U.S., *Rashomon* was embraced quite quickly and its mark was eventually seen in films and even stage plays. In 1952, the National Board of Review named it Best Foreign Film and it was given an honorary Oscar by the Academy of Motion Picture Arts and Sciences. By 1959 it was adapted into a Broadway play starring Rod Steiger, and in 1964 it was turned into a made-for-TV Western with Paul Newman as the bandit and directed by Sidney Lumet.

What must also be noted when looking at *Rashomon* is not only how Akira Kurosawa first made an impression on world audiences, but how well he collaborated with Toshiro Mifune. As Stuart Galbraith explains in his book on the careers of the two men, it is nearly impossible to separate them when discussing their contributions to cinema. Mifune, in fact, stars in all four of the key Kurosawa films that most influenced American films. But they had worked together before *Rashomon*. Mifune starred in a Kurosawa film for the first time in *Drunken Angel*, playing the tubercular gangster and the film's symbol of self-destructive freedom. In *Quiet Duel, Stray Dog*, and *Scandal*, Mifune had also taken starring turns. The two men made sixteen films altogether before a troubled rift on the long, much-delayed production of *Red Beard* drove them apart for the rest of their careers. Their partnership had often been compared to such legendary collaborations as the John Wayne and John Ford partnership or Martin Scorsese and Robert DeNiro.

Mifune's own persona and influence on both Japanese and world action cinema is often as highly regarded as Kurosawa's. Once dubbed "the most Japanese man in the world,"[38] Mifune had come to symbolize the quintessentially stoic Japanese man of strength, resolve and action. Whereas John Wayne, considered by most critics and action fans as his main Hollywood counterpart, was the prototypical American cowboy — or soldier — Mifune was the world's image of the perfect Japanese samurai. Interestingly, just like Wayne, Mifune, too, had a similar dual image as a larger-than-life World War II leader of men. In fact, he played Admiral Yamamoto an astonishing four times. Although the roles he played throughout a very long career were quite varied — it can be argued that Mifune was actually allowed a greater versatility by producers than a lot of the iconic American action heroes, from Wayne to Clint Eastwood, or even Sylvester Stallone and Arnold Schwarzenegger — Mifune had forever been cast in the minds of world audiences as the wandering lone warrior.

In *Rashomon*, however, one can see the impressive range and versatility of Mifune's skill as an actor. Whereas a lot of American leading men, especially heroes and men of action/adventure, would develop a rather narrow persona, limited acting styles and ranges, Mifune could always modulate from stoicism and self-control to explosive, barely-contained emotion, pent up kinetic energy exploding into either focused action that yielded results, or ineffective buffoonery, the hysteria of the inconsequential peasant or simpleton. In *Rashomon*, for example, he dominates the film with a wild-eyed, animalistic, capering energy as the bandit. In *Seven Samurai*, he is once again the most volatile, outlandish member of the group. Here he is often a clown, a comic relief, the lowly peasant who rages to escape his past and remake himself as a samurai. These are performances John Wayne or Clint Eastwood would never have attempted. By the same token, the stoic, steely Mifune of *The Hidden Fortress, Yojimbo,* the *Macbeth* adaptation *Throne of Blood* (*Kumonosu-jo,* 1957), or *Red Beard,* as well as the scores of admirals, generals and captains — not to mention a role no less regal than Emperor Meiji in *203 Kochi* (1980) — he played were always realized with flawless perfection.

Seven Samurai

If *Rashomon* brought Kurosawa world recognition, *Seven Samurai* gave him a masterpiece most aficionados of Japanese cinema consider perhaps the greatest Japanese film ever made.

Seven Samurai is certainly the most well known of all of Kurosawa's films. Its plot is familiar to most filmgoers with a passing knowledge of action/adventure classics. Set in feudal Japan — although near the end of the Tokugawa period when outside influences like guns and gunpowder were creeping in — the story finds a group of farmers routinely terrorized by a gang of roving bandits. Like a locust invasion, the bandits usually raid the village when crops and harvests are aplenty, pillaging the hapless peasants. Realizing that they can not survive under the bandits' endless plundering, the villagers decide to hire seven *ronin,* or masterless samurai — who were in ever greater numbers by the late Tokugawa era — to protect them. The samurai go to work fortifying the village, training the peasants and reconnoitering the bandits' weaknesses and tactics. Eventually, the bandits are wiped out, the village is saved, but only three of the samurai survive the final battle. Life, in the end — or life for the peasants at least — goes on as it always has. The samurai, in turn, wander away, still alone, still on the fringes of society, not given any meaningful reward for their work or, perhaps, even much thanks by the peasants they fought so hard for.

Of all of Kurosawa's films, *Seven Samurai* usually got the strongest comparison to the American Western. This was so even before John Sturgis adapted the story into *The Magnificent Seven.* Although Kurosawa had often readily confessed his fandom of the American Western film, one should take note of a deeper connection between American and Japanese mythologies than whether or not filmmakers from the two countries were copying each others' films. The fact is that there had always been a remarkable similarity between such American and Japanese cultural icons as the cowboy and the samurai. For example, when Sturgis and producer/star Yul Brynner attempted their conversion of *Seven Samurai* into an American film, it wasn't merely a random choice to use cowboys as the new version of Kurosawa's heroes. There really was no better alternative for an Americanization of the Kurosawa film than a Western because cowboys had been imbued with the same value systems in the West as the samurai had by Japanese history, legend, and popular culture.

This similarity in national heroes, of course, is ironic and remarkable. Samurai films had been the number one target of the Allied Occupation censors after World War II. Samurai were supposed to have represented all that was undemocratic and fascist in the Japanese cultural mythos.

In truth, both the Americans and the Japanese use their cowboys and samurai as representations of morality, chivalry, and honor, essentially all that is best in their respective societies. These are the heroes who represent a higher, transcendent morality. Both the samurai and the cowboy are men of action, skilled in combat and the killing arts, yet these abilities are governed by iron-clad codes of personal conduct. Both of these warriors use their abilities to enforce justice, to bring peace, to protect the weak and the innocent, to battle evil and ensure the safety and survival of the civilization and the social order. Both characters even swear by a code of honor that most often forces them to live solitary lives, devoted essentially to themselves and the honing of their combat skills. The fictional cowboys and samurai are all flawlessly honest characters, they always do the honorable thing because their personal codes demand it, not because the rule of law hangs over their head or standards of proper behavior are imposed upon them from the outside. Robert Warshow draws a perfectly accurate summary of the generic American "westerner" and it is remarkable how "westerner" could just as well be replaced by "samurai:"

> What does the Westerner fight for? We know he is on the side of justice and order, and of course it can be said he fights for these things. But such broad aims never correspond exactly to his real motives; they only offer him his opportunity. The Westerner himself, when an explanation is asked of him (usually by a woman), is likely to say that he does what he "has to do." If justice and order did not continually demand his protection, he would be without a calling. Indeed, we come upon him often in just that situation, as the reign of law settles over the West and he is forced to see that his day is over; those are the pictures which end with his death or with his departure for some more remote frontier. What he defends, at the bottom, is the purity of his own image — in fact his honor. This is what makes him invulnerable.[39]

In the greater equation, such stories focusing on men of violent skills reluctantly employing those skills in defense of the social order, the defense of peace, is the key to why the greatest patterns of influence can be seen between American cinema and all the foreign cinemas, be they Japanese samurai films or the Chinese and Hong Kong martial arts films that deal with action and combat. The underlying values of all these stories are uncannily similar.

Kurosawa wound up making *Seven Samurai* because he had long been interested in telling a story of the quintessential samurai. As he had recalled in interviews and his biography, he first wanted to make a film about the typical day in the life of a typical samurai. He wanted to put flawless historical detail on the screen. By the mid–1950s, the ban on samurai films had been lifted and filmmakers and audiences were eager to revisit this iconic historical figure from a new perspective. For Kurosawa, making the perfect samurai picture also had the added appeal of examining his own family's heritage. While the typical-day-in-the-life-of-a-samurai film did not happen — Kurosawa was never quite satisfied with writer Shinobu Hashimoto's day-to-day, moment-by-moment details of a samurai's routine — *Seven Samurai* is not only one of the most exciting films ever made in the genre, it's also a subtle examination and critique of the stratified Japanese society created by centuries of the samurai functioning as a privileged social class.

The key of the *Seven Samurai*'s complexity and power is ultimately in the relationship between the samurai and the villagers they protect. This relationship, in fact, is strained throughout. The protected, we find out, fear, if not resent, their protectors. The villagers find themselves terrorized by the bandits, yet they can not be sure that the seven warriors who've come to their aid are any better than their tormentors in the end run. The peasants' wives and daughters are hidden when the seven arrive. The villagers can't be sure the samurai won't try and take advantage of them. When Kambei (Takashi Shimura), the leader of the seven *ronin*, finds this out, he remarks with quiet dismay that after all his group is trying to do for the farmers — not only defending them but doing it for no more payment than three meals of rice a day — at least the warriors' honor could be given the benefit of the doubt. At that point, the audience is sure to feel the same way. They must clearly be wondering if the peasants are worth saving at all. Soon enough, however, a more complex social relationship between farmer and samurai is revealed and Kurosawa goes past the traditional boundaries of this action genre to make a strong, critical social statement about Japan's revered past and traditions. Kurosawa, a descendant of samurai, uses the Mifune character, the wild, angry Kikuchyo, to remind that the history of samurai and farmers has been one of long exploitation.

The pivotal scene comes when Kikuchyo discovers a trove of old samurai armor hidden in the village. Ever driven to impress the other six warriors he has been desperately trying to join, he presents them with the armor as a gift. Hopefully, he has now earned their respect for his resourcefulness. Most likely, though, he is told, those are the armor of samurai the villagers had killed

Seven Samurai (1954) is not only one of the most imitated of all of Kurosawa's films, but considered the greatest Japanese film ever made.

and robbed in the past. Indeed, the film reminds, those peasants can be treacherous, thieving and deceitful. Once again, the issue of how worthy they are of help is floated about. Kikuchyo, however, explodes in retort, accusing his partners — and informing the audience — of the samurai's role in the injustice and exploitation farmers have lived under for generations:

> What do you think farmers are? Saints? They are the most cunning and untrustworthy animals on earth. If you ask them for rice, they'll say they have none. But they have. They have everything. Look in their rafters, dig in the ground, you'll find it. Rice in jars. Salt. Beans. Sake. Look in the mountains, hidden farms everywhere. And yet they pretend to be oppressed. They are full of lies. When they smell a battle they make themselves bamboo spears. And then they hunt. But they hunt the wounded and the defeated. Farmers are miserly, craven, mean, stupid, and murderous beasts.... But then, who made animals out of them? You. You did — you samurai. All of you damned samurai. Each time you fight you burn villages, you destroy the fields, you take away the food, you seduce the women and enslave the men. And kill them if they resist.

The speech is a short, yet effective, deconstruction of the myth Japanese society had built around the samurai. History has proven that the larger-than-life, ethical warriors, the men who lived by their own ironclad codes of honor, were very much later-day samurai, and perhaps greater part legend, folk tales and mythology than fact. Much that has been written about the samurai's warrior code, the *bushido* code, in fact, had been written near the end of the samurai era. The code of the noble fighting man had been solidified in the Japanese imagination once the civil wars of the feudal era had ended and the samurai settled down as a privileged ruling class. The original samurai in the late twelfth century were little more than hired fighters for warlords. In effect, they began as thugs and mercenaries, fighting and killing for the highest price. The original samurai "code" might have been closer to the law of the jungle; kill or be killed, do whatever it takes to get ahead and win.

Concurrently, American culture — popular culture more precisely — had done much the same mythologizing of the frontier gunfighters and cowboys. Thus, yet another parallel existed between the Japanese historical action genre and the Hollywood Western at the time *Seven Samurai* premiered. Just as the samurai had been overhauled by Japanese fiction and entertainment, so Hollywood turned frontier characters who either might have had very limited exposure to action, violence or gun battles of any sort, or were little more than thugs, mercenaries or hired hitmen, into romantic heroes.

Frontier historians today are often amused by how the cowboy has been adopted by American art and culture as its chivalrous hero of honor, representative of decency, truth and democratic values. The real frontier "cowboy" was little more than a ranch hand. If one were to take a close look at the day-to-day routines of most of these men, one would find a rather mundane, if not boring, life. These men tended herds, fixed fences, worked a farm or went on cattle drives. The life of action, adventure and the selfless defense of truth and justice was something utterly alien to the "real" cowboy of the American West. Nevertheless, as anime historian Patrick Drazen argues in his comparison of Japanese and American myths in popular culture, "American culture ... deviates from its European roots in several respects, notably the American belief—almost an article of faith—that the unsophisticated common people possess an innate common wisdom unequaled by the upper class elite. This has manifested itself in a variety of ways, from America's first independent act of political dissent (the Whiskey Rebellion, 1794) to books like *The Adventures of Huckleberry Finn*."[40]

Hollywood mythologizing of a common, semi-literate manual laborer as a knight errant in chaps and spurs, however, is more benign than glossing over the true history of "gunfighters" in the real West. Much like the early samurai, the gunfighter was little more than a hitman, a thug with a set of guns who usually killed for the right price. In fact, a lot of the earliest "lawmen" were themselves former criminals—ones who turned on their comrades in the last moment to avoid the end of a rope.

Seven Samurai and its quiet deconstruction of Japan's most cherished mythic heroes premiered at a time when some American filmmakers were also starting to feel that romanticized Western clichés might soon be ripe for some critique and debunking. The later half of the 1950s, in fact, started seeing a maturation of the Western in Hollywood. The genre had slowly started moving away from the simplistic, childish shoot-'em-ups or the grandiose celebrations of "the greatness of American civilization that had tamed the wild frontier and subjugated the blood-thirsty red savages." By the later half of the decade, Westerns started turning up in the form of the "message picture." Films like *High Noon* (1952) used the Western's conventions as a critical commentary not only on the past but on contemporary American life and society as well. Even as early as 1943, *The Ox-Bow Incident* aimed its critique at injustice and the lynch mob mentality. *High Noon* condemned McCarthyism and American timidity in the face of the Communist witch-hunters who, the film charged, were little more than a modern day gang of assassins. Future filmmakers, the Baby Boomers who would discover Kurosawa in film schools in the 1960s, would likewise take his lead and turn out a series of films that made the later years of that decade and the early '70s memorable for the unrelenting parody and demythologizing of all that was old, traditional, revered, and cherished.[41]

The first example of the powerful influence of *Seven Samurai*, though, can be seen through *The Magnificent Seven*. However, the American adaptation of *Seven Samurai* had to contend with key cultural and historical differences between feudal Japan and the 1800s American frontier. Mainly, the rigid class divisions of Tokugawa Japan that separated samurai from peasants had no American equivalent. John Sturges' film focuses instead on the forces of modernity rapidly altering American society in the later half of the nineteenth century. At the same time, the film resonates powerfully in the early 1960s because, Sturges charges, the modern world America changed into at the closing of the frontier was flawed, corrupt, and morally compromised, much as it appeared to be in 1960. The sort of self-satisfaction and optimism Americans felt at the end of World War II was giving way to a growing sense of cynicism and wariness as the years passed. The paranoia of the Cold War and McCarthyism, for example, brought into doubt the notion that the U.S. was the home of freedom, individuality, and free expression. Much as movies like *High Noon* and the science fiction/horror classic *Invasion of the Body Snatchers* (1956) suggested, America was becoming a world of apathetic compromisers, unquestioning followers, the pod-people of Don Siegel's science fiction allegory, spineless cowards who couldn't stand up for what was right. The malignant state of racial inequality, segregation, and bigotry made America look ever more like a nation of hypocrites. *The Magnificent Seven* speaks directly to these specific American cultural concerns.

The film's plot is set up in a standard enough fashion. It involves a group of gunmen being hired by a Mexican village to defend it from regular raids by a gang of bandits. Essentially, the Kurosawa plot of seven samurai warriors hiring themselves out to protect a similarly besieged village is transplanted to the barren American and Mexican deserts. In the course of the film, the gunmen attempt to fortify the village, train the locals to defend themselves, square off against the bandits in several skirmishes, and eventually decide to make a final stand in a battle where they are far outnumbered and outgunned. As the case has usually been in the typical Western, there comes a moment for the heroes where the decision to fight is the morally correct one. There is even a very brief elegiac flavor to the relationship between the gunfighters and the villagers that, for a fleeting moment, recalls the older tradition of John Ford Westerns. We see that while the gunfighters save the town, they are also in essence saving civilization, saving a new way of life that will eventually put an end to the tough loner's untamed, ungoverned existence.

So far so good — except that what makes *The Magnificent Seven* stand out is that the film does not seem to be entirely happy with what is happening to the untamed, rugged, macho individualist. There is no golden glow of a sad, yet inevitable, resignation to the passage of time like we see in Ford's Westerns.

In Sturges' film, the progress from the old-fashioned warrior code of the gunfighter in the wilderness to the modern world is presented in harsher tones. The traditions of one generation of rugged fighting men are not kept alive in the world they had created. The ending of Sturges' film implies that the new world is not entirely so pure, even if the progression from one to the other may still be the natural evolution of human society. Here the gunfighters save a town the audience is not entirely sure is worth saving. As a matter of fact, we are not entirely sure if any town, any outpost of modern civilization, is worth saving after the film's opening scene.

The tone of the story to follow is set by an opening sequence in which Yul Brynner and Steve McQueen decide to make a few extra dollars in a small town by driving a hearse and its coffin to burial. The problem, it seems, is that an Indian is inside the coffin, and many of the locals object to the burial's taking place in an all-white cemetery. The opposition is so strong, in fact, that no one dares drive the hearse, lest they be shot by the local bigots. Brynner and McQueen, though, take the challenge for the money and ride a gauntlet of snipers perched in windows and on rooftops along the main street.

Modern society, civilization and the organized, close-knit community has been hopelessly corrupted, *The Magnificent Seven* says. The brutal, Wild West where gunfighters used to square off in duels over honor has been replaced by a sneaky, quiet, insidious form of brutality. In the new world, the macho man, the fighter, the tough guy with the gun has become a frowned-upon outsider, but he has now been replaced by racists and cowards. The killing and brutality is now done from a distance, from the shadows. This is no longer a world where a man does what he feels he's got to do, right or wrong, and stands up for his beliefs and is ready to be shot down for it. The modern man, the supposedly civilized and enlightened man, free of old-fashioned macho nonsense, will snipe from the shadows and rooftops, he will stab his enemies in the back. This is much like the world of 1950s America Sturges' audience could still recall vividly. This is like a world where so-called patriots could destroy others' reputations by whispering allegations about disloyalty and Communist sympathies.

After the hearse prologue — functioning as the "hook" of the film, and establishing the atmosphere of action to follow and the character of the heroes and the film's dismay with "civilized" society — the story proceeds in gathering its seven gunfighters. A group of peasants from the besieged village appears and the roundup is much like the hearse sequence. The gunmen are up for the work because they need the money and there is little else they are qualified to do. They sympathize with the peasants' cause, but they are mainly willing to commit to the mission because they are bored and they have nothing better to do. Getting into the little war with the bandits might be a way to have a bit of bloody fun. One of the most ironically humorous scenes in the beginning of the film has McQueen's character considering what else he could do, other than work as a hired killer. He was told by a man in another town that he could have a prosperous future as a "crackerjack clerk," if he took advantage of the opportunity. Not likely.

Thus the seven head out for the town and eventually start fighting for the peasants, despite the fact that their employers betray them several times. Much like the townspeople whose cemetery was too good for an Indian corpse, the peasants are cowards and compromisers. Eventually, in the final battle, all but three of the gunfighters are killed. The ending, however, sets the world of the gunman side by side with that of the "civilized" peasants. Here, the civilized side is a field being worked by the peasants. The field, ready to be picked of its harvest, bears new life — whatever it may turn out to be — whereas the world of the gunfighters is one of death — no matter how idealistic the killers might have the capacity to become. Then, one of the gunmen (Horst Buchholz) actually starts to look at the peasant life longingly, especially since he had been attracted to one of the peasant girls. He considers laying down his gun, and soon enough does so. He hangs it up on a fence post and joins the girl picking crops in the field. This gunfighter is the youngest member of the group, commonly referred to as "The Kid." He is the next generation of men, he is the future, whereas the other two survivors, Brynner and McQueen, are a pair of older, weathered, leathery gunmen, too old for anything other than riding away into the distance and obsolescence. When McQueen looks at the peasants in the fields, an exchange lifted right out of Kurosawa follows. "So, I guess we won," McQueen says. Brynner replies, "No, we didn't win. We lost. *They* won. We always lose."

Before directors like Sam Peckinpah and Robert Altman would begin their debunking of Western myths, what film scholars would call "postmodern genre deconstruction," *Seven* took shots at the moral ordering of Westerns and action films a lot like Kurosawa critiqued samurai myths. It toyed with and mocked the old concept of heroes fighting evil so civilization, law, order and morality would triumph. The heroes of this new world fought because it was the most fun they could have at a particular moment in time. The world was simultaneously both screwed up and self-righteous. Such a world did not exactly need, or deserve, self-sacrificing, courageous heroes to come to its rescue.

As the 1960s progressed, the impact of *Seven Samurai* was seen in the emergence of the action subgenre where a team of adventurers are recruited to carry out a near impossible mission. Although *The Magnificent Seven* would spawn three sequels (1966's *Return of the Seven*, 1969's *Guns of the Magnificent Seven*, and 1972's *The Magnificent Seven Ride!*), closest in tone and intention to the Kurosawa original was Robert Aldrich's 1967 war film, *The Dirty*

Dozen. The film spelled out Kurosawa's message about the dark side of his heroes much louder and clearer than any American adaptation had done before. The heroes, or more accurately antiheroes, of *The Dirty Dozen* are a collection of hardened, dangerous criminals. The world is evil and unstable in the universe of the *Dozen*, a chaotic world of brutality where each side must do what it can to win. This is no longer the World War II of the 1940s and '50s Hollywood epics where a virtuous America fought a morally uncomplicated war against absolute evil. The "good guys," the Allies in this version of World War II, must rely on whatever it takes to achieve victory, even if it takes promising a collection of sociopaths, murderers, rapists, scum of every stripe and every crime, freedom if they attempt to pull off an impossible mission behind enemy lines. Of course, what made this sort of open nihilism acceptable and believable to the *Dozen*'s audience was the Vietnam War's ever more chaotic spiraling into a quagmire. As the country would first question, then loudly oppose, the war in the coming years, as traditional value systems and traditional morals would be questioned and challenged by the younger generation, the critical perspectives of these films — the *Dozen* and Kurosawa's *Seven*— would prove to be the most accurate visions of a world where no easy answers could be found, where good guys and bad guys could no longer be so easily distinguishable.

In 1969, committed Kurosawa fan Sam Peckinpah took his turn at the same theme with *The Wild Bunch*. Although Peckinpah's film would diverge from Kurosawa's source material a great deal — his main characters are not heroes or protectors in any sense — *The Wild Bunch* does stay true to the theme of a society in transition. Peckinpah's Western, just like *The Magnificent Seven* and most of the noteworthy Westerns from that era and through the 1970s, shows the spread of destructive modernity. The modern world in Peckinpah's film, just like in Sturges' vision, is one of corruption, impersonal, exploitive big government and big business. Peckinpah, however, presents his gang of outlaws as much darker, more vicious and violent than Sturgis' gunfighters or Kurosawa's ambiguous samurai. Peckinpah's outlaws kill indiscriminately when the situation calls for it. Innocents often get caught in the gunfire. The effect of the film, however, just like Kurosawa's intended effect, is to deconstruct a past that has been mythologized in clean contrasts of black and white.

Ultimately, even as its critical nihilism would be toned down, the team of heroes on a mission would become a staple of action films in Hollywood for decades. Even without the critical edge, this type of film's heroes would at least be outsiders, rebels, "screwballs," or "misfits," people who could not find their place in mainstream society — just like Kurosawa's *ronin* could not — but who still possessed the lethal fighting skills and wherewithal needed to save that society when it was threatened.

In fact, in 1980, Kurosawa's film was remade again, but this time as a low budget science fiction film, *Battle beyond the Stars*, by exploitation master Roger Corman. Of interesting note is that Robert Vaughn, who played Lee, the gunfighter who loses his nerve in *The Magnificent Seven*, plays Gelt, a space gunfighter in the Corman film. On television in the 1970s and '80s, variations on the same formula would be seen in the Stephen J. Cannell action series *The Black Sheep Squadron* and *The A-Team*. In 1998, CBS premiered a short-lived TV series based on *The Magnificent Seven*.

Yojimbo

Kurosawa's second most noteworthy contribution to the evolution of the American Western and action/adventure genres came in the form of *Yojimbo*. Interestingly enough, the film's impact started when it was plagiarized by Italian director Sergio Leone as *A Fistful of Dollars* (1965).[42] "The idea is about rivalry on both sides, and both sides are equally bad," Kurosawa explained. "We all know what that's like. Here we are, weakly caught in the middle, and it is impossible to choose between evils. Myself, I've always wanted to somehow or other stop these senseless battles of bad against bad, but we're all more or less weak—I've never been able to."[43]

Evil spreads around to all sides in a battle, *Yojimbo* suggests, and it offers an adventure story where one is hard-pressed to find good guy and bad guy distinctions anywhere. Were the film not leavened by a large helping of dark, ironic humor throughout, it would be one of Kurosawa's darkest, most cynical films.

The plot involves Mifune's title character—Yojimbo means bodyguard—Sanjuro Kuwabatake, wandering into a town besieged by the feuding households of the local silk merchant and the sake merchant. Both sides have collected small garrisons of henchmen and they are intent on wiping each other out. It becomes immediately obvious that there is no virtuous side in this war. All are equally greedy, unscrupulous, power-hungry and murderous. However, the film's grizzled anti-hero, Kuwabatake, is beyond caring about virtue. He sees an opportunity to make money instead. He can craftily start manipulating the two sides into wiping each other out. He hires himself out to one side, collects money, but never really puts himself into too much danger while he provokes deadly confrontations between the two parties.

The only danger he does find himself in, though, is one he brings upon himself when he gets too soft and sentimental. It seems the only people in town worth saving are a lowly farmer and his wife and small child. But when he lets the three of them escape the anarchic town, Kuwabatake's manipulation is discovered and he is nearly killed. Thus, the film darkly suggests, not

Clint Eastwood's star-making film, *A Fistful of Dollars* (1964), is based on Kurosawa's *Yojimbo* (1961).

only is there little order, little goodness or natural justice in the world, but those who give in to such fanciful notions put their own lives at risk. No good deed in this film goes unpunished.

The suitability of Yojimbo's adaptation into a Western is more obvious, perhaps, than in any other Kurosawa film. Kurosawa's own fandom of the Hollywood genre comes through loud and clear. From the desolate, besieged town to the wandering lone warrior who saunters into the middle of the action, to the sudden violent showdowns in the middle of the main street, Yojimbo unmistakably echoes films like *Nigh Noon, Shane* (1953), and all the countless generic horse operas about ambiguous gunfighters who amble into wild frontier towns and single-handedly clean them up. As Kurosawa was a director most filmmakers all over the world kept on eye on now, an adaptation of *Yojimbo* as a Hollywood Western appeared inevitable. The odd turn of events was that the remake — still a "Western" — came from Italy.

Sergio Leone, the director of the "sword-and-sandal" epic *The Colossus of Rhodes* (*Coloso de Rodas*, 1961), was the first one to take a turn at *Yojimbo* because he, too, was not only fascinated by the traditional Western but also frustrated with the hoary clichés of right and wrong, simplistic good guy and bad guy morality plays in Hollywood films. Leone's approach to the Western has been documented by film historians as being shaped by his pre–World War II experiences of American literature, then contact with the American occupation forces during the war and a heavy influx of American cinema after the war's end. Leone is quoted by Christopher Frayling as having experienced a moment of disillusionment on meeting American soldiers during the war: "they were no longer the Americans of the West. They were soldiers like any others.... Men who were materialist, possessive, keen on pleasure and earthly goods.... GIs who chased after our women and sold their cigarettes on the black market, I could see nothing that I had seen in Hemingway, Dos Passos or Chandler.... Nothing — or almost nothing — of the great prairies, or of the demi-gods of my childhood."[44] Leone was also bothered by the mannered, unrealistic execution in the classic Hollywood Westerns:

> The man of the West bore no resemblance to the man described by Hollywood directors, screenwriters, cineastes.... One could say all the characters they present to us come from the same mold: the incorruptible sheriff, the romantic judge, the brothel keeper, the cruel bandit, the naïve girl.... All these molds are mixed together before the ending, in a kind of cruel, puritan fairy-story. The real West was a world of violence, fear and instinct.... Life in the West was not pleasant or poetic, at least not in any direct sense ... the law belonged to the most hard, the most cruel, the most cynical.[45]

His films were a result of his outsider's eye cast on these revered American conventions, taking them apart, exaggerating them to the point of absurdity, parody and commentary. As Richard Schickel analyzes:

> Leone and his several writing collaborators had scraped away the western's romantic, poetic and moral encrustation, leaving only its absurdly violent confrontational essence. It was very close to an act of deconstruction, for it might be said that instead of offering metaphors for moderns, as the "message" Westerns did, the Leone films were postmodernist in their very essence. Like grander and more self-conscious works in this tradition, they were fully, wickedly aware of the conventions they were sometimes rendering as ironic abstractions and sometimes completely subverting.[46]

Leone's version of the film turned out to be a blockbuster success, of course, remaking Clint Eastwood's career from that of a TV supporting player to A-list movie star. As a result, Kurosawa had inspired what would be another standard-setting Western classic and helped alter the face of the genre, perhaps forever. The hard, amoral, cynical loner had replaced John Wayne's idealistic, romanticized Western hero of upstanding moral virtue as the new prototype of the Old West gunslinger. After Eastwood and Leone followed the success of *A Fistful of Dollars* with *For a Few Dollars More* (1965) and *The Good, the Bad and the Ugly* (1966), Eastwood returned to Hollywood where his American Westerns started resembling the Italian films more than the classic Wayne formula.

Tracing Eastwood's career all the way to the 1990s and beyond, one can find this sort of revisionist impulse as the connective thread among many of his films, especially the ones he directed. His first Oscar-winning film — and final Western, sort of a capstone statement on his entire career as a cinematic gunfighter — *Unforgiven* (1992), is a powerful myth-shattering statement about the genre. It basically makes explicit what an entire career had been alluding to. The grandiose myths of righteous, heroic gunfighters in the West were always a sham, an outrageously inaccurate apotheosizing of killers, sociopaths and mercenaries. Eastwood's second Best Picture Oscar winner, *Million Dollar Baby*, is a gritty, bleak boxing drama that starts out enacting all the uplifting, *Rocky*-esque fantasies often seen in sports films, then suddenly turns on the genre and demolishes its success myth with the wrenching paralysis and slow, graphic deterioration of its main character. With *The Flags of Our Fathers* (2006), Eastwood takes aim at wartime propaganda, attacking the public relations campaigns governments orchestrate — even the American government and even during a "good war" like World War II — and the degrading effects it can have on real heroes.

But the template for the irony, the ambiguous heroes and ambivalent tones of the films had been set by Akira Kurosawa and his quietly critical reexamination of Japan's own cherished myths and legendary warriors.

The Hidden Fortress

Although made before *Yojimbo*, *The Hidden Fortress* deserves a separate examination from the Kurosawa movies that changed the look and the feel of American Westerns. *The Hidden Fortress* is an interesting film for the (largely inaccurate) impression it has made on many film fans as the sole inspiration for one of the most successful and influential Hollywood franchises in history.

A lot of film and science fiction fans believe that *Star Wars* was a direct adaptation of *The Hidden Fortress*. Although it was not, several themes of the Kurosawa film, as well as a couple of opening scenes, did make enough of an impression on George Lucas — an avid Kurosawa fan and admirer of Japanese art — to have him pay homage to yet another samurai epic that critiques and deflates the glorious warrior legends.

The Hidden Fortress is set in a time of civil war. A strong, willful and self-reliant princess (Misa Uehara), along with a cache of gold, is being pursued. She is protected by Toshiro Mifune's stoic, fearsome General Rokurota Makabe. On their quest to reach a safe haven, the hidden fortress, they are accompanied by a pair of bumbling peasants (Minoru Chiaki, Kamatari Fujiwara) the general captured. Unbeknownst to the peasants, they are the ones carrying the gold hidden in bundles of firewood. The gold, once the group reaches the fortress, will be used to turn the tide of the war.

Several basic *Star Wars* parallels already become obvious in this synopsis. In the first *Star Wars* film, *Episode IV: A New Hope*, an intergalactic battle is also raging. An equally strong, willful and self-reliant princess (Carrie Fisher) is trying to reach a hidden rebel base, a fortress of sorts, accompanied by heroic protectors Luke Skywalker (Mark Hamill) and Han Solo (Harrison Ford). They are also joined by a pair of comic relief droids, one of whom carries the plans to the enemy's Death Star. The plans could possibly lead to the discovery of a weakness in the defenses of the Death Star, its ultimate destruction and the turning of the tide of the war in favor of the rebellion.

But the plot parallels between the two films are best left at this level. As Kevin J. Wetmore, however, argues in *The Empire Triumphant*, influences from Kurosawa, as well as Asian art, mythology, the martial arts and religion permeate the themes, character profiles, look and narratives of both sets of *Star Wars* trilogies. The *Star Wars* films pay a more general homage to Kurosawa's greater body of samurai-themed work than to what goes on in *The Hidden Fortress*. In many ways, though, the two filmmakers also had markedly different agendas behind their films.

Kurosawa, much as he did in *Seven Samurai* and *Yojimbo*, used *The Hidden Fortress* as a deconstruction of the warrior mythologies of the traditional *jidai-geki* films, whereas Lucas faithfully enacted all the traditional derring-do and heroism of the genre. The opening and plot setup of *The Hidden Fortress* is very nearly a complete farce. In the midst of what should be a rousing civil war epic foregrounding feuding clans, fearless warriors, thrilling battles, chases and pulse-pounding escapes, Kurosawa chooses to focus on a pair of bumbling, whining, inconsequential peasants. From the first scene of the film, the epic battles are in the distance and daring warriors are doing their thing far in the background. As the warriors gallop in and out of the battles, they ride around the hapless peasants, a couple of lowly wretches who are not even worth killing or throwing out of the way. To defile traditional heroic story-telling even more, once the audience finds out more about the peasants, they like them less and less. Not only are they clumsy and weak, but they are petty, greedy, utterly lacking any sense of honor, treacherous, deceitful and even perverted. In one scene, they very obviously contemplate what it would be like to overpower and rape the princess. R2D2 and C3PO they are not.

Only after General Rokurota Makabe is introduced and his full personality is revealed, however, does Kurosawa go to the ultimate length in turning the heroic honor mythos of the samurai stories upside down. Rokurota had allowed his sister to be used as a double, a decoy for the princess, and, as a result, he let his own sister die. The princess, in turn, was horrified by this and by Rokurota's coldness, his inhuman dedication to honor and duty that would allow him, without emotions or regret, to let his own sister walk to her death. Kurosawa, basically, dares to critique the very notion of samurai honor here. Whereas the metaphysical core of all *jidai-geki* epics are founded on the warrior "code of honor," the inviolate ethics that command samurai to achieve near-impossible feats of heroism, in Kurosawa's film "the code" is what makes Rokurota a cold-blooded monster. A lesser person, someone who would allow themselves such feelings as fear, anger, longing or love would be a more compassionate and virtuous human being. As Kurosawa manipulates these characters, he ultimately never makes Rokurota an entirely sympathetic character at any point in the film. The film's full title can even be translated more accurately as Three Bad Men in a Hidden Fortress. Not only are the peasants bad men, but so is Rokurota.

Lucas, of course, likewise invests his heroic Jedi Knights with such epic codes of honor and duty, yet *Star Wars* presents all of it with dead seriousness. In fact, in the greater analysis, Lucas' intention with the two *Star Wars* trilogies is mythmaking, whereas Kurosawa skewers myths with sharp, darkly comic irony.

The analyses of the origins and social, political, psychological and religious meanings of the *Star Wars* films have already produced a veritable cottage industry of both mainstream and academic books. Here, it is enough to say that George Lucas' approach to crafting the *Star Wars* epic was the creation of a filmic version of a study in comparative mythology disguised as a science fiction action story. But many, if not most, of the concepts, plot devices, characters and themes of Lucas' film are influenced directly by Asian culture, Asian films and, in particular, Kurosawa's films.

"Through anthropology I had gotten interested in folklore and mythology and in their role as an anchor for societies," Alan Arnold quotes Lucas in *Once Upon a Galaxy: A Journal of the Making of The Empire Strikes Back.* "I came to realize that America has no modern fairy tales. You could say that the western movie is the last of our myths."[47]

Drawing particularly on the work of Joseph Campbell, the *Star Wars* films are an updating of the traditional quest formulas of ancient myths and most world religions. These formulas always present the journeys of self-discovery and apotheosis of an archetypal hero who grows as a spiritual figure, an enlightened man, one who becomes a redeemer and savior of his world.

Campbell, in turn, a fan of the *Star Wars* films, had also often spoken about how the films perfectly synthesize his major arguments.

Star Wars, essentially, is a redemption story, Luke Skywalker becoming the enlightened, redeeming hero through his rediscovery and mastery of the ancient spiritual and martial codes of the Jedi Knights. The Jedi, as Wetmore analyzes, are a space fantasy version of the Japanese samurai. Other parallels that might be drawn to the Jedi would include China's Shaolin monks, likewise versed in the spiritual and martial arts. Furthermore, if one wanted to find the closest religious version of the Force, the lynchpin of Lucas' Jedi mythology, Wetmore argues that Taoism, or perhaps Buddhism, might be its closest equivalents. The main point Wetmore makes, quite correctly, however, is that Lucas builds his films' mythology off of an Asian template and he completely venerates the spiritual warriors and their "code." In *Star Wars*, redemption is achieved only through the embrace of the ancient traditions. Those who have fallen to the Dark Side of the Force are saved by the rediscovery of the principles of a true Jedi Knight. Luke redeems his father by becoming a perfect Jedi. Anakin Skywalker, in turn, fell because he rebelled, broke the rules and rejected the teachings of the Jedi tradition.

Although, in form, the *Star Wars* films owe an immense creative debt to Akira Kurosawa — the mythology of the Force and the Jedi (even their name, derived from the *jidai-geki* genre), the parallels between the Jedi and the samurai, costumes and sets that look unquestionably Asian, the names of characters that sound Japanese (Obi-wan, Anakin, Yoda) — their overall thematic accomplishment is a narrative that is very conservative, whereas Kurosawa's approaches to the subjects of warriors, codes of honor, and ancient traditions are quietly skeptical, critical and revisionist.

Legacies

As is often the case with many innovators, an artist who might garner a reputation as a cutting-edge visionary one day might be written off as a representative of old guard, staid conservatism by the end of his life. Unfortunately, such was the case in the later half of Kurosawa's career.

Akira Kurosawa's career, his box office and critical prestige, peaked in 1965 with *Red Beard*. Even though he would make films for over three decades afterward, controversy, financial difficulties and contentious studio politics impeding his artistic vision and ambitions would haunt his professional life throughout this time.

Red Beard, his last film with Toshiro Mifune, would, ironically, also be Kurosawa's biggest critical success in Japan. Overseas, however, it was largely dismissed as a sentimental and predictable melodrama. It was considered a surprising misstep from the creator of edgy, hard-hitting films like *Seven Samurai, Rashomon* and *Yojimbo*. Indeed, the film is a rather slow-moving tale of a young, impatient and conceited Tokugawa-era doctor (Yuzo Kayama). The young man is looking forward to serving as a physician in the shogun's court but is given a posting in an impoverished country clinic instead. But just as the Western critical consensus pointed out, almost all of the film's plot points are quite predictable. Worst of all, they border on the mawkish and sentimental. By the film's end, the callow youth has been, naturally, converted by Toshiro Mifune's gruff, iron-willed doctor with a heart of gold into a compassionate advocate for his downtrodden patients. Not surprisingly, when the youth finally gets the opportunity to transfer to the shogun's court, he elects to stay and work with the poor.

The film's troubled production turned out to be a foreshadowing of three difficult decades to come. *Red Beard* took nearly two years to complete because of Kurosawa's obsessive perfectionism and requirements for impeccable historical details. With his reputation as one of the world's most influential filmmakers, Kurosawa could — as powerful directors and stars can in any film industry — bend the studio brass to his will. As a result, the film's budget skyrocketed like none of the budgets on his other projects had ever done before. His relationship with Mifune also soured in the meantime. Mifune had, by then, started his own production company, but could do nothing with it while tied down with the seemingly endless *Red Beard* shoot. *Red Beard*, in effect, was a financial liability for the actor.

Calamities kept following Kurosawa after *Red Beard*. A director who had influenced Hollywood as much as Kurosawa had should have been courted by the American studios. In fact, Kurosawa did receive invitations from Hollywood, the most prestigious one being the offer to co-direct Twentieth Century–Fox's Pearl Harbor epic *Tora! Tora! Tora!* (1970). It was to have been one of the most ambitious and expensive reenactments of the attack ever staged. David Lean was originally attached as the director of half the film, telling the American point of view of the events. Kurosawa was to helm the story of the Japanese. But, unfortunately, Kurosawa could not bend Hollywood to his will. He quickly found himself in the position of countless filmmakers before — and generations of young, independent filmmakers to come — who are courted by studios impressed by their "vision," yet prevented from realizing that vision. The Fox leadership interfered with Kurosawa's plans for his half of the film at every turn, at one point forcing a complete rewrite of the script he wanted to shoot. Chafing at the indignity, Kurosawa let his shooting schedule fall so far behind as to force the studio to fire him.

In Japan, Kurosawa's next project nearly cost him his life. After starting his own production company with directors Keisuke Kinoshita, Kon Ichikawa, and Masaki Kobayashi, he embarked on *Dodesukaden* (1970) about a group of slum dwellers who are able to make their bleak lives endurable by constructing elaborate fantasy worlds. When the film failed at the box office, Kurosawa attempted suicide by cutting his wrists. For Kurosawa, compounding the problems of the failed *Dodesukaden* was the depressing reality of the reasons that had forced him to try the route of independent production. By 1970, the Japanese film industry was struggling to stay alive. The dual problems of television and the influx of foreign films — namely American films — had cut into the profits of the studios so seriously that most were risking bankruptcy with every production. Japanese audiences were either staying home to watch the small screen or only venturing out to theaters to watch the latest big-budget, big-star American blockbuster.

The Japanese studios, in turn, focused all of their resources into smaller-budgeted, sure-fire, predictable genre entertainment. Two of the most popular genres that still seemed to draw audiences spanned a strange spectrum from the tawdry to the ridiculous. The so-called *Roman Pornography* genre drew audiences in with sex, even if it turned lurid and violent, with frequent regularity. The other sure-fire audience draw was the giant monster, or *kaiju*, genre. Spawned by Ishiro Honda's 1954 classic *Godzilla* (*Gojira*), these films were basic assembly-line films. Endless stories of Godzilla coming back again and again to demolish Tokyo, or Godzilla joining other giant monsters to demolish Tokyo, could be churned out by Toho studios to capitalize on the steady yet fast-diminishing stream of yen the Japanese were willing to spend at the box office. The only interesting turn in the Godzilla formula came as the giant, angry reptile slowly morphed into a hero monster. As more giant creatures were dreamed up by hard-pressed screenwriters, Godzilla eventually turned into Japan's protector, its guardian giant that showed up when a new monster from space, from the depths of the ocean, from under a volcano or under the ice showed up with hostile designs on Tokyo. Godzilla's transformation, though, made quite perfect metaphorical sense to the heads of Toho studios. A fantastic character that had been dreamed up as a symbol for Japan's destruction by the atom bomb, Godzilla had become the Japanese film industry's savior in real life. Soon enough, other filmmakers jumped on the *kaiju* bandwagon, with Daiei studios making its series of *Gamera* films about a giant flying turtle. Toho studios, however, would be the most successful home of giant monsters. Its *Rodan*, *Mothra*, and *King Ghidorah* films, as well as all various entries where the monsters met, fought or joined forces, turned out to be Toho's top earners for decades to come.

What Japanese studios did not have the resources for, however, or the inclination to gamble on, were temperamental, uncompromising directors who needed to realize their personal visions on screen, no matter the cost.

Five years would pass after *Dodesukaden's* failure until Kurosawa could make another film. He could get *Dersu Uzala* (*Derusu Usara*) off the ground, however, only with the help of foreign investment. Depicting Russian explorer Vladimir Arseniev's exploration and charting of the Russian-Manchurian border with the aid of an aging hunter named Dersu Uzala, the film was financed by the Soviet government. Although it was well-received by critics, another five years would pass until a new Kurosawa film would make it to screens. This time it took the help of fans George Lucas and Francis Ford Coppola to help Kurosawa secure funding for *Kagemusa*.

Kurosawa directed four more movies after *Kagemusa*. In 1985 he made *Ran*, an adaptation of King Lear, his last samurai-themed film. With *Dreams* (1990), *Rhapsody in August* (*Hachigatsu no Kyoshikoku*, 1991), and *Madadayo* (1993), he made films as different, respectively, as an abstract, filmic representation of dream sequences, a family's attempts at coming to grips with their country's past and their own vague understanding of the atom bomb, and an episodic, drolly comic tale of a retiring professor. As Kurosawa told his daughter, Kazuko, shortly before his death, he couldn't spend all of his life just remaking *Seven Samurai*.

Aggressive reactions to Kurosawa's films in Japan began in the late 1960s when, just as in Hollywood, a new generation of filmmakers was attempting to break into the industry. But whereas the young American aspirants and film students were adopting Kurosawa as a role model and mentor, their Japanese counterparts were turning on him. As director Masahiro Shinoda, a member of the late '60s "Japanese New Wave," said, "My generation reacted against the simplistic humanism of Kurosawa in, for example, *Rashomon*, *The Bad Sleep Well*, and *Red Beard*."[48] For the new generation of Japanese artists, Kurosawa was too formal a stylist, too populist, not political enough. Plus, Kurosawa was just too successful. As Shinoda adds, "Kurosawa has also been resented by the younger people not only because they were looking for a new metaphysic, but also because he had the advantage of large sums of money to spend on his films and they did not.... Kurosawa has exhausted himself pursuing the traveling camera."[49]

Although there had always been dualities in Kurosawa's films, interrogations of traditions, a deeply felt compassion for people crushed by the weight of their calamities and the unjust circumstances of life, Kurosawa had always insisted on films of hope. Perhaps for this reason, too, to compound his characteristically un–Japanese love of individualism and his success in the West, Kurosawa had to face the later half of his career contending not just with a difficult film industry but with a hostile artistic community. Kurosawa, perhaps, was too fond of the proverbial happy ending, in giving hope that an individual's struggles had worth, that the individual will could accomplish positive results. While Kurosawa might have revealed the dark side of the samurai legacy in *Seven Samurai*, for instance, the oath his title characters take to protect their peasant employers produces a virtuous result. Truth, reality, and experience might often be relative, *Rashomon* demonstrates, yet good and evil are not. In the final moments of the film, the woodcutter's choice to save a baby redeems him from his own greed and dishonesty. His actions, inspiring a young priest not to lose his faith in humanity, also promote something — no matter what it may turn out to be — positive for the future. Points of view, hidden agendas, human fallibility might cause pain and misery in the world, but when a baby's life is saved in *Rashomon*'s last moments, that one act of mercy and compassion has a value that is real and uncomplicated.

As unfortunate as it is that such sentiments were not cutting-edge enough for the new wave of Japanese artists, these sentiments, nevertheless, touched audiences for generations and changed world cinema like the works of few directors have.

3

Dragon Rising: The Power of Hong Kong Martial Arts

While a few of Akira Kurosawa's films had been instrumental in altering the American action/adventure and science fiction genres, the rest of Japanese popular culture did not seem to be able to travel to much of the world successfully for several decades. "Serious" filmmakers besides Kurosawa — directors like Yasujiro Ozu, Mikio Naruse, or Keisuke Kinoshita — were hardly known outside of critical and academic circles in the West. Various Japanese popular genres just did not take hold as well as the Hong Kong martial arts films would.

Among these genres the Godzilla-style *kaiju* giant monster films, for example, were never embraced as anything more than cheesy B-level entertainment for kids on local TV channels or on video tape. *Chambara* sword-fight films, but for a few exceptions like the *Zatoichi* films, were also mainly unknown by film goers in the U.S., apart from the hard-core action buffs and connoisseurs of Asian cinema.

With the disintegration of the Japanese film industry by the late 1960s, its chances of staying a force of cultural influence in the world dwindled. Almost at the same time, Hong Kong action cinema and its martial arts films were able to rise to world-wide prominence.

As the next chapter will detail, Bruce Lee, perhaps more than any other Hong Kong filmmaker, was responsible for the global explosion of Hong Kong films. In fact, discussing Hong Kong and martial arts films is almost impossible without including Bruce Lee. However, aside from having an indelible impact upon Chinese and Hong Kong cinema, he was also the product of an old and very rich tradition of filmmaking and theater art. Before one can look at Bruce Lee's impact, this history of Chinese filmmaking needs to be examined.

The Stage Is Set: Shaolin Wu Shu
and Modern Cinema

The martial tradition had been a part of Chinese film from its earliest days. Much like Japanese films have always made use of *jidai-geki* historical melodramas based on warrior legends, or the earliest American silents already featured cowboys and Indians shooting it out on the frontier, the earliest Chinese films already worked kung fu into their plot lines.

Some, however, claim that a clear connection exists between Chinese film and the very originators of the first martial arts fighting styles in the legendary Shaolin temple of the Hunan Province. This is a connection that is supposed to have come by way of the Peking Opera where performers were the first to be initiated into the ways of the Shaolin martial arts *and* the first to be featured in early twentieth century Chinese films. The martial arts are more than an easy, aggressive effort to exploit audience hunger for quick, cheap violence in Chinese cinema. The martial arts are a continuation of a tradition that is at the core of Chinese art as a whole. It is the continuation of a tradition that has as much chivalry, ethics, spirituality and philosophy as it has kicks, punches, sword-slashing and clashing armies of warriors.

Chinese history — and more than a bit of legend and mythology — claims that Shaolin Wu Shu, often referred to as just "kung fu," had been developed at the temple by its Buddhist monks, from where it spread throughout Asia by way of the Peking Opera. What would become the martial arts were, in fact, a set of exercises introduced to the monks by Indian monk Bodhidarma. Supposedly disturbed by the poor health of the Shaolin monks, Bodhidarma taught them exercises to strengthen their muscles, improve their breathing and, generally get them into shape. As even the monks in their secluded keep couldn't isolate themselves entirely from the worst parts of the secular world — namely raiding parties of bandits — Bodhidarma's exercises were modified into self-defense moves. Although the monks had to remain men of peace and couldn't take up weapons to fight, it was still decided that they had a right to defend themselves.[1] Thus, the first fighting styles were developed, sets of exercises called *wuqinxi*, or "five pure rivers." The moves of these exercises were fashioned after the movements of five animals: the tiger, the snake, the crane, the eagle and the monkey. In turn, entire self-contained systems would grow around these five animal styles.[2]

A standard plot device in countless martial arts films involves battles between artists trained in one or more of these animal styles. Films would also often center plots on the development, modification or resurrection of esoteric, ancient or "secret" styles of kung fu.

Some of the films dealing with the animal arts include *Snake and Crane*

Arts of Shaolin (She Hao Ba Bu, 1978); Snake-Crane Secret (She Hao Dan Xien Zhen Jiu Zhou, 1978); Snake Deadly Art (She Xing Zui Bu 1979); Snake in the Eagle's Shadow (Se Ying Diu Sau,1978) — notable for being Jackie Chan's first comedic martial arts film; *Ten Tigers of Kwangtung (Guangdong Shiu Hu Xing Yi Wu Xi,1979); Ten Tigers of Shaolin (Guangdong Shi Hu,1978);* or *Eagles' Claw (Ying Zhao Tang Lang, 1977)* among scores of others.

To appreciate the centrality of the Shaolin temple to martial arts films, one need only look at the very long list of films focusing their plots on the monks, the history of the temple, and its fighting secrets. Among these films are *Shaolin and Wu Tang (Shao Lin yu Wu Dang, 1979); Ten Brothers of Shaolin (Shi Da Di Zi, 1979); Shaolin Chastity Kung Fu (Shao Lin Tong Zi Gong, 1981); The Shaolin Drunken Monk (Shao Lin Zu Ba Quan, 1983); Shaolin Fist of Fury (Long Huo Chang Cheng, 1987); The Shaolin Invincibles (Yong Zheng Ming Zhang Shao Lin Men, 1979); The Shaolin Kids (Shao Lin Xiao Zi, 1977); Shaolin King Boxer (Tie Quan, 1976); Shaolin Mantis (Tang Lang, 1978); Shaolin Master Killer (Shao Lin San Shi Liu Fang, 1978); The Shaolin Temple (Shaolin Si, 1979); Shaolin Traitor (Shao Lin Ban Pan Tu, 1976);* or *War of the Shaolin Temple (Shao Lin Shi San Gun, 1980)*, again among dozens of others.

In the Shaolin lore, the monks did not stay completely withdrawn from the world forever. In fact, they were drawn into the most dangerous of all "worldly" affairs: politics. As early as A.D. 618, the Emperor Kang, having been impressed by the fantastic fighting abilities of the monks, called on an army of 128 monks to help rescue a prince from a rebel group. Over the centuries, the Shaolin monks would be called on to help quell various insurrections, terrorist plots, pirate threats and a Japanese invasion.

The turning point in the history of the Shaolin came, supposedly, during the Qing dynasty — established by the invading Manchurians — and at some point during the reign of the Emperor Yong Zheng. Fearing the monks' hostility to the Qing rulers, the emperor is reputed to have ordered the temple destroyed. Although the martial arts were outlawed since the Manchurians took over in 1644, it was widely — and quite correctly — believed that the monks were secretly carrying on their Wu Shu training and teachings. The destruction of the temple was supposed to have been the most effective final solution.

In Shaolin-centered martial arts cinema, the destruction of the temple is another oft-recurring theme. *Executioners from Shaolin (Hung Hei Kwun, 1977)*, for example, and *The Blazing Temple (Feng Shiu Siu Lam Chi, 1976)* depict the temple's end. Shaolin monks dedicated to preserving Wu Shu, spreading it outside the temple, and resisting the despotic Qing rulers, are likewise the heroes of many historical martial arts films. *The 36th Chamber of Shaolin (Shao Lin San Shiu Liu Fang, 1978)* deals with San Te, one of the most famous monks of the temple. The film traces the tutelage of a tough and skilled, but arrogant, youth in the martial and spiritual ways of Wu Shu. After having successfully completed his long road of trials through the temple's 35 chambers — each one outfitted with a customized set of weapons and physical challenges the student must learn to defend himself against — an enlightened, humbled San Te is ready to teach the sacred fighting arts to the world outside. He eventually sets up his own school in the Xichan Temple in Canton.

The cinematic legacy of the Shaolin legends, Kevin J. Wetmore argues, is as apparent when looking at the *Star Wars* films as the Japanese samurai influences from Kurosawa and the *jidai-geki* dramas. The mythology of the Jedi Knights seems to bear a very close resemblance to the Shaolin monks and the fate that befell them under Manchurian rule.

The similarities are especially apparent in the second trilogy, the prequel films presenting the background story of the Jedi. Much like the Shaolin, the Jedi are an ascetic, monastic order, dedicating their lives to the spiritual contemplation and control of the Force and the development of their fighting skills. Like the Shaolin, the Jedi, too, live by strict ethical codes. Although the Jedi are not active in the legislative matters of the Old Republic, they are, on occasion, used as a peace-keeping army. Like the Shaolin fighters called upon by the Emperor Kang, the Galactic Senate uses the skills of the Jedi for particularly dangerous missions.

Evil forces, however, eventually overthrow the Old Republic in episodes I, II, and III of the *Star Wars* series, establishing a dictatorial Galactic Empire, much like the Manchu invasion took over China in 1644. In *Star Wars*, to further the parallel, the Jedi must be eliminated for the Sith Lords to establish the Empire. The Jedis' fighting skills and control of the Force are too dangerous for the Sith to contend with as they consolidate their rule. To carry out their plan, the Sith must recruit and use a traitor from within the ranks of the Jedi. According to Shaolin legend, an evil monk named Ma Fuyi helped orchestrate the overthrow of the temple, then attempted to hunt down and exterminate the remaining monks. So, too, in *Star Wars*, Anakin Skywalker betrays his master and betrays the Jedi Knights, personally killing most of the Knights, even the "youngling" child trainees.

In the aftermath of the Sith takeover and the establishment of the Empire, the two remaining Jedi, Obi-wan Kenobi and Yoda, go into hiding, waiting for the right time to help Anakin's son, Luke, take up the battle against the Empire and learn the ways of the Force. In Shaolin legend, a handful of monks likewise escape the destruction of their temple, form secret societies, and begin teaching martial arts and fomenting anti–Manchu resistance.

One of the legends connecting martial arts to entertainment claims that many of the fugitive monks ran away with and hid among traveling opera troupes. There they diligently taught their martial arts techniques since the performers could disguise the moves of Wu Shu as the routine acrobatics and stylized moves of their stage performances.[3]

Over the centuries, however, Shaolin temples would be rebuilt — and destroyed — many more times, with a southern temple destroyed during the war of 1928 by the warlord Shi You San. Unfortunately, after the Communist takeover of China, religion was outlawed and adherents of Shaolin Chan Buddhism had, once more, to practice their faith underground.[4] The religious ban lasted until 1980; in 1983 Communist China even produced the martial arts film *The Shaolin Temple*. It starred a 17-year-old Jet Li and he became the first martial arts movie star hailing from mainland China.

In an interesting turn of events, the smash hit success of *The Shaolin Temple* prompted the Chinese government to restore the site of the original temple as a tourist attraction. Monks even perform daily Wu Shu exercises for the visitors.

However, much of the origins of the Chinese martial arts, the details of how they developed among the Shaolin monks, and the destruction of their temple are well wrapped up in legend and myth. Some historians contend that little evidence exists for the famous core of the temple legend and its destruction.[5]

When supernatural elements enter the story, one interested in historical details is even harder pressed to decide how much can be believed and how much is pure invention. For example, before setting up the Shaolin monks' fitness regimen, Bodhidharma was supposed to have sat and meditated in a cave for nine years, staring at a single spot on the wall until a hole burned through it. His successor at the temple, the monk Hui Ke, was supposed to have proved his devotion to spirituality by chopping off one of his own arms. He remained, nevertheless, a formidable martial artist.

While much of this sounds quite fanciful, the stories turned into plot devices martial arts films would often revisit, to great box office success. The one-armed-monk legend, for example, was the basis for *One-Armed Swordsman* (*Dubei Dao*, 1967), the first million-dollar-grossing Hong Kong martial arts film. Although the film was not a direct adaptation of the Hui Ke legend, its themes of moral and spiritual purification through kung fu and codes of honor, sacrifice and duty are all in place.

What is fact, however, is that the Peking Opera did incorporate martial artistry into the training of its performers, and Chinese cinema did originate as the filmed version of opera performances. Since the Peking Opera — actually a wide coalition of various regional opera troupes and styles that performed throughout China — was the country's favorite form of entertainment going back to 1790, early Chinese film exhibitors found they could stand a chance of drawing crowds only if they projected filmed versions of the prestigious plays.[6] Typical opera performances involved the reenactments of legends and mythic stories, music, poetry, singing, as well as acrobatics and martial arts.

While some opera purists would frown on the celluloid reproduction of the stage performances, the economies of scale would ultimately be in favor of the film exhibitors. Reshowing a film several times was cheaper than staging original theatrical productions. Moreover, admission to a film was also much more affordable than a theater ticket. Therefore, all those who found the opera beyond their means could opt to see the motion picture version.

In fact, films would prove to bring the ultimate demise of the Peking Opera. The improvements in film technology by the late 1950s and '60s had all but put the traditional Opera out of business.[7]

The legacy of the Peking Opera, however, is two-fold. On the one hand, before its obsolescence, the Opera provided the last generation of its classically-trained performers to the film industry. On the other, the subject matter of the Opera led to the sharp stylistic dichotomy of both mainland Chinese and Hong Kong action films.

The Peking Opera performers who migrated to film were the generation trained in the early '60s. Jackie Chan and Sammo Hung would prove to be the superstars of this generation, as well as Yuen Biao and action directors and fight choreographers Yuen Woo-ping and Corey Yuen.

Glimpses of the classic Peking Opera still available on DVD and VHS today include the film versions of the plays *The Kingdom and the Beauty* (*Jiang Shan Mei Ren*, 1959), *The Bride Napping* (*Hua Tian Quo*, 1962), *The Three Smiles* (*San Xiao*, 1969) and *The Last Woman of Shang* (*Da Ji*, 1964).

Depictions of the darker aspects of the Opera and the treatment of its performers are also available in several films. Controversy had always surrounded the Opera's training of children, as a top performer had to begin his tutelage by ages six or seven to fully condition his body to the rigorous demands of the martial arts and acrobatic performances. Accepted at the typical Opera school for no less than a seven-year commitment, children were basically sold by their families, all parental rights relinquished for the length of the contract. At that point, the instructors of the Opera school had full legal rights to treat the students as they saw fit. The contract even gave them the right to punish the students as long and as harshly as they felt was required, with no legal liability if the children were injured, maimed or even killed. The most graphic and shocking recollections of the brutalities in a typical Opera school are recounted in Jackie Chan's autobiography, *I Am Jackie Chan: My Life in Action*. In 1988, Sammo Hung, Chan's former classmate — and bullying nemesis—appeared in a highly sanitized look at life in an Opera school in the film *Painted Faces* (*Qi Xiao Fu*). Acclaimed Hong Kong director Tsui Hark's 1986 *Peking Opera Blues* (*Do Ma Daan*) also incorporates the Opera in its whimsical, comic story. Mainland Chinese director Chen Kaige's Golden Globe–winning 1993 film, *Farewell My Concubine* (*Ba Wang Bie Ji*), focuses on the lives of two actors brought up in the Peking Opera, highlighting the brutal training and constant beatings the children have to endure.

The operatic roots of Chinese film, however, also established the basis for the sharp contrasts between the realist and the fantastic schools of filmmaking. Because the Opera based so much of its entertainment on ancient legends and folk tales, so too did a lot of early films, gravitating toward stories based on such larger-than-life, hyperbolic stories. These old stories would be joined by original productions that likewise used classical settings, extravagant period costumes, swordplay action, solemn and traditional heroes, as well as stories of ghosts, demons and magic.[8]

Nevertheless, Chinese cinema would not only exist in the realm of the fantastic. Once Hong Kong became the capital of Chinese-language filmmaking, trends would alternate between the fantastic and realistic schools of cinematic story telling. Bruce Lee, for example, was mainly fond of the realist approach. Once the martial arts craze subsided by the 1980s, however, a new generation of filmmakers, the Hong Kong "New Wave," would apply state of the art, American-style special effects to new stories of fantasy, magic, ghosts, vampires, and monsters.

Overall, what most film scholars trying to pinpoint the metaphysical core of the Hong Kong cinema, trying to understand the *gestalt* of these films, all eventually agree on is the fact that the fantastic, the slightly larger than life, is always present in Hong Kong films. As David Bordwell writes, "Hong Kong films can be sentimental, joyous, rip-roaring, silly, bloody, and bizarre. Their audacity, their slickness, and their unabashed appeal to the emotions have won them audiences throughout the world."[9]

He adds:

> What Western fans consider "over the top" in Hong Kong movies is partly a richness of stylistic delivery—an effort to see how delightful or how thrilling one can make the mix of dialogue, music, sound effects, light, color, and movement. Realism is less important than a bold expressiveness in every dimension. In particular, physical activity can achieve a real magnificence when it is sustained and embellished. This delight in expressive technique is a local elaboration of the sensuous abundance sought by popular filmmakers everywhere.[10]

In an interview on the American DVD release of *Iron Monkey* (*Siu Nin Wong Fei Hung Ji: Tit Ma Lau*, 2001), Quentin Tarantino also brings an interesting interpretation to what might appear to be, to the uninitiated, a schizophrenic combination of emotions in typical Hong Kong films. When a Chinese audience goes to see a film, he argues, especially to something that is supposed to be escapist entertainment, it expects to see literally everything on screen. They want to see comedy *and* intense drama. Hence, many films will take whiplashing turns from broad, burlesque comedy to very realistic moments of tragedy. Martial arts films will veer from realistic fights to wildly outrageous and wholly unrealistic acrobatics.

This sort of clash between the sublime and the absurd, in fact, is an aspect of many Hong Kong films that American audiences might often be befuddled by. Americans like their emotions or stylistic approaches strictly segmented. Screwball comedy and tragedy do not mix in a Hollywood film. A good illustration of the standing gulf between Eastern and Western sensibilities is Sammo Hung's martial arts comedy *The Magnificent Butcher* (*Lin Shi Rong*, 1979). A film that is otherwise a collection of broad slapstick shtick — complete with a pants-fall-off-the-fat-clown routine — suddenly takes a dark and uncomfortable turn with the shockingly explicit attempted rape and eventual murder of a woman.

The Hong Kong Studios: MP&GI and the Shaws

The globalization of the Hong Kong film industry was a result of a diaspora from Mainland China; the industry functioned largely as a provider of entertainment beyond its own shores. Hong Kong studios have always, primarily, made films for export. Most of the product, however, went no further than the Pacific Rim countries. Even among these, their main markets were the Chinese immigrant communities. It would be Bruce Lee's career that would change all this.[11]

After film arrived in China and the exhibition of motion pictures as a money-making enterprise proved successful, film studios opened in Shanghai, Taiwan and Hong Kong. The Shanghai studios became the most dynamic and successful since Shanghai was also the center of Chinese business and finance.[12]

Hong Kong's role in the early days of Chinese filmmaking was as a center for Cantonese-language cinema. Mainland Chinese and Taiwanese films were almost exclusively made in Mandarin. With Mandarin the official language of the government, the upper classes and the intellectuals, films increased their prestige as a new art form and stood a better chance of being accepted by the elite if made in Mandarin.[13] Cantonese-speaking artists, as a result, flocked to Hong Kong. Cantonese was spoken largely in southern China and among the blue-collar working classes. Hong Kong's strategy for serving this market with entertainment, in turn, veered toward films high in thrills, sensational plots, violence, and supernatural spectacle. It was purely populist entertainment.[14]

But this changed with the political upheavals of the early twentieth century. With the outbreak of the second Sino-Japanese war in 1931 and the Japanese occupation of Hong Kong until the end of World War II, the film industry was badly hit. Filmmaking in Hong Kong nearly collapsed. After the war's end, more turmoil swept China as the nationalist Kuomintang government fought Mao's Communists for control of the country. With the nationalist defeat and the Communist takeover, waves of refuges spread across Southeast Asia. Many of them flooded into Hong Kong. Throughout, the colony's economy was depressed enough for the film studios to remain teetering on the edge until the end of the 1940s.[15]

The Chinese diaspora would also have profound effects on the structure of the Hong Kong film business once it did get back on its feet. To finance films, studios realized that the most efficient way to secure investment was to pre-sell unmade projects to theater chains across the Pacific Rim. With the large numbers of Mandarin-speaking Chinese now living in these areas, the exportation of Mandarin, rather than Cantonese, films became a safer investment. Soon enough, the odd situation developed where a largely Cantonese-speaking island was turning out the bulk of Asia's Mandarin-language films.

The turning point that got the Hong Kong film business back on its feet came in 1949. This was a point when a new type of film took Asia by storm. Of course, it was a martial arts film.

That year, director Wu Pang made a film he hoped would raise the spirits of moviegoers during the difficult times. It would be a heroic action film, he decided, centered on a fierce, patriotic and ethical hero who fought to right wrongs, fought for Chinese pride and helped the underdogs and victims of society. Best of all, the film would be based on a real person.

Wu's two-part action film *The True Story of Wong Fei Hung* (*Huang Fei-hong Chuan*) was such a blockbuster success that it spawned 98 sequels, running until 1970. The film was based on a real martial artist, herbalist healer, patriot and Confucian scholar who lived from 1847 to 1924 and ran the Po Chi Lam clinic/martial arts school in Foshan. For Chinese audiences, Wong Fei Hung was one of their most important and revered folk heroes. Someone on par with Davey Crockett, he was said to have embodied all the virtues of a philosopher/martial artist and Chinese man of unflagging national pride. Wong Fei Hung's mastery of the martial arts was supposed to have been so flawless that for generations martial artists could lay claim to immense honor and respect by tracing their lineage of teachers all the way back to him. Martial arts director Lau Kar Leung, for example, has boasted that he is only five masters removed from Wong Fei Hung.[16]

The Wong Fei Hung movie juggernaut was so powerful that in certain years the only martial arts films made in Hong Kong were Wong Fei Hung movies. In 1956, for example, 25 Wong Fei Hung films were made.

These films still had a connection to the Peking Opera in their popular lead actor. Kwan Tak Hing, star of the decades-long series, was a former Opera performer himself and an accomplished martial artist. And he literally was the star of the entire series! Kwan starred in every single one of the Wong films. After the series came to an end — not because of waning popularity, but because the producers decided that 99 was a lucky number to bring Wong Fei Hung's adventures to a close — Kwan occasionally reprised the role, making cameo appearances in films based on the (highly fictionalized) lives of Wong's most famous pupils. He turns up in *The Magnificent Butcher* to dispense sage advice and beat an opponent in a calligraphy-brush duel. The film was based on a supposed episode out of the early years of Wong disciple Lam Sai Wing. Lam, a butcher turned famed martial artist, became a highly respected teacher in his own right. Yuen Biao, another of Jackie Chan's Opera cohorts, made 1981's *Dreadnaught* (*Yong Zhe Wu Ju*), based on the life of Wong student Leung Foon, and offered another opportunity for Kwan Tak Hing to reprise his famous role. These appearances would be akin to Sean Connery making special guest appearances as James Bond in other action stars' pictures.

In an interesting turn of events, Kwan became an herbalist in real life after finishing the Wong Fei Hung movies, and also taught martial arts. In effect, he *became* Wong Fei Hung.

But if Wong Fei Hung saved Hong Kong cinema, a group of entrepreneurial brothers would make the island colony's film industry synonymous with martial arts films.

In 1957, the Shaw Brothers studio opened the largest filmmaking facility to date in Hong Kong. Named Movie Town, it rested on forty-nine acres, encompassing massive sets, editing facilities, film and acting schools and dormitories for its actors, trainees and production staff. It was a literal filmmaking factory, designed to rival anything in Hollywood. It was also the vision of film producer Run Run Shaw for turning his family's cinematic enterprise into the most powerful company in Hong Kong.

The "Shaw" family — originally Shao — made its first fortune in China's pre-war textile industry. Shao Zuiweng — theatrical name Runjie Shaw — however, had also worked briefly as a theater manager and had an accurate sense for the profit-making potential of film. In 1925, with brothers Runde, Runme and Run Run, he opened the Tianyi Film Company in Shanghai and began turning swift and steady profits in such popular genres as horror, fantasy, and sword-fighting action pictures.[17]

The company's successful horror and supernatural-themed films, though, soon clashed with the Nationalist government's social theories. The Kuomintang regime was committed to pressuring and censoring filmmakers into abandoning all films that promoted old-fashioned, superstitious, mystical and occult themes. These were outdated, backward-thinking films, the argument went, and unhealthy for a modern culture.[18]

The Shaws, in response, relocated to Singapore, establishing their new Nanyang Film Company. They also opened a chain of theaters throughout Asia and invested in a production facility in Hong Kong. By the early 1950s, they realized that the future of Asian filmmaking lay in Hong Kong and shifted their center of operations to the British island colony.[19]

The Movie Town facility was eventually run exactly like the filmmaking factory it was conceived as. The Shaws' approach to film was highly populist and their crowd-pleasing genre films could be turned out quickly, cheaply and according to easily repeatable plot formulas. These film facilities, critics commented, were not much different from the textile mills that first made a fortune for the Shaws.

Not surprisingly, the business plan worked flawlessly. The Shaws turned enormous profits from tightly controlling their overhead and churning out a high volume of popular fantasy, romantic, and adventure films. The profits were also wisely invested in the constant incorporation of the latest technologies, making polished, good-looking production values a mark of a typical Shaw Brothers film.[20]

The final step in the Shaws' ascendance to the top of the Hong Kong film world was their battle with rival Motion Pictures and General Investment Corporation. MP&GI was the filmmaking arm of one of Malaysia's most powerful business conglomerates, run by Loke Wan Tho. The MP&GI approach to film, however, was the artistic opposite of the Shaws' product. Whereas the Shaws made popular, escapist genre entertainment, MP&GI tried to create prestigious art. Loke's vision for his studio was to turn out films that sophisticated, cosmopolitan sensibilities could embrace. Quality films, he believed, were the key to getting the attention of a new generation of Chinese filmgoers. For MP&GI, money was to be no object in establishing themselves as the most sophisticated and classy of Hong Kong filmmakers. Generous exclusive contracts were offered to established writers, directors and stars to woo them to MP&GI. The company also aggressively courted the most promising of the Chinese cinema's up-and-coming new talent.[21]

Until 1964, these two top film companies of Hong Kong were locked in a war for the domination of the local and Southeast Asian film market. They often attempted to steal talent away from each other. They also made many of the same films, racing to beat each other to the box office. The first one to exhibit one of these films usually enjoyed blockbuster success and wind-fall profits, while the other's version floundered and died.

But the war between the studio giants came to an end in 1964 when Loke died in a car accident. Apparently he really was the most important creative driving force behind the studio's success. Without his guidance at the studio's helm, MP&GI — now renamed Cathay Organization Hong Kong — quickly went out of business.[22] The Hong Kong film world now remained for the Shaw Brothers studio to dominate.

For a while they did. Specifically, Run Run Shaw wanted to use the martial arts to dominate that market. Although the Shaw Brothers Studios' massive quota of films included a lot of popular genres, the fact was that Run Run Shaw, personally, did not much care for many of them. He did not like melodramas, romances and general women's films. More importantly, as a business man, he felt that a new generation of martial arts films, a whole new approach to the martial arts, would be the key to captivating a new generation of moviegoers. Referred to as the *wuxia* films, or martial and spiritual films, they were about both action and nobility of character. A studio marketing executive, in turn, came up with the phrase "New Century of *Wuxia*." A new slate of films peopled with noble fighters, and two important directors, would put the accent on action.

Run Run Shaw's first director to reimagine the venerable martial arts genre was Hu Jinquan. Working under the professional name King Hu, he brought a harder edge to *wuxia* films, a grittier, faster-paced, more action-oriented approach. He took a suggestion from Shaw, in fact, and paid very close attention to the Japanese *jidai-geki* and *chambara* films. Both of those genres were highly successful all across Asia at the time, well known for their realistic depictions of violence and fast, frantic action. The Shaws and Hu were especially inspired by Kurosawa's samurai films.[23]

Hu's landmark film from this period was *Come Drink with Me* (*Da Zui Xia*, 1966). Starring former ballerina Cheng Pei Pei, the film borrowed the Peking Opera's tradition of the woman warrior story. While the film might have had the period setting and its protagonist was still a woman — and though Run Run Shaw's growing disdain for women's pictures prompted the original edict for a whole new type of *wuxia* film — King Hu shot the rest of the film through with a high dose of adrenaline heretofore not seen in the genre.

Come Drink with Me is also the first film to put special emphasis on crediting the work of the martial arts director. Soon, fight choreographers like Lau Kar Leung and Yuen Woo-ping would become as famous as the directors they worked for and the stars they made look good with the fancy fighting moves. Both men would also move on to lucrative directing careers.

When it came to specific plot devices in the new-school *wuxia* films,

Come Drink with Me is credited by fans as introducing a fight sequence that would almost become a standard requirement in the genre: the teahouse fight. In countless martial arts films to follow, massive, intricately choreographed brawls in a teahouse would break out, most often using chairs, tables and tea pots as improvised weapons. Unlike the anarchic bar-room mêlée that became a similar staple of so many Hollywood Westerns, the teahouse fight of a *wuxia* film is always a skillful, fluid, acrobatic affair. More than merely smashing chairs and tables over each other's heads, the *wuxia* combatants routinely punch and kick each other while balancing atop the furniture, sometimes even as they teeter and sway atop precariously stacked scaffolds of chairs, stools and tables. Hot tea is also nearly always splashed in someone's face in the *wuxia* teahouse fight.

King Hu's tenure at Shaw Brothers did not last long past *Come Drink with Me*, however. Much like the demanding and temperamental Kurosawa whose style he studied, Hu was too much of a perfectionist for the Shaws' conveyor-belt film operation. He wanted to be an *auteur*, whereas the Shaws were looking for a proverbial "traffic cop." They wanted someone to put a group of actors through their moves as quickly as possible, with no deviations from predictable plot formulas.[24]

Hu might have departed the Shaws' operation soon after *Drink*, moving on to the Union Film Company, but the films he made with his new company, *Dragon Gate Inn* (*Long Men Ke Zhen*, 1966) and *A Touch of Zen* (*Hsia Nu*, 1969), are both regarded as masterpieces and they brought him attention from the world film community.

Following Hu's departure, the Shaw brothers' new star director to continue revamping the martial arts formula was Chang Cheh. A novelist-turned-screenwriter, Chang found a comfortable partnership with the Shaws because he shared Run Run Shaw's disdain for feminine films and he had no problems churning out a quick succession of studio-bound action spectacles.[25] In fact, not only did Chang Cheh helm nearly 100 films in his entire career, but he soon courted controversy for the amount of explicit, bloody violence he put in his films.

Chang Cheh's *One-Armed Swordsman* (1967) is unanimously considered one of the turning-point films in the martial arts genre. In many ways, it also established conventions Bruce Lee would expand upon and use to create his screen persona. The film was Chang's answer to the specific needs of the quickly-growing youth-film market and it was very strongly influenced by some of his favorite Hollywood films.

Chang Cheh, although 44 years old at the time, had an uncanny affinity for youth films. He was especially fascinated by the troubled-teenager pictures and the rebellious-juvenile-delinquent films Hollywood had been making since the '50s. He was also an avid fan of both James Dean and Marlon Brando. As film critics David Chute and Andrew Klein discuss on their DVD commentary for *One-Armed Swordsman*, Chang was so enamored of rebels that he liked working with leading men who were difficult to get along with. He had the greatest affinity for those actors who did not listen to him. Apparently he must have felt that a contentious relationship with a temperamental leading man gave his films the sort of verisimilitude they needed. On *Swordsman*, he found such a star in Jimmy Wang Yu. A former polo champion, Wang was also a brawler off the set. He was a real-life tough guy from a rich family who had the resources to live the Hong Kong fast life and enjoy the parties and the clubs, and he missed few opportunities to get into scrapes on the various party circuits. On the set, Wang also liked to butt heads with authority figures. But this suited Chang Cheh just fine. With *Swordsman*, he was committed to trying his version of the youth rebellion theme, as grafted onto the requirements of the *wuxia* genre.

On its surface, *Swordsman* is faithful to most of the central motifs of the martial arts genre. There is a requisite feud between rival schools. Martial artists are committed to defending the honor of their teacher. There is a storyline of treachery, betrayal and revenge. There is even a teahouse fight.

In terms of iconic fight scenes, *Swordsman* even sets up a brand new tradition that *wuxia* films would emulate for decades. Here, audiences are introduced to the street festival fight. As *Swordsman* sets the template, the generic street festival sequence involves the virtuous, peaceful citizens of a rural community wanting to have some fun in a bustling village square. The place is invariably filled with vendors and/or street performers. The good times are soon interrupted, however, by belligerent thugs who push people around, overthrow apple carts, make passes at and grope other men's girlfriends, and take things from vendors without paying for them. The thugs are usually affiliated with an unethical martial arts school whose guiding principle is doing anything it takes to win. Once it looks like the thugs' abuse knows no bounds, the hero steps in to challenge them.

Chang Cheh's approach to the *wuxia* film, though, introduced nuances that had never been seen before. The film's hero, Fang Gang, is a slowly-stewing young man at a prestigious martial arts school catering to the sons of wealthy families. He is uncomfortable there and unhappy with his circumstances as the master's charity case. Years ago, Fang's father was a servant at the school who saved the life of Master Qi (Tin Fung) during an attack by a rival martial artist's thugs. When Fang's father died, Master Qi swore to raise and take care of his son. Today, a grown Fang Gang might be the school's best martial artist, but he doesn't feel like he fits in among the rest of the students there. Complicating matters, Master Qi's spoiled, bitchy daughter, Pei-er (Pan Yin Tse), enjoys putting him further ill at ease by making insincere romantic overtures at him. Knowing that she is only trying to lead him on, Fang is usually sullen and withdrawn, the perennial outsider among elitist snobs. Fang, essentially, is as close to a martial arts version of James Dean's Jim Stark character from *Rebel Without a Cause* (1955) as one could possibly get in a wuxia film. These kind of dysfunctional relationships at a martial arts school were completely new to the genre. While there had been plenty of plots about traitorous students and warriors betraying each other, *Swordsman's* approach to the issue of infighting among martial artists is radically different. Here Fang is on the brink of rejecting the school and its culture. There is corruption within the system and the only virtuous stance to take is rebellion.

Fang eventually loses his arm when a confrontation with Pei-er and two elder students goes awry. Taunted by the girl into testing his mettle against his elder "brothers"—the students of a martial arts school are considered surrogate brothers—Fang quickly shows his superiority with a few moves, but he refuses to keep fighting. Then he once again rejects the girl's advances. Seeing this as arrogance and condescension, she lashes out at Fang, slicing off his arm with her sword.

Although typical martial arts conventions are soon back in play for the rest of the plot—Fang learns to fight with his left hand and even comes to defend the honor of the school he was so uncomfortable in—*Swordsman* breaks rules that have been heretofore sacrosanct in the *wuxia* world. The hero questions the character of the honorable teacher's school, for example. He does not treat his elder brothers with respect. At the end of the film, although he saves the school from the murderous Long Armed Devil's gang, Fang turns his back on the master's invitation to become the new teacher and he walks away from the martial artist's life.

Chang Cheh's approach to the revision of the martial arts film paid off, though. As mentioned before, *Swordsman* was the first million-dollar-grossing *wuxia* film ever made. The youth market indeed responded to the *Rebel Without a Cause* of kung fu and the film helped establish the subgenre of the crippled martial artist. Jimmy Wang Yu reprised the role in *Return of the One-Armed Swordsman* (*Du Bei Dao Wang*, 1969) and also played the *One-Armed Boxer* (*Du Bei Chuan Wang*, 1971). *The Crippled Avengers* (*Can Que*, 1978) were a team of martial artists joining forces to avenge their injuries at the hands of villainous Master Dao.

Something else worth noting about *Swordsman*, when searching for the connections between Asian and Hollywood cinema, is its uncanny parallel to so many bedrock Western plots and thematic archetypes. Perhaps more that any other *wuxia* film of its time, *Swordsman* is the closest to being a Western with swords and fists instead of six-shooters. The treatment of the martial artist, his place in society, his relationships to others — namely women — repeatedly echoes Hollywood Westerns. More than just self defense skills, *Swordsman* uses martial arts skills to define the practitioners' profession and social standing. Although the reasons are somewhat vague, fighting skills and martial arts training seem to destine a man to wandering the land and getting mixed up in fights of honor, vendettas, or wars, or, at best, becoming a freelance do-gooder, a righter of wrongs and champion of justice. The martial artist in this film is also as much of a loner and outsider as Kurosawa's samurai and the archetypal "westerner" outlined in Warshow's essay. The fighter's connection to others, to any community, except when he opens a school, seems to be tenuous. His relationship with women and families is also problematic because women can't seem to understand the warrior codes and obligations. In this respect, Chang completely discards a great deal of tradition going back to the earliest films and the Opera, where women were, most often, equally adept at the kung fu and had no problems joining the masculine world of fighting. Nevertheless, in Chang's film, the problem is ever present. After Fang Gang has been nursed back to health by Hsiao Man (Chiao Chiao), a beautiful farm girl who falls in love with him, his desire to train himself to fight with his left hand and become a martial artist once more is met by fear and disdain. The girl loves him too much to want him to be a fighter again. She wants to have a new life with him and if he becomes a martial artist again, all of that will be automatically jeopardized. Quite inexplicably, in this film the farming life, the peaceful simple life, seems incompatible with training to fight. It takes a lengthy explanation by Fang, and a curious lull in the action, to make Hsiao Man understand that, even if he trains and regains his fighting skills, he does not necessarily need to use them or be in any way involved in the life of a wandering fighter. Martial arts skills here are almost like a gun a nervous spouse is afraid to keep in the house, lest an accident happen. Fang, though, needs to work hard to explain that kung fu skills are better to have and not need, than need and not have. In other parallels to the Western, the martial artist here is like the gunfighter who is either challenging others to tests of skill or is being challenged and attacked by old foes coming to settle a score. The film's opening sequence, and Fang Gang's position as an orphaned ward of Master Qi, is motivated by such a grudge match. A fighter Qi defeated in the past is coming to get even, killing Fang's father in the process. Furthermore, Fang's new love, we find out in a highly coincidental plot twist, likewise lost a father to the martial life when she was a small child. Ever since then, just like her mother, the girl had grown to fear and loathe the life of a martial artist.

With the close similarities between *Swordsman* and American Westerns, it is surprising that the film did not find a larger mainstream audience in the U.S. once the martial arts genre finally crossed the ocean. Although it is almost a canonical film even among American kung fu aficionados, it was not discovered by a wide audience the way Bruce Lee would be or, decades later, Jackie Chan and Jet Li.

Chang Cheh also revolutionized the look of the martial arts film. Whereas the Peking Opera roots of the genre had often been all too evident — fight scenes that were *too* balletic and stagy, stilted, stylized performances — Cheng put the focus on the most vicious aspect of the martial arts. The martial arts are, after all, about fighting and violence and Chang had no qualms about shedding copious amounts of blood on screen. When Chang's characters use knives, swords, and spears, they deliver wide, gushing, spurting wounds. Limbs are sliced off and people run through with spears, swords and arrows. Often referred to as the "king of stomach wounds," Chang would often like to show the losers of fights in his films get their guts sliced open. They might, on occasion, find their intestines unraveling at their feet. In such situations, the most gallant fighters would do their best to tuck their innards back inside and keep fighting to their very last breath. Moreover, borrowing from Kurosawa, Chang also liked to let moments of intense violence linger in drawn-out stretches of slow motion. John Woo would later also list Chang as an inspiration for some of his own more memorable sequences of slow motion carnage.

At the turn of the decade in the early '70s, films like these, along with other Shaw Brothers hits like *The Golden Swallow* (*Jin Yan Zi*, 1968) and *The Chinese Boxer* (*Long Hu Dou*, 1970), had, as Run Run Shaw hoped, rebooted the martial arts film, gave it a new look and a new set of rules. The films ignited the "kung fu craze." However, most of the "craze" raged in Asia and Asian communities in the rest of the world. The martial arts were taken mainstream everywhere in the world because Bruce Lee was not satisfied with even the Shaws' innovations, and he would play only by rules he established.

4

The Little Dragon

Today, Bruce Lee belongs in a rare pantheon of celebrities whose power, impact, charisma, *relevance* seem to defy death itself. Like Elvis Presley, Marilyn Monroe, James Dean or Princess Diana, these are true immortal celebrities who continue to captivate and fascinate even from beyond the grave. They continue attracting new legions of fans, devotees, and acolytes who might not even have been born when the celebrities' stardom reigned.

Gauged by the sale of merchandise, books, magazine articles in various martial arts publications, and internet discussion forums and tribute pages, Bruce Lee literally lives on. A cursory look at any handful of books that are still being published about him gives evidence that Lee is special even among the most elite of immortal superstars. Lee captivates fans who feel he has a direct impact on their everyday lives. Besides numerous biographies, there are works on Bruce Lee and his guide to physical fitness, good health, longevity, and, of course, martial arts excellence. In effect, Bruce Lee is still teaching and guiding his pupils in the ways of the martial arts. But that is just the tip of a very large iceberg. Bruce Lee still instructs his fans in a lot more than just fitness and fighting. He tells them how to live. There are books about the words and thoughts of Bruce the philosopher, the spiritual advisor, the self-help guide to inner peace, self-mastery and enlightenment. There is also Bruce the sex symbol, Bruce the rebel and Bruce the champion of racial equality and justice. There is even Bruce Lee the subject of that peculiarly twentieth and twenty-first century phenomenon, the conspiracy theory. There are also plenty of revisionist works written about him. There are attempts by acquaintances, former colleagues, friends and rivals to "set the record straight," claiming to uncover hidden truths about "the real Bruce Lee." But while a great deal about Lee has, indeed, been mythologized, there is one truth about his life that is incontrovertible. Above all else, there is Bruce Lee the innovative filmmaker and star. Lee shares the distinction of being one half of the two-man team that did more than anyone to expose the West to the art and culture of Asia. If the world's eyes had been opened to Japanese culture by Akira Kurosawa, Bruce Lee was his counterpart when it came to bringing Hong Kong and Chinese films to the world.

As an actor, Lee is also a lot like Toshiro Mifune. Just as Mifune has been etched in the minds of film fans as the image of the quintessential Japanese samurai, Lee is the template for the supremely-skilled Chinese kung fu fighter. On screen, Lee was a master of unarmed combat whose entire body was a devastating weapon and whose mind ruminated on the subtleties of spiritual truths and the martial arts as a path to enlightenment. Bruce Lee was also the original one-man army. A decade before Sylvester Stallone and Arnold Schwarzenegger stripped off their shirts and, muscles bulging and glistening, wiped out battalions of evildoers, Lee flexed an incredibly powerful shirtless physique and took on hordes of martial-artist killers. With his shirt ripped off at least twice in each film, Lee would cockily saunter into enemy territory, wiping out twenty or thirty or forty men with kicks and punches that blurred before the eye.

Much like Japanese cinema before 1951, Chinese and Hong Kong films had largely been ignored by mainstream audiences outside of Asia. But once Lee destroyed box office records seemingly overnight with three low budget films between 1971 and 1972, Hollywood immediately took notice. Although Lee died almost literally at the moment he achieved international stardom, that small handful of his films, plus one of his American films, *Enter the Dragon* (1973), would send ripples through American filmmaking for decades to come. Just like Kurosawa, Bruce Lee was single-handedly able to leave a lasting impression on Hollywood, the wealthiest and most powerful film industry in the world.

David Carradine once discussed that he was so captivated by what he saw in *Enter the Dragon* that he quickly urged everyone working on his *Kung Fu* TV series to see it immediately. It would be unlike anything they had ever seen before, he promised. One of the first bits of feedback he got from a colleague was a simple comparison to the standard James Bond film. "He's a Chinese James Bond," the man simply remarked. And, indeed, on a superficial level, the film really is a martial arts version of any number of Bond films. The hero has to infiltrate the impregnable island fortress of a criminal mastermind named Han and thwart a diabolical plan before it wreaks destruction and havoc on the world. But the film was much more than that and Carradine knew it. Bruce Lee, he sensed, was not the Chinese James Bond but the Chinese James Dean.[1]

The parallels between Lee's and Dean's careers are almost eerie. They both did something very original, captivated audiences with larger-than-life charisma, and just as they were about to achieve global megastardom, they died in inexplicable strokes of bad luck. Most of all, they both embodied the same feelings of restlessness and rebellion. But while Dean played the teen misfit, the simmering rebel a decade away from the upheavals of the coming global youth culture movement, Lee screamed and unleashed defiance. Whereas Dean was a tragic figure in each of his films, a victim who inspired unrest because of the mistreatment he endured at the hands of the system's hypocrites, because he was a representative of the sheer unfairness of it all, Lee took action.

Bruce Lee's career proved that in show business true success is always a matter of perfect — or, perhaps more accurately, *lucky*— timing. It doesn't matter so much *what* a performer does in the world of film, music or any of the popular arts, as *when* he does it. Lee, in effect, was a true creation of the late '60s and early '70s. In the worlds of film and the martial arts, he was a loud, brash, uncompromising innovator.

In no uncertain terms, he told producers, directors and all the critics who would listen what was wrong with the martial arts genre and action films. He was also loud and clear about his criticism of Hollywood, the film industry's treatment of race, and its depiction of Asians. In the wake of the American civil rights movement, Lee's films put the accent on racial pride. His characters would refuse to back down from a fight when they were persecuted for their heritage.

Likewise, as a fighter, Lee did not hesitate in criticizing the extremely conservative martial arts culture. In a world that puts paramount importance on tradition, on reverence for history, on the wisdom of the oldest masters, where martial arts styles make a case for their supremacy by proving how old they are, Lee, in his twenties, declared that all the martial arts styles were flawed. He glibly rejected tradition and deemed himself worthy of creating his own art. Lee personified cocky, youthful impertinence in an age when young people around the world were breaking rules, protesting and threatening to overthrow the system.

Bruce Lee was born to Li Hoi Cheun and his Eurasian wife, Grace, on November 27, 1940, in San Francisco's Jackson Street Hospital. His father was a member of an opera troupe from Hong Kong, touring the U.S. at the time. A year after Bruce's birth, the family returned to Hong Kong, where Bruce grew up. In a life that would be mythologized to epic proportions, even his birth was surrounded by what his more mystical, superstitiously-inclined devotees describe as uncanny omens. For instance, he was actually given two names by his mother. For years Grace had believed that hostile spirits had designs on the family. For example, the Lis lost their first child soon after birth. Since that child was a boy, threats from the spirit world seemed imminent. To make sure their second child was a girl, the couple adopted daughter Phoebe. When their second son, Peter, was born, all seemed to indicated good luck, or, as Hong Kong lore termed the whims of fortune, good "joss." Upon the birth of their third son, the family wanted to take no chances, so they gave him a girl's name at first. He was called Sai Fon. Soon after, Grace renamed him Jun Fan. The physician on duty at the time nicknamed him Bruce. As an adult, he would anglicize the family name to Lee.[2]

While otherworldly influences on Bruce Lee's life are a favorite topic for speculation among his fans, what is known as a fact is that his rebellious, energetic streak was evident since childhood. Early on, Bruce was loath to follow rules. Even in the strictly authoritarian Chinese family, traditionally controlled by a strong-willed father, in time it was just accepted that Bruce would do certain things his own way if he set his mind to it.[3]

Among the things Bruce set his mind to were an active resistance to school, and an interest in fighting, show business, and, surprisingly enough, learning. Bruce might have hated the regimentation of school, but he loved knowledge. According to his family, as energetic and hyperactive as Bruce could be, he could also be found withdrawing and reading books for hours on end. Fighting, however, would cause problems for years, especially as his teenage years witnessed a string of expulsions from various schools. While a student at LaSalle "College," a Catholic school he started attending at twelve, he became a leader of a gang that actively sought out street brawls, especially with the British students of the King George V School. As his street fighting became more intense, his contacts with the rougher criminal street elements of Hong Kong more violent, scrapes with the law and visits by the police to the Li household increased. The one thing in his life that provided a positive direction for Bruce, though, was his own involvement in performance. Through his father, who had long aspired to a steady career as a film actor and even appeared in a number of the Wong Fei Hung films, Bruce got entrée into the Hong Kong film business by the time he was six. As it was becoming apparent that school could not control Bruce, his father hoped that entertainment would become an effective substitute.[4]

Bruce Lee made twenty films between the ages of six and eighteen, appearing under the screen name of Li Hsia Lung (Little Dragon). In an interesting example of art imitating life, most of his roles included street urchins, tough little orphans and juvenile delinquents. Whereas school antagonized him to no end, as a small child he had already declared that he would grow up to be a famous film star. But the one thing that continued to interfere with order in Bruce's life and peace of mind for his family was his compulsion to get into trouble.

After Bruce got the worst of a particularly violent street fight, a friend of his family introduced him to Master Yip Man, an instructor of the Wing

Chun style of kung fu. It was a fighting style emphasizing pared-down movements, efficient techniques that could be learned quickly and put to use in real-world fights, as opposed to the stylized movements of traditional kung fu used in tournaments and exhibitions. It also happened that Bruce was a natural at martial arts, taking to most of the techniques much quicker than most of the other students. A lot of the ideas Bruce would later expand upon once he became a teacher himself were planted by Yip Man. The ideas of reflection, the critical analysis of effective fighting methods, and a philosophical approach to the meaning of combat were all a part of Master Yip's tutelage. Unfortunately, so was the edict that everything one learned had to be tried in a realistic arena. Furthermore, Yip Man was also a strict traditionalist who believed that the martial arts could be taught only to the Chinese. The first of these ideas served as an effective encouragement for Bruce to continue as a street brawler. The second would eventually drive him out of Master Yip's school. Once his fellow students learned of Bruce's mixed heritage, they demanded that he be expelled. Although reluctant to do so, Yip Man got rid of Bruce to keep all of his other students.[5]

By the time Bruce Lee was nineteen, his show business career might have given him the stability and future his street fighting and "gang banging" threatened to wipe out. Run Run Shaw had taken note of his films and saw promise in Lee. The producer wanted to offer him a contract. Lee's parents, however, saw a more likely promise of jail, or worse, for him in Hong Kong unless he radically changed his life. Their son, they feared, was out of control and spiraling toward some tragic end.

In 1959, Bruce returned to San Francisco on the urging of his mother to continue his education. Perhaps crossing an ocean, she reasoned, would remove him from the dangers of Hong Kong and his own most self-destructive impulses. Having only himself to rely on in a foreign land, Grace hoped, might force Bruce to discipline his impetuous energy and focus it on something in a way he hadn't been able to do at home. In fact, Lee's first intention as he headed to the U.S. was to become a doctor. He planned to learn English well enough to complete high school and go on to college.[6]

Luckily, Lee's hyperactive, aggressive personality was coupled with an equally forceful drive to complete any task he set his mind to, the ambition to attain goals he visualized for himself. It also turned out that Grace Li's hopes for the shock from her son's having to fend for himself in America also came true. Instead of putting his energies into fighting and stirring up trouble, Lee put them into work and education. He eventually finished high school and moved from San Francisco to Seattle where he enrolled in the University of Washington, studying philosophy.

To put himself through college, Lee began teaching martial arts. But he also followed Master Yip Man's advice about the intellectual approach to the fighting arts. He attempted to couple that with the philosophy he devoured so voraciously from the books he was constantly reading, trying to understand the core meaning behind the moves of kung fu. He tried to teach his students how the martial arts were a path to a more virtuous and fulfilling life. In the most ironic turn of fate, the rebel who had fought with all his energy to escape school as a child, the delinquent who enjoyed starting fights, had now become a teacher instructing others on the value of the martial arts as a way of self-improvement and not belligerent violence.[7]

Nevertheless, Bruce Lee's ideas and practices as a martial arts philosopher and teacher soon courted controversy.

For one, he rejected the prejudice that originally drove him from Yip Man's school. When Lee taught, his classes were open to anyone who wanted to learn. He began teaching Americans of every race and ethnic group.

Unfortunately, that prejudicial, exclusive attitude that martial arts purists held in Hong Kong followed Lee over to the melting-pot country. The California Chinese martial arts community found out about his heresy and issued an edict for him to stop. The martial arts belonged to civilized Chinese persons only, they declared. The barbarians would not be taught their secrets.

When he defied this order, Lee was forced to partake in one impromptu tournament. He had to fight for the right to teach his way.[8]

That match, he handily won. But more controversy would linger about *what* Bruce Lee taught. The philosophy behind his teachings, the meaning behind kung fu, continued to rankle purists and traditionalists.

While most martial arts still clung to traditions, venerated the masters from centuries ago and followed strict styles, Lee declared that such thinking was erroneous. He had, essentially, brought the counterculture to the rigid, immovably conservative world of the martial arts. Rules laid down by others, Lee argued in the spirit of the times, were to be questioned and challenged. The path to martial arts mastery was not the perfection of others' systems and others' rules and the ideas of masters who had been dead for centuries. Mastery of the martial arts was to be found in self-mastery.[9] In Lee's view, to be a true kung fu adept, you needed — in the words of the hippies and radicals — to "do your own thing."

Lee called his new martial art Jeet Kune Do, or the way of the intercepting fist. His style, he explained in numerous TV interviews, articles for martial arts magazines and his own books, was to have no style. His form was to have no form. The perfect martial artist is like water: completely flexible to any situation, apparently formless and soft, yet also the most powerful force on Earth.

Aside from adapting counter-cultural, anti-authoritarian musings to the martial arts, Lee's motivation was also purely practical. He brought the experience and sensibilities of a former street brawler to the martial arts. He brought real street experience to a world that was largely, he believed, peopled with theoreticians and athletes with little fighting experience outside of the gym or the highly structured and regulated tournament arenas. Lee wanted to teach his students how to win real fights quickly and decisively, not score points in a contest.[10]

Lee backed up his claims by impressive demonstrations at martial arts tournaments. It was at one of these tournaments that his path back to the world of entertainment began.

By 1964, as Lee was making waves in the martial arts community with his brash iconoclasm and the ways of Jeet Kune Do, he had relocated with his new wife, Linda, to Los Angeles. His teaching had caught the attention of celebrity martial arts enthusiasts, among them actors John Saxon, Steve McQueen and James Coburn, and L.A. Lakers basketball star Kareem Abdul Jabar. But, of course, he made the move south because his childhood dream of becoming a major film star had started motivating him again. More than anything, Bruce Lee wanted to get back into the world of films. But he wanted to outdo himself. He wanted something much bigger than the venue where he had been a child star. He wanted a bigger arena than his father's Hong Kong film world. Hollywood was the top of the film mountain and Lee was determined to win here as he had against the other opponents he had picked fights with before.

But Hollywood, as Akira Kurosawa was discovering just around the same time, was a much more difficult opponent to conquer. Lee's ultimate hurdle, though, was not creative and corporate inertia, but racism. Lee wanted something much bigger than even Kurosawa. He would not be behind the camera, an unseen force, a reputation, a creative hand invisibly controlling the final product that would make it onto the screens. Bruce Lee wanted to act. He tried to put himself in front of American audiences, where it immediately became obvious that he was so different.

Lee's first forays into the Hollywood film world were not unimpressive. Martial artist Ed Parker had shot some footage of Lee performing his Jeet Kune Do moves and his tournament demonstrations and passed them to Hollywood hairstylist Jay Sebring. Sebring, in turn, brought Lee's incredible physical prowess and striking charisma to the attention of TV producer William Dozier. Dozier was in a unique fix at just that time; he needed an Asian martial arts expert quickly. He was producing *Batman* for ABC television and the show was a smash hit success. The network, in turn, wanted to multiply its superhero success and Dozier was tasked with bringing the *Green Hornet* to the screen. The *Green Hornet* had an Asian martial artist sidekick named Kato.[11]

Bruce Lee (far left) gets his first taste of Hollywood as Kato, the Green Hornet's sidekick, in a late 1960s episode of *Batman*, with Van Williams as the Green Hornet, Adam West as Batman and Burt Ward as Robin.

Bruce Lee, seemingly overnight, had broken into the Hollywood big time. Although Kato might have been the Green Hornet's sidekick, he was fast developing a cult following. Just like all who met Lee or saw his startling martial arts moves, audiences knew they were seeing something completely new. No other action star had fought like this before.

But audience tastes had also always been fickle. Smash hit successes one day proved to be flashes in the pan the next, and such was *Batman*'s fate after three seasons and, in turn, the *Green Hornet*'s. From pop culture phenomenon to blink-of-an-eye flameout, superheroes proved ephemeral in prime time television.

Lee's successive attempts at building a career in Hollywood seemed to bring ever-diminishing returns. After the *Green Hornet*, he had various walk-on roles and guest appearances in TV shows and films. Stardom, however, looked ever more elusive. While TV producers would listen to his ideas, told him they loved the kung fu, they all stopped well short of giving any of his projects a green light. They listened, for example, to his pitch about a Chinese martial artist wandering the Old West, righting wrongs and quietly opening the eyes of American audiences to the richness of Chinese culture. It was a great idea, Lee was repeatedly told — except the final commitment never came.

Counterculture, civil rights movements, youth rebellions and changing attitudes or not, television has always been the most cautious and conservative mass medium. Especially in times of sudden upheaval, in times when radical ideas were making people the most nervous, Americans looked to the TV set as a reassuring symbol of normality and predictability.[12] Therefore, if TV audiences had never seen an Asian hero before — Kato's mask had well concealed his "different" features for much of the show — TV executives were not going to chance antagonizing them with a Chinese hero now.

Things, though, were much different across the ocean. In Hong Kong, the *Green Hornet* was a smash hit on TV, rerun over and over again. On Hong Kong television, in fact, the Green Hornet wasn't even the star as far as audiences were concerned. Kato was. The program was called *The Kato Show*. For Hong Kong audiences, Bruce Lee was already a star.

In 1970, Lee moved back to Hong Kong to try films once again. He approached the Shaw brothers, hoping a film contract would again be extended. But this time, he also brought some ideas. He also hoped to negotiate.

It didn't work. As in most of his endeavors, Lee wanted to exercise control over any films he made. This was a major demand he placed before the Shaws. He wanted to make a martial arts film where he had a hand in the script, where he could tell a story he wanted told and communicate his personal philosophies about kung fu. But, most of all, he had to bring his own vision of combat to the screen. He wanted to choreograph his own fight scenes. Plus, he demanded a HK$100,000 salary.[13]

Run Run Shaw immediately balked. Above all, he was able to run such a profitable movie empire because he kept a tight control over budgets and salaries. One of the reasons Shaw employees, even most actors, most *stars*, lived in Movie Town housing was their salary was so low they couldn't afford housing anywhere else in Hong Kong. While making *The One-Armed Swordsman*, Jimmy Wang Yu made HK$2,000. Bruce Lee's demand for HK$100,000 was outrageous and out of the question.

Although Lee would make another return to the U.S. for a guest appearance on the soon-to-be-short-lived *Longstreet* TV series, Hong Kong would call back once more. There were other people who were unhappy with Run Run Shaw's stewardship of the Shaw Brothers Studios and they wanted to give Lee a try.

Good Joss Three Times

Raymond Chow had been an executive at Shaw Brothers and he did not like Run Run Shaw's "dutiful" obligation to his female staffers and starlets. Shaw's use of his casting couch had become legendary in the Hong Kong film industry. This outraged Chow, but not entirely on moral grounds. He was angry because he had been short-changed for a promotion in favor of a beautiful woman who slept with Shaw. After Mona Fong, a singer under contract at the studio, had been promoted over Chow following a series of Shaw's private coaching sessions, Chow walked out. Along with producer Leonard Ho, he set up his own studio, Golden Harvest.[14]

Desperate to secure talent as he tried to set up a company in the shadow of the Shaw Brothers film powerhouse, Raymond Chow offered Bruce Lee HK$15,000 for two films, along with a promise of the creative input he was so eager to exercise.[15]

Bruce Lee's first starring feature already looked like something markedly different from most of the standard *wuxia* films. *The Big Boss* (*Tang Shan Da Xiong*, 1971; later released in the U.S. as *Fists of Fury*), shot in Thailand, was not a period picture, as most of the Shaw Brothers films were. It certainly had a stark, shoestring budget look and it did not even try to set its action in a far off past of swordsmen and legendary warriors and warlords and such. Raymond Chow and Leonard Ho didn't have the money for such fanciful trappings. Back in Hong Kong, their studio consisted of a compound of run-down shacks and shabby office buildings on the outskirts of town. The movie, basically, looked as gritty and desperate as its story.

The Big Boss has a very simple crime thriller plot. It involves a once-rebellious youth named Cheng Chao-on sent to work with his uncle in an ice factory in Bangkok. As he and his cousins soon discover, the factory is used as a front for a drug smuggling operation run by their "big boss," a Japanese businessman named Mi (Yin Chieh Han). After two of the cousins start asking too many questions and nosing around Mi's operation, they mysteriously vanish. Suspecting foul play, Cheng begins investigating himself, eventually leading to a showdown with Mi and his henchmen.

That Chow and company allowed Lee a hand in the development of the story is obvious. Cheng's back story is nearly Bruce Lee's own autobiography. Just like the film's star, the character carries around his demons. Like Lee's own forced trip to San Francisco, Cheng had to flee his home because of his brawling and scrapes with the law. As the film begins, we find Cheng often fingering a jade amulet around his neck, something given to him by his mother as a symbol of his solemn vow never to fight again.

The fact that Lee got a great deal of creative control over the film, though, is more of a testament to the often-chaotic nature of low-budget kung fu filmmaking at the time, and to the state of disarray in the Chow organization, than to Golden Harvest's artistic magnanimity. Lee could work on imposing order and some vision on *The Big Boss* because leadership was sadly lacking from the project. The director of the film, Wu Choi Wsaing, was both disorganized as filming began *and* a loud, tantrum-throwing martinet who quickly alienated the entire crew. A worse problem, though, was that there was no script to work from. Wu had various rough, nearly incoherent outlines jotted on loose sheets of paper, and they were literally making up the film as they went along. Of course, such had been the modus operandi on a lot of low-budget Hong Kong films, so the beginning of *The Big Boss* project was not entirely unusual. Exacerbating matters for Lee, however, who cared about the project and saw it as a way to make or break his career, was the fact that Wu Choi Wsaing did not. The director was a good representative of the rank-and-file Golden Harvest team that had been lured away from Shaw Brothers: burnouts and hacks putting films through their paces for a quick paycheck.[16]

Soon enough, Wu was replaced with Lo Wei. Although the film's new producer was less of a tyrant, he did not care much more about the quality of the film than Wu did. Lo Wei's unique problem was his compulsive gambling. Often he would have a radio on the set to help him keep track of the racing results while the cameras rolled.[17]

In its final form *The Big Boss*, therefore, can be considered very much a Bruce Lee film. It was a result of his own vision, ideas and direction much more than anyone else's at Golden Harvest. In turn, the film started breaking box office records across Asia the moment it was released.

Lee revolutionized martial arts filmmaking with *The Big Boss* because he managed to make the genre relevant again. It can even be argued that he made martial arts films relevant in a way they had *never* been relevant before. By placing the story in the present, by involving characters and situations that were realistic, *The Big Boss* could speak to the lives of its audiences clearly and honestly. Here was a film that was not set in fifteenth-century China, did not involve Shaolin monks or noble warriors on their quests to defend the honor of their emperor. Such films said very little to the young people of the '70s. In *The Big Boss*, audiences saw a working-class family toiling away in a dead-end job, trying to scrape by and make it from one day to the next. They were surrounded by the familiar denizens of the lowest strata of the working-class world. They had to contend with street punks, crooked gamblers, pimps, prostitutes, and organized crime gangs. The ice factory they worked in was run by a corrupt boss and they were abused by his vicious foreman. *The Big Boss* offered its audiences untempered reality instead of escapist fantasy.

But the film also offered a hero restless young people of the early '70s wanted to see. There was only so far Cheng would be pushed before he did what the youth of that generation were burning to do: he fought back once injustice had gone too far. Here was a hero who would not tamely accept the faults, flaws, crimes and slights of the world. Cheng would not get along and go along. The young audiences of *The Big Boss* wanted to see a hero who was true to his ideals, who could not be bought off, bribed by the boss' henchmen or promoted until he sold out and supported the system. Cheng was a character the radicalized could cheer for, he was a hero for the counterculture movement. He was the personification of the darker, dangerous side of the hippie generation. Although the late '60s and early '70s are now romanticized as a time when a generation "stood for peace and love," it was also a time of revolt. Bruce Lee in *The Big Boss* can be read as an epitome of this impulse to rebel and overthrow the system. He stood for the impulse to throw rocks and riot when handing out flowers did not work. Just like Martin Luther King had a counterpoint in Malcolm X, Bruce Lee represented the clenched fist of the counterculture movement when turning the other cheek and passive resistance failed.

The fighting style, the physical presence, the moves Lee displayed in his films, in fact, are most often described by film analysts as being animalistic, dangerously primal, yet seductive and attractive. It is also interesting to see how all the trademark Lee moves he would repeat in his following films are already on display in *The Big Boss*. One of the most accurate summaries of Lee's repertoire of mannerisms, trademark moves, comes from David Bordwell:

> In every film fight, Lee boldly expresses his changing emotions and his unique personality. Of course he is capable of ferocious rage, although usually it is compressed into a fierce glare and a stabbing forefinger. For unworthy opponents he shows undisguised contempt, cocking his head, strolling around them, rolling his eyes. Yet even when dispatching the lesser fighters, he seldom loses that brooding scowl suggesting a strange mixture of detachment and self-absorption. Sometimes his eyes turn from his enemy to fasten on something off-screen, and his blows seem merely to play out a pure pattern of elegant movement, largely indifferent to their devastation of the opponent. At other moments, after he delivers a punch his brows knit, his head swivels, and his mouth opens in astonishment at the damage he has done or draws into a grimace mixing strain, anger, and anguish.[18]

All of this is seen in *The Big Boss*.

As mentioned before, another Bruce Lee trademark, setting the example for future action stars like Sylvester Stallone, Arnold Schwarzenegger and Jean-Claude Van Damme, was the fetishization of the male body. In *The Big Boss*, Lee is already fighting in either a very tight tank top or bare-chested once his shirt is torn off. This move, of course, was revolutionary in two respects.

On the one hand, the conspicuous display of the male body, the objectification of well-proportioned musculature of an actor, had not been a regular feature of action films. In either the American films of action icons like John Wayne or Gary Cooper or Clint Eastwood, *or* the traditional Chinese *wuxia* films, men were not given to showing off how good-looking their bodies were. Although Chang Cheh included a scene of Jimmy Wang Yu chopping wood shirtless, sweaty muscles glistening, in *The One-Armed Swordsman*, martial arts films were not meant to show off men's brawn. Kung fu was all about skill and speed, not brute strength. What little objectification of the male body occurred took place in the cult cinema of Italian Hercules and Roman strong-man movies. That was the first and only genre that put bodybuilders in leading roles. Former professional musclemen like Steve Reeves, Reg Park or Mickey Hargitay starred as Sampson or Hercules or various brawny gladiators and mythic heroes. These were the only films at the time that made sure their stars' muscles glistened and flexed and bulged at just the right time and just the right angles for the cameras. But these were rather fringe genres and would remain on the fringes, almost dying out, in fact, until Arnold Schwarzenegger briefly revived them with the *Conan* films of the early 1980s.

On the other hand, the objectification of Lee's body is of importance on the racial level. For the first time, a film was quite consciously and aggressively positioning its Asian star as a sex symbol. The fact that audiences outside of Hong Kong and Southeast Asia, that Caucasian audiences in America, would accept Lee was revolutionary. In essence, once Lee's films would play to packed movie theaters in the U.S., to a broad racial cross section of the country, he would have the final say about Hollywood's racism. The actor they had rejected as unsellable to mainstream America would become one of the most influential male film icons of the twentieth century. This level of success in fetishizing and sexualizing Lee shattered a very long and very demeaning tradition of Asian male stereotypes that had been created mainly by Hollywood. The most prevalent of the stereotypes presented Asian men as being weak and asexual.[19] Although pulp novels, dime novels, comic books and early adventure cinema used the stereotype of the Asian male as the menacing, cruel, conniving invader, the warlord or the criminal mastermind, there was also an undercurrent of weakness, an effeminate softness to these characters. While the Asian criminal masterminds — cemented in the popular imagination by Sax Rohmer's 1912 to 1930s Fu Manchu novels and subsequent movie serials and feature films, not to mention volumes of the early twentieth century's virulently racist "yellow peril" literature — plotted to take over the world, invade America or flood its streets with crime, drugs and vice, they did it while cowering in the shadows. The stereotypical Asian male was dishonest, underhanded, physically weak and either sexually inadequate or somehow perverted.

But Lee's success in this respect, it should also be noted, repudiates more than just Hollywood racism. It is true that many of early Hollywood's depictions of non–Caucasians are inexcusably offensive, but the fact is that even in Asian cinema there has not been any tradition of strong, hard-bodied, muscle-flexing alpha males. As Galbraith writes in his history of Akira Kurosawa's and Toshiro Mifune's careers, Mifune's image of the strong, rough, physical Japanese man of action was a captivating surprise not only to American and European audiences, but to Japanese as well. Asians have always liked their leading man softer, more effete than Americans. In the martial arts film tradition, the veneration of the Shaolin monks again suggests an uneasy relationship with sex and sexuality. While Shaolin monks might have invented one of the deadliest fighting styles in the world, they were also celibate. Self-consciously sensuous, seductive, hyper-masculine muscle flexing had no real precedent in kung fu films.

Reading Bruce Lee's screen persona aside from counter-cultural, radical and gender concerns, one also sees a more complex action hero making his appearance in the martial arts genre. This was the type of protagonist already taking over a lot of the action genre in the U.S. Lee's characters took what Chang Cheh started in *One-Armed Swordsman* one step further. The roles Lee played personified a new breed of action hero painted in morally ambiguous shades of grey. The past of the *wuxia*, of all martial-arts-oriented Asian story telling, had been peopled largely by noble warriors. Nobility, essentially, was the only mold for generations of swordsmen and warriors and questing martial artist heroes and sage Shaolin monks. Much like the duty-bound, noble samurai of Japanese legends, and the heroes of the *jidai-geki* and *chambara* films before Kurosawa, the martial artists on film have always been uncomplicated, upstanding, honest, selfless, temperate and true. Bruce Lee, however, did what Toshiro Mifune did for the samurai. He did what Clint Eastwood did for the equally noble tradition of the cowboy. Lee complicated the generic hero. Lee's typical characters had a darkness to them, a dangerous menace lurking not far beneath the surface. Unlike *wuxia* protagonists who had come before, Lee's characters were bound to fight for reasons other than honor, duty or the protection of the weak and virtuous. A Lee character had it in him to fight — to kill — out of rage. An audience knew that a Lee protagonist, although he might have been a hero and he might have fought on the side of right, could still hold a grudge. A Lee character could fight out of anger, he could break rules if need be. He was a realistic hero in a complicated world that was losing its faith in myths. He was the kind of hero audiences could relate to when they no longer trusted in a just, orderly universe. Audiences could cheer for a Bruce Lee hero when they felt the justice system, the authorities were a nest of corruption. If you couldn't believe in society's leaders, its authority figures, you could root for a Bruce Lee character. When moviegoers were no longer sure that crime did not pay, that evil would be punished and the virtuous get their just rewards by some benevolent design of the universe, a seething, edgy hero like Lee became attractive. Like films featuring Clint Eastwood as Dirty Harry or the dangerous rabble of *The Dirty Dozen*, Bruce Lee films showed a world where badasses and bullies were put in their place not by noble piety and a just, divine providence of an attentive and kind God, but by a bigger, tougher and meaner badass who just happened to fight on the right side.

But if swaggering, ambiguous machismo didn't have precedent in martial arts cinema, strong Chinese nationalism — chauvinism even when it came to the Japanese — certainly did. The perennial villains of countless martial arts films, both before and after Lee, were the Japanese.[20] To be certain, the Chinese have endured invasions and occupations from the West, imperial control and humiliation — namely the Opium Wars and the British Crown's forcing the Chinese government to tolerate the sale of the dangerous narcotics to its people — but they suffered particularly under the Japanese. The occupation of Chinese lands, including Hong Kong, by the Japanese during World War II and the repression, brutality and mass murders committed by the Japanese army linger painfully in the not-so-distant memories of Chinese throughout Asia. The *wuxia* film, thus, has been a symbolic battle ground between patriotic Chinese and villainous, sadistic, murdering Japanese invaders. Lee's second film, *Fist of Fury* (*Jing Wu Men*, 1972; released as *The Chinese Connection* in the U.S.), fully exploited this anti–Japanese animosity.

The film is also Lee's only period piece. It is set in 1908 Shanghai, and the Japanese presence is becoming unbearable for a growing number of patriotic Chinese. The Japanese are exerting an ever-increasing influence over the local government and they treat the Chinese police forces as their puppets. They also quite openly and regularly describe the locals as "the sick men of Asia." But one of their strongest critics and most fervent crusaders for Chinese national pride and independence is Master Huo Yuan Jia of the Jin Wu school of Wu Shu. In the opening scene of the film, however, we are told that something has gone terribly wrong — Master Huo, the seemingly invincible marital artist, has just been killed in a tournament.

Lee plays Huo's pupil, Chen Zhen, returning to Shanghai and hearing of his master's death. After flying into a hysterical rage at Master Huo's funeral, flinging himself into the grave and clawing the dirt off the coffin, Chen decides that it would have been impossible for his teacher to have been killed so easily. The old man was a devastating martial artist; strong, agile and nearly invincible with his technique.

Sure enough, a rival school of Japanese karate experts barges into the Jin Wu school, promising the students that they will be put out of business. Burning for revenge, Chen soon repays the favor, going to the Japanese dojo and single-handedly beating up all of its students. Eventually proving that Huo Yuan Jia was poisoned before the tournament, Chen instigates a new series of confrontations with the Japanese. But this earns a retaliation and all of the Jin Wu students are killed. Chen eventually faces off with Suzuki (Riki Hashimoto), the sadistic head of the dojo, killing him handily. All the while, however, the hotheaded Chen seals his own fate, ending up in the hands of the Japanese-manipulated police. Knowing there is nowhere left to go during a final showdown with a massive contingent of well-armed cops surrounding his school, Chen launches into one last act of defiance. With a shrieking battle cry, he hurls himself at the phalanx of cops. The last image is a freeze frame of Lee lunging through the air, à la *Butch Cassidy and the Sundance Kid* (1969). The scene fades out as we hear gunfire erupting.

Aside from several impossible leaps through the air and a completely ridiculous rickshaw-lifting scene, *Fist of Fury* is a perfect testament to another Bruce Lee trademark: realistic martial arts. One of Lee's agendas had always been the propagation of his martial arts philosophies and the tenets of Jeet Kune Do. To get people to take the martial arts seriously, Lee felt, they had to see *real* martial arts. They had to be shown the true physical prowess of a supremely skilled technician on screen. To do so, Lee had to eschew a lot of kung fu film traditions that dated back to the earliest silent film roots of the genre, namely the glaringly unrealistic screen combat.

Matching the epic, legendary subject matter of so many early martial arts films, the staging of fights had long been accomplished with an accent on over-the-top, unrealistic and, more often than not, physically impossible combat moves. Many an artist had been seen flying incredible distances through the air, jumping tens of feet over opponents, leaping over walls or carrying on extended swordfights while seemingly suspended in mid-air. Needless to say, wires and trampolines had been used — often times quite crudely — to approximate what looked like period Chinese versions of *Superman.*

Lee, on the other hand, wanted to thrill his audience with his own incomparable fighting skills. He wanted to stun his fans with moves they had never seen before, but he wanted to make sure they saw the *real* Bruce Lee on screen. His audiences should have been made to realize that Bruce Lee was a living superman. In other respects, Lee's preference for the realistic approach to martial arts filmmaking was also rooted in his days in Hollywood.[21] The American approach to filmmaking was similarly of the realist school. For Hollywood directors and American audiences, there had to be a great degree of verisimilitude to even larger-than-life situations. Sure, the stories of lightning-draw Western gunfighters were pure fantasy, but they *looked* real. Ultimately, this reality in Lee's films would help contribute to their eventual blockbuster success and influence in the U.S. as well.

While others have also had objections to the wire-propelled, fantastic school of martial arts — Run Run Shaw told his directors to study Kurosawa and the Japanese action films for their realistic look, and even the old Wong Fei Hung movies opted to show only fighting moves that could be done without special effects — no other actor had ever moved and fought like Bruce Lee. As a number of editors had often recalled when giving interviews about work on Lee's films, he was so preternaturally fast that his hands and fists could lash out quicker than the cameras could capture the movement. While cameras often had to be speeded up to photograph other martial arts actors, the opposite was true for Lee. They had to *slow* the cameras in order for his movements to properly register.[22]

Unfortunately, *Fist of Fury* is still occasionally marred by the results of arguments Lee lost with returning director Lo Wei. There are several scenes where Lee is seen springing through the air in leaps that could be accomplished only with the aid of a trampoline. The worst of these relapses to the old-style martial arts film, though, is a scene where Chen threatens a lackey of the Japanese by single-handedly lifting the man's rickshaw high overhead.

Audience reception of the film, however, ensured that Lee's future cinematic endeavors could proceed unencumbered by hack directors. As Bruce Thomas' Lee biography recalls, seeing *Fist of Fury* almost became a patriotic obligation for Chinese audiences throughout Asia. Lee went for the nationalistic nerve with his film and he hit it with virtuoso accuracy. A scene where Chen smashes a sign reading "No dogs or Chinese allowed" inspired standing ovations. In most of the theaters where the film played, it shattered all previous box office records. In Singapore, *Fist of Fury* was withdrawn for a week until the police could formulate adequate crowd control techniques to handle the mobs descending on the theaters. In the Philippines, the government also pulled the film after it looked like the locally-produced movies would not make any money as long as *Fist* was playing.

As a result of *Fist of Fury*, Lee also set a precedent in star power that had been seen only in Hollywood. After becoming the most successful actor in Hong Kong history, he used his clout to make demands no one else had ever been able to make.[23] He became the first actor to demand and get the right to script and direct his own films and form his own production company within the studio he worked with. In what he planned to be his third and fourth films, now as a producing partner with Raymond Chow in Concord Pictures, Lee would attempt to use all this creative freedom.

The first of these two films became *Way of the Dragon* (*Meng Long Guo Jiang*, 1972; retitled *Return of the Dragon* in the U.S.). As with all Bruce Lee films, several major precedents were set. Not only was he now completely in control of the film, but it was the first Hong Kong film to shoot on location in Europe.[24] The film is also lighter in tone than *The Big Boss* and *Fist of Fury*. *Way of the Dragon* is a tongue-in-cheek story of a virtuoso martial artist coming to Rome to save his family's restaurant from extortion by the mob. It concludes with a fight between Lee and the mob's American martial artist hitman, Colt, played by karate world champion Chuck Norris. Filmed partially on location in the Coliseum and mainly on soundstages, the fight is, indeed, one of the most impressive martial arts spectacles on film. Lee's driven perfectionism and ongoing insistence on a realistic approach to screen combat makes the fight sequence unforgettable.

In making *Way of the Dragon*, Lee quite shrewdly exploited the same elements for success as he did in *Fist of Fury*. He knew that *Fist*'s nationalistic flavor made it a smash hit and turned him into a household name throughout Asia. He had a very specific fan base, Lee knew, and he knew that audiences had to be carefully nurtured and pleased. The Bruce Lee fan base was a largely working-class youth audience, an audience that might have seen itself as powerless, a group without a voice in the world and little to take pride in. In turn, when people like that went to the movies, they wanted to see a larger-than-life, fantasy version of themselves doing all the things they knew they could never get away with. In *Way of the Dragon*, as in *The Big Boss* and *Fist of Fury*, the Lee character is another volatile, edgy, working-class youth who will no longer be pushed around. Traveling to Rome to visit his besieged family, he is a representative of all the Chinese communities scattered throughout the world. Just as real immigrant communities faced battles to assimilate into foreign cultures, to be accepted and allowed to live on their own terms and try to preserve their heritage, the characters of *Way of the Dragon* fight for the right to establish a new life in a foreign land.

Lee planned on following *Way of the Dragon* with a film that would put the accent on his martial arts philosophy in a way none of his previous films had. Although he had remade himself as a film star, Lee's ambitions, as always, remained outsized. He yearned to be established in wider venues. He wanted to fuse his former life of teaching martial arts and studying philosophy with his film work. Of course, with his new platform as Asia's number one box office star, he would be able to teach and expound his revolutionary designs on the fighting arts.

Game of Death (1978) was envisioned as Lee's tour de force of filmmaking and martial arts philosophy. It would be a filmic representation of all he had been teaching through Jeet Kune Do. Its plot was a metaphor for the concept of overcoming styles, abandoning traditions, defying pre-set limitations, of finding one's self.[25] The plot should have involved a group of martial artists recruited for a mission to raid a pagoda whose upper tier housed a trove of gold. Challenging the team, however, are several groups of martial artists, all masters of various styles of combat. In effect, the pagoda would have been a multi-level martial arts school, with each floor housing one of the major martial arts. The top floor, though, has a single treasure guardian. This is a fighter with no one style, no constricting set of fighting rules and traditions that control him. Of the raiders, the only one who could stand a chance of reaching the treasure would be the one who could likewise abandon his adherence to styles, who could become completely fluid, completely free and improvisational.

Filming on the *Game of Death* began in 1972, but it would never finish. Lee decided to put the project on hold because another opportunity came up to conquer the ultimate film obstacle. By then, word of his phenomenal ascent to stardom had reached Hollywood.

The martial arts craze sweeping Asia was also gaining attention in America. Some had begun to speculate about whether the kung fu fad could take hold in U.S. movie houses as well. The Shaw Brothers' *One-Armed Swordsman, The Chinese Boxer* and *Five Fingers of Death* (*Tian Xia Di Yi Quan*, 1972) had all been released in the U.S., all turning sizable profits. Furthermore, following Richard Nixon's 1972 visit to China, an interest in Asian culture was on the rise. At the same time, the counterculture movement had also been discovering Eastern philosophies, spirituality and Asian religions. From meditation to Buddhism, the youth movement was finding Asian culture and Asian beliefs to be the hip new "trip." After the Beatles traveled to India to meditate with the Maharishi Mahesh Yogi, the Transcendental Meditation movement quickly swept Hollywood.[26]

Warner Bros., in turn, wanted to gamble on what stood a good chance of becoming a new film trend. Rather than paying to distribute Hong Kong films, they wanted to try and make one of their own. It might finally be time, they decided, to give Bruce Lee his chance to star in a Hollywood film.

By this time, though, what had become the added insult to the injury of Hollywood's previous prejudicial rejections of Lee was also on TV. The "Eastern-Western" Lee had hoped to interest producers in had made it to the airwaves at last. Titled *Kung Fu*, it was a martial arts version of *The Fugitive* about a Shaolin monk roaming through the Old West, wanted for a justifiable killing, righting wrongs with his martial arts and dispensing sage proverbs and philosophical musings.[27] Despite the rising interest in the East, the lead role was still not played by an Asian actor. The CBS network chose David Carradine, who had no previous martial arts training, to play the Shaolin monk Kwai Chang Cain. The Cain character was prominently identified as being half Anglo and half Chinese, lest audiences be too rankled. Although Bruce Lee himself was of mixed racial heritage, Carradine's casting was telling of CBS' timidity. In the show's frequent flashbacks, a teenage Cain is also played by a Caucasian actor who looks even less Chinese than Carradine.

Enter the Dragon, Warner Bros.' project for Lee, filmed in Hong Kong and co-produced by the American studio, Raymond Chow, and Lee, was both the first serious commitment by a major Hollywood studio to bringing Asian heroes and the martial arts to American audiences *and* a project that few of the American principals had faith in. Nearly everyone had passed on the offer to direct the picture and screenwriter Michael Allin had expressed open disdain for the project even as filming began.[28] According to actor/martial artist Bob Wall, director Robert Clouse routinely made comments denigrating Lee's acting skills, well within earshot of the other cast and crew. By all of the accounts of the production, the atmosphere on the set quickly deteriorated into nearly open warfare, with Lee on one side and Clouse and Allin on the other. To the creative personnel on the American side of the production, the film was rarely more than a cartoonish B-movie, a "chop socky" exploitation picture casting a martial artist as an Asian James Bond. To Lee, the exacting perfectionist who approached films as a reflection of his values, his character, in essence, the creatively lax and uninvolved attitude was maddening. At one point, the hostilities between Lee and Clouse escalated to the point that Lee demanded Clouse be barred from the set when the fight sequences had to be choreographed and filmed.[29]

As chaotic and contentious as the filming of *Enter the Dragon* had been, however, Lee's streak of box office success remained unbroken. The film quickly performed as all three of his previous ones had, rocketing to block-buster success upon release. *Enter the Dragon* not only opened as a hit in the U.S., but it would eventually make over $200,000,000 in its worldwide release. As in all of his battles, Bruce Lee had again won, had proven true to his boasts to become a bigger success than all of his former star pupils.

But, unfortunately, David Carradine's comparison had proven to be the truest. Bruce Lee did become the Chinese James Dean. Just like Dean, Lee didn't live to see his crowning achievement. He could not see *Enter the Dragon* become not just a hit, but an eventual cultural phenomenon, something that had a tremendous impact on Hollywood, a film that realized his dream of giving American audiences a Chinese hero.

Bruce Lee died on July 20, 1973, in Hong Kong. The peculiar circumstances of his death made it pass into legend, into martial arts pop culture mythology. After Lee passed out in the apartment of his mistress, actress Betty Ting Pei, his demise came as a shock to a world of fans because it was so unlike the way a larger-than-life hero, a fighter who was as close as one might get to a real superhero, was supposed to die. The official coroner's report ruled that Lee died of an allergic reaction to the prescription pain killer Equagesic, which, according to Betty Ting Pei, he took shortly before collapsing.[30]

Unknown to his fans, Lee, the epitome of perfect health and superb physical conditioning, had been badly deteriorating in the months leading up to his death. The stress of finishing *Enter the Dragon*, coupled with the business pressure of an increasingly

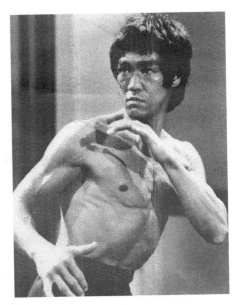

The Dragon triumphant! Bruce Lee returns to Hollywood as an international superstar in *Enter the Dragon* (1973).

contentious and difficult relationship with Raymond Chow and Lee's own compulsion to push himself to the extremes of exhaustion with work and exercise, had been gradually tearing the seemingly invincible actor down. Those closest to him had been concerned over his drastic weight loss and increasingly temperamental, erratic and unpredictably volatile behavior. Throughout this period, he was known to have complained about the sudden onset of excruciating headaches. While dubbing *Enter the Dragon*, Lee passed out and had to be rushed to the hospital with a severely swollen brain.[31]

But these were details the world did not know. To his millions of stunned fans, it seemed impossible that a man who was so much stronger, so much more perfect than mere mortals, could suddenly be felled by the most banal of circumstances. It was a death millions could not accept. And thus, Bruce Lee passed into the special realm of that late-twentieth-century social phenomenon, the conspiracy theory. To this day, in Hong Kong and throughout Asia, among martial arts fans and Bruce Lee devotees, there are more conspiracy theories circulating around his death than the U.S. has conspiracy theories about the John F. Kennedy assassination. Lee was murdered by the criminal triads controlling so much of the Hong Kong film industry, some argue, because Lee crossed them. Lee was killed by disgruntled martial artists, others counter, because the movie star belittled their art. Or Lee was killed by Japanese assassins because his film disparaged Japan. Or Lee was killed by martial arts instructors still holding a grudge over his teaching of secret techniques to Westerners. Or Lee did not die at all, but faked his own death to escape the pressures of celebrity, withdrawing into a monastic life in the Chinese wilderness to practice his kung fu in peace. Or, perhaps the most fantastic of all theories, the demons Lee had evaded as an infant with his first feminine name caught up with him at last.[32]

Regardless of the outlandish speculation, the fact is that Bruce Lee drastically changed martial arts filmmaking in the East *and* the West. Lee had become the embodiment of modern martial arts cinema. For a very long time to come, all films dealing with the martial arts would exist in the shadow cast by Lee. They would imitate Lee and his films, they would pay reverent homage or even parody them, they would try to follow in the stylistic and thematic footprints left by Lee's work, or they would react to them and try to force the genre to grow and change, but Bruce Lee and his films would always remain the standards of the genre.

Impact on America

It is fitting, of course, that Hollywood would be affected by Bruce Lee as much as Hong Kong was. The man the American film industry had previously rejected was still making the rules Hollywood had to — at least for a while — abide by. Until the "kung fu craze" subsided by the mid to later half of the decade, Hollywood was as much in Lee's grip as was Hong Kong. Just as people in Bruce Lee's orbit had to follow his rules, follow his tempo, bend to his will or get out of the way, so American producers were still in the temperamental star's grip from beyond the grave.

Bruce Lee's impact on Hollywood and American culture was threefold. He helped inspire a greater interest in the real martial arts, the success of his films brought more Asian films into the U.S., and American filmmakers even started shooting projects centered around Asian cultures and the martial arts.

Just as he had dreamed of doing from the moment he started teaching in Seattle, Lee got Westerners involved in the martial arts en masse after his death. With the kung fu craze in the theaters and on TV, more and more Americans wanted to learn the fancy moves themselves. Kung fu, Karate, Judo, Tae Kwon Do, and various other Chinese, Japanese and Korean martial arts schools started cropping up across the country. Bruce Lee, of course, presided over many of them — or at least he did in spirit. Aside from Bruce Lee T-shirts becoming a fashion fad of the '70s, his posters led the crush of posthumous merchandising efforts. At least one Bruce Lee poster decorated most martial arts schools after his death. People wanted to learn martial arts to *become* Bruce Lee.

To fuel American audiences' newly developed and insatiable appetites for the martial arts, Hollywood's film distributors decided to go back to the source and import more kung fu films. There had to have been, after all, more like Bruce Lee in Hong Kong. Or, if not in Hong Kong, perhaps in Japan.

For a brief moment, the 1970s saw the opening of Hollywood's doors to Hong Kong–produced martial arts films in the effort to find the next Bruce Lee. For a while, some of the best works of directors like King Hu, Chang Cheh, Lau Kar Leung, and Yuen Woo-ping made it to the U.S. Both Shaw Brothers and Golden Harvest films were available to American audiences. While the two studios were in cutthroat competition in Hong Kong, they turned out enough movies to satisfy American — and world — appetites for swordfights, fistfights, the honors of schools offended, teachers who needed to be avenged, promising young martial artists who needed to learn secret techniques and villainous clans that needed to be destroyed.

Even countries like England, Italy, and Australia went in pursuit of all the kung fu money to be made. Their own theaters, after all, were packed by cheering fans when the projectors unrolled Asian martial arts films. Just like Warner Bros. had done with *Enter the Dragon*, some of these countries also entered into co-production deals with Hong Kong studios. The British produced *Legend of the Seven Golden Vampires* (1974) and *Shatter* (1974). The Italians made *Blood Money* (*El Karate, el Colt, y el Impostor*, 1974). The Australians cast one-time James Bond George Lazenby opposite Jimmy Wang Yu in *The Man from Hong Kong* (1975).[33]

But the martial arts influx did not come only from Hong Kong. Although the Japanese film industry continued struggling throughout the late '60s and '70s, one fearsome, scowling, morally ambiguous Japanese Karate master attained, for a brief period, an enthusiastic fan base that almost rivaled that of Bruce Lee.

Shinichi "Sonny" Chiba, born Sadao Maeda in 1939 in Fukuoka, Japan, rocketed to world-wide fame with the 1974 release of *The Streetfighter* (*Gekitotsu! Satsujin ken*). While Bruce Lee displayed fluid grace and raw animal power in his moves and sudden, deadly strikes, Sonny Chiba displayed just plain brute power. If Bruce Lee was the Clint Eastwood of the martial arts — lean, brooding, subtly dangerous — Chiba was the Charles Bronson of the genre. Chiba was not graceful, he was not positioned as a sex idol. He was a compact, glowering, silent blunt instrument. Even in the roles he played, Chiba took moral ambiguity into much darker, much more dangerous territories than Lee ever did.

As the '70s martial arts films got more and more violent, as the general

American action genre became increasingly brutal, cynical, and amoral, Chiba's *The Streetfighter* pushed the limits of on-screen bloodletting past what anyone had ever seen before. Not only are Chiba's opponents given vicious, bone-shattering beatings, but a crude bit of X-ray–like special effect shows bones breaking as a result of a hit. In *The Streetfighter*, throats are ripped out, eyes are gouged out, and testicles torn off. Moreover, Chiba's character is an amoral, unfeeling antihero. He is a freelance hitman who kills for the highest price. Which side is in the right is hardly a concern for him. The fact that he winds up on the "right" side in the course of the film is by pure chance.

The Streetfighter was such a shock to the American ratings board, the Motion Picture Association of America, that it became the first action film to get an "X" rating for violence.

Although Chiba earned a sudden cult fan following, he did not have the sort of staying power in the American popular memory as Bruce Lee did. While his follow-up films, *The Return of the Streetfighter* (*Satsujin Ken 2*, 1974) and *The Streetfighter's Last Revenge* (*Gyakushu! Satsujin Ken*, 1974) were all successful (and heavily edited to tone down the blood and gore), the entire martial arts genre started faltering within a few years. The downturn in these films' popularity ultimately served to compromise Chiba's longevity in the American mainstream.

The reason the martial arts genre started fading also bears taking a brief look at. For one, while some excellent films were imported in the '70s, the quality was quickly outweighed by the dreck. For every *Five Deadly Venoms* (*Wu Du*, 1978), or *Master Killer* (*Shao Lin San Shi Liu Fang*, 1978), audiences were treated to dozens of films like *The Amsterdam Connection* (*He Lan Du Ren tou*, 1978) or *Dumb Boxer* (1973) or *The Bloody Fight* (*Quan Men*, 1972) or *Kung Fu-ry* (1975). The dreck, after all, came cheaper. Thanks to films like these, the martial arts cinema was quickly on its way to turning into a punch line for scores of jokes and fodder for (largely accurate) parody. Bad acting, bad fight choreography, bad camera work, bad plots, and cheesy special effects of swordsmen swinging around on the ends of ropes all helped undermine a once-exciting and dynamic genre. Of course, the worst (and funniest) offenses these films committed were sloppy gaffes like stilted, stiff dialogue dubbed over lips whose movements did not match the words, or ridiculous sound effects where an actor's every movement, no matter how slight, was matched by a loud *whooshing* sound.

But what almost killed the martial arts genre was Hong Kong's own reaction to Bruce Lee's death. Lee had always looked to kung fu films as a way of introducing the world to the Far East, as a first step in whetting the appetites of film audiences for a much larger dose of Asian culture and all it had to offer. Hong Kong studios, however, hardly had such an ambitious cultural agenda. When Lee died, their response was a frantic search for not simply a replacement, but a clone. Their efforts were an exercise in absurdity.

The wake of Bruce Lee's death saw the beginning of "Bruceploitation" and the Bruce Lee imitators. A handful of actors with enough of a resemblance to Lee were quickly groomed to take over the duties of single-handedly dispatching hordes of evil on screen. They were given Bruce Lee haircuts, they were photographed in Bruce Lee poses in advertising art, and they were given laughable new screen names. This was the new era of Bruce Li, Bruce Le, Bruce Lo, Bruce Lai, Bruce Leung, Bruce Chen, Bruce Thai, Tiger Lee, Dragon Lee, Conan Lee, Rocky Lee, and Bronson Lee. In turn, they starred in films like *Blind Fist of Bruce* (*Mang Quan Gui Shou*, 1979); *Bruce, King of Kung Fu* (*Zui She Xiao Zi*, 1980); *Bruce Has Risen* (*Shen Long*, 1978); *Bruce and the Iron Finger* (*Da Jiao Tou Yu Sao Niang Ze*, 1979); *Bruce the Superhero* (1979); *Bruce and the Shaolin Bronzemen* (*Shen Long Meng Hu*, 1982); *Bruce Lee Fights Back from the Grave* (*America Bangmungaeg*, 1976); and *Bruce Is Loose* (*Qing Long Ke Zhan*, 1977). As Hong Kong film historian Ric Meyers writes, this was akin to making a series of Dirty Larry films starring Clint Westwood.

But the worst piece of Bruceploitation actually involved Bruce Lee himself. In what amounted to cinematic grave robbery, Golden Harvest tried to squeeze every last cent it could from every last frame of film that Lee was on. Hiring Robert Clouse to do the job, they took the footage Lee had shot for *Game of Death* and tried to assemble it into a film. But, as it turned out, Lee had shot only scenes for what would have been the film's climactic pagoda fight. Clouse and Golden Harvest remained undaunted, however. They hired Kim Tai Chung and Chen Yao Po to stand in for Lee and they tried to create the film's first two acts by shooting the actors from behind, in shadows, in very distant long-shots or wearing dark glasses or motorcycle helmets. The film's most infamous scene involves one of the actors standing in front of a mirror; a photo of Lee's head is pasted onto the glass to create the illusion of the actor's neck and shoulders extending from Lee's head.

Most of what has been written about *Game of Death* over the years usually involves the terms "travesty," "garbage," "insult," and "fraudulent."

Importing foreign kung fu films could take Hollywood only so far, though. The most powerful filmmaking and distribution organization in the world had to make its own films as well. American-flavored martial arts, it was reasoned, might not only keep filling the hole left by Lee but, perhaps, add something more uniquely local to the genre that the Hong Kong and Japanese fare lacked.

Interestingly enough, the first American films to continue where Lee had left off also continued in their rebellious, counter-cultural tradition.

With the blockbuster success of *Enter the Dragon*, several producers reasoned that some of the other martial artists who had shared the screen with Lee might now stand a good chance of winning over audiences on their own. However, John Saxon, the most obvious choice for this position in the eyes of critics and fans at the time — given the fact that Saxon's character makes it until the end of the film and that Saxon was a well-established actor before *Enter*—wouldn't appear in a kung fu film until 1978's forgettable *The Glove*. As Bruce Thomas remarks, it was odd how no one at Warner Bros. even wanted to make a spin-off film about the Roper character Saxon played in *Enter*.

Instead, the first *Enter* alumnus to make a kung fu film was the African-American actor Jim Kelly. Kelly, a former International Middleweight Karate Champion, plays Williams in *Enter*, an American fighter who comes to the evil Han's island for the martial arts tournament and eventually joins forces with Lee in trying to put an end to the villain's nefarious drug-running activities. Although Williams is killed about midway through the film, the athletic and charismatic Kelly, it was speculated, helped the film draw a large black audience. Throughout the '70s, Kelly made a series of martial arts films in the "Blaxploitation" cinema mold. Mixing martial arts with the Black Power themes of Blaxploitation, Kelly arguably followed Lee's formula quite closely, using the martial arts as a vehicle for messages about racial pride.

From 1974 until 1982, Kelly made *Three the Hard Way* (1974), *Black Belt Jones* (1974), *Golden Needles* (1974), *Take a Hard Ride* (1975), *Hot Potato* (1976), *Black Samurai* (1976), *The Tattoo Connection* (1978), and *One Down, Two to Go* (1982). Of these films, *Three the Hard Way* and *Black Belt Jones* and its oddly titled sequel, *Hot Potato*, are generally the most well known. In all of these films, Kelly plies his martial arts as he fights his way through plots by evil white racists to either swindle, subjugate or kill blacks.

Three the Hard Way, for example, joins Kelly with former football players and Blaxploitation regulars Jim Brown and Fred Williamson to stop a megalomaniacal white villain from poisoning America's water supply with a chemical agent designed to kill only blacks.

Surprised by the film's very strong box office, Warner Bros. immediately wanted their *Enter the Dragon* costar to come back and make *Black Belt Jones*. They even put *Enter* director Robert Clouse at the helm of the project. This time, Kelly displays yet more coolness, supremely self-confident machismo, and a very big, bulbous afro. He plays a free-lance secret agent with a social conscience who comes to the aid of his former martial arts school in a South Central Los Angeles ghetto. As it turns out, the dojo's admirable Asian teacher — catering to black youths, doing his best to make a positive difference in the community — is being pressured by the local mob to sell the property. Knowing that the city's major redevelopment plans will drive up the price of real estate, the gangsters want to make a killing on the land deal.

Less militant and confrontational with whites, the *Jones* sequel, *Hot Potato*, put the Kelly character in yet a bigger, international stage. His character fights to rescue a U.S. senator's daughter from a crime lord trying to influence American foreign policy.

Martial arts, in fact, became an often-used staple of Blaxploitation films. Along with Kelly, who became the most well known as a black martial artist in the '70s, numerous films in the genre armed their tough guy protagonists with kung fu skills. Ron Van Clief, for example, a New York State Full Contact Karate Champion, made *Black Dragon* (1974), *Black Dragon's Revenge* (1975)—about a Bruce Lee conspiracy theory—*The Squeeze* (1978), *Kung Fu Fever* (1979) and *The Bamboo Trap* (1979). Carl Scott, another black actor and martial artist who also worked in Hong Kong on occasion, like Van Clief did, made films like *Soul Brothers of Kung Fu* (1976) and *Sun Dragon* (1979). Even October 1969 Playboy Playmate of the Month, Jeannie Bell, got into the act in 1975, playing the title character in *TNT Jackson*. Comedian and musician Rudy Ray Moore brought the martial arts to his Blaxploitation farces *Dolemite* (1975), *The Human Tornado* (1976), *Petey Wheatshaw* (1977) and *Disco Godfather* (1978).

Aside from the racial pride messages in Bruce Lee's films, martial arts have, from their earliest appearance in the U.S. and their depiction in popular culture, had an especially strong appeal to African-Americans. Theorizing about the reason, Mikel J. Koven writes a list of possible appeals to this audience:

> 1. the vast number of young black men who had served in Vietnam had come in contact with this art form and were eager to propagate it in the States; 2. martial arts give one discipline, structure and spirituality, in addition to being able to defend oneself—a major theme in a number of Blaxploitation films—and therefore, karate gave black youth an active and positive alternative to the drugs and street crime which plague inner cities; 3. martial arts do not depend on brute strength or size, and therefore create an equality between opponents, which other forms of street defense do not; and 4. it was non-white—and perhaps more subconsciously (or not!) was an acceptable way in which to kick whitey's ass.[34]

What should be added to this hypothesis is the fact that the martial arts are often seen as the little man's weapon. In real martial arts schools, first-time initiates or visitors are routinely shown demonstrations of how a small, willowy or very old martial arts expert can almost magically overcome enormous, muscle-bound opponents. In any number of kung fu films, tiny, wizened masters can handily defeat much younger and stronger fighters. Although the truth behind this lies in the very real fact that the martial arts are basically the arts of biomechanics, the use of leverage and balance against opponents, the defeat of strength by the *miraculous* powers of a much smaller and weaker adept carries profound psychological, even political, weight. The martial arts would be attractive to those who have always felt small, disenfranchised and powerless. Seeing a supremely skilled fighter on screen use lightning-quick moves, flailing, jabbing fists and feet to defeat a phalanx of bigger, tougher, better-armed opponents is metaphorical for the outsider, the impoverished, the marginalized minority without resources taking on and challenging an oppressive status quo. Even Bruce Lee, although always having taken good care that each of his films show off his well-developed muscles, was still a small man. He is always photographed at such angles and framed against opponents in such a way as to make sure the audience notices that his main opponents are *much* bigger and stronger.

The Blaxploitation kung fu film, or the Blaxploitation genre as a whole, however, did not last long in the seventies. Ultimately they were a product of a time when counter-cultural, radical movements came to prominence because of the country's growing dissatisfaction and anger with the Vietnam War. The war turned out to be an event that set a stage for factions of angry, dispossessed and disenfranchised groups to speak out against the injustices of a society that purported to be free and democratic. The civil rights movement, in turn, inspired a period in black filmmaking where African-American artists could independently make the films the big studios were loath to touch. When films with black heroes asserting their independence and power proved successful, even mainstream studios came around and joined the "black power" movement, just like they opened their doors to Bruce Lee when they saw there was money to be made. The money, however, ran out quickly, especially for Blaxploitation. The reasons were various.

For one, as M. Ray Lott argues, many of the Blaxploitation "classics," from *Three the Hard Way* to *Black Belt Jones* to *Black Samurai*, were fundamentally hypocritical about their commitment to equality. If anything, Lott argues, these films engaged in very bitter reverse racism. The black heroes openly hated whites. Whites were overwhelmingly racist, fascistic maniacs. Reviewing, quite accurately, *Black Belt Jones*, a film that likes to wear its commitment to social justice and its Marxist statements about "capitalist pigs" proudly on its sleeve, Lott writes:

> Money, literally, becomes the root of all evil, and business becomes analogous to corruption, the bigger the business the more corrupt.... Contrasted with this is the presentation of the have-nots. Those who are poor or without large sums of money are shown in a positive light, as decent folks committed to their neighborhoods, while the wealthy or well-to-do are depicted as criminals who prey on the people. All, that is, except Kelly. Kelly is a secret agent with a million dollar house on the beach, plushly furnished right down to the beautiful

woman who caters to him. He drives a fancy sports car and wears the hippest threads in town. Kelly is clearly a raconteur, not a proletarian working man, and spends his time at political gatherings that promote Third World affairs. His occupation leaves him long amounts of idle time, some of which he spends training a group of women in gymnastics. In fact, Kelly has so much money that he actually turns down missions from the government.[35]

Moreover, while this sort of militancy, even in films released by a major studio like Warner Bros. in the case of *Black Belt Jones*, might have alienated even the most liberal-minded white audience, Blaxploitation found just as many detractors among African-Americans. At best, these films degenerated into ever-more-cartoonish kitsch, quickly abandoning all pretense at creating a cinema of pride and empowerment. One-dimensional caricatures of black macho men, pimps, hookers, hustlers, and racist "whitey" cops and "the man" soon ruled. At worst, Blaxploitation could be seen as the propagator of some of the most vulgar black stereotypes one is likely to find in film. For example, the empowered heroic black male these films were supposed to have been championing — characters like Shaft — degenerated into the stereotype of the belligerent, sex-obsessed black thug. The typical Jim Kelly character, for example, bears a disturbing resemblance to what film historian Donald Bogle calls "the buck" in his study of the most prevalent racist stereotypes in American film. The buck is always a large, muscular black man, usually hot-tempered, impulsive and violent. Attempts to rein in his aggression are usually fruitless and reasoning with him does not work. The buck is basically unintelligent and constantly given to challenging the white man's authority. He also has an insatiable sex drive, perpetually lusting after young white women.[36]

Indeed, not only can the typical Jim Kelly hero mow his way through armies of white goons, but he can usually devour women with a near-supernatural sex drive. In *Enter the Dragon*, this is already on display. In a scene where the martial artists arrive on Han's island and are treated to a lavish banquet, each man is given a choice of a prostitute for the night. The Kelly character, naturally, picks three. Then he says, "If I've missed anyone, I'm sorry. You have to understand — it's been a long day. I'm tired."

When any film genre becomes so hot so suddenly that studios rush to fill a demand any way they can, the seeds of that genre's demise are planted within its success. Soon enough, the dross outweighs the quality. The teen horror genre saw this phenomenon, for example, by the late 1980s. The glut of Jason and Freddy sequels and mindless and unimaginative rip-offs ensured the genre's downfall for nearly another decade. Between the fourth-rate Hong Kong dreck, the Bruce Lee clones and the bad Blaxploitation, the martial arts genre, too, had flamed out by the middle of the decade.

Bruce Lee's icon status, nevertheless, had not diminished. As mentioned earlier, a Bruce Lee industry is still alive and well. Books about his philosophies, his martial arts style and teachings, collections of his letters to friends and recollections by the people who knew him are still being published.

While countless biographical films have been made about Lee in Hong Kong, even Hollywood revisited Lee with one major film homage in the 1980s and a big-budget Warner Brothers biopic in 1993.

The first of these films, 1985's *The Last Dragon*, is a cult favorite, fusing very broad comedy and a Blaxploitation homage with a slick MTV-video-style look and sound. Produced by Motown Records boss Berry Gordy at the height of the 1980s music video craze, when everything from commercials to films and hit TV shows like *Miami Vice* was imitating the look, sound and editing style of videos, *The Last Dragon* is a sort of self-conscious postmodern fusion of a lot of things other media had done before. The film, though, has a sense of humor about its pastiche and seems to laugh at its own corniness, at the sources of its inspiration, all the while enacting everything it parodies.

At the core of *The Last Dragon* are Bruce Lee and his teachings. These the film takes very seriously, even as it pokes reverential fun at them. The plot involves a black teenager in Harlem, Leroy Green (Taimak), who is so devoted to the martial arts and his fandom of Bruce Lee that he dresses only in silk Chinese peasant outfits, wears a big coolie hat, eats all his food — even popcorn when he goes to see Bruce Lee films — with chopsticks and talks in a stilted martial-arts-speak that could only have come out of a stylized Hong Kong *wuxia* epic. His friends, in fact, have taken to calling him Bruce Leroy. Leroy, though, is also a virtuoso martial artist, training with his Master (Thomas Ikeda) and in pursuit of the ever-elusive "glow," the final phase of martial arts mastery where all of his moves will become natural, instinctive, beyond all conscious thought or control. In the course of the film, Leroy becomes embroiled with a crooked record promoter (Christopher Murney) trying to force the sexy host (Vanity) of an *American Bandstand*-type dance music TV show to play the videos of his talentless protégé (Faith Prince). Compounding Leroy's problems is a local thug — and leader of an interracial(!) gang — named Sho'nuff (Julius Carrey III), who calls himself the "Shogun of Harlem" and wants to challenge Leroy to a fight to determine who's the best fighter in town.

The film's other major inspiration — besides Bruce Lee, who seems to hang over the proceedings as a sort of patron saint, showing up in film clips projected onto screens in the background of two major sequences — is Blaxploitation kung fu cinema. The entire venue of the film is the Harlem inner city. Furthermore, except for the record promoter and several of his hoods, a couple of white members of Sho'nuff's gang and a trio of Chinese fortune cookie factory workers, all of the major characters are African-American. Leroy, in the genre's best tradition, is socially conscious and devoted to bettering the lives of the kids in the community. This he does, of course, by teaching kids in a local community center, imbuing them with such positive martial arts tenets as self-confidence, self-reliance, and a prayer for self-control to avoid fights, violence and aggression. *The Last Dragon*, refreshingly, also makes the point of avoiding the most offensive aspects of the Blaxploitation genre. The violence, for example, is not graphic or bloody, there are no racial and ethnic slurs and black pride is not coupled with the virulent anti-white contempt of many of the Blaxploitation films. Moreover, *The Last Dragon* dispenses with the "black buck" stereotype altogether with its saintly hero. Whereas Blaxploitation icons like Jim Kelly made a point of highlighting their machismo by letting the audience know what oversexed studs they were, "Bruce Leroy" Green is almost peculiarly *undersexed*. When he's not a spectacularly skilled martial artist, Leroy is wholly innocent, naïve and awkward in every social situation. He becomes shy and tongue-tied almost every time he's around Laura Charles, the dance show host, and his little brother (Leo O'Brien) — reminiscent of Blaxploitation's jive-talking, street hustler stock characters — routinely mocks him for his lack of experience with the ladies. In fact, as Leroy confesses to Laura early on, he has *no* experience with the ladies at all.

Ultimately, though, the metaphysical core of *The Last Dragon* is still Bruce Lee and the tenets of Jeet Kune Do. The mastery Leroy seeks can be attained only when he is in the mental and physical state Bruce Lee instructed his students to reach. He has to become completely instinct-driven, formless, and free of all styles, dogma and restrictive rules. When Leroy can't accept the fact that he has learned all there is to learn, when he can't yet reach the "glow" because he can't believe that there are no more "techniques" to master, his teacher sends him on what amounts to a wild goose chase in search of the ultimate Master. Believing that the ultimate Master is ensconced somewhere in a fortune cookie factory, Leroy has to find a way to get past the establishment's three employees who are set on keeping all trespassers out. Taking his cue, naturally, from a Bruce Lee film (*Fist of Fury* and the scene where Lee disguises himself as a phone repairman to sneak into the Japanese dojo), Leroy makes it into the factory and finds out that the "Master" is nothing more than a computer automatically generating "sage" little catch phrases for the cookie inserts. Stunned, Leroy eventually realizes what his teacher intended by tricking him into this pointless mission. *He* is his only true master. Just as Jeet Kune Do instructs, a person can be free and perfect only when he has learned to live and act on his own terms, when he can find out his own truths for himself.

In 1993, Hollywood at last mounted the big budget, major studio production of the sort of epic Bruce Lee biography his fans had always been hoping for. The result was *Dragon: The Bruce Lee Story*. It had everything fans were looking for and everything they were dreading.

What the film had going for it was its polished, well-produced Hollywood scale. The film had good-looking fight sequences and a long, decade-spanning scope. It followed Lee from the time he left Hong Kong for San Francisco, through his years of struggling to break into show business, his relationship with wife Linda, his eventual rise to stardom in Hong Kong and the start of production on *Enter the Dragon*. The film's star, newcomer Jason Scott Lee (no relation; Bruce Lee's son, Brandon, was approached to play the lead role, but he turned it down), did a very convincing job of mimicking Lee's moves and mannerisms and he sculpted the same sort of lean, sinewy physique Bruce Lee had. In many sequences, especially its various fight scenes, the film did, to an extent, look almost like a brand new Bruce Lee film.

Unfortunately, for those familiar with Lee's biography and the consensus opinion of his personality, *Dragon* is also quite disappointing. At the core of the problem is the fact that the film endeavors to create a Bruce Lee hagiography rather than tell the story of a complex, multifaceted and often difficult individual. The film follows a very standard rags-to-riches formula, depicting a noble, decent, unbreakable optimist who holds to his dreams in the face of overwhelming obstacles, unfair circumstances and nearly impossible odds against success. While this certainly had been a part of the real Bruce Lee's life, and the film does put a great deal of emphasis on America's and Hollywood's racism in the '60s, it ignores the darker aspects of Lee's life and personality. "You can't change people with your fists," the cinematic Lee tells Linda (Lauren Holly) on their first date, just after they are refused seating at a swanky restaurant by a racist maitre d.' This film's version of Lee is a noble soul from beginning to end, a man well in control of his passions, his anger, someone who remains decent and gentle, zenlike even, in the face of blatant unfairness and injustice. That, of course, from all accounts, even his own family's, is quite unlike the real Bruce Lee. Most people who dealt with Lee usually told of his volatile and intimidating temper. The hothead, the juvenile delinquent who enjoyed picking fights, is nowhere in evidence in *Dragon*. For fans reasonably aware of Lee's biography, the scene where he is first set on his journey to American is blatantly, amusingly unrealistic. In *Dragon's* version, Lee's flight from Hong Kong is necessitated by an altercation at a night club. As the scene is set up, it presents a happy-go-lucky kid on his way to do some dancing and have some fun, minding his own business and causing no harm. Things go awry, though, once a group of thuggish, racist American sailors show up at the club and start causing trouble. After the sailors push the Chinese around, make swinish passes at the girls, call the locals "gooks," and generally do everything possible to provoke a fight, there is nothing for Lee to do but defend himself. A brawl ensues and the police are soon looking for Lee.

Aside from sanitizing Bruce Lee's personality, the film's fight scenes are also too far over the top for martial arts purists. For anyone who knows the tenets of Jeet Kune Do and Lee's ideas about how a cinematic fight should try to be as realistic as possible, *Dragon's* acrobatic, over-choreographed fight scenes are frustrating. Certain scenes, in fact, look like they had been copied from the Jackie Chan school of acrobatic kung fu. The worst offender in these respects is a scene where Lee gets into a fight with the kitchen staff of the restaurant he works for after arriving in the U.S. The initial flying fists and kicks soon escalate to all-out acrobatics as Lee and his assailants are spinning through the air on metal poles and ladders criss-crossing the alley behind the restaurant. Such a scene is wholly unrealistic, unlikely to ever occur in any fight anywhere, and it would never have been filmed for any Bruce Lee movie.

The most peculiar aspect of *Dragon*, though, is its heavy emphasis on mysticism and the "curse" theory behind Lee's death. Throughout the film, Lee is shown having nightmarish visions about being attacked by an enormous demon, some evil, vengeful spirit trying to claim him because he did not die upon birth. Such dream sequences, though they interrupt the flow of the story, give *Dragon* the opportunity to insert more fight scenes.

Ultimately, therein lies the big problem *Dragon* creates for Bruce Lee purists. While the film does have the expensive Hollywood production values, the great-looking fights and special effects, it ultimately makes the same mistakes as the countless Hong Kong biopics do. The agenda of this film is not so much to tell of Bruce Lee's life or to examine his personality, but to make a new Bruce Lee action film. Essentially, just like the Hong Kong films, *Dragon* tries to show that Lee's real life was basically one big action film, no different from the movies he made. In this version, Bruce Lee is an action hero who is as perfect, pure, virtuous and admirable as any movie protagonist. His real life, according to this film, was as exciting, dangerous and action-packed as anything seen in *Enter the Dragon* or his other three films. To that extent, we are given a perfect, larger-than-life version of the real man and we are shown exploits and epic battles that never happened in real life. *Dragon* is akin to a bio-pic of Sylvester Stallone with apocryphal scenes of his involvement in boxing in some youth league or community center as a teenager in Philadelphia, committing to a grueling training regimen and fighting a long-shot match against an overwhelming opponent.

But perhaps a realistic film about the real Bruce Lee can not even be made anymore. Popular culture in America, China, across Asia and all over the world has placed him in the realm of myth. As far as generations of fans are concerned, there is only Bruce Lee the legend and the hero.

5

Chuck Norris: Right Turn ... Or, a Masculinity Crisis and the Man Who Saved the Martial Arts

A devastating blow was delivered to fans of martial arts films and Asian cinema in 1973. On the twentieth of July, Bruce Lee died in Hong Kong. The circumstances of his death would remain surrounded by controversy for decades. However, not only was a popular film star lost that day, but tremendous damage done to an entire genre of action/adventure films. In his meteoric rise to stardom, Bruce Lee had come to personally represent martial arts on film.

The martial arts genre was the hardest hit in the United States, however. American audiences had been very slow to embrace an Asian actor like Lee to begin with. Americans have, after all, always been slow to warm to foreign cultural influences. Even with Bruce Lee's momentary stardom, the martial arts had not taken a permanent foothold in mainstream American popular culture. When Lee was gone, the martial arts seemed to go with him.[1]

The one man who could save the martial arts in American movies and give it mainstream attention had to be a Caucasian American actor. It had to be a "local" personality to adapt this import from the East. This local turned out to be former Karate World Champion Chuck Norris.

In the annals of martial arts and action/adventure films, Chuck Norris is now known for successfully fusing the exotic-looking moves and warrior codes of the Eastern martial artist with the look of the American Western film, police and political thrillers and war films. His standout films are the Spaghetti Western and martial arts combination of *Lone Wolf McQuade* (1982), the police thriller *Code of Silence* (1985), the Vietnam War/conspiracy trilogy, *Missing in Action* (1984, 1985, 1988), and the terrorist-themed *Delta Force* 1 and 2 (1986, 1990) and *Invasion U.S.A.* (1985) films. After his film career waned in the early 1990s, he made a comeback by starring in the surprise hit TV series *Walker, Texas Ranger*, for eight seasons.

But to understand why Chuck Norris had to "save" the martial arts, one must further understand what exactly happened to the martial arts film after Bruce Lee died.

Things Change

The genre suffered two major assaults after Lee's passing. The first one came from the Hong Kong film industry itself. The second blow was delivered by a change in the American cultural and political landscape.

The aftermath of Bruce Lee's death was the start of all the Bruce Lee impersonators. Simply, not only was the most charismatic star of martial arts films gone, but the genre he made so popular was reduced to a joke.

In the meantime, the second blow to the martial arts genre was being delivered in the U.S. The American film scene had suddenly changed. Or, more to the point, American tastes had changed. The receptiveness to new ideas and new visions that had opened the door to foreign filmmakers in the '60s was disappearing. The American consumer's interest in the avant-garde, in the exotic and counter-cultural, was waning. In fact, by the middle of the 1970s, movie-goers were again gravitating toward the big-budget, traditional studio spectacles they so vehemently rejected in the late '60s. With the spectacular successes of films like *Jaws*, *Rocky*, *Close Encounters of the Third Kind*, *Star Wars*, *Saturday Night Fever* and *Superman*, old fashioned, all–American blockbuster entertainment was back.

One notable Caucasian martial arts filmmaker with a brief flicker of popularity in the early years of the decade was hammy independent director and actor Tom Laughlin. Tying the martial arts to the counterculture, much as Blaxploitation had, Laughlin's series of *Billy Jack* films used the Korean fighting style of Hapkido to deliver Laughlin's left-wing, anti-establishment polemics. The first *Billy Jack* (1971) film dealt with a Native American ex–Green Beret Vietnam vet using his Hapkido skills to battle racists, corrupt cops, politicians and businessmen. The film actually proved to be one of the most profitable independent films of the era. It spawned a respectably successful sequel, *The Trial of Billy Jack*, in 1974. However, by 1977 the third entry in the series vanished from the theaters seemingly overnight.

Overall, Bruce Lee's death left a major hole in the action cinema. Moreover, what was also hurting the chances of the martial arts being established in mainstream films was their minority orientation, their radical implications. Since the counterculture chic of the early '70s had quickly faded away, even a Caucasian radical like Tom Laughlin could hardly take the martial arts into the mainstream. For the martial arts to find blockbuster audiences again, they needed a very thorough, very extensive Americanization.

Against All Odds

This Americanization of the martial arts film was eventually orchestrated by Chuck Norris. His rise to Hollywood stardom, however, turned out to be as unlikely and colorful as the plot of an underdog action film.

Born Carlos Ray Norris in Ryan, Oklahoma, on March 10, 1940, Norris had been a six-time World Professional Middle Weight Karate Champion who retired undefeated in 1974. In 1969, he held the Triple Crown for most tournament wins and was named the Fighter of the Year by *Black Belt* magazine. Norris, however, hadn't intended to become an actor until he was well into his thirties.[2]

Norris' introduction to the martial arts came by way of a stint in the Air Force from 1958 to 1962 and being stationed in Osan, South Korea. As Norris detailed in his two autobiographies, *The Secret of Inner Strength* and *Against All Odds*, a soldier at Osan Air Base had three options for spending his free time: "(1) booze it up, (2) enroll in an academic class, or (3) study martial arts. I'd never been a drinker and academic studies weren't my forte, so delving into the martial arts seemed the best way to pass the time."[3]

Through the Judo Club on the air base, Norris got his first taste of the Asian fighting arts. Later, at a street demonstration in Osan, he was intrigued by the high-kicking, acrobatic style of a group of Tang Soo Do practitioners. While simultaneously training in judo, Norris began studying in the local Tang Soo Do dojo. By the end of his tour at Osan, he had earned a black belt in Tang Soo Do and a third-degree brown belt in judo.

It was also in the service that he would adopt the nickname that would become his professional name. Carlos, it had been remarked, was an unusual name for someone who was obviously not Hispanic. Norris' blond hair and blue eyes always made the name sound odd. He is, in fact, equal parts Irish and Cherokee Indian. His name is derived from the Reverend Carlos Barry, the family's minister in Ryan, and his father, Ray. After enlightening a fellow serviceman that Carlos' English equivalent was Charles, Norris was called "Chuck" by his friends. Today he is actually referred to as Carlos by his closest friends and family.

Norris would often mention his tour in the Air Force and contact with servicemen as an inspiration for his reverent treatment of soldiers in his films. Off screen, his charity work includes fund-raising efforts for the Veterans Administration. In terms of thematics, he has always insisted on overtly patriotic messages in his films. This approach, in fact, had played a strong role in giving the once-exotic martial arts film a distinctly American, pointedly conservative overhaul. He has also insisted on the crafting of his characters and overall screen persona as a larger-than-life, often paternal, role model of positive masculinity. Aside from the military, Norris had often readily talked about his impoverished childhood and turbulent relationship with an alcoholic father. His father, he has often been quoted as saying, was a role model in reverse. Chuck had seen the drunken Ray Norris as an example of what a man should never be. In his films, Norris has insisted on characters that could be looked upon by kids as positive role models.

Norris' actual exposure to the film business, however, was accidental. Following his Air Force service, he had planned on joining the Los Angeles Police Department. Because of a long waiting list for new hires, he worked at the Northrop Aircraft company as a file clerk to support his wife and newborn son. To supplement his income, he began teaching martial arts. With his tournament wins gaining publicity for his school, Norris decided to put his energy into full time martial arts instruction instead of pursuing a position in the LAPD.

Through the martial arts championships, he became an acquaintance and frequent training partner of Bruce Lee's. The two met after Norris won the 1967 All-American Karate Championship. Talking martial arts as they returned to their hotel after Norris' bout at Madison Square Garden, the two started an impromptu sparring and workout session in the hotel hallway — lasting until 4:00 A.M.

By that point, Norris' karate school attracted the attention of prominent Hollywood power players as well. His notable celebrity clients included James Coburn, Priscilla Presley, the Osmond family, and Steve McQueen.

McQueen contacted Norris for private karate lessons for his son, Chad, following the young McQueen's schoolyard scrapes with bullies. McQueen, in fact, would also urge Norris to seriously consider acting as a new career.

"If you can't do anything else," Norris recounts McQueen's suggestion in the autobiography, *Against All Odds*, "you might as well try acting."[4]

Before McQueen's urging, however, came Bruce Lee's suggestion that Norris give Hollywood a try.

Lee introduced Norris to the trade of film-fight choreography and cameo appearances as a martial artist villain. Lee, after all, had also worked in Hollywood as a fight coordinator and appeared as a heavy in small TV and film roles after the *Green Hornet* show went off the air. Through Lee's suggestion, Norris choreographed a martial arts fight sequence for Dean Martin's Matt Helm spy spoof, *The Wrecking Crew*, in 1968. Along with working out the fight sequences for the film, Norris plays one of Martin's opponents. Although Norris was the reigning Karate World Champion in 1968, Matt Helm, naturally, wins the fight.

Norris' more notable early appearance, however, came in Lee's film *Way of the Dragon* (1973). It was only after appearing in *Way of the Dragon* that Norris decided to seriously pursue acting. But, as it turned out, neither he nor Hollywood envisioned him as the next major action star and savior of Asian-influenced marital arts cinema. "Chop-socky movies are dead,"[5] he quotes a film executive in *The Secret of Inner Strength*. As Norris began acting lessons and embarked on the customary rounds of auditions, he was told that his range was hopelessly limited and his presence stiff and unnatural. He was merely a former jock who happened to be famous in the martial arts community, casting agents and producers told him. Unfortunately, Hollywood was no longer interested in the martial arts.

If Hollywood was not writing roles for martial artist leading men anymore, Norris' response was to develop a film idea of his own that would be suited for a martial artist. With input from several of his martial artist friends and Joe Fraley, an aspiring screenwriter, a script called *Good Guys Wear Black* was put together. Norris then embarked on a round of pitch sessions to film producers.

Interestingly, this approach was quite similar to what Sylvester Stallone would later do in his development of *Rocky*. As Stallone had repeatedly recounted, he, too, had been constantly pegged as being uncastable because of his face, his physique and his voice. In turn, he wrote the script for *Rocky*, creating a role only an actor of his body, looks and voice could play believably.[6]

Ironically, Norris' first starring film role did not turn out to be the one he created for himself. The *Good Guys Wear Black* script was being rejected by every producer he contacted. However, he was approached to put his martial arts skills to use in a low budget, independent film called *Breaker! Breaker!* (1977).

Although *Breaker! Breaker!* had minimal input from Norris, the character and plot do contain many of the elements that would later be integral to the Norris oeuvre. The film, in essence, is a modern day Western. It uses truckers, country music and Citizens Band (CB) radios in place of the traditional cowboys and horses of the generic oaters. The plot involves the corrupt mayor and police force of a backwoods speed-trap town imprisoning and robbing truckers. Once his kid brother falls victim to the kidnapping scheme, Norris goes looking for payback.

The Western style of *Breaker! Breaker!* fit well with Norris' own ideas on an American adaptation of martial arts. The film, in fact, was a reflection of an emerging country-western pop culture trend in the mid– to late 1970s. This trend would eventually make mainstream stars of country musicians like Kenny Rogers, Dolly Parton and Tanya Tucker. Other country-flavored entertainment that would attain smash-hit success would be Burt Reynolds' *Smokey and the Bandit* films, the TV show *Dukes of Hazzard*, and Sam Peckinpah's *Convoy* (1978), starring country music star Kris Kristofferson.

On the basis of his role in *Breaker! Breaker!*, Norris' *Good Guys Wear Black* script eventually got the attention of a group of producers and investors who would found the American Cinema company. They, in fact, gave him a great degree of freedom in molding his character and a lot of input as the story was adapted from the original script.

The real reason behind the success, or failure, of any film is the turn of a series of chance events. Ultimately, it's good or bad luck, timing, circumstances or serendipity that makes or breaks movies, that creates beloved celebrities or destroys their careers. Similarly, that Chuck Norris should wind up resuscitating the moribund martial arts genre was an uncanny turn of luck. This turn of luck was the decision to imitate the style of old-fashioned Western films.

Norris' first film cast him as a martial artist because, he and his investors reasoned, he had name recognition in the martial arts community. He had a potential core audience American Cinema hoped to capitalize on. But Norris was also interested in fashioning his films and his characters after the traditional Hollywood Westerns. He had always loved Westerns; and if he was making action films, he explained in a number of interviews about his early years on screen, he wanted to be a sort of new-generation John Wayne. As he writes in his autobiography, *Against All Odds*, Norris' enchantment with the Westerns as a child was rooted, for very personal reasons, in the moral code of its strong, masculine heroes. This was a moral code decidedly missing in his own volatile, unpredictable and verbally and emotionally abusive father. "I loved those Saturdays when I escaped into another world," he writes. "The Westerns, starring John Wayne, Gene Autry, and Roy Rogers, provided me with positive examples of proper and moral behavior.... Their behavior in those films was governed by the 'Code of the West'—loyalty, friendship, and integrity. They were unselfish and did

Chuck Norris: the martial artist in the form of the Western cowboy.

what was right even when the risk was great. Years later I would recall those Western heroes when I developed the kind of characters I wanted to play as an actor."[7]

In the era of the new blockbuster films, where the thematic trends set by hits like *Jaws, Rocky* or *Star Wars* were all about a celebration of traditional adventure stories and classic heroic archetypes, Norris' melding of the martial arts with the format of the all–American Western proved to be a winning formula. The martial arts film was successfully Americanized at last when it was rewritten according to the rules of the most American of all film genres. The influence of the Western can be seen in the first three films Norris made with American Cinema.

The plot of *Good Guys Wear Black* involves a Vietnam-era conspiracy, where the surviving commandos of a rescue operation are being assassinated after the war. John Booker, the Norris character and one of the former commandos, must race to track down the last living members of the team before government assassins are able to eliminate them.

Much in line with the Western tradition of the ex-warrior who has long retired and put his violent ways behind him, the Booker character is introduced as an unassuming college professor. He has put his Vietnam experience behind him, save for occasionally answering a student's inquiries about the war with a terse denunciation of the policies that brought about the conflict.

The same retired warrior theme is revisited in Norris' third film, *The Octagon* (1980). There he must face a group of Japanese Ninja assassins working as terrorist subcontractors. Tying *The Octagon* even more closely to conventions of the Western, the film closes with an arena showdown. In the final battle, Norris takes on a hit-squad of ninjas in an obstacle course inside their training camp. The showdown is as ritualized as the Western's typical hero in the middle of Main Street squaring off against a cadre of villainous gunmen. One of Norris' costars is Spaghetti Western veteran Lee Van Cleef, who played opposite Clint Eastwood in *For a Few Dollars More* (*Per Qualche Dollaro in Più*, 1965) and *The Good, the Bad and the Ugly* (*Il Buono, il Brutto, il Cattivo*, 1966). Van Cleef was also one of Gary Cooper's nemeses in *High Noon* (1952). This helped further tie *The Octagon* to the venerable Western tradition.

A notable aside about *The Octagon*'s melding of Eastern and Western film archetypes is the use of the ninjas as villains. Here the mythologized, black-hooded assassins of feudal Japan turn up in an American film for only the third time. Western audiences first saw ninjas in the James Bond film *You Only Live Twice* (1967) and the Sam Peckinpah conspiracy film *The Killer Elite* (1975). By the 1980s, ninjas would be rediscovered by the Hollywood

B-movie industry and a long list of ninja epics would thrive in the martial arts theater.

While both *Good Guys Wear Black* and *The Octagon* revolve around a military/political thriller storyline, his second film, *A Force of One* (1979), involves a police thriller. The police thrillers and the military adventures would be the main thematic concerns for much of Norris' career. In *A Force of One*, he is a karate instructor recruited to help the police track down a cop-killer who appears to be a martial arts expert. Along with putting a greater emphasis on the martial arts as a sport with a strong ethical value system, the character development of *A Force of One* allows Norris to play an idealistic character much in the way of the Western heroes he idolized as a boy. Matt Logan, the Norris character, is not only a fearsome martial arts champion, but the adoptive father of an orphaned black teenager he saved from a life on the streets.

Aside from his films' abundantly borrowing from the Westerns, Norris' success can also be attributed to the fact that he actually looks very natural in the role of the archetypal American cowboy. In fact, some of Norris' previous weaknesses that had turned acting classes and auditions into ignominious failures had suddenly become not only negligible but, if anything, actual strengths. The unexpressive, taciturn, if not outright stiff, impression Norris makes is extremely effective for the old-fashioned action hero he portrays. Critical derision to the contrary, the very essence of an effective action hero is precise and well-controlled *action*. Action heroes, whether they are cowboys, soldiers, cops or martial artists, should be doers, not talkers. No one really wants to see an action hero wasting screen time talking. A true hero, as fans of action films will attest, does his job and shuts up. He does not need to *tell* anyone how good he is.

Norris' mustachioed, Marlboro Man looks, his sturdy, compact body, serve to give him a very satisfying everyman quality. Norris' appeal lies in the fact that he looks believable when he is in the thick of the action; he looks real. In Norris, there is an effective lack of hyperbole. He does not have the over-the-top muscularity of a Sylvester Stallone or an Arnold Schwarzenegger that always made those actors seem slightly cartoonish and unrealistic. Most importantly, Norris fits the action hero role because he exudes a very crucial, very solidly masculine "presence" on screen.

Steve McQueen's advice to Norris, as a matter of fact, was founded on the observation that Norris had a "presence." He has that quality casting directors call the "it" factor; the charisma that determines a performer's success in front of an audience.

Perhaps more important than even the "it" factor to Norris' success as an action hero is a certain ferocious, explosive intensity his eyes can signal in scenes of mounting tension. Although all accounts and close acquaintances of Norris have described him as a truly gentle man — his autobiography, *Against All Odds*, foregrounds his Christian faith — Norris has admitted that he had always been told that he can exude a very intimidating air of danger. There is a volatility evident in his eyes when he is provoked beyond his breaking point. Despite critics generally dismissing Norris' acting skills, that volatility, the explosive quality in his eyes, has been enough of an edge to make him a highly effective action hero.

If one wants to characterize the Chuck Norris screen persona, it can be summed up as a modern day cowboy. The typical Chuck Norris character is straightforward, uncomplicated, simple perhaps, but reliable and honest. He is an exact updating of the John Wayne/Gene Autry/Roy Rogers era of heroes who wore the proverbial white hat, who talked straight and shot straight. Of course, in the modern film world, this sort of a character is an anachronism. Critical expectations now are that even heroes need to be nuanced and complicated. They need to have multiple facets, they need to have dark sides. Since a Chuck Norris character does not, it is fairly obvious why critical respect has largely eluded Norris for much of his career. His presence, though, that "it" factor, his obvious hardness, still gives him the qualities that produce the classic, Western-style masculine hero, his lack of nuanced acting abilities to the contrary.

A true appreciation for why it can often be harder to become an effective action performer than a "good actor" can be gained by observing some of today's very skilled actors who have repeatedly proven to be unconvincing as action heroes. Tom Cruise, for example, while an excellent actor and always in fine physical shape, is lacking the hardness, the grit, to look anywhere near convincing as a tough guy in his *Mission: Impossible* (1996, 2000, 2006) films. Sure, he has often attempted the intimidating stare, the dangerous look in the eyes, but he has never come anywhere close to the real thing. Unfortunately, he didn't get it quite right even when he was cast as a professional killer in *Collateral* (2004). Similarly, serviceable actors like Brad Pitt, Keanu Reeves, Ben Affleck or Matt Damon have had to rely on special effects and computerized film trickery to make them appear tougher than they could possibly be on their own.

Social Commentator (?)

It can be argued that true blockbuster films, pictures that resonate so well with audiences as to become iconic, become so successful because they touch a sensitive cultural nerve. In Stephen King's terminology when analyzing the landmark horror films, smash hit popular entertainment always speaks to one of society's "areas of unease."[8] Chuck Norris' films that connected most effectively with sensitive social pressure points were *Lone Wolf McQuade* (1982) and his *Missing in Action* (1984, 1985, 1988) series. *Lone Wolf McQuade* can be interpreted as a reflection on a time of swiftly changing gender politics and the social redefinition of masculinity. The *Missing in Action* films spoke to the anxiety Americans in the 1980s still had about the Vietnam War.

In *Lone Wolf McQuade*, a film Chuck Norris cultists hold in very high regard and the film that would later inspire his TV series, *Walker, Texas Ranger* (1993–2001), Norris is a Texas Ranger both deadly efficient in meting out instant justice and hopelessly at odds with police bureaucracy. The titular Lone Wolf moniker is the disparaging nickname Ranger J. J. McQuade is given by his ever-image-conscious superiors. The scruffy, unkempt McQuade not only does not look as clean and well-groomed as a police officer should, but his violent, insubordinate and unorthodox law enforcement style no longer has a place in modern police work. His chief is sick and tired of his lone wolf attitude, he is told in an early character-establishing scene. The exchange is reminiscent of Dirty Harry being lectured in each of his films about being a Neanderthal and an anachronistic misfit in a kinder, gentler, more liberal police department. But soon enough, a murderous gang of gun runners sets up a base camp in McQuade's neck of the woods and threatens his daughter and ex-wife. Naturally, this time McQuade's brand of frontier justice is the only hope the police have.

Although the Western archetypes, from the characters to the setting in the parched Texas desert, are stronger than in any of Norris' previous films, the Asian influence is retained in various key scenes. McQuade is fonder of his guns in this film, but he is still a martial arts expert. The main villain of the film is played by David Carradine in an inspired bit of casting. Carradine, of course, had edged out Bruce Lee for the lead role in the *Kung Fu* TV series. At the end of the film, Norris and Carradine fight to the death using martial arts.

The majority of reviews of *Lone Wolf McQuade* compared Norris' performance and character to Clint Eastwood in his iconic Spaghetti Western and *Dirty Harry* roles. This, of course, was an apt comparison because the resemblance was intentional. The film's opening score is reminiscent of the strains of an Enio Moricone theme. The first shots of the arid desert could have come from any of the Man with No Name films. The opening scene of McQuade single-handedly dispatching a gang of horse thieves recalls the first scene of *A Fistful of Dollars*. McQuade is, at once, every bit as aloof and taciturn as Eastwood's Man with No Name and as rebellious and hostile to ineffective authority as Dirty Harry.

There is an important difference between *Lone Wolf McQuade* and all of Norris' previous films, however. This difference might actually have contributed to the film's remarkable success and enduring popularity among action aficionados. Precisely, the nature of the Norris character is slightly different from his previous reluctant fighters. His relationship to the police bureaucracy is also quite different from previous efforts. The sum total of these qualities also lets the film speak to an issue of obsolete masculinity.

In *Lone Wolf McQuade*, Norris is not quite as reluctant a hero as before, although he is quite a lonely one. His methods are unorthodox, politically incorrect and basically an embarrassment to the Rangers. While the police force is attempting to project a clean-cut, modern image, McQuade is a brutish, anti-social throwback. His superiors waste few words telling him he does not fit in. Although he is more than skilled in doing his job—taking down dangerous, homicidal criminals of every stripe—the modern world is not so much concerned with results as with good P.R. McQuade, unfortunately, is not polished, politically astute, media-savvy or well-versed in the social graces. Not too surprisingly, this type of grungy outsider behavior has broken up his marriage and he now lives alone—but for his pet wolf—in a dilapidated desert shack. Although his teenage daughter might love him and appreciate him for what he is under the rough exterior, she is not allowed to live with him and he has very limited visiting hours. This kind of a ragged-edge loner, however, has emerged as the new archetype in the American action cinema since the late '60s and early '70s.

Since the earliest days of that decade, the new man of action has been taking shape as the unappreciated, downtrodden burnout. Action heroes, taking perhaps the strongest cues from the phenomenally successful *Dirty Harry* films, have been showing up in the form of the brutish, unpleasant social anachronism. They might have what it takes to bring down armies of psychos, drug dealers, or terrorists, but they are also unappreciated by their superiors, their women, and genteel, white-collar America at large. A decade before J. J. McQuade's bosses tired of his lone wolf attitude, Dirty Harry's bosses were outraged by his maverick attitude toward law enforcement. They regularly chewed him out and put him on suspension instead of giving him commendations for cleaning up the streets.

Social commentators, anthropologists, feminists, and film theorists have all given this disrespectful treatment of action heroes considerable scholarly attention.[9] Why have the tough men of action, the only men strong enough to take on the worst threats to society, been getting such a drubbing in these films? According to an emerging theory of a late twentieth-century crisis of masculinity, unappreciated outsiders are exactly how many American men feel. In a post–Vietnam, post-feminist world, American culture is no longer treating strong, traditional machismo as a necessity for the survival of society. Hard-fighting, hard-bodied macho masculinity that might have built a nation out of the wild frontier, that might have fought and won wars, is not so useful on the domestic front. To more radical sensibilities, strong, hard-fighting masculinity might even be a dangerous, destructive liability. Strong masculinity, such a point of view says, might have started and botched such unnecessary wars as Vietnam. Traditional masculinity, according to the masculinity crisis theory, is under the gun in modern day America. As famed anthropologist Lionel Tiger argues, a cultural landscape has come about where exclusively male spheres of influence have disappeared. Control over families and offspring has been taken away from men.[10] Masculinity, in effect, has become obsolete. Action films, in turn, have become symbolic ruminations on the diminishing social status of the American male. As sociologist Neal King writes about the modern action film, "cop action fixes on arguments over the privileges that so many men feel they have lost to moral and economic decline, and it tells a story of workers in a diminishing world ... (movie) cops may be all that stand between their communities and chaos, yet they have a hell of a hard time making their bosses respect them as valuable workers."[11]

Lone Wolf McQuade is Chuck Norris' most potent entry into this masculinity-crisis cinema. It effectively recasts the once vaguely radical martial arts film in a right-leaning elegy to traditional, strong, white American masculinity.

Following *Lone Wolf McQuade*, Norris made a pair of films that would tap into the Zeitgeist of the 1980s. These films virtually established an entire action subgenre. As Norris recounts in his autobiographies, he had been interested in a film dealing with Vietnam. He wanted to make a film that would serve as a personal dedication to his brother, Wieland, who had been killed in the war in 1970. Although the plot of *Good Guys Wear Black* is put in motion by a conspiracy rooted in Vietnam, much of the film is not dealing with the war itself. But a problem with putting Vietnam on screen until the late 1970s was the fact that the highly divisive and unpopular conflict was too much of a financial risk. Americans wanted to forget the war, not pay money to see it all over again in theaters. Only a few films, like Francis Ford Coppola's *Apocalypse Now* (1979), or the drama *Coming Home* (1978), attempted to address the Vietnam experience. By the 1980s, however, particularly because of the popular Reagan presidency's inspiration of a new national atmosphere of pro–American and pro-military patriotism, action films could attempt to weave Vietnam into their plots. They used military and ex-military characters as their heroes. On television, Vietnam veterans in shows like *Magnum, P.I.* and *The A-Team* had already proven successful.

Norris's back-to-back films, *Missing in Action* and *Missing in Action 2:*

The Beginning, exploit the sensitive questions about the fate of hundreds of U.S. servicemen missing and unaccounted for in Vietnam. The films then suggest that many of these men could still be alive, held captive in slave labor camps. Their fates, the films accuse, are well known to the American government. The truth, however, has been covered up for the sake of political expediency as the government was eager to withdraw from the war and the nation was hoping to forget the calamitous events as fast as possible.

In the first of the two films, the Norris character, Col. James Braddock, a Vietnam vet and former POW, stumbles onto the conspiracy. He promptly returns to Vietnam and single-handedly rescues a group of Americans.

The prequel, *Missing in Action 2*, tells Braddock's back story. It deals with his capture and imprisonment during the war and vicious battle of wills with a sadistic camp commandant.

Film critics have written volumes about these films' appeal as a symbolic rewriting of the Vietnam War.[12] In *Missing in Action*, Norris wins the war the way Americans wish the real war could have been won. The martial arts perspective, however, is a lot more ironic. The two films, along with their 1988 sequel, *Braddock: Missing in Action III*, present a slightly discomfiting image of a Caucasian martial arts expert rampaging over hordes of Asian villains. Although the films were popular with audiences, critics have often complained about a quiet racist subtext to these Vietnam action films.

The first two *MIA* films, however, turned out to be blockbuster hits, igniting a mid–eighties back-to-Vietnam-to-rescue-the-POWs subgenre of action. The first sequel to Sylvester Stallone's *First Blood* (1983), in fact, "borrowed" this same formula. But the back-to-Vietnam plot made it one of the most successful films of the decade and put the name "Rambo" in the American pop culture lexicon.

The circumstances behind the two *MIA* films are notable because many Norris fans have argued that they helped set him up for an early big-screen career demise. With these two films, Norris started a long-term partnership with the Cannon Group production company. Run by Israeli producers, and cousins, Menahem Golan and Yoram Globus, the Cannon Group was essentially managed as a large-scale, fly-by-night exploitation film factory. Golan and Globus bought the company in 1979, after briefly thriving and quickly failing as producers of "serious" dramatic fare. They operated Cannon as a quick, cheap conveyor belt of B-grade sex and violence sagas distributed to the global market. Some of their notable filmmaking modus operandi included commissioning elaborate poster art for unmade films, displaying them at prominent film festivals like Cannes, and raising money for the hypothetical films on the basis of the posters. Most often the artwork promised plenty of violence and explicit sex. They were also able to lure big-name actors to their films by offering them a great deal of creative freedom. Golan and Globus allowed these stars to often write and direct projects. Ultimately, although Norris' Cannon films could occasionally tap into the national mood with uncanny accuracy, as was the case with the first two *MIA* films and later the terrorist hijacking epic *Delta Force* (1986), the production quality of many of these films gives evidence of a cheap, quickie company that was incapable of aspiring to anything more than exploitation status.

To fully appreciate the quality to which Norris could have risen in the 1980s, and where he was stuck for far too long, one might be well-served to compare his *MIA* 1 and 2 follow-up, *Code of Silence* (1985), to such Cannon films as *Invasion U.S.A.* (1985), *Firewalker* (1987), *MIA 3* (1988), or even *Delta Force 2* (1990).

Code of Silence, a thriller about police corruption in Chicago, turned out to be Norris' one film that got almost unanimous praise from the critics. Most importantly, *Code of Silence* is not a Cannon production. Helmed by Andrew Davis, who would later make the Oscar-nominated *Fugitive* (1993) with Harrison Ford, *Code of Silence* is not only a rousing action film, but quite a complex morality tale. It examines the difficult choices cops face pledging loyalty to their fellow officers while often encountering corruption in the insular police culture. Although the film gives Norris' fans the expected showdowns with guns and bone-jarring martial arts fight sequences, it also balances the mayhem with a smart plot. The characters are complex, layered and realistic. Solid, believable performances are delivered by the entire cast, including Norris.

This film, unfortunately, highlights what Norris could have been capable of in the hands of a strong director. Andrew Davis, as it turned out, could be exceptionally skilled in pulling good performances out of macho action heroes of limited acting range. He would do the same in 1988 with Steven Seagal, guiding him through his first film, *Above the Law*. *Above the Law* likewise believably mixed the whimsical world of the martial arts and a gritty, realistic police-and-political-corruption thriller. In 2001, Davis was also able to get the first realistic, dramatic performance out of Arnold Schwarzenegger in *Collateral Damage*.

Norris' return to the Cannon Group after *Code of Silence* marks another important turn in the orientation of his image. From that point, he was becoming more of the gun-wielding action hero and less of the martial artist. Although he would deliver a roundhouse kick or two in each of his films, the emphasis would always be on the firepower. The main gimmick of *Invasion U.S.A.*, for example, is a customized shoulder rig supporting a pair of UZI machine pistols. In the age of high-octane action epics like *Rambo*, Norris' own *MIA* films, the *Die Hard* and *Lethal Weapon* films, men with guns and explosives were in vogue. Fireballs and demolished buildings had become more attractive to audiences than hand-to-hand combat.

However, the martial arts and the fascination with Asian combat would still remain a strong staple of 1980s B-cinema. Although mainstream audiences seemed to prefer men with guns, Norris' original martial-arts-loving fan base could still be counted on to support the bountiful crop of ninja and kickboxer epics debuting throughout that decade—even if many of them went straight to video.[13]

It's Hip to Be Square

By the late 1990s, Chuck Norris experienced a career resurrection. This time, it came by way of TV after several big-screen failures. Although the quality of his films had severely eroded—fine examples are family-oriented duds like *Sidekicks* (1992) and *Top Dog* (1995)—CBS convinced him to try the midseason replacement show *Walker, Texas Ranger* in 1993. A much-sanitized, bureaucracy-friendly and family-oriented updating of *Lone Wolf McQuade*, the show turned out to be a surprise smash hit for CBS. The show ran for eight seasons, performing well in the ratings until the end of its run. Just as Norris compared the show to his martial arts tournament career, *Walker, Texas Ranger* performed well from beginning to end and went out a winner.

The oddest turn Norris' career has taken yet, however, has been in the early to mid–2000s. Since *Walker, Texas Ranger* went off the air, Norris has become a sort of postmodern, tongue-in-cheek cult icon of indestructible, completely old-fashioned macho masculinity. Norris seems to have a sense of humor about the fact he represents an image that is completely anachronistic, or at least *un-hip*, with deadly, straight-faced seriousness. The postmodern Norris has had a cameo appearance in the Vince Vaughn/Ben Stiller comedy *Dodgeball: A True Underdog Story* (2004), playing, of course, himself, and spoofing his image alongside corny celebrities like William Shatner and David Hasselhoff. In a similar vein, he has repeatedly appeared on *Late Night with Conan O'Brian*, poking fun at *Walker*. On *Saturday Night Live*, a skit entitled "The Young Chuck Norris" has further lampooned his stalwart tough guy persona. Norris himself has also given his blessings to the internet humor site ChuckNorrisFacts.com that lists parody "facts" about his superhuman toughness. The site runs facts like "There is no theory of evolution, just a list of animals Chuck Norris allows to live," "Chuck Norris doesn't read books, he stares them down until he gets the information he wants," and "When the Boogeyman goes to sleep every night, he checks his closet for Chuck Norris." This new "Chuck mania" has also been profiled in *Rolling Stone*.

The reason behind this unlikely career turn for Norris as a pop culture icon, one can guess, is the fact that he very much seems to be serious about his positive, upstanding, two-fisted, traditionally strong male image. In an era of irony, boyish, sensitive men, and self-referential media, Chuck Norris is completely without irony. In a time when celebrity duplicity is exposed every day, when people seem to be reminded that public figures are not what they appear to be, Norris seems to be exactly what he appears to be. How can one tell? Because most of the things he does and says are completely contrary to every current rule for what one should do to appear hip, what one should do if they *want* to be famous, get attention and become a cool pop icon. For example, in the very liberal film industry, Norris is not only vocally conservative, but he has been an unflagging supporter of both Bush presidencies. Even as the war in Iraq energized liberal Hollywood's vehement anti–Bush animosity, Norris is proud to be a personal friend of George W. Bush. In the 2008 presidential primaries, he endorsed social conservative candidate Mike Huckabee. Norris is also vocal about his Christianity. He has repeatedly molded the plots of *Walker, Texas Ranger* episodes to espouse traditional, conservative Christian family values. He talks about starting each day by praying with his wife. His second autobiography, *Against All Odds*, is in great part a rewrite of *The Secret of Inner Strength*, this time taking key turning points in his life and recounting them in a series of homilies about God's plans for a person's everyday life. While actors who occasionally play heroic roles usually try to defend their "serious artist" credentials by explaining how they *really* want to play dark, edgy, ambiguous anti-heroes, Norris has always very clearly explained that he has no interest whatsoever in being edgy, in playing anything dark or anti-heroic. In fact, Norris once passed on a role in a major Hollywood film because of his insistence on maintaining his heroic image. He was originally approached for the role of the evil karate instructor, Sensei John Kreese, in the first *Karate Kid* (1984) film. He turned it down because he did not want to play the leader of a group of martial artist thugs. In essence, according to the current rules of celebrity cool, Chuck Norris is doing everything very willfully, very purposefully, wrong. The end result is pure irony from someone who consciously tries to avoid irony; he appears to be so square that it makes him hip and colorful.

Chuck Norris' final credit in the history of action-oriented entertainment deserves to be that he revived the martial arts on film at a moment when they might have faded into obscurity. The revival, though, was possible for an American audience because Asians were removed from the lead roles in films using Asian martial arts. Chuck Norris' career, basically, is a product of its time. It came at a turning point in American cultural history when the turbulence of the late '60s and early '70s was dissipating. It came, perhaps, when mainstream American audiences were no longer willing to accept a foreigner of a different race, like Bruce Lee, as a heroic leading man. Nevertheless, Norris' films did preserve a small connection to Asian culture through the martial arts. Consequently, as Norris' mainstream stardom was at its height in the 1980s, the B-grade action film industry continued focusing on the martial arts. Ninjas, kick boxers and martial artists of every style and background — even race — thrived in a highly profitable straight-to-video market in the '80s. Norris's stardom, in fact, begat the careers of Jean-Claude Van Damme and Steven Seagal. They, too, capitalized on the formula of the Caucasian action hero with ties to Asian culture. Steven Seagal has even focused the plots of most of his films around the types of police/military/political thriller scenarios Chuck Norris was always fond of.

Critical praise for Chuck Norris' work has been scarce, but that rarely fazed him. Politically correct mockery of the strict moralism in his films has also been loud and spirited. In an age where "sophisticated" films were supposed to depict right and wrong on a relative, sliding scale, Norris still insisted on making both his films and his TV show as unambiguous as the Westerns of his childhood. Once more, he stays unconcerned by the critical derision. As a result, he appears to be more popular today than ever.

6

Asian Action in the '80s: Ninjas and Karate Kids

In the 1980s, fandom of Asian-influenced action, Asian actors and film-makers, and the martial arts seemed to be peculiarly confused and conflicted. Many films of that decade are filled with martial artistry, yet the trend started by Chuck Norris' ascent to fame continued. Audiences seemed interested in the Asian marital arts, in films with themes and locales incorporating Asia, yet, more than ever, following the Norris precedent, they wanted Americans exclusively at the center of the stories and Americans practicing the deadly Asian arts.

In fact, many film and popular culture historians will speak of an ongoing martial arts boom in the '80s. They will remark about the "ninja craze" of that decade. They will identify the craze as starting with 1981's *Enter the Ninja*, a B-level success, and culminating with the *Teenage Mutant Ninja Turtles* toy, comic book, cartoon and live-action film phenomenon by the decade's end. After all, there would be plenty of other ninja toys, ninja novels and even a ninja TV show in the '80s. By the later half of the decade, by the time Chuck Norris reinvented himself in the roles of gun-wielding commandos and cops, new martial arts stars like Jean-Claude Van Damme and Steven Seagal were on the path to A-list action/adventure movie stardom. Other new actors attempting to carve out a niche on top of the A-list, actors who had formerly gained attention in supporting roles and who were eager to carry films on their own as leading men, likewise turned to the Asian fighting arts for help. For example, Patrick Swayze might have established himself as an ensemble player in such "Brat Pack" pictures as *The Outsiders* (1983) and *Red Dawn* (1984), and even attained heartthrob status in *Dirty Dancing* (1987), but he ultimately tried to turn into an action/adventure leading man and martial artist. He hoped to show off some martial arts moves in *Road House* (1989) in an effort to earn a place among the wealthiest and most powerful of Hollywood's leading men. After fighting Sylvester Stallone in *Rocky IV*, Dolph Lundgren also started showing off his martial arts skills in films like *Red Scorpion* (1989) and *The Punisher* (1989).

Nevertheless, considering the 1980s an altogether prosperous era for the martial arts and Asian influences in American pop culture is not entirely accurate. The fact is that nearly all of the ninja films were made by B-level exploitation factories like the Cannon Group production company, and the films turned the bulk of their profits from video rentals and foreign distribution. The ninjas, in straight action films, were more of a cult-level fan following than a serious American cultural phenomenon. It would eventually be up to kids who couldn't even get into R-rated films to really propel the ninjas to the forefront of the popular imagination — and to the bank with substantial profits. But, by then, it would be ninja *turtles* and not the fearsome Japanese assassins that truly created the ninja success story.

Moreover, any serious attempt to help Asian films and Asian filmmakers break into Hollywood seemed to have been taken off the agenda in the 1980s. As will be discussed later, Jackie Chan was an exception, but American producers' efforts to help him cross over to the U.S. mainstream were thoroughly wrong-headed. The first Jackie Chan experiment was doomed to failure from the start. Other Hong Kong martial arts pictures continued languishing in the video rental market or in sporadic appearances in the low-rent inner city "grind house" theaters and out-of-the-way discount theaters. Even more disappointingly, while the 1980s actually saw a motion picture renaissance in Hong Kong, the establishment of a "New Wave" of young directors and actors making not just martial arts and action films but high-quality art films, fantasies and dramas, those films went largely unnoticed in the U.S. outside of cineaste circles and film festivals.

Understanding Hollywood's relationship to the Far East in the 1980s is important, however, because it does give an interesting glimpse of the process by which factors like local and international politics, cultural trends and even gender and racial issues and attitudes intersect to shape the content of popular entertainment.

The 1980s started out promisingly enough for fans of Asian cultural influences, particularly Japanese influences. For one, on April 23, 1980, Akira Kurosawa returned to the top of his form with *Kagemusha*. The film, made with George Lucas' and Francis Ford Coppola's financial assistance, took the master back to the kind of historical dramas many of his fans had been eager to see. The film also bore the Kurosawa signature of a flawless balance when it came to handling an epic subject matter. The film not only had the proverbial sweep, the large-scale, grandiose tableau one expects of the historical drama, but at the same time it was compellingly personal and character-driven. The story involves a thief recruited to be a warlord's double. Drastic complications arise soon, however, as the warlord dies just as two of his enemies are marshalling forces to overrun his territories. From that point on, a tug of war ensues between the thief's baser nature — his treachery, his cowardice, his self-interest — and his realization of how the greater good would be jeopardized if the warlord's demise is found out. The warlord's followers need a figurehead to rally behind, and the hapless, miserable little thief soon finds himself transformed by a nobler side of his character. Echoing previous Kurosawa themes, however, the director's virtuoso balance of disparate moods, the film is at once grave, morally ambiguous, and ultimately run through with sad, bitter irony. Just as the bumbling thief finds it within himself to grow into the role of the fierce, inspirational leader, the ruse collapses and he is found out. Soon after being turned away from the lord's court, the thief's adopted clan suffers a crushing defeat. Without their leader, the lord's army is systematically crushed. The thief, seeing this with dismay, sacrifices himself for the cause as well, rushing into battle, soon to be killed.

Although regarded by Kurosawa devotees as one of his best works, the film, ultimately, did not reach as big an audience in the U.S. as his earlier classics had. The most profound impact made by Japan on the U.S. in the 1980s came through television.

Premiering on September 15, 1980, *Shogun* became the second-highest-rated miniseries ever broadcast on TV, riveting viewers to a four-part story of a British sailor's experiences in feudal Japan. Bearing testament to both the skills of the filmmakers and the country's surprising attraction to Japanese culture is the fact that audiences were not discouraged by *Shogun*'s very long segments filled with nothing but Japanese dialogue, *minus any subtitling*.

Shogun is based on a massive 1210-page novel by author and filmmaker James Clavell. The book had previously seen the same success as the miniseries would, enjoying a long stay on the *New York Times* bestseller list. Clavell, an Englishman who had relocated to Hollywood in 1953, first gained fame as the screenwriter of the original, 1958 version of the horror film *The Fly* and for writing and directing the Sidney Poitier drama *To Sir, with Love* (1967). His creative legacy, however, is his "Asian Saga" series of books dealing with Japan (*Shogun*, 1975; *Gai-jin*, 1993), China (*King Rat*, 1962), Hong Kong (*Tai-pan*, 1966; *Noble House*, 1981) and late '70s, revolutionary Iran (*Whirlwind*, 1986). Clavell was originally inspired to write by his experiences in the East during World War II, and his books are all massive, detailed — and often melodramatic — accounts of the contentious interaction between Asians and Europeans. His first novel, *King Rat*, is a semiautobiographical account of his captivity in the Japanese-run Changi prison in Singapore during the war. His follow-up novels reach further back in Asian history, tracing the establishment of the first European trading companies in Japan and Hong Kong. *Tai-pan* and *Noble House* deal with Hong Kong, fictionalizing the Jardine-Matheson trading company's establishment. Clavell substitutes the Scottish Struan clan's romantic and political intrigues in Hong Kong for Jardine-Matheson as they battle fellow European traders and pirates to become the most powerful European presence in Hong Kong. In *Noble House*, the Struans' descendants are revisited in 1963, still maneuvering to remain the dominant European corporation in the colony, evading American corporate raiders, battling the heirs of their family's old enemies, the Brocks, and contending with KGB spies plotting to wreck the Hong Kong economy. *Noble House* was also filmed as a TV miniseries in 1988, starring a pre–James Bond Pierce Brosnan as Ian Struan Dunross, "tai-pan," or supreme ruler, of the Noble House company.

Shogun was a similar fictionalization of European traders vying to control trade with Japan in the 1600s. This time, Clavell took the real exploits of William Adams as his inspiration. Adams was a British navigator in the employ of Dutch trading companies, widely believed to have been the first Englishman to set foot in Japan. Adams was embroiled in the fierce colonial competition between the Catholic Spanish and Portuguese trading powers and the Protestant British and Dutch companies. In Japan, in fact, where the Portuguese traders and Jesuit missionaries had already established a trading beachhead, Adams was initially imprisoned and came close to being executed upon the counsel of the Jesuits. Fearing potential competition from the Protestant powers, the Jesuits accused Adams and his men of piracy and strongly urged the *daimyo*—warlord—of Mikawa, Ieyasu Tokugawa, to crucify all the men. Adams, however, eventually gained the trust, and even liking, of the *daimyo*, becoming his chief advisor for all affairs relating to trade with the West once Tokugawa became the shogun—military leader—of all Japan. Moreover, Adams also became the first non–Japanese to be given the title of samurai.[1]

The Clavell book and the miniseries follow this general history fairly closely, while renaming Adams "John Blackthorne" and Tokugawa "Toranaga," granting the storytellers just enough room for creative license. For example, a great part of the emphasis in both the book and the film is placed on Blackthorne's romance with his beautiful, but married, interpreter, Mariko. In real life, Adams, too, lived the rest of his life in Japan and married a local woman, leaving a wife and children back in England. *Shogun*'s Blackthorne is single, leaving the adjustment to Japanese customs and his feelings for Mariko the only sources of creative tension.

While the cast of *Shogun* was filled with high caliber talent, including Richard Chamberlain, the star of the 1960s TV series *Dr. Kildare*, the film's real coup was getting Toshiro Mifune for the Toranaga role. As Mifune had already been anointed in the world's eyes as the "most Japanese man in the world," with his image cemented in his long line of general, war hero and, most importantly, samurai roles, the film could not have had a more fitting shogun than Mifune.

Aside from the romantic intrigue and political maneuverings between Blackthorne, the Jesuits, and Toranaga and his rivals, *Shogun* is remarkable for its detailed focus on the intricacies of Japanese customs and strict ethical codes. The four nights of *Shogun* were, to a great extent, an education in Japanese culture. As the closing credits declared, *Shogun* received the endorsement of the National Education Association and many a high school student was required to watch the entire miniseries for history classes. The sharp increase in the popularity of Japanese restaurants, especially sushi houses, around the time of the broadcast is usually attributed to the runaway success of *Shogun*. The program's coupling of the carefully-rendered cultural details with the action and melodrama served to give rise to a greater interest in and awareness of Japanese culture in the U.S. during the early 1980s.[2]

But in the early '80s, other literature focusing on Asia would likewise find enthusiastic audiences, occasionally leading to film adaptations. In 1980, fantasy author Eric Van Lustbader published *The Ninja* to bestselling success, spawning a lengthy series of successful sequels. The books present the story of half–American, half–Japanese businessman Nicholas Linnear getting caught up in the cutthroat maneuverings of Asian and American corporations, assassins, Communist bloc spies and a great deal of extremely graphic sex in each of the entries in the series.

Although *The Ninja* books, interestingly enough, were never adapted to the screen, the first entry in the series did have a plot line that would appear to be a template of sorts for a lot of the ninja films made in the 1980s. The main character in these stories is not pure Japanese, for instance, and soon after his training is completed, he relocates to the U.S. This hero is also the first Westerner — or, in Nicholas Linnear's case, half–Westerner — to master the ancient fighting techniques of the ninjas. As we find out in a series of flashbacks, reminiscent of the *Kung Fu* TV show where almost half of each episode consisted of flashbacks to Kwai Chang Cain's training in the Shaolin temple — many of the other ninjas are not happy with the initiation of a foreigner, a "barbarian," into the ancient arts and esoteric secrets of their order. Even as the American trainee shows as much, if not more, aptitude for the ninja arts as the Japanese, the animosity is still there and some of his fellow students might even conspire to stop him from finishing his training. In Lustbader's book, Nicholas Linnear's own cousin, Saigo, is his most brutal rival. He despises Nicholas for his aptitude in the martial arts and for his American heritage. As the two are growing up, Saigo routinely rallies groups of bullies to harass and terrorize Nicholas when he dares to venture into the hallowed, and what should be racially-exclusive, territory of the dojo. In other Americanized ninja entertainment, just as *The Ninja*'s major plot twist reveals, years after the foreign hero has left the dojo, now fully recognized as a ninja, his most hated rival will attempt to hunt him down and execute him. In essence, this villain will try to remove the foreign taint from the culturally and racially pure world of the Japanese martial arts. In *The Ninja*, a series of ninja-style killings in New York City are being committed by Saigo, trying to track down and eliminate his despised cousin.

Other martial arts influences in the forms of ninjas and secret societies of Asian assassins making inroads into American popular literature in the 1980s could be found in a genre best described as the modern dime novel. First appearing in 1968, these were series of short, 200- to 250-page, action/adventure novels published each month. The novels told the ongoing stories of larger-than-life heroes, usually spies or Vietnam veterans, who wage a one-man vigilante campaign against organized crime or terrorists. The first of these series of adventures was called *The Executioner* series. Written by Don Pendleton, the books recounted the ongoing saga of Vietnam veteran Mack Bolan waging a one-man war against the Mafia. The books were published starting in 1968 by Pinnacle, an imprint of former porn publisher Bee-Line. The books used the device of numbering each entry in the series, reminiscent of the *Doc Savage* male adventure books of the 1930s.[3]

The most memorable and successful of these series adventure novels were the *Destroyer* books written by Richard Sapir and Warren Murphy. They focus on bumbling ex-cop Remo Williams, recruited into a super-secret government agency and trained in the ancient (and fictitious) Korean martial art of Sinanju to be a top-flight assassin. Although the first *Destroyer* novel was published in 1971, the series, like the entire genre, truly reached its heights of success in the 1980s. The typical male adventure novel's stories of a one-man army avenging the wrongs and crimes of society, striking back at terrorists and various foreign enemies that weak-willed government bureaucrats and bleeding hearts didn't have the gumption to stand up to, found a much more receptive audience in the Reagan era. What is the most remarkable about the *Destroyer* books and their runaway success, however, aside from their hero (who is an unarmed martial artist in a category of books populated by heavy-artillery-bearing commandos), is the fact that they are a pure, out-and-out mockery of the entire genre.

Although the satire of the *Destroyer* series could often turn out to be scattershot, the books are memorable because they lampoon everything in adventure literature and action movies. From spies and tough-guy government agents to every wing and orientation of politics and, most importantly, a lot of the classical trappings of martial arts stories, everyone is on the receiving end of Sapir and Murphy's satirical barbs. As in scores of Shaw Brothers, Golden Harvest, and every other martial arts studio's typical fare, the *Destroyer* books are, first and foremost, about the relationship between the student and his sadistically demanding — yet loving and concerned — master. Once recruited into CURE, a shadowy government agency dedicated to "defending the Constitution," Remo must live day and night with Chiun, the wizened Korean martial arts master tasked with turning him into the deadliest fighter in the world. Chiun, the greatest living master of Sinanju, the "sun source of all martial arts," is both a superhumanly tough and agile old man and a hen-pecking Jewish mother to Remo. When Chiun doesn't torment Remo in torturous training sessions, he usually berates him for his immaturity, his lifestyle and ignorance. The (humorous) verbal abuse is usually qualified by comments that Remo, after all, can't help not having been blessed by the Creator with the privilege of being born Korean. Chiun's usually disapproving jabs at American culture — servicing Sapir and Murphy's impulses to comment on contemporary lifestyles and whatever the more outlandish pop culture fads of the time might have been — are balanced by his fanatical love for soap operas, particularly for *As the Planet Revolves*. As Warren Murphy had remarked about his instincts when it came to creating adventure heroes — a long line of them, as a matter of fact, as he also wrote the *Trace, Digger* and *Grandmaster* series of paperbacks as well as dozens of stand-alone mysteries, and co-wrote screenplays like *The Eiger Sanction* for Clint Eastwood and *Lethal Weapon 2*—"Basically, I've always made a living writing about heroes who were a little bit dopey."[4]

The *Destroyer* books, however, left their best shots for the martial arts and the larger-than-life, often absurdly complicated plots of most thrillers other authors always presented with poker-faced solemnity. Surely, Remo and Chiun would also go up against world-threatening nemeses in each of their books, but their problems would also come from sources like vampires, ancient demon goddesses, shape-changing robots, voodoo practitioners and crooked auto manufacturers whose nefarious plots included a hoax about creating a new car powered by garbage. Furthermore, Chiun's and (eventually) Remo's martial arts skills are so perfect as to make them virtually deadlier and more indestructible than Superman. Through the development of hyper-acute senses, Remo and Chiun could see the minutest twitches in any gunman's muscles that made them both unkillable by any shooter alive. A true Sinanju master could also be observant enough to tell not only that a man was carrying a gun simply from the balance of his body, but how many bullets were in the weapon. Simply, the *Destroyer* books were a comical, mocking riff on all the secret techniques, sage, indestructible masters, enlightenment-seeking students and megalomaniacal super-villains of hundreds of Hong Kong martial arts epics. In their absurdist, blatantly unrealistic action, they were the literary equivalent of Jackie Chan films.

In 1985, Orion Pictures adapted the *Destroyer* characters to the film *Remo Williams: The Adventure Begins*. Unfortunately, neither Sapir nor Murphy was involved in its production. As faithful as director Guy Hamilton and screenwriter Christopher Wood — James Bond alumni both, with Hamilton having directed *Goldfinger* (1964), *Diamonds Are Forever* (1971), *Live and Let Die* (1973), and *The Man with the Golden Gun* (1974), and Wood writing the scripts for *The Spy Who Loved Me* (1977) and *Moonraker* (1979) — tried to be to the books, *Remo Williams* just doesn't work. Both Hamilton and Wood simply appear to be oblivious to the absurdist parody in the Sapir and Murphy work. The end result is a movie that's an unsteady combination of straight-faced action conventions — serious, committed government agents pledging their lives to the good of the country, the free world, our way of life and so forth, and icy, sneering corporate villains — and outlandish action sequences like running on water and fighting on the face of the Statue of Liberty.

To give Hamilton and Wood the benefit of the doubt, one might hypothesize that the mid '80s were just the wrong time for mixing absurdity and big-budget action heroics. Twentieth Century–Fox, for instance, was very unhappy when director John Carpenter tried it with *Big Trouble in Little China* (1986). As Carpenter explains on the film's DVD release, he had always been a fan of martial arts films and he was interested in the genre's supernatural roots. He was hoping to pay homage to these types of films with *Trouble*, but he was also hoping to up the ante by adding satire to the mix. Much like Sapir and Murphy had done in their books, Carpenter wanted to lampoon the generic steely-jawed, super-cool, super-competent action heroes. He wanted to take the oft-seen buddy action formula and completely invert it, teaming a rugged, man's-man action hero type with a comic-relief Asian sidekick and tweaking the relationship in such a way that the action hero is a self-important, yet clueless, buffoon and the sidekick is the one who really gets things done and saves the day. In fact, Carpenter's film, succeeding in its mission of satire, is very much like the *Destroyer* books in tone, humor, and irreverence. Unfortunately, the film did not work for audiences at the time.

As Carpenter discusses *Trouble*'s failure with the film's star, Kurt Russell, on the DVD, Fox executives were unhappy with the finished product. Although the executives didn't even understand Carpenter's intentions, they were, to their credit, in all their Philistine ignorance, actually correct in predicting *Trouble*'s imminent box office failure. Action audiences in the mid '80s did not want to see heroes lampooned. This was the time of *Rambo*, *The Terminator*, and one-man-army action heroes mowing down legions of ruthless opponents with icy, humorless precision.

One can guess that perhaps *Remo Williams*' creative team might have found itself in a similar quandary. They might have even been forced to find a way to blend quintessential *Destroyer* elements like the outlandish action with a straight-up Rambo-esque tone. In the '80s, even Hamilton and Wood's old Bond franchise was being retooled and given a slightly more serious face. Since 1981's *For Your Eyes Only*, the producers were trying mightily to distance themselves from the juvenile humor of the earlier Roger Moore entries.

Remo Williams, ultimately, is a disappointing conversation piece for *Destroyer* cultists. It is something to reflect on and analyze how it went wrong. For those not familiar with the novels, it is simply a "weird," "unrealistic" action film. It seems to want to be a serious thriller, more or less, but then it has ancient little Koreans spinning from the paths of bullets with superhuman speed and running on water.

The Ninja Craze

Martial arts in the 1980s were very good to B-movie kings Menahem Golan and Yoram Globus, however. Not only did they secure Chuck Norris' services for a multi-picture deal, but when they brought ninjas to the big screen and to millions of VCRs the world over, their investment paid off in spades. Their 1981 thriller, *Enter the Ninja*, birthed a cash cow and ignited the career of a new B-movie star.

Enter the Ninja is very much like a classic Western peopled with martial artists. Martial arts purists would compare the plot to *Way of the Dragon*, except with a title pilfered from Bruce Lee's last film. The story involves Frank Landers (Alex Courtney) and his beautiful wife, Mary Ann (Susan George), operating a ranch in the Philippines and running into trouble with the corrupt Charles Venarius (Christopher George), the head of a local corporation. This crooked businessman has information that the Landers' ranch is sitting atop a massive oil field. Naturally, he wants to force the couple to sell, just as Western-film land barons have been trying to run peaceful independent ranchers off their lands in hundreds of Hollywood oaters. When Landers refuses to sell, Venarius sends his goons to administer some violent persuasion.

Luckily for the Landers couple, Frank's Vietnam War buddy, Cole (Franco Nero), also comes by for a visit and Cole has been trained in the vicious arts of the ancient ninjas. Much like Nicholas Linnear in the Lustbader novels, Cole is the first Westerner ever to penetrate the secret society of Japanese assassins and gain enough of their respect to learn all their skills. In the Philippines, Cole, just like Bruce Lee's character in *Way of the Dragon*, becomes Landers' equalizer against Venarius' thugs.

But, just like in Westerns, the big boss' goons can be beaten up and humiliated only so many times. The slimy Venarius refuses to back down and demands that the Landers' ninja protector be matched by a ninja of his own. When Venarius' henchmen go to Japan to find another ninja, they find one in the perfect mold of the American ninja plot formula. It turns out that there is an embittered Japanese ninja, Hasegawa (Sho Kosugi), in Cole's graduating class, outraged that a Caucasian was initiated into the traditionally Japanese secret order. Hasegawa is basically an angry, racist version of the Chuck Norris character in *Way of the Dragon*. Even the ending of *Enter the Ninja* is reminiscent of the dénouement of that Bruce Lee film. Whereas *Way of the Dragon* ends in the Coliseum, *Ninja* presents its final battle between Cole and Hasegawa in an empty kickboxing arena.

The success of *Enter the Ninja* did not, however, launch a new American career for the film's lead. Although Italian actor Franco Nero had, indeed, made various attempts to break into American films — his most significant Hollywood role is that of the drug lord, General Esperanza, in *Die Hard 2* (1990) — the rugged-looking star of several Spaghetti Westerns and adventure films never seemed to master English well enough for a successful crossover. *Ninja*, instead, proved to be a career-making vehicle for its star villain, Sho Kosugi.

Kosugi's own introduction to Hollywood, purportedly, resembled something that might have come out of a martial arts film. A karate champion by age 18, he moved to Los Angeles, intending to search for a college to study business and economics. Taking a wrong bus upon arrival, Kosugi ended up in the middle of Watts, not speaking any English, a suitcase in his hand and a camera around his neck. Soon enough, he had to put his karate to use against a group of punks trying to relieve him of his belongings.[5]

After the rough introduction to the streets of L.A., Kosugi did begin his education at Pasadena City College and later at California State University. In the meantime, he also ran a successful business teaching karate. In the heart of the film business, though, opportunities soon came up for appearances as an extra in various low-budget films needing martial arts adepts. Kosugi's moves eventually came to Menahem Golan's attention, and the road to *Enter the Ninja* and the ninja craze had begun. As Kosugi himself said, "A car called the 'ninja boom' passed in front of me as I was driving down the road, so I took it for a ride."[6]

Soon after *Enter the Ninja*'s success, Kosugi was used again by Golan and Globus to great success in *Revenge of the Ninja* (1983). Although not a sequel to *Enter* per se, it is generally regarded as a second entry in the Cannon ninja "trilogy." Apparently Kosugi had come across so well in *Enter*, and audiences had reacted so strongly to his character, that in *Revenge* he became both the headlining star *and* the hero. Kosugi plays Cho Osaka, a widowed Japanese man — and secret ninja — who relocates to Los Angeles with his son and opens an art gallery. He soon discovers, though, that the business is being used by his new partner as a drug-smuggling front. Attempting to extricate himself from the clutches of the gangsters who hijacked his business, Kosugi must eventually face the crime ring's ninja-trained boss in a dual to the death.

The next entry in the "series," *Ninja III: The Domination* (1984), took an ill-conceived turn into high absurdity. This time, Golan's and Globus' true natures as unalloyed exploitation masters came to the surface in tacky, garish glory. The third ninja film, apparently, was not satisfied with only one "craze," but moved to exploit *four*. At the same time, it even tried its best to rip off *The Exorcist* (1971). Joining the ninjas in *The Domination* were break dancing, MTV-style editing, and the aerobics and health-club movement. The plot of the film involves Lucinda Dickey as an aerobics instructor possessed by the soul of an evil ninja. Kosugi plays Yamada, who must take up the battle to rid the girl of the ninja "domination."

The film's garish lighting techniques, neon-glow colors, and synthesized dance music soundtrack could have left some audiences wondering whether the people involved in *Ninja III*'s production actually believed that "MTV ninja" was a cutting edge idea or if they were worried the "craze" might have been showing signs of abatement and a need for a quick overhaul with the most recent musical fad of the day. Whatever the case might have been, the Cannon team had shown its fondness for music and dancing throughout the '80s and '90s. They had also produced the high-camp classics *Breakin'* and *Breakin' 2: Electric Bugaloo* (both in 1984), also starring Lucinda Dickey. (*Breakin' 2* actually seems to have had a longer staying power in the pop cultural memory, perhaps because of its subtitle. "Electric Bugaloo" has often turned up as a punch line to a number of jokes about campy '80s films). Then, in 1990, they gambled on the lambada dance's becoming the next big thing to sweep American night clubs. To consolidate their position as the lambada leaders of film, Cannon rushed *Lambada* (1990) through a break-neck production schedule to beat a rival film, 21st Century Film Corporation's *Lambada: The Forbidden Dance* (1990), to the theaters. In the final analysis, Cannon might have won the race to the theaters, but it lost its bet on the lambada being the next pop culture craze of the '90s. Badly.

Sho Kosugi and ninjas, on the other hand, remained relatively popular throughout the decade. Although Kosugi left Cannon after *Ninja III*, he played ninja roles in *Pray for Death* (1985) and *Nine Deaths of the Ninja* (1985). In *Rage of Honor* (1987), he went without the ninja's black jumpsuit and hood, but valiantly battled South American drug lords. Returning to Cannon in 1988, he played a martial artist government agent locked in a race against Russian agents to find a high-tech missile tracking device in *Black Eagle*. Although the film was utterly forgettable, lacking in suspense or imagination, it is somewhat notable in that Kosugi's final match is against a lethal Russian martial arts assassin played by future action star Jean-Claude Van Damme.

The Cannon Group, in the days it had to make do without Kosugi's services, put plenty of effort and resources into exploiting the ninja boom for all it was worth. After Kosugi's departure, they made a martial arts star out of Michael Dudikoff, a former model and triathlete with almost no previous martial arts training. The boyish Dudikoff, with his blond surfer looks, became the *American Ninja*. From 1985 until 1993, Cannon turned out five *American Ninja* epics, Dudikoff reprising the title role in all by parts 3 and 5. Playing Joe Armstrong, a soldier stationed in the Philippines, Dudikoff seems to be stricken with amnesia, having no recollection of his childhood and how he picked up a deadly repertoire of martial arts skills. Once his memories do come back, he realizes that he is one of the very few Westerners ever trained in the arts of the ninja. As an orphaned child, he was found and raised by a Japanese World War II vet (John Fujioka). The soldier, of course, passed his ninja skills on to Joe.

The various entries in the *American Ninja* series had Joe and his buddy, Curtis Jackson (Steven James), the base's hand-to-hand combat instructor, get mixed up in corruption among the Army brass, drug smuggling schemes, and rescue missions to save hostages from Arab terrorists. In the third film (1989), where Dudikoff is replaced by David Bradley (playing Sean Davidson, not taking over the Armstrong role), a rogue scientist's plot to create an army of genetically engineered ninjas is thwarted by the heroic duo.

There is one unsatisfying footnote — for die-hard *American Ninja* fans at least — in part five (1993) of the series. Although David Bradley is back, he plays a completely different role and the film is the only PG(!)–rated entry in the franchise. For some reason, the Cannon exploitation machine, always comfortable with courting fans of R-rated blood, gore and sex, had decided that the family-oriented route was the way to go for the series. But the film was not satisfied with just toning down the action, but, in a move that brings to mind the general early '90s trend of teaming action heroes with precocious kid sidekicks, Bradley is given a martial artist teenager to tag along on a mission to save his girlfriend from a South American crime ring. Needless to say, not only was the film the least successful in the *American Ninja* cannon, but it's thoroughly reviled by the saga's fan base.

In the meantime, Sho Kosugi, by all accounts a very ambitious actor and good businessman, went on to establish his own production company.[7] He attempted bigger projects on his own and tried to test his acting limits. *Aloha Summer* (1988) was perhaps his most ambitious move, a drama where he played an embittered Japanese veteran of World War II. In 1992, he produced and starred in his most prestigious vehicle, *Journey of Honor*. This samurai-era historical epic even included Toshiro Mifune as Ieyasu Tokugawa, along with Mifune's Shogun costar, John-Rhys Davies, and Christopher Lee rounding out a high-caliber cast.

Although Kosugi liked playing heroic lead roles in most of his films, he also took the time to go back to the evil ninja roles that required him to play angry purists outraged by Westerners learning ninja techniques. This was, essentially, another version of Hasegawa from *Enter the Ninja*, repeated enough times to qualify it as a signature Sho Kosugi role. For example, when NBC tried to cash in on the ninja craze in 1984 with its series *The Master*, it turned to Kosugi to play a virtual clone of Hasegawa.

The Master revolved around an American martial artist (Lee Van Cleef)—of course, the only American to ever have been initiated into the ways of the ninja—traveling across the country *Fugitive*-style (or *Kung Fu*-style) looking for his long lost daughter. In the first episode of the series, the Van Cleef character teams up with a fast-talking "all-American" young cool guy (Timothy Van Patten) who lives in a van. From there on, the two of them travel from town to town, righting wrongs and helping people in trouble, all the while trying to evade Kosugi's various assassination attempts.

The series, in theory, should have been a smash hit. Lee Van Cleef was a Spaghetti Western icon and he should have been the draw for older viewers. His sidekick was obviously molded as a teen idol heartthrob type. Teenage boys should have loved his tricked-out van while the girls were supposed to swoon over his rebellious attitude and his seductive charms. Martial arts and ninja fans, in turn, should have been drawn by the weekly showdowns between Van Cleef and Kosugi. The first episode of the series was even directed by Robert Clouse.

To NBC's chagrin, this foolproof formula didn't quite work out. Perhaps the problem lay with the sanitized violence prime-time broadcast standards and practices required. This was, after all, the time of *The A-Team*, where commandos could spray thousands of rounds of ammunition at each other every week—when not lobbing grenades or spewing fire from jerry-rigged flame-throwers—yet no one could ever be shown getting killed. Or, perhaps, it lay with the fact that it made no sense that a pair of ninja masters like Van Cleef and Kosugi could go at each other week after week, but neither could finish the other off. After a while, Kosugi came to resemble Wile E. Coyote, waiting to spring a trap on Van Cleef every week, seeing it fail, then getting up, dusting himself off, and swearing vengeance come their next confrontation. Perhaps the bubbly, disco-style Bill Conti score that sounded like a reworking of the *Hawaii Five-0* theme had something to do with it. No matter which of these reasons was behind *The Master*'s not clicking with audiences — or, perhaps, in a way they all were — the show quickly ran out of ratings steam.

Although *The Master* might have vanished from the airwaves, Kosugi returned to the vengeful ninja villain one last time to menace Rutger Hauer in 1989's *Blind Fury*. This film is noteworthy because it was an attempt at adapting the very long-running Japanese *chambara* series, *Zatoichi the Blind Swordsman* (*Zatoichi Monogatari*, 1962) to the American action cinema. Hauer, famous for playing a murderous android in *Blade Runner* (1982) and Sylvester Stallone's nemesis in *Nighthawks* (1981), as well as starring in several of Paul Verhoeven's Dutch films, plays Nick Parker, a blind Vietnam veteran. Nick, after losing his sight in the war, was nursed back to health by an indigenous tribe that taught him swordsmanship skills and the way to harness all of his remaining senses. While Nick might be a happy-go-lucky drifter today, he also carries a razor-sharp sword sheathed inside his cane and he knows how to use it. Once he gets involved in the mob's plot to kidnap the son of a Vietnam War buddy, Nick, naturally, wreaks havoc through the ranks of the criminals until they have no choice but to call on Kosugi's ninja assassin to even the odds.

Although the ninja and martial arts juggernaut continued rolling along throughout the 1980s, its historical analysis needs to try to understand why these films seemed to be stuck in this B-movie pop culture ghetto. It was a decade, after all, when high-octane, high-budget action and adventure ruled the box office, and the *Rambo, Die Hard, Terminator, Lethal Weapon* and *Dirty Harry* films topped the box office charts. In the '80s, the record-setting salaries were paid to action stars like Stallone, Schwarzenegger, Mel Gibson, Clint Eastwood and Bruce Willis. But the mainstream of Hollywood, the major studios, wanted their action dished out by gunmen and not fighters. A stigma still remained on the martial arts to a large degree.

The source of the stigma can be spotted in several places. For one, the martial arts were still identified with the sort of tacky, witless schlock the genre degenerated into in the '70s. Chuck Norris' career was the exception that proved the rule. But even Norris, of course, had been working hard since *Code of Silence* to remake himself as a gunman and not a puncher and kicker. Martial arts still brought to mind the bad Blaxploitation films, the laughable Bruce Lee clones, and the endless import of terrible Z-grade Hong Kong martial arts dreck playing in the grind-house theaters.

Moreover, the fact is that even in their American incarnations, martial arts films were still just poorly-made exploitation vehicles. In the hands of people like Cannon's Menahem Golan and Yoram Globus, the genre hardly ever aspired to anything resembling art. Even in the eyes of most fans, the martial arts films are simply a low-rent genre. They are a "guilty pleasure" genre. These are the "so bad it's good" films. As DVD reissues of many of these films have been released over the past several years — sometimes even meriting "special edition" or "collector's edition" releases — the typical user comments on online film sites like the Internet Movie Database or sellers like amazon.com or martial arts fan community pages invariably read along the lines of "pure '80s cheese" or "much worse than I remembered."

Indeed, the lack of creative ambition in most of these films helped stamp a formulaic template onto the genre that cast them as artistic dead ends. Most of the American martial arts films were one-dimensional revenge melodramas. Although a major draw for a martial arts film needed to be the combat, one could hardly expect the genre to go too far into the mainstream once the perception had been created that such films could never *be* anything more than scowls, threats and flailing fists. As Roger Ebert said in a review of *The Karate Kid*— in a review where he discussed how surprisingly *good* the film was — most have long come to expect the martial arts film to be about nothing more than grunts, screams and threats like "You have offended my honor," and "Prepare to die!" Even at times when some of the films tried to make their plots more intricate, as was the case in the *American Ninja* films, too much of the end result was hackneyed, contrived ridiculousness. For example, *American Ninja 3* starts out by informing its audience that the mad scientist building his army of genetically engineered ninjas funded part of the operation by sending his henchmen to rob the box office at Philippine martial arts tournaments. From there, the film could only go further downhill, with no hope of recovery.

More importantly, too many of the martial artists groomed for stardom, especially by the Cannon people, had clearly been given their breaks because of their physique, looks and fighting skills alone. Not only were actors like Michael Dudikoff and Sho Kosugi stiff and bland as performers to begin with, they never seemed to improve much. When it came to physical abilities, Sho Kosugi was perhaps even more of a puzzler than Dudikoff. Dudikoff, at least, had his baby-faced, former-model looks. Sho Kosugi, while adept at the martial arts, had an utterly bland, nondescript face and cardboard screen presence. When he played his vengeful ninja villains, the seething traditionalists on a personal mission to kill the Western impostors to ninjahood, he had, at least, a certain dead-eyed, icy menace. As a leading man, however, a sympathetic hero, he was utterly useless. As action film historian Marshall Julius writes in his assessment of *Black Eagle*, Kosugi has absolutely no star quality whatsoever and he is devoid of charisma.[8]

But the martial arts genre's subsistence on the B-level of '80s action cinema has to have more complex reasons than simply bad movies and uninteresting stars. Perhaps a major reason was the Vietnam War itself. At first, America tried to put the disastrous war behind it as quickly as possible. Hollywood, in its function as a cultural mirror, largely ignored the conflict for years. Then, as the country was ready to reassess its experience in Southeast Asia, ready to reassess its *losses* in Southeast Asia, the war started showing up in TV shows and films in compensatory fantasies of heroes like Rambo and Chuck Norris' Col. Braddock refighting the war. The fact that the martial arts happen to originate in the same part of the world where Americans suffered this scarring, traumatizing defeat carries a glaringly obvious symbolic meaning.[9]

At this point it should be emphasized that a connection between popular entertainment's refighting of Vietnam in the 1980s and the marginalization of the martial arts film is purely hypothetical. Research on '80s action fans and their feelings about Asian cultures and the martial arts is sadly lacking. However, I hereby offer the suggestion that, as the new breed of '80s action heroes stood as a symbolic representation of the country's regaining of its resolve and self-respect after a beating received in an Asian country, at the hands of Asians, American moviegoers — more than just wishing to see Caucasian heroes getting tough and annihilating their enemies — did *not* want to see anything Asian influencing those heroes. The action hero of the 1980s fought with his fists, American-style, and did not use weird-looking, balletic moves from a strange foreign race that had humiliated him in Vietnam.

There is a telling example of this sentiment in Gene Hackman's *Uncommon Valor* (1983), the first film to use the back-to-Vietnam-to-rescue-the-POWs formula. When a fight breaks out between a young soldier and a grizzled, "old school" Vietnam veteran, the younger man (Patrick Swayze) readies for the fight by taking a karate stance. His arms even snake back and forth in an exotic, stylized preparatory move. The older man (Randall "Tex" Cobb), however, the "all–American" soldier, just scoffs at this and replies, "Don't give me any of that Oriental martial garbage!" Then, sure enough, with a big, John Wayne–style roundhouse punch, the veteran knocks the younger man senseless with little effort. An American hero of the '80s didn't need anything from the East. He could fight his battles the American way, with American boxing and American moves, and, more than anything, the guns, bombs, tanks, helicopters and various high-tech weapons prepared by the American industrial system.

In the final analysis, one might even be surprised to see the Japanese ninja become as successful as he had in the B-movie market. As Japan went through a very strong period of economic prosperity in the '80s and early '90s, a new form of Asian stereotyping turned up in popular entertainment. One of the new villains of the decade was the Japanese corporate raider.[10] Cold, sinister, and vengeful, usually motivated to avenge the atomic bombings of Hiroshima and Nagasaki, these Japanese villains sought to overwhelm Americans on the corporate battlefield, to "buy up America." When underhanded, corrupt business techniques were not enough, the Japanese villains were not above murder to get their way.

Looking for a Father: *The Karate Kid*

Such reactionary sentiments, however, would not entirely dominate the whole of the decade. In fact, not only is one of the most popular films of that era a martial arts film, one of the "quintessentially '80s favorites," but it is widely considered one of the *best* films of that time and one of the best martial arts films made in the U.S. *The Karate Kid*, made in 1984, at the height of Reagan-era patriotism, is the thinking martial arts fan's film.

The success of *The Karate Kid* is remarkable because the film uses so many archetypal situations, characters and themes from martial arts films, coming-of-age dramas and even teenage love stories, yet it nevertheless makes all of the archetypes feel completely original and relevant. As only the best genre films can, *The Karate Kid* manages to bring nuance and depth to a story that could so easily have been hackneyed, flat, and predictable.

The basic story of *The Karate Kid* is a simple one. Daniel LaRusso (Ralph Machio) is forced to move to Southern California from Newark, New Jersey, because his single mother found a better job there. But even in California, the LaRussos have a long way to go until they can start living the good life. For the time being, they have to make do in a run-down, low-rent apartment complex. Daniel, though, quickly finds himself to be a fish *way* out of familiar waters. Not only is he a new kid in town, but he is a dark-complexioned, ethnic-named kid in a high school full of preppy rich kids. The locals all have names like Johnny, Dutch, Bobby and Ali, they're all blond, many of them live in expensive homes and their parents frequent country clubs. Daniel, though, quickly finds himself drawn to Ali (Elisabeth Shue). While she's one of the local rich girls, she seems to be interested in him and she doesn't mind that Daniel lives in a working class neighborhood or that he doesn't drive a flashy car like the other kids. Unfortunately, Ali's ex-boyfriend, Johnny (William Zabka), is a violent punk who doesn't want to accept the fact that she has broken up with him. Once Johnny realizes what's going on between Daniel and Ali, he and his gang of karate-trained bullies set their sights on terrorizing Daniel. After Daniel gets beaten up one too many times, his apartment's superintendent, a quiet little Japanese man named Mr. Miyagi (Noriyuki "Pat" Morita) takes him under his wing and begins teaching him karate.

Most of the plot points of *The Karate Kid* are fairly obvious, and the emotional buttons the film tries to push are also easy to see. The film finds its tensions in class and ethnic conflicts. Daniel, the poor but decent Italian kid, is quickly humiliated and pushed around by the rich, arrogant suburban WASP kids. The girl of his dreams appears to be far out of his league. He is a weakling and an underdog in every way. After all the abuse heaped on him, his one chance to earn some respect comes with the big karate tournament. At that point, probably no one who has seen at least one *Rocky* film or any number of Hong Kong martial arts films or any sports underdog stories doubts for a moment that Daniel will win, that he will beat the worst of the bullies, and get the girl. The film rolls along like the most well-oiled and well-tuned of formulaic machines. However, it never fails for a minute. While it should quickly have alienated all the jaded 1980s moviegoers, even the most hardened cynics of the time praised it for its power to uplift and inspire.

The Karate Kid, basically, works because it is completely true to its material. It never tries to be hip or smarter than its story. It's not postmodern or self-mocking or slick in any way. Furthermore, it uses its karate in a way scores of other martial arts films have only paid lip service to. According to the canon of all martial arts systems, the fighting arts are but a path to self-improvement, character, and maturity. What is more, the canon instructs that the martial arts should be practiced not to make deadlier, more destructive people, but to train people to avoid fighting and avoid violence. Perfect martial arts are, in the words of Bruce Lee in *Enter the Dragon*, "the art of fighting without fighting." *The Karate Kid* comes closest to these tenets by a symbolic structuring of its drama and action. The film essentially foregrounds its characters and their relationships and not the fighting. In fact, there really is very little fighting in *The Karate Kid*. Moreover, a very critical martial arts aficionado would also notice that much of the fighting is not as smooth and spectacular and "expert" as the action in Hong Kong films. Of course, this is so because hardly any of the actors playing the lead roles had any martial arts training before the film. But the agenda of *The Karate Kid*, after all, is to elevate its archetypal characters to well-fleshed-out, believable, three-dimensional human beings. To truly appreciate why this approach puts *The Karate Kid* close to the state of a truer representation of the essence and spirit of the martial arts, one might try to do something almost heretical — or heretical at least to the martial arts film world. One could compare it to *Enter the Dragon*. Bruce Lee's magnum opus, after all, is considered by many the greatest mar-

THE
MOMENT OF
TRUTH...

The Karate Kid PG

COLUMBIA PICTURES Presents
JERRY WEINTRAUB Production of a JOHN G. AVILDSEN Film
"THE KARATE KID"
starring RALPH MACCHIO · NORIYUKI "PAT" MORITA · ELISABETH SHUE
Music by BILL CONTI Director of Photography BROOKS ARTHUR
Executive Producer R.J. LOUIS Written by ROBERT MARK KAMEN
Produced by JERRY WEINTRAUB Directed by JOHN G. AVILDSEN

**With Oscar and Golden Globe nominations,
The Karate Kid (1984) is the gold standard
of '80s Hollywood martial arts films.**

tial arts film ever made. It's certainly the most influential one. Yet, despite a couple of philosophical meanderings by Lee and his Shaolin master in the beginning of the film, it quickly gets down to business and lets its fists and feet do all the talking for the rest of the film. *Enter* is *not* about the art of fighting without fighting. It's about how cool it looks when a perfectly-tuned human killing machine kicks, crushes, stomps, gouges, and pummels hundreds of faceless comic book thugs into insensibility.

Another of *The Karate Kid*'s agendas is actually well in line with what cultural studies scholar Susan Jeffords has identified in her book, *Hard Bodies: Hollywood Masculinity in the Reagan Era*, as an oft-recurring theme in 1980s action cinema. The film is about a boy's quest to find a father figure and a guide to show him how to nurture his inherent masculinity and how to grow into self-sufficient, strong, confident manhood. At the same time, a strong, traditionally-masculine male is in search of a son to pass his values, his skills, on to. The film addresses men's need to be fathers, to have a way of influencing their offspring, especially their male children, to have a way of securing their legacies and making sure their values will live on. Jeffords compares these themes to the cultural conservatism of the time and Ronald Reagan's calls for the culture to honor its traditional values, its traditional past of strength, self-sufficiency, and manly, "hard-bodied" patriotism. These were all values that have, after all, been attacked and mocked by the Vietnam-era counterculture. Traditional masculinity, hard-bodied, physically strong and self-assured masculinity had all been attacked by a generation of counterculture hippies and feminists. As a result, America had been badly weakened. Its image had been damaged in the eyes of the world, its enemies no longer feared it and its allies no longer respected it.

Jeffords' thesis is almost perfectly realized in *The Karate Kid*. From the moment we meet Daniel LaRusso, we find a frustrated kid with a chip on his shoulder. Not only must he move to a new place he does not like, not only is he poor and an outsider, but his mother seems to be perpetually oblivious to his problems and needs. But, most of all, Daniel is weak and victimized. He can not take care of himself, he can not defend himself, because he's never had a father figure who could have taught him those skills, who could have taught him how to be a man. Because Daniel's masculinity has never been nurtured, he is preyed upon by enemies and he quickly loses the respect of his friends. The very title of the film comes from a mockery Daniel suffers after getting beaten for the first time by Johnny. The confrontation comes just as Daniel thinks he has made some new friends in California and after he first talks to Ali. Johnny suddenly shows up and begins knocking Daniel around. After Daniel tries to challenge him with a clumsy karate stance, Johnny handily beats him up. From then on, not only is Daniel a target for Johnny and his gang, but the kids he thought were his friends laugh at his weakness and ineptitude, mocking him with the "Karate Kid" moniker.

While Daniel is in search of a father, Mr. Miyagi is in search of a surrogate son. It is, of course, relevant that Daniel is not merely "adopted" by a strong father figure, but by a Japanese father figure, a representative of a culture where traditions and the passing on of values and the "ancient ways" are paramount. In fact, Mr. Miyagi explains several times that he has learned all of his karate skills from his father. Miyagi's father, in turn, learned them from his and so the skills have been passed from father to son for generations. Miyagi, however, could not continue this legacy. His own wife and unborn son died from complications during childbirth. Miyagi, thus, needs Daniel as much as Daniel needs him.

It must be noted, however, that *The Karate Kid* is not merely a bellicose lesson in violent manhood, disguised by self-help platitudes. Mr. Miyagi pointedly makes it clear to Daniel that for a true martial artist, for a truly superior man, learning karate is a way to avoid fighting. While those sentiments could easily be used as hollow pacifist clichés in lesser films, *The Karate Kid* follows through with its message by paralleling a positive father/son relationship with a negative one. While Daniel looks for and finds an ethical father figure in Mr. Miyagi, Johnny and his buddies also look for their masculine role model, and they find him in the evil Kreese (Martin Kove), the head of the Cobra-kai karate school. The film, in effect, acknowledges that masculinity can just as easily be toxic as it can be empowering and nurturing. Whereas Mr. Miyagi teaches Daniel not only how to be self-reliant and strong, but decent and respectful of others, Kreese merely teaches his charges to be strong and domineering. The Kreese karate ethos is "show no mercy to the enemy." His students are taught that only winning counts, no matter the cost, no matter how the rules are broken. During the climactic tournament, Kreese orders his students to try to break Daniel's knee when he appears to be a serious contender for the championship. In Johnny's hysterical, dysfunctional relationship with Ali, the film raises the specter of spousal abuse and domestic violence as the byproduct of toxic masculinity.

The Karate Kid was a blockbuster success in 1984, spawning two sequels that decade: 1986's The Karate Kid Part II and The Karate Kid Part III in 1989. In 1994, the formula was repeated again in The Next Karate Kid. Unfortunately, by the fourth entry in the series, the formula had been worn too thin for fans. Generally, the film is dismissed by the fan base — as it was ignored in the theaters, written off as a sloppy attempt to wring a few more dollars out of an overused franchise — and its only point of interest is future Oscar-winner Hillary Swank playing Mr. Miyagi's new pupil. Other than the basic problem of the exhausted premise, the fourth film also had to make do without the writing and directing team of John G. Avildsen and Robert Mark Kamen. The two had maintained a continuity of style and quality throughout the first three episodes. Avildsen, the director of the first Rocky, obviously had the talent to take material that could very easily have turned maudlin or betrayed its derivative, formulaic structure and shot it through with perfect sincerity. Avildsen, above all, knew how to make an audience root and cheer for an underdog. Kamen, in turn, a martial artist in real life, knew how to explore the values and philosophies behind the fighting in a compelling way.

Of the 1980s Kid sequels, Part II actually took a very interesting approach because it put the emphasis on Asia and the Japanese cultural traditions of honor, face and obligation. The film follows a general plot structure similar to the first film. Once again, Daniel tries to mind his own business but becomes the target of a superior foe; he trains with Mr. Miyagi, learns and grown as a person, and eventually has to step into an arena and fight a battle that is much tougher and more brutal than anything he has ever dealt with before. But through the Asian setting and a greater focus on Mr. Miyagi and his past, the film was original enough to keep the fans interested.

While action ruled the box office in the 1980s, these kinds of ambivalent feelings about the East and martial arts persisted for several years. The interest in the Asian martial arts could always be revived with a very well-made movie, but audiences seemed to be unable to accept the sort of racial diversity they were open to in the early 1970s. Before the decade was over, two more Caucasian action heroes who used the martial arts emerged, yet their careers would point to major cultural changes on the horizon as the 1990s approached.

7

The Rise and Fall of
Jean-Claude Van Damme
and Steven Seagal

The Americanization of the martial arts in the 1980s continued as it made major A-list stars out of Jean-Claude Van Damme and Steven Seagal, both of whom buttressed their careers on their martial arts abilities and credentials as champion fighters. Van Damme, for example, often touted his past as a multiple-championship-winning kickboxer in Europe. Seagal's publicity always stressed the fact that he was the first Westerner ever to operate a dojo in Japan. The implications behind both biographies were clear: both of these men were the real deal and they were among the toughest customers in the ranks of professional fighters and tough guys. One had the tournament titles to prove it. The other one was so good in the fighting arts that he, even as an outsider, could command enough respect in the notoriously insular home of the martial arts to run his own school. Audiences could trust such men to give them the best martial arts action for their money. Van Damme and Seagal followed in the footsteps of Bruce Lee and Chuck Norris because they were not just actors pretending to play a role. The fact that both men's tenures as stars were relatively short lived, however, signaled yet another pole shift in cultural attitudes and Americans' perceptions of the East.

Jean-Claude Van Damme, born Jean-Claude Camille François Van Varenberg in Sint-Agatha-Berchem, Brussels, Belgium, in 1960, had always molded his image and career as a combination of Bruce Lee's and Arnold Schwarzenegger's. He had the martial arts moves, but he cultivated a massive, rippling physique that was as defined and pumped as a smaller competitive bodybuilder's. Ever fond of catchy nicknames, Van Damme encouraged "The Muscles from Brussels" as one moniker. According to celebrity gossip sheets, he also liked to be called "Van Damage." His early life, according to

Van Damme, actually makes him sound a lot like a real life Daniel LaRusso. A sickly weakling as a child, a perennial target for bullies, young Jean-Claude Van Varenberg turned to the martial arts to defend himself and gain self-confidence. By age 18, in fact, he had acquired skills good enough to compete in major martial arts tournaments throughout Europe. He also taught martial arts in his own gym as his tournament wins added up, and he began bodybuilding to transform a scrawny physique into the sort of bulging powerhouse he would very proudly display in his movies.[1]

Movies, in fact, quickly crystallized as the number one life goal for the highly ambitious Van Varenberg. They prompted him to change his name as he made plans to head to either Hong Kong or Hollywood and put his muscles and fighting skills to use on film. Worrying that Van Varenberg was too much of a mouthful for non–French and non–Flemish speakers, he adopted a childhood friend's more streamlined surname. Oddly enough, at one point after coming to the U.S., he briefly auditioned as Frank Cujo. Luckily for his career, a casting agent was able to make him see the error of his ways. Frank, he was told, sounded like the name of a truck driver, and Cujo was a crazy dog in a Stephen King book.[2]

Van Damme toiled in Los Angeles for five years, doing the customary odd jobs actors often take to make ends meet until the big break comes along. Among them was pizza deliveryman, bouncer, and, at one point, carpet-layer. His martial arts pedigree and his striking, model good looks did help him make contacts and start forging inroads into the film business. In 1984, Chuck Norris gave him a role as an extra in *Missing in Action*.

Things, however, took a turn for the more promising in 1987, when he was hired to wear the bulky, rubbery *Predator* costume for the Arnold Schwarzenegger science fiction film. But Van Damme's mission was to become a martial arts action star. The best place to do this, of course, was at Menahem Golan and Yoram Globus' Cannon Group. The home of ninjas, Sho Kosugi and Chuck Norris was the place, Van Damme reasoned, to start his ascent as the next major martial arts superstar. In fact, hearing about his role in the Schwarzenegger picture, Golan and Globus suddenly thought him a promising prospect as a new leading man as well. They though he might even be perfect for a martial arts tournament movie called *Bloodsport*.

For Van Damme fans, looking for his name in *Predator*'s credits will be a futile exercise. He did not stay with the *Predator* project too long. In fact, he was soon fired. Depending on versions of the story, Van Damme either was fired because of a difficult attitude or — according to the Van Damme version, which actually sounds perfectly plausible — he got himself fired on purpose. For one, the *Predator* costume was painful to wear, uncomfortably hot and difficult to move in. Van Damme, unintentionally or as a part of a ploy, became ever more vocal about his frustration with the project and the treatment he was given. Furthermore, the action sequences in the unwieldy costume were dangerous and put him at risk of injury before he got to move on to his own starring role at Cannon. Getting himself fired for this reason does make sense. Besides, Van Damme was also bothered by the fact that in *Predator* no one would get a chance to see his face.[3]

Life at the Cannon Group, however, did not go smoothly for Jean-Claude Van Damme for several years. *Bloodsport* was shot, yet Golan and Globus were so unhappy with the finished product that they decided not to release it. Van Damme, in turn, was moved on to the proverbial Z-grade schlock of *No Retreat, No Surrender* (1986), a low budget martial arts film directed by Hong Kong director Corey Yuen. The film did triple duty by ripping off *Rocky IV, The Last Dragon* and *Fist of Fury*. Here, to save his school, an underdog martial artist (Kurt McKinney) must fight a brutal match against a cold, machinelike, murderous Russian fighter named, of course, Ivan. Van Damme plays Ivan. As the McKinney character trains, he is inspired by the spirit of Bruce Lee. As a follow-up, it became apparent that the Cannon management must have thought that Van Damme's Belgian accent was close enough to Russian to cast him as yet another sadistic, soulless Soviet killer opposite Sho Kosugi in *Black Eagle*. With both films vanishing into the netherworld of videotape and grind-house theaters the world over, Van Damme decided to take things into his own hands and began campaigning mightily for *Bloodsport*'s release. After enough nagging, Golan and Globus agreed to recut and release the film in 1988.[4]

To the stunned surprise of many film industry watchers, *Bloodsport* turned a shockingly large profit. Shot for $1.5 million, the film went on to gross $30 million. Jean-Claude Van Damme's career had, at last, taken off.

Bloodsport actually wound up being a showcase for various themes and elements that would keep recurring in his later films. The most notable was his signature move of the very wide leg-split. Van Damme's remarkable flexibility allowed him to perform perfect splits, with both legs reaching so far out to the sides as to form a straight line from one foot to the other. In most of his films, as in *Bloodsport*, he likes to perform stunts where he balances on top of two objects like chairs or crates, one leg on each support, forming the perfect split. Furthermore, making Golan and Globus' decision to shelve the film all the more surprising, Van Damme already displays what would be his trademark affable charm. Although he can get adequately tough, steely-eyed and iron-jawed when vicious opponents are closing in, Van Damme also often brings an easy-going, good-humored performance to his best films. This is not so much a Schwarzenegger-style sense of ironic, deadpan humor, but something closer to the kind of clever, boyish charm Burt Reynolds or Mel

Gibson could affect in their lighter films. Something like this might even account for *Bloodsport*'s surprising success in the mid-to-later half of the 1980s. By that time, much of the action genre's cadre of usual heroes had been getting ever more grim, grimy, humorless and charmless. With the growing body counts, expanding muscles and expanding explosions in the *Rambo* school of one-man-army action films and all of its adherents and imitators, Van Damme might have struck a chord with filmgoers looking for someone to lighten up. Furthermore, Van Damme, more than other action heroes save perhaps for Mel Gibson, appeared to try to actively court the female audience. As his career took off, attendance profiles of his films seemed to bear out the success strategy. Women liked Van Damme. What has been

Jean-Claude Van Damme rises to stardom in the American martial arts film movement of the 1980s.

described as his *GQ* looks no doubt helped this. Plus, as he does in *Bloodsport*, Van Damme is frequently given to showing off his bare backside in most of his films.[5]

The martial arts tournament storyline of *Bloodsport* would also turn out to be a Van Damme favorite. Supposedly based on a real incident in the life of controversial martial artist Frank Dux,[6] the film involves Van Damme's character going AWOL from the Air Force to compete in an underground Hong Kong tournament called the "Kumite." In the best tradition of Hong Kong martial arts epics, Van Damme must fight the battle for his childhood teacher's honor. With a beautiful American reporter tagging along to tell his story, he evades government personnel hot on his trail and, against all odds, beats the most fearsome of the Kumite fighters to become the first Westerner to win the championship title.

It is interesting that Van Damme's main opponent in this film, the mountainous, sadistic, and treacherous Chung Li, is played by one of the Hong Kong martial arts cinema's favorite villains, Bolo Yeung. Sometimes working under the stage name of Yang Sze (his real name), Yeung first gained fame as one of Han's main henchmen in *Enter the Dragon*. In fact, in *Enter* he was billed as Yang Sze and his character's name was Bolo. That character, though, made such an impression on martial arts fans that Yeung apparently adopted his name as a new professional name for most of his films thereafter. Yeung, a former professional bodybuilder and holder of the "Mr. Hong Kong" title, is, indeed, usually the most remarkable physical presence in any of his films. His massive muscularity, his sheer overwhelming size, is seldom seen in Asian actors. Furthermore, his face also lends itself well to sadistic henchman roles, villains' ruthless chief lieutenants who enjoy meting out beatings and torture. With full lips that appear to be perpetually pursed and eyes that give off a disdainful glare, Yeung's face always has a condescending arrogance etched on it. He is a truly effective villain because he is someone audiences can wholeheartedly despise. Van Damme worked with Yeung again in *Double Impact* (1991), the two men once again squaring off in a climactic fight to the death.

Van Damme returned to the martial arts tournament milieu in films like *Kickboxer* (1989), *Lionheart* (1990), and *The Quest* (1996), even as he experimented with various other genres like science fiction in *Cyborg* (1989), *Time Cop* (1994), and *Universal Soldier* (1992), and crime thrillers like *Death Warrant* (1990), *Double Impact* (1991), *Sudden Death* (1995), *Maximum Risk* (1996) and *Knock Off* (1998). It is also notable that he always kept the martial arts prominent in all of his films. Whereas Chuck Norris had often downplayed the hand-to-hand combat in many of his '80s films, as Steven Seagal would also often do, Van Damme's martial arts prowess is always well on display in all of his films.

Van Damme's career, ultimately, can be divided into three parts. There is the Cannon Group period, then his mainstream period, and finally what could be called his fall and subsequent banishment to the direct-to-video world.

His early successes, like *Bloodsport*, *Kickboxer*, *Cyborg*, and *Death Warrant* were all made under the Cannon banner. By the time his contract with Menahem Golan and Yoram Globus was up, though, he had become the first actor who actually left the studio a major mainstream star. Until then, Golan and Globus either made B-movie careers for unknowns like Sho Kosugi and Michael Dudikoff who could never rise above the exploitation level, or signed established stars like Charles Bronson and Chuck Norris to multi-picture deals. Unfortunately, Bronson's long string of *Death Wish* sequels at Cannon helped reduce a once-thriving career to self-parody. Chuck Norris, as previously discussed, was also left to languish in formulaic B-movies. But Golan and Globus' skills as career-killers were never better evidenced than by their courting of Sylvester Stallone for *Cobra* (1986) and *Over the Top* (1987). At the height of his popularity following the successes of *Rambo: First Blood Part II* and *Rocky IV* in 1985, Stallone agreed to a then-record salary offered by the Cannon executives and made a pair of films that were shameless, witless rip-offs of his two signature roles. While *Cobra* did average business, *Over the Top*—a mawkish arm-wrestling drama—crashed and burned under humiliating box office numbers and insulting reviews. After the Cannon debacle, Stallone's career and image appeared to go into a sharp freefall.[7] Jean-Claude Van Damme, on the other hand, turned out to be the only performer who managed to leave Menahem Golan and Yoram Globus as a success.

What happened afterward was a mixed bag. With a large mainstream fan base, Van Damme made a series of films for Universal Studios. Several of them were inventive and entertaining. In the best of them, the sort of charm he affected in *Bloodsport* was on display to crowd-pleasing results. Moreover, in a number of films, Van Damme seemed to be making an impressive attempt at growing as an actor.

In *Double Impact*, for example, his first post–Cannon film, he plays twins separated at birth who reunite as adults to avenge the murder of their parents at the hands of Hong Kong gangsters. One of the twins, Chad, had been raised in wealth and luxury in Southern California. The other one, Alex, was abandoned in a Hong Kong orphanage, growing up on the streets and becoming a smuggler and low-level criminal. To pull off the illusion that the audience is watching not just two separate men, but two men who have grown up under radically different circumstances, requires superb timing and physical performance. Van Damme manages to do so with remarkable skill. In fact, he does such a good job that an audience is willing to ignore obvious questions like: How did it happen that both men devoted themselves to similar bodybuilding regimens and sculpted identical physiques? Or, why do they *both speak with a pronounced Belgian accent?*

Other films of his mainstream period display high quality production values, impressive stunts and special effects, and often have well-established, A-list directors controlling the action. Directors like Roland Emerich (*Universal Soldier*)—who would go on to helm science fiction epics like *Independence Day* (1996), *Godzilla* (1998) and *The Day After Tomorrow* (2004)—John Woo (*Hard Target*), Stephen E. DeSouza (*Street Fighter* [1994], and the writer of such action classics as *48 Hours* [1982] and *Die Hard*), and Peter Hyams (*Sudden Death* and *Time Cop* and the director of *2010: The Year We Make Contact* [1984] and *The Relic* [1997]) all bring some of their best efforts to make Van Damme look like the reigning action film champion. It is also interesting that Van Damme very actively sought to bring some of the biggest names in Hong Kong cinema to Hollywood. Called "the human green card" by Jeff Yang, Van Damme helped facilitate deals for John Woo to make *Hard Target*, Tsui Hark to make *Double Team* and *Knock Off*, and Ringo Lam to make *In Hell* (2003).[8]

As Ric Meyers claims in his *Drunken Master* DVD commentary, though, Van Damme's relationship with all of the Hong Kong directors quickly turned contentious. Apparently the actor liked dominating his directors and telling them how to do their jobs. As Meyers argues, Van Damme would always have the good sense to pick very good filmmakers for his projects, but then he would turn around and stifle their creativity. After making one film with Van Damme, Meyers says, all of the directors would swear never to repeat the experience again. It is interesting to note, however, that Tsui Hark, who also has a reputation in Hong Kong for being a difficult director and even more difficult producer (someone allegedly given to interfering with his directors), would choose to work with Van Damme twice.

It was also in his mainstream period that Van Damme tried his hand at directing. Helming his own film in 1996, he went back to the martial arts tournament formula in *The Quest*. Much like in *Bloodsport*, he put himself into a greatest-fighters-in-the-world-face-off plot, except now the time period is the 1920s and the fight tournament is held in a mysterious Asian jungle sanctuary. With a lavish budget, good-looking locations and special effects, and even a high-class supporting cast like Roger Moore playing a rakish pirate and con man, the film can be considered a qualitative success. Its reviews were also generally positive, with most critics praising the well-choreographed and exciting fight sequences.

But the film's box office numbers did not do so well, and this was an issue with most of Van Damme's mainstream-period films. Although well-made and garnering fairly good reviews, none of Van Damme's A-list films had been blockbusters hits. At best, they did respectable business. But by the mid–1990s, Van Damme appeared to be a diminishing asset. After the failures of *Maximum Risk, Double Team* and *Knock Off*, his career took its biggest blow. Twentieth Century–Fox released *Legionnaire*, another sweeping period action film set in 1920s Africa, straight to video. His follow-up effort, *Desert Heat*, could get only video distribution. Although he was given the chance to redeem himself on the big screen again in 1999 in a sequel to *Universal Soldier*, the film's failure has kept Van Damme out of the movie theaters since.

The stalling and eventual crash of Van Damme's mainstream film career can be seen as a result of various factors coming together at just the wrong time. A lot of bad joss, in Hong Kong terms. Mistakes in choosing the kinds of roles he played had a lot to do with it. So did a period of turmoil in his private life. But, most importantly, the American film scene, audiences, and the world film market also conspired to bring Van Damme down.

A major problem Van Damme seemed to create for himself in this period is that he just appeared either too careless or too cynical in his approach to roles. Although in the mid '80s he attempted to bring some charm to films like *Bloodsport* and, for a while, he appeared to be pushing himself to grow as an actor, by the '90s he looked content to go through the motions as a stone-faced, monosyllabic fighting machine.

The first step in this direction was 1992's *Universal Soldier*. A science fiction/action film co-starring Dolph Lundgren, the film gives Van Damme little to do but stare ahead blankly and kick and shoot a lot of people. But the zombie-like performance is motivated by the fact that Van Damme is supposed to be literally dead. He is a soldier killed in Vietnam and reanimated by a top secret government project that turned fresh corpses into immortal assassins. When it comes to plot and execution, the film commits two major offenses. For one, the script inadvertently raises moral and philosophical issues it is either too unimaginative or just too lazy to deal with. Thus, the film compensates by trying to distract its audiences by quickly introducing a fight, a chase, or a shootout, hoping to numb the viewers into insensibility with a lot of noise and quick editing. The second major offense is that the action sequences are tired and unimaginative.

The film's basic premise is that science has, at last, found the key to immortality. What moral, ethical and religious/spiritual questions this raises, *Universal Soldier* and its creative team could apparently not care less about. The film seems to be content to use this concept of immortality as simpleminded excuse to show drone-like soldiers shoot and beat each other, then get up and shoot and beat each other some more. This is the sort of action film fans might expect from a Golan and Globus exploitation conveyor belt. But even the beatings and shootings are done in a lazy, stale, perfunctory manner. Every single scene in this film proves completely predictable. When Van Damme finds himself in a roadside diner staffed and patronized by a collection of redneck stereotypes, the kind of setting that reminds viewers of hundreds of movies and TV shows where a fight breaks out in the redneck diner, sure enough a fight is not too far behind. In a scene where trucks drive along a desert road skirting a cliff, the audience might wonder if one of the trucks could lose control and fly off the cliff. Within minutes, one of them does exactly that. In a fight between Van Damme and Lundgren on a farm, a quick glimpse of a combine's cutting mechanism shows a metal spike sticking ominously into the air, glistening like a knife. Soon enough, Lundgren finds himself impaled on it.

Universal Soldier's ultimate ambition was no greater than to imitate the

Terminator films. The team behind Van Damme's film must have been especially motivated by *Terminator 2* that had premiered to record-setting grosses one year earlier. If *T2* presented Arnold Schwarzenegger as an unstoppable automaton fighting another automaton, a corporate board meeting somewhere in Hollywood must have decided that Jean-Claude Van Damme as an unstoppable automaton fighting an entire army of similar automatons could easily replicate *T2*'s success. Unfortunately, the *Universal Soldier* creative team did not notice that James Cameron had no problems addressing the moral and ethical issues his film raises, all the while staging one fresh, exciting and unpredictable action scene after another.

Van Damme's blank, one-note performances continued even after *Universal Soldier*. In the case of *Hard Target*, for example, the real star of the picture is John Woo and his signature balletic, over-the-top Hong Kong battle choreography. Van Damme is back in a stony, monosyllabic, fighting-machine mode throughout much of the film. In an even stranger development, he followed *Hard Target* with *Street Fighter*, an adaptation of a video game and not a remake of the Sonny Chiba film. Here Van Damme removes himself from center stage and shares the film with a lot of other actors who show no more personality or nuance than the digital avatars they are supposed to be representing.

In a series of dull performances, the only brief flashes of the old Van Damme sense of humor and charm resurface in *Time Cop* and *The Quest*. In *Time Cop*, he plays not just a tough futuristic cop, but a husband. The script gives him a few good scenes with co-star Mia Sara and lets him appear as if he cares about what is happening around him. In *The Quest*, the fact that it was such a personal film and he was directing the project might have re-ignited a sense of fun and excitement in Van Damme.

The Quest (1996): Van Damme's (last) triumph. He wrote, directed and starred in the epic martial arts tournament film.

By the time he made *Maximum Risk*, *Double Team* and *Knock Off*, though, his presence barely registers on screen. He is as flat, cold and emotionless as the stalest 1980s one-man-army action heroes that had long gone out of style.

In his book *The American Martial Arts Film*, M. Ray Lott tactfully remarks that in *Knock Off*, Van Damme looks prematurely aged and inappropriate for the raconteur role he is supposed to be playing. In fact, Van Damme looks almost as bad in *Double Team*, his effort to help eccentric NBA star Dennis Rodman try his hand at action film stardom. But in the 1990s, Van Damme had also been suffering from several bouts of drug and alcohol addiction. As odd as that sounds, for someone who had always been fanatically committed to exercise and fitness, Van Damme did struggle for years with an addiction to cocaine and alcohol.[9] These afflictions, one might assume, could have played a role in his sub-par performances and maybe even in his judgment when it came to picking several roles.

But a much bigger challenge facing Van Damme was the fact that by the turn of the decade, audience tastes were changing. In fact, the entire world film scene was changing. By the time Van Damme had broken out of the Cannon basement, the entire one-man-army action film was going out of style. The one-man-against-hordes-of-evil formula had worked well at the heights of the Reagan era when it stood as a symbolic representation of a country feeling like an underdog, a loner trying to regain respect and prove itself after its disastrous loss in Vietnam. A lot of the turgid, angry subtext of those films spoke to that feeling of national disappointment, the need to regain self-respect. The template for these films had been set by Sylvester Stallone and Chuck Norris in their back-to-Vietnam films and the formula proved to be so potent that it thrived for almost an entire decade. But by the early 1990s, audiences were ready to move on to something new. The Cold War was over, the nation's number one enemy had collapsed and the one-man-army's role as a political allegory had grown old. Furthermore, even the genre's function as a symbolic statement about compensatory masculinity, a statement about the need to respect traditionally strong, muscular, warrior manhood, had also grown tiresome. Plus, aside from politics and gender statements, the whole formula had grown stale, cliché-ridden, simplistic and predictable. There were only so many times a muscular, rampaging ex-commando could take on an entire army (usually in a climactic showdown in an abandoned warehouse). Even the one-man-army offshoot of the "location-specific action film" — otherwise known as the *Die Hard*–style action film about a specific location being taken over by a team of villains and saved by one lone hero trapped inside — was seeing the end of its days by the time Van Damme tried doing it in *Sudden Death*. Almost immediately called *"Die Hard* at a hockey game," *Sudden*

Death was not so much a bad film as it was an old film. It was a stale film. It merely moved through the paces without doing anything new. By the time *Sudden Death* rolled into theaters, audiences had already seen *Die Hard* on a plane (*Passenger 57*), *Die Hard* on a battleship (*Under Siege*), on a train (*Under Siege 2*), in Beverly Hills (*The Taking of Beverly Hills*), on a bus (*Speed*), on a cruise ship (*Speed 2*), in a number of straight-to-video *Die Hard* clones, and two sequels to *Die Hard* itself.

And, as the following chapter will detail, by the 1990s audiences were ready to move beyond the Americanization of Asia and the martial arts. A Caucasian co-opting Eastern traditions like the martial arts had become passé, if not vaguely racist. Ironically enough, the time had come for the Asian filmmakers Van Damme himself championed and helped break into Hollywood to introduce a whole new style of action, a wholly authentic Asian flavor to the American action scene.

The Sensitive Warrior

Van Damme's career trajectory is very similar to that of 7th degree black belt Aikido expert Steven Seagal. Seagal was another attempt at Americanizing Asian martial arts. Seagal, however, had a much more auspicious beginning than Van Damme. Although he made connections in Hollywood much like Bruce Lee and Chuck Norris did, Seagal started performing at the very top, which made his fall by the mid–'90s all the more precipitous.

Steven Seagal fell in love with the martial arts by the time he was seven years old. By the early 1970s, after finishing college, he moved to Japan to continue his training in Aikido. As his publicity materials suggest, he was, in fact, the first Westerner to teach Aikido in that country. As his detractors — and there are a number of them — point out, he didn't open a school himself on the strength of his reputation as a master fighter. Rather, he married the daughter of the school's master. Aside from how he got to teach in Japan, Seagal's days in that country would fuel a lot more controversy after he hit the big time in Hollywood. But Seagal never did intend to stay in Japan too long. In the mid '70s, he moved to California and, like Bruce Lee and Chuck Norris had done before, started teaching martial arts and building up a high-powered Hollywood client list. Many of his film acquaintances, in fact, started calling on him to serve as a fight choreographer on action films.[10]

With Seagal's filmic ambitions growing exponentially, he got lucky enough to have Michael Ovitz, the founder and head of the Creative Artists Agency, sign on as an Aikido student. Creative Artists Agency was, at the time, the premiere Hollywood talent agency, representing the A-list of the film business, from writers to actors, directors and producers. Many, in fact, considered Ovitz one of the most powerful men in the industry. Whatever film Ovitz wanted in production would usually get a green light from any studio with few problems. Looking at Seagal, Ovitz envisioned another major action star on par with Sylvester Stallone and Arnold Schwarzenegger.

Seagal, with his powerful patron behind him, got a chance to bypass the B-movie bush leagues Chuck Norris and Jean-Claude Van Damme had to fight so hard to get out of. Seagal debuted in 1987 in the Warner Bros. film *Above the Law*, supported by a major publicity blitz touting his background as one of the greatest martial artists in the world.

The publicity blitz, however, included certain claims and generated controversy that would dog Seagal for years. Often it would give ammunition for ridicule once his career began faltering and various allegations about his private life and business dealings started making gossip headlines. How much of the hyperbole was Seagal's idea and how much Warner Bros. invented is not known for certain, but the actor did participate in spreading a colorful line of rumors and insinuations in his early rounds of publicity interviews. Since the plot of *Above the Law* involves a CIA drug-running conspiracy, Seagal and the Warners publicity department started suggesting that, while in Japan, the future actor worked with the CIA as an anti-terrorist operative. The CIA, according to the P.R. campaign, was aware of the fact that Seagal was one of the deadliest Aikido practitioners in Japan and they recruited him into the fold to train operatives and carry out missions throughout Asia.[11] On other occasions, Seagal would add to his own mythology by claiming that while in Japan, he liked to hone his fighting skills by provoking members of the Yakuza organized crime families into fights. In fact, he claimed that the dojo he ran was at one point gambled away by his father-in-law and he had to fight Yakuza gangsters to get it back. His first wife, Miyako Fujitani, has bitterly disputed this.[12]

Such claims could be dismissed as the usual Hollywood publicity hype taken to new, perhaps absurd, levels. But they did take on a darker edge when *GQ* writer Alan Richman made claims about Seagal's harassing and threatening him. According to the writer, after Seagal was angered by an unflattering article Richman wrote, questioning the actor's CIA ties, Richman started receiving a series of death threats. As Richman alleges, Seagal claimed to have close friends in the Mafia and he would put a hit out on the writer in retaliation for the humiliating *GQ* piece.[13] Although nothing ever happened to Richman, years later journalist Anita Busch also claimed to have been under surveillance by private investigators in Seagal's employ following her stories about the mob connections of Seagal's business partner, Jules Nasso.[14]

Looking at *Above the Law*, one can see that there really are autobiographical parts in it. Although the CIA claims can't be proven or disproven — the

CIA has officially denied Seagal ever worked for them — the film opens with a voice-over giving us the Seagal character's early life story. Nico Toscani, the Chicago cop Seagal plays, immigrated from Italy as a child and developed an early interest in the martial arts. As a teenager, he traveled to Japan, just like Seagal, to learn from the masters. The voice-over is accompanied by a montage of still photographs of Seagal as a child, a teenager, and an adult in Japan. Once the story veers into action/adventure territory and CIA recruitment, viewers are left to decide how much of the hype, the rumors and suggestions they want to believe.

Above the Law was a hit and Seagal's screen presence can largely be credited for it. Aside from director Andrew Davis' coaxing a decent, natural performance out of the rookie actor, Seagal's bearing and overall impression are very effective. In many ways, he comes across almost as a martial arts version of Clint Eastwood. Not only is Seagal tall (6'5") and rangy, built a lot like Clint Eastwood, but he even has a similar squinty-eyed, vaguely sinister look. He has an aloof manner, again like Eastwood, and speaks in a soft near-whisper, but it's all shot through with a suggestion that very dangerous things lie just beneath the surface. Seagal speaks softly, but he packs a very big punch. Furthermore, given the time Above the Law was released, Seagal, much like Chuck Norris, looked refreshingly realistic. In a time when nearly every action hero, save perhaps for Bruce Willis and Clint Eastwood, pumped iron and looked like bodybuilder perfection, Seagal's physique was not imposing at all, aside from his height. Furthermore, Seagal's receding hairline and real-looking face — handsome, yet not in a matinee idol or male model way — helped make him seem real in an action film landscape that had been taken over by superheroes.

Another major difference in Above the Law was its political orientation. Whereas the '80s school of Rambo and Missing in Action back-to-Vietnam sagas and Top Gun–style pro-military films placed the genre squarely in the camp of Reaganesque conservatism, Above the Law is very liberal. Coming on the heels of the Iran/Contra scandal, it offered an angry indictment of super-patriots, rogue intelligence agents and an entire CIA establishment that was too powerful and unaccountable to lawmakers, the media and the public. In the course of the film, Seagal's Nico Toscani stumbles onto a drug-running ring run by the CIA to fund its Central American anti–Communist operations. If action films until then glorified rogue agents, rogue commandos and soldiers who were willing to break the rules to fight enemies, Above the Law countered by showing the results of such lawlessness. If anything goes, the film argues, when government agents decide their mission is so righteous that even the subversion of laws and the checks and balances of the democratic system are excusable, what is to keep such people from becoming a gang of criminals just as bad as the threats they purport to be fighting? But *Above the Law* is also shrewd enough to give its own version of the rule-bending rogue cop. Action fans, after all, have long come to expect to see heroes who are also rebels, outsiders who take matters into their own hands and play by their own rules. In this traditional mode, though, born of the Reagan conservative movement's crusades against big government and "big bureaucracies," the government, law enforcement, the courts and the intelligence and military establishments all have their hands tied by weak-willed liberal desk jockeys who don't have the gumption to take on the country's enemies. Nico Toscani, therefore, just like Dirty Harry or Rambo or any number of right-wing action heroes who have disobeyed officials and wrong-headed bosses, who kept investigating even after being put on suspension, starts breaking rules to bring down the corrupt CIA drug ring. In *Above the Law*, the government, law enforcement, and the intelligence services are being subverted by vast right-wing conspiracies. The only way to achieve justice is for a liberal hero to take things into his own hands and bring down the enemies of democracy. Of course, deciding whether or not the film, in its agenda as a critic of Iran/Contra–style conspiracies and super-patriot zealotry, is actually being hypocritical can only lead to a long, circular and futile exercise. If the film condemns the Reagan administration's subversion of laws against the funding of the Contras in Nicaragua, is Nico Toscani not being just as bad when he disobeys rules and acts like a vigilante one-man army? But, then again, are the traditionally right-wing rule-breaking action heroes not hypocrites themselves, along with all their conservative fans, if they present themselves as the "law and order" party while championing vigilantism?

Some of these themes would continue showing up in later Steven Seagal films, however. Most often, the Seagal characters try to manage their better, more peaceful and liberal impulses — usually as sensitive family men and spiritual environmentalists — and their urges to turn into vigilante wrecking crews when peace, law, and order don't work. After *Above the Law*, Seagal's two most political films are *On Deadly Ground* (1994) (which he wrote and directed) and *Fire Down Below* (1997). Both films deliver strong environmental messages, indicting oil corporations and a government that has been bought off and subverted by big business interests. Just like in *Above the Law*, Seagal fuses liberalism with vigilantism in these films. The defense of the environment is not possible, the films charge, because of a system where corporate money can corrupt the government agencies that should be protecting the land. The only recourse is to do what action heroes do best. In *On Deadly Ground*, Seagal becomes a one-man army to destroy an oil company's dangerous oil rig before it can go online and defile the pristine Alaskan wilderness. The authorities, as usual, are of no help. They are all in the pocket of big business. Furthermore, as the Seagal character, the heavy-handedly-named Forrest Taft, accuses, massive business conspiracies have long suppressed various clean air and clean energy technologies in order to keep profiting from oil. As the evil oil company's drilling platform is about to be activated, an entire private army of mercenaries is in place to protect it. Forrest Taft's righteous rage and Aikido, however, are more than a match.

In *Fire Down Below*, big business is again the enemy. This time, illegal chemical waste dumping is endangering the lives and the health of an Appalachian community. Seagal, playing a conscientious and dedicated EPA agent, Jack Taggart, goes undercover to find out the facts. He soon learns that the polluters are too rich and too well connected in the corridors of power to ever be brought to justice. Moreover, even by the time Seagal is able to bring a case against the head of the dumping ring, Orin Hanner (Kris Kristofferson), the laws are so toothless that justice can not be achieved. Although Hanner and the gang made $30 million dumping hazardous waste, they face only a $100,000 fine. "What a great country!" Hanner gloats, strutting out of the courthouse after paying his dues. But if Hanner will be let off the hook by the system, he won't be let off by Steven Seagal's sense of justice.

Although in the early 1990s Seagal had reached the pinnacles of A-list, big-studio success, he too fell victim to the same cultural changes and audience tastes that put an end to Van Damme's mainstream career. Oddly enough, Seagal's downward slide started with a sequel to his biggest hit. In 1992, he attempted his own version of the location-specific action film in the *Die-Hard*-on-a-battleship thriller *Under Siege*. Re-teaming with director Andrew Davis, he took the highly-derivative story and turned it into a smash hit success. Naturally, in 1995 the formula was repeated (minus Davis' direction) in *Under Siege 2: Dark Territory*. However, fans, by then, seemed indifferent to yet another variation on the terrorist takeover plot. From that point forward, Seagal's career was stuck in a very fast and very sharp downward trajectory. Within a few years, he would exclusively be making straight-to-video films.

The disintegration of Seagal's mainstream career is curious, as he was one of the martial artist action heroes who might have been able to fuse more Asian culture and Asian influences to his films than a lot of other action stars. Seagal, after all, boasted of a much stronger connection to the East than other Hollywood action heroes. He missed few opportunities in interviews to discuss the fact that he is a Buddhist and a devout follower of the Dalai Lama. Not that this revelation, much like his alleged CIA connections, didn't take a couple of odd turns. For example, in 1997, he declared that His Holiness, Penor Rinpoche, one of his Buddhist spiritual advisors, had revealed Seagal to be the reincarnation of a Buddhist Lama.[15] Again, much like the CIA issue, or even more so, it's a claim that can never be proven or disproven. Seagal, however, had often said that his Buddhism was a strong influence on his films and that he would always work hard to use the tenets of the religion to shape the contents of his films. Whether or not he was able to do this is debatable. In films where his religion becomes an issue, like *The Glimmer Man* (1996), Buddhism goes no farther than the Seagal character's reciting a few homilies about being peaceful and finding serenity and trying to find enlightenment. Since most of these declarations come just before Seagal is moved to beat up and shoot people, the sincerity of his efforts can be called into question. If anything, talking of peace and serenity just before battering a group of people into insensibility might almost be interpreted as a mockery of Buddhism. The ways of peace and harmony, according to these films, obviously don't work in the real world. What does work is busting heads and breaking bones.

In another somewhat odd choice when it came to finding a connection to another race, Seagal used two of his films — his last two films to date to be released theatrically — to connect with African-American hip-hop culture. In both *Exit Wounds* (2001) and *Half Past Dead* (2002), his costars are prominent rappers and the films have a large black cast. In *Exit Wounds* he plays opposite rap star DMX and in *Half Past Dead* he is teamed with Ja Rule. The overall look and sound of both films is also largely influenced by hip-hop videos. The soundtracks of both films are also replete with rap music.

Seagal, though, had one more trait in common with Van Damme that aided in the demise of his career. The quality of his performances steadily deteriorated with each film he made. Moreover, his appearance and demeanor in a number of these films just kept getting either stranger, ill-suited to an action hero, or outright antagonistic to action fans.

For one, Seagal seems to have developed a weight problem. Especially as the 1990s wore on and his age approached 50, he had started getting noticeably portlier. Although he had never been the chiseled bodybuilder type, and in the '90s the body-oriented action star went out of style, an action hero should still not have been fat. By the time he made *On Deadly Ground*, he had taken to wearing mid-thigh-length, loosely-tailored jackets to help hide the size of a quickly-spreading middle-age paunch. Chinese audiences might have come to accept an overweight martial artist like frequent Jackie Chan costar Sammo Hung, but the body- and fitness-obsessed Americans did not.

Furthermore, the type of characters Seagal insisted on playing had also grown tiresome very fast. While he might have started his career by making *Above the Law*'s Nico Toscani seem somewhat realistic and human, his subsequent roles kept getting more and more superhumanly invincible. And this despite their expanding girth! Most reviews of Seagal films would sum up the action by remarking how any character Seagal ever plays is a completely unbeatable superman. The typical Seagal hero could hardly be touched by any number of bad guys. Ultimately, a hero who stands virtually no chance whatsoever of losing is not very interesting; his indestructibility removes the feeling of tension and suspense from a film.

But when indestructibility is coupled with arrogance, the effect is even more off-putting. In a typical Seagal film, his characters enjoy taunting and humiliating their opponents, not simply beating them. To be fair, the intention is obvious in most of his films. But the execution has still served to chafe fans after a while. Seagal is always pitted against the biggest and the baddest of villains. His opponents are usually so vile, so corrupt, so sadistic and oblivious to the suffering they inflict on others, that it should become exciting and cathartic to watch these creeps get a taste of their own medicine. Nevertheless, this intention has often been lost on critics and, more important, on ticket-buying audiences. To many, Seagal is not a hero who beats bad guys but an arrogant, preening bully.

But Jean-Claude Van Damme's and Steven Seagal's problems were merely emblematic of bigger changes unfolding. By the time the 1990s arrived, slow, yet steady, social currents appeared to be undermining the martial arts in films. Aside from Sho Kosugi, for a decade audiences always seemed to prefer Caucasians co-opting Asian martial arts and Asian culture. Yet, as the very action genre itself showed signs of weakening, the repetitive formulas of the invincible one-man-army tiring, damage was being done to the American martial artist films as well. For example, by the time Patrick Swayze tried to break into the martial arts action hero role, he failed badly with the bizarre *Road House* (playing a "legendary" bouncer with a degree in philosophy from Harvard). Dolph Lundgren likewise floundered in a handful of theatrically released films, usually showing off his skills as an expert in karate, before departing to the straight-to-video world.

Within a few years, however, Asian-influenced entertainment would make yet another comeback in the U.S., but this time it would not be so homogenized, so Americanized. In fact, even Bruce Lee's legacy would make yet another brief mark on American cinema.

8

A New Decade and a New World

One sign that a mainstream Hollywood star's days of A-list prominence are numbered might be the failure of his imitators. By the earliest days of the 1990s, the indicators were everywhere that the Americanized martial arts movement was close to imploding. Although Jean-Claude Van Damme and Steven Seagal might have been enjoying what would soon prove to be the halcyon days of their careers, there was no successful new wave of martial artists burning up the movie screens in their wake. In fact, aside from Van Damme and Seagal, nearly all of the American martial arts cinema had migrated to the video market. A number of new actors attempting to follow in Van Damme's and Seagal's footsteps failed to generate much attention outside of a small market of martial arts enthusiasts. The decade, it appeared, was bound to head squarely in the direction of special effects fantasies and very big, very expensive, very safe mainstream "all–American" studio blockbusters. The one exception that could possibly have revitalized the martial arts genre, Bruce Lee's son, Brandon, came to a sad and tragic end.

Ultimately, the decade would witness one of the most dramatic Asian influences on Hollywood action/adventure films ever seen. But its beginnings saw the failures of a lot of entertainment attempting to rely on the martial arts.

The '90s: Days of Robots and Dinosaurs

Hollywood in the 1990s was swept by the digital revolution. The impact of this new visual effects technology would, eventually, be both positive and negative. For one, computer graphics could render a whole new dimension of reality in films dealing even with the most outlandish and fantastic of concepts. However, many critics — and filmmakers as well — would also lament a dumbing-down effect on story-telling and character development by the fancy new computer effects.

Certainly, directors and special effects technicians had dabbled in and experimented with computer animation since the early '80s. In 1982, Disney's *Tron* was the first film to include long segments of its story and pivotal action sequences animated entirely by a computer. Scenes of space flight and space battles would also have various levels of computer enhancement added throughout that decade. For example, 1984's *The Last Starfighter* used computer animation to render all of its scenes of interstellar battles between warring alien races. However, for years, the flat, smooth, arcade look of computer-generated images prohibited them from meshing effectively into the textured scenery of any realistic settings. Computer imagery, essentially, needed to exist in another plane of reality. It could work only in outer space sequences or alternate dimensions or in any context where the scenery was alien and unrealistic. For example, buildings, airplanes, cars or any number of *real* objects could not be rendered convincingly by the early computer animation technology.

Nevertheless, computer effects that would approximate perfect reality had been the Holy Grail for filmmakers like George Lucas and James Cameron. Lucas, in fact, had withdrawn from directing after the first *Star Wars* and devoted himself largely to overseeing the development of special effects technology in his Industrial Light and Magic company. Flawlessly realistic computer animation was the prize he quested for. James Cameron, likewise, founded the Digital Domain company to perfect the use of computerized image manipulation in films.

The first breakthrough in integrating a realistic setting with a computer-animated image, an entire computer-animated character, appeared in Cameron's 1989 film *The Abyss*. Cameron successfully placed a computer-drawn alien water-creature into the grungy, industrial setting of an underwater drilling rig. Integrating the real world and computer animation saw its most successful effort, though, in Cameron's 1991 hit *Terminator 2*. Whereas the water creature was seen for only a few brief moments in *The Abyss*, in *T2* Arnold Schwarzenegger's main nemesis was a computer-generated liquid metal T-1000 robot. While most of the T-1000's scenes were still performed by actor Robert Patrick, he could be seen flawlessly "morphing" back and forth between living flesh and glistening metal, changing from one human form into another, and carrying on a hand-to-hand fight with Schwarzenegger while in the computer-generated liquid metal form.

With *T2*'s blockbuster success, the development of ultra-realistic computer effects became the goal of most action and science fiction/fantasy films for the rest of the decade. Specifically, filmmakers competed in topping each other in the use of longer, more elaborate and more realistic computer effects. The second most successful standard-setter of the decade was Steven Spielberg's *Jurassic Park* (1993). Here, computer animation created perfectly flawless renditions of the textured skins of scaly, leathery dinosaurs. As a result of the so-called "mind-blowing" possibilities of digital special effects technology, action and adventure-oriented filmmaking in the '90s was aiming for otherworldly spectacle, much as it did in the late '70s following *Star Wars* and *Superman*. American filmmaking simply could not sustain an interest in films where two fighters face off and throw punches and kicks. Martial arts seemed to be too earthbound for Hollywood's digital ambitions. It would eventually take Asian filmmakers and stunt coordinators with films like *Crouching Tiger, Hidden Dragon* (2000) to show their American counterparts why martial arts and computers might really have been made for each other.

But in the early years of the decade, American martial artists had to get used to their place at the B-movie level. Some of them, to be sure, tried their best to rise higher and a few producers and studios did attempt to help them. A notable example in this period is Jeff Speakman, an expert in American Kempo karate. After a few years of doing bit parts in B-movies and a guest role on the TV show *Hunter*, Speakman got the attention of Paramount studios. While the Van Damme and Seagal money-making machineries rolled along nicely, Paramount decided to use Speakman's similar pedigree as a high-ranking Kempo black belt to try to establish a new action star of their own who could dazzle with lightning-quick fighting moves. Speakman was set up in a revenge film called *The Perfect Weapon* (1991) and given a Seagal-like publicity sendoff, touting his reputation as one of the best Kempo practitioners in the sport. Although Speakman's film is not bad and he had adequate acting skills and a likable demeanor — much more agreeable, in fact, than Seagal's smug arrogance — the film only did mediocre business. Perhaps because he waited two years to make his second film, *Street Knight*, with the Cannon Group, a career that didn't really ignite much excitement in the first place just faded away. The Cannon people certainly didn't put much effort into publicizing *Street Knight*'s theatrical release. Perhaps if they had, Speakman might have been able to rise to greater prominence, especially since *Street Knight* did attempt to be somewhat topical in its plot. Coming just a year after the Rodney King riots in Los Angeles, the film deals with a group of corrupt cops attempting to provoke a full-scale gang war. They hope the war will lead to all-out anarchy and riots in the streets of L.A., giving them adequate cover to rob a jewelry store. The leader of the cops even bears a striking resemblance to L.A.P.D. officer Stacey Koon, one of the two cops in the King incident who received federal jail time for their roles in the beating. To Jeff Speakman's bad luck, however, the film received almost no marketing support aside from a few newspaper ads before its debut. Had *The Perfect Weapon* been a major hit, with Speakman well established as a star, *Street Knight* might have stood a chance at the box office.

But, then again, the new, high-tech blockbuster atmosphere of the '90s might have prevented Speakman from ever attaining A-list status despite his talents. Speakman, like Van Damme and Seagal, was attempting to gain a reputation for the dazzling physical feats he was capable of performing. Audiences of the time, though, were anxious to be dazzled by the moves of computer programmers and special effects technicians.

Despite the fact that Speakman's big-screen career stalled, he continued making films in the direct-to-video market. Although the video market was far from the prestige of big studio, big screen, A-list stardom, it was — and still is — quite lucrative for its star performers who have managed to carve out a niche of fan followers. Speakman continues to make direct-to-videos as of this writing and has an established fan following. The most successful of today's direct-to-video performers, the A-list of this film venue like Van Damme, Seagal and Dolph Lundgren, regularly command seven-figure salaries for their films.[1]

A few other notable martial artists of this era who were able to carve out a successful niche in the direct-to-video market include Cynthia Rothrock, Don "The Dragon" Wilson, Olivier Gruner, Daniel Bernhardt, Sasha Mitchell, Billy Blanks and Marc Dacascos.

Among this list, Cynthia Rothrock is perhaps the most noteworthy. She is a wildly popular performer among martial arts fans, with a world-wide cult following, who nevertheless still could not crack the mainstream theatrical markets in the U.S. Timing, again, might be the main culprit behind her almost exclusively direct-to-video career. However, she does bring to mind some questions about the role gender plays in action stardom in the eyes of both the Hollywood production community *and* American fans.

Rothrock certainly has impeccable credentials as a martial artist. She is a five-time undefeated World Karate Champion (1981–85) and she holds five Forms Championships and five World Weapon Championships. She has been inducted into both the *Black Belt Magazine* and *Inside Kung Fu Magazine* halls of fame. She first gained the attention of the martial arts film community in the early '80s after showing off some of her moves in a Kentucky Fried Chicken commercial. While a part of the West Coast Demonstration Team, she was invited to an audition held by a Hong Kong company looking for American *male* martial artists to appear in a film. Rothrock impressed the casting team so much that they decided to hire her instead of any of the men. Although the company put off actually making the film, ABC's *World News Tonight* did a story on Rothrock and how she made an impression on the

Hong Kong martial arts film world. After fight choreographer/director Corey Yuen and actor/director Sammo Hung saw the feature, they decided to buy her contract and Rothrock was on her way to making action films in Hong Kong.[2]

Rothrock's stay in Hong Kong from 1985 to 1990 proved remarkably successful. Not only was she able to measure up to the Hong Kong audiences' standards for martial arts performers, but she became the most popular Westerner ever to appear in local films. A testament to how well she impressed Hong Kong audiences is the fact that she was one of the very few Caucasian performers in Hong Kong to play hero roles in films. American and Caucasian actors in Hong Kong films are usually cast as villains.[3]

In 1990, Golden Harvest, the company she had been working for, decided to try to crack the American market by producing films in the U.S. with American actors in starring roles. Rothrock, naturally, became their first choice for the project. The film they put her in was called *China O'Brien* (1990), directed by Robert Clouse, about the martial artist daughter of a rural Utah sheriff who must avenge her father's death. A year later, Rothrock and Clouse followed up with *China O'Brien II*, this time about the eponymous Rothrock character trying to rid her Utah town — where she's now the sheriff — of a drug gang. Although both films found a solid following of martial arts fans, that fan base was still not enough to help convince any major Hollywood studios of Rothrock's A-list potential. Unlike Van Damme or Norris, who were given the money and a big studio's backing to try to cross over to a mainstream audience, Rothrock eventually settled into a series of straight-to-video films.

One might also wonder if Rothrock's American introduction might have produced more profitable results if it had been attempted later in the decade. The later half of the 1990s and the turn of the millennium witnessed a rise in the popularity of female action heroes. On the heels of several hit TV programs like *Xena: Warrior Princess*, *La Femme Nikita* and *Dark Angel*, Hollywood took notice of women as the potential equals of men when it came to the creation of mayhem and destruction. In films like *Lethal Weapon 3* (1992), Mel Gibson not only falls in love with a tough, martial artist female cop (Renée Russo) after she proves she's just as tough as he is and has as many battle scars as he does, but marries her in *Lethal Weapon 4* (1998). In action franchises like *The Matrix* films (1999, 2003) and the *Charlie's Angels* films (2000, 2003), women use martial arts and handily beat scores of men who dare to take them on.

But Hollywood's attitude toward action heroines and tough women has always been strikingly schizophrenic, leaving any speculations about whether or not a bona fide martial artist of Rothrock's caliber could ever have gone completely mainstream without definitive answers. The inability to figure out what to do with women in action/adventure films became even more obvious in the '90s. While female action heroes had been around for a long time, going as far back as the adventure serials of the 1930s, they actually found a more usual home in T&A exploitation films like *Faster, Pussycat! Kill! Kill* (1966), *H.O.T.S.* (1975), *Sheena* (1984), *RoboC.H.I.C.* (1990), *Hard Hunted* (1992) or any number of women-in-prison films. In the '90s, filmmakers appeared to be incapable of deciding what to do with women when it came to heroic cinema. For example, did women belong in straight thrillers like Jamie Lee Curtis' *Blue Steel* (1990) or Bridget Fonda's *Point of No Return* (1990) (a remake of the popular French film *La Femme Nikita* that also inspired the American syndicated TV show), or in a big-budget T&A camp fest like Pamela Anderson's *Barb Wire* (1996)? Apparently American audiences didn't always know what they wanted either. They largely ignored *Blue Steel*, while they enjoyed *Point of No Return*. They were fans of Anderson's cheesy TV show, *Baywatch*, which often included action and adventure storylines, yet they didn't take her seriously as a big-screen star. One of the toughest female characters on screen in the '90s was Linda Hamilton's Sarah Connor in *Terminator 2*, lean, strong and as muscular as perhaps an amateur bodybuilder. In turn, taking a cue from this, Jean-Claude Van Damme (who is married to former female bodybuilder Gladys Portugues) cast six-time Ms. Olympia bodybuilding champion Cory Everson in *Double Impact*, yet Everson could not interest any other producer in backing her big-screen ambitions ever again. Sharon Stone could also be cast as very tough women in supporting roles in straight thrillers like *Total Recall* (1990) and *Basic Instinct* (1992), yet when she got top billing in a film like *The Quick and the Dead* (1995), she found herself in a campy imitation of Clint Eastwood's Spaghetti Westerns. But, overall, as the decade progressed, audiences seemed to be more accepting of the action heroine as the main protagonist in a film, carrying the story on her own and taking on the villains as men had done before.

So, might Rothrock's career have been different had she made *China O'Brien* perhaps five years later? As she had experienced in Hong Kong, heroic female leads who are adept at combat had a very long history in Chinese-language martial arts cinema. Technically, the very first martial arts film stars — or, really, any type of film stars — of Chinese cinema were women. In the earliest days of film in China, many of the male Peking Opera stars considered film an inferior art form and beneath their stature. Many of the first performers to work in Chinese films were women. In fact, there was such a shortage of male performers in early film that women would often play male roles.[4] This openness to strong, fighting women, of course, was incomprehensible to American culture even in times as supposedly enlightened and modernized as the 1990s. Furthermore, one might argue that even the most successful female action films and TV shows of the time were not all that they appeared to be. Most of them, like the *Xena* TV show or the *Charlie's Angels* films, were so campy that they might actually have been more of a mockery and parody of women's empowerment than its straight presentation. In fact, if one were to compare them with the original late '70s/early '80s *Charlie's Angels* TV show, one might find the old version of the story taking its empowered women much more seriously than its descendant a generation later. Even James Cameron's show, *Dark Angel*, that tried to take itself seriously, had to present its female lead as not merely strong and capable, but as a model-perfect piece of eye-candy. Most of the '90s and 2000s breed of heroines were definitely skewing more toward cheesecake and subtle male domination fantasies than any realistic representation of a strong woman who could hold her own in a man's world. But Rothrock's films are exactly that. She is at once tough and capable at dealing in violence, yet she is not an angry, hard-case feminist spewing politically correct slogans. While she is also attractive, she does not have the sort of glamorous, ex-model looks of Cameron Diaz or Jessica Alba.

Ultimately, Rothrock's career settling into the direct-to-video market in the '90s was yet another sign that Americanized martial arts were falling off the radars of mainstream audiences. Highly accomplished, multiple-black-belt-holding and championship-winning martial artists like Don "The Dragon" Wilson, who thrived in B-movie king Roger Corman's *Bloodfist* series, made a lucrative living in the video market. Sasha Mitchell and Kevin Bernhard might have taken over Van Damme films in their *Kickboxer* and *Bloodsport* sequels, but they could not replicate the originator's career. French kickboxing champion and ex–Marine Olivier Gruner also tried to replicate Van Damme's success with films like *Angel Town* (1990) and *Nemesis* (1993), but could not. Billy Blanks made direct-to-video films but became a household name only when he began selling his Tae Bo exercise program. Mark Dacascos found mainstream success as the "Chairman" of the Food Network series *Iron Chef America* in 2006.

The one exception who could have bucked this trend in the American martial arts film might have been Brandon Lee. Being the son of a martial arts legend, of course, still had a very powerful cachet, even to kung fu fans who might not have been born when Bruce Lee made his films. However, upon examining the film that led to Brandon Lee's tragic demise, one can speculate that the young actor understood why the martial arts genre was faltering and what he needed to do if he wanted to establish a thriving, A-list action career.

At first, however, Brandon Lee's name did not automatically open doors to the decision makers in Hollywood, even though films and acting were career paths he was always sure he wanted to pursue. Films and martial arts, the younger Lee knew, he would always be associated with. However, as is the case with many children of iconic celebrities, he had been forced to spend a great deal of time figuring out how he would let these two legacies shape his life. To what extent would he be a captive to his father's image and where could Brandon Lee assert his own identity? Lee, by all accounts, had no problems with movies. He always *wanted* to be in films. But the martial arts were something he had a harder time coming to terms with. His father might have been a movie star, a phenomenally successful one certainly, but that stardom all stemmed from one thing: he was considered the greatest living martial artist of his time. The martial arts cast a much more formidable shadow over Brandon Lee's life. The martial arts and fighting, in fact, were the first things that gave Lee a very early taste of what life would be like as the son of a legendary fighter. That taste came when Lee was just nine years old, just after his father's death. Unfortunately, it was not a pleasant taste. Once he and his mother and sister moved back to California, he found himself on the receiving end of taunts and challenges to fight. A long string of expulsions and school changes followed as Lee received some instruction, on and off, from Dan Inosanto, one of his father's former students. The troubled and angry Lee, however, found himself wrestling with the question of whether or not he wanted the martial arts a part of his life at all. At one time, he was about to join a martial arts school until he walked through the door and found a big poster of his father staring him in the face. He immediately turned around and left.[5]

By the time he went to Boston's Emerson College, Brandon Lee had come to make peace with the martial arts as he pursued a degree in drama. Knowing he had a legacy looming over him, something he was unlikely ever to escape completely, he decided that fighting the past would not work. Instead of aspiring to be a martial artist actor, though, he set his mind on becoming an actor who could do realistic martial arts if a role called for it.

As much as Lee might have been troubled for so long about his father's impact on his life, he actually realized after college that the Lee name did *not* open a lot of Hollywood doors. His first job in the industry was as a script reader. A casting agent, though, eventually took notice of him and suggested he try out for a role in a made-for-television movie. At that point, ghosts from his family's past reappeared.

Ironically, the TV movie was *Kung Fu: The Movie*. Plus, as if that was not strange enough, the role he wound up getting was that of an angry young man believed to be Kwai Chang Cain's son. For a follow-up role, Lee even got a part in a second *Kung Fu* TV movie that was going to be a modern day updating of the story. It was going to follow the lives of Cain's descendants and it was intended as a pilot for a new series on CBS. Although the network ultimately passed on the pilot, the modern day *Kung Fu* idea would reappear in 1993 as a syndicated series starring David Carradine as a Kwai Chang Cain descendant and Chris Potter as his policeman son. That show ran for four seasons.

From 1986 until 1990, though, Lee found himself in the B-movie arena, making a film called *Legacy of Rage* (*Long Zai Jiang Hu*, 1986) in Hong Kong and the micro-budgeted *Laser Mission* (1990) in South Africa. *Legacy of Rage* is noteworthy for martial arts aficionados because Lee appears alongside Bolo Yeung.

But the road to Hollywood prominence really began with Lee's role as a sidekick to Dolph Lundgren in *Showdown in Little Tokyo* (1990). Although it was an odd film, modestly budgeted, it was theatrically released. *Showdown* was one of Lundgren's last theatrical films, the boost his career got from 1985's *Rocky IV* just about having lost its entire momentum. Much of the film involves Lee's acting as a straight man to Lundgren in a fairly standard cop-buddy action picture. Lee plays the nervous, officious, by-the-book young partner to Lundgren's rebellious, lone-wolf veteran cop. The film attempts to derive humor from the two characters' relationship to and knowledge of Asian culture. The Lee character is of Japanese ethnicity, but he grew up in Los Angeles. He knows nothing of his heritage other than the martial arts. The big, blonde, Teutonic Lundgren, on the other hand, grew up in Japan and he is much more Japanese than Lee. As the two cops get embroiled in a Yakuza plot, the most amusing moment of the entire film might actually be the climactic showdown in the gangsters' lair, offering some unintentionally funny sight gags. Before going into battle, Lundgren, like a superhero changing into his crime-fighting costume, dons a headband and a samurai outfit and takes up a very big sword. Seeing the towering Lundgren in his diaphanous samurai pants might have elicited more laughs from the audience than all the preceding banter between the two buddy cops.

Lee's follow-up to *Showdown* was much more satisfying, however. In *Rapid Fire* (1992), he stands in center stage, taking on organized crime hoods in Chicago. Of note in this film are some of the semi-autobiographical strains playing throughout the story. Much like Brandon Lee himself, his Jake Lo character is struggling with memories of his dead father. Jake is a sullen college student, angry that he had to lose his father to idealism. The elder Lo used to be a pro-democracy activist who was killed in Tiananmen Square. Angry over the loss of his father and convinced that idealism can only lead to tragedy, Jake is embittered and disaffected, scoffing at any notions of noble activism. Soon enough, of course, he is forced into putting his life on the line for principles after witnessing a mob hit. Prodded by an FBI agent (Powers

Booth) into doing the right thing and helping bring the gangsters down, Jake has to come to terms with his father's memory and forgive him for getting himself killed for a cause. The relationship between Jake and the FBI man, not surprisingly, is constructed as a sort of surrogate father/son relationship.

But in 1993 history tragically repeated itself. *The Crow* became Brandon Lee's biggest hit, but it was a film he would never live to see. He was killed on the Wilmington, North Carolina, set, close enough to the end of filming that the final product — upon the insistence of Lee's mother — could be edited into a complete film. The similarities to *Enter the Dragon*'s posthumous success were so uncanny that they revived speculation of a family curse and conspiracies again. Moreover, the subject of *The Crow* and the way Lee died kept adding to the morbid intrigue. The plot of the film involves a rock star being murdered, then coming back to life to avenge his own death. Lee's fatal accident, furthermore, happened during the filming of his murder scene when a mishap with a gun sent a chunk of metal tearing through his abdomen. Rumors immediately circulated that the shooting was no accident, that someone had intentionally replaced the handgun's blank round with a live one. Then, the most bizarre twist to the story came when Bruce Lee fans realized that the gun accident was similar to a plot point in *Game of Death*. In the finished version of that film, the Bruce Lee character is an actor who fakes

Brandon Lee in *The Crow* (1994). Tragedy struck as Lee was poised for Hollywood stardom.

his own death by making a gun stunt on the set of his film look like a fatal accident.[6]

Adding to the uncomfortable coincidences, *Dragon: The Bruce Lee Story* was also released later in 1993. That film, as previously discussed, put an inordinate emphasis on the curse issue. The most unnerving part of the film, in fact, is Bruce Lee's final fight with the demon-vision haunting him. In this scene, the demon notices that Bruce has a son and sets its sights on the nine-year-old Brandon. Realizing this, a badly beaten Bruce gets his second wind, gaining enough strength to defeat the demon. As the vision fades out, Bruce is happy knowing that he saved Brandon's life.

What is also noteworthy about *The Crow*, and an indicator that Brandon Lee could have become the next generation of American martial arts stars, is the way the film seems to have understood what was wrong with all other Hollywood fighting films and how they needed to be changed. The American martial arts films were still stuck in the format of using a thin plot skeleton to move characters from one fight scene to the next. *Rapid Fire*, although acquitting itself well at the box office, was an example of that dying formula. The story is basic, spare and, without a doubt, unoriginal and unremarkable. But, according to this old formula and its assumptions about audience tastes, the plot would barely register in the backs of the minds of the audience anyway. Martial arts fans, this analysis argued, came to the theater only to see fights. The best plots were those that gave their characters a reason to mix it up, then get out of the way and let fists and feet fly. *The Crow* became a much bigger success because it was much smarter than that. Had Brandon Lee lived and continued along the *Rapid Fire* route in the age of special effects and digital fantasies instead of more films like *The Crow*, he might have wound up in the direct-to-video ghetto, living next door to Jean-Claude Van Damme, Steven Seagal and Jeff Speakman. *The Crow* brings imagination, intrigue and something more to think about and look at than good guys and bad guys fighting. It creates a "mythology" for its character, it builds its own stylized, self-contained world of magic and mysticism.

Magic, mysticism, special effects and other-worldly fantasies, in fact, would reappear in a few more films in the '90s where martial arts were used by the main characters. The mid '90s would also see a brief series of martial arts video-game-based films made. One of these was Van Damme's *Street Fighter*. Other games where players controlled martial artist characters included *Double Dragon* and *Mortal Combat*. Both games were adapted as films, with *Mortal Combat* (1995) proving to be the most successful. In fact, it spawned a 1997 sequel called *Mortal Combat 2: Annihilation*.

But the biggest Asian impact of the 1990s was ultimately delivered by Asian filmmakers. This was the decade of the second Hong Kong invasion.

9

Mayhem in Slow Motion: The Viral Cinema of John Woo and the Hong Kong New Wave

When John Woo was twelve years old, a teacher asked him to draw the cover for the Easter pageant staged by the Lutheran school he attended in Hong Kong. Although he was a shy, unassuming kid by nature, Woo's artistic abilities, nevertheless, had gotten the attention of his teachers quickly. Excited by the invitation, Woo, who had quickly fallen in love with the spirituality and mysticism of his religious schooling, put his best effort into drawing a picture of Christ on the cross. The end result startled his teachers. Woo's drawing was very good, exceptionally good, in fact, and exceptionally detailed. He had drawn exactly what a man suffering the horrendous torture/execution of a crucifixion would look like. Agony was etched on his face. The crown of thorns tore his flesh, spilling voluminous trails of blood. "His pain must be seen to be understood," Woo explained when asked why he made the picture so startlingly explicit.[1]

This earnest approach to the most shocking, most brutal and violent aspects of life would eventually make John Woo not only one of the most influential action directors in the world, but perhaps one of the most thoughtful ones. In a genre that could often let itself be overwhelmed by its hyperbolic spectacle, John Woo's action films always match the spectacle with ruminations about honor, loyalty, and characters who balance on the thin edge dividing good and evil in a violent and chaotic world. But such artistic impulses had been shaped by having grown up a sensitive and introspective individual in a chaotic and brutal world.

He was born Wu Yu-Sen in Ganchou, the Canton province of China, in 1946. Much of John Woo's early life had included trying to flee from and survive the chaos and brutality of the world. After the Communist takeover in 1951, Woo's father, like millions of other Chinese, fled the country to Hong Kong. The former philosophy professor and his family wound up living in a slum that was so depressed and desperate, the dilapidated shanty they were forced to move into was too small to house the entire family. Woo's father had to sleep outside most of the time.[2] That so many Chinese refugees would continue pouring into and electing to live in such conditions, however, speaks to the hopelessness of their former lives under the Communists on the mainland. Coupled with the grinding, overwhelming poverty of the Hong Kong slums, Woo's most intense recollections of his childhood were always the constant, unpredictable moments of vicious street violence and crime all around him. He had seen all too close the gangs, the street hoods, the Triad mobsters, the pimps and prostitutes and, most vividly, the violence and casual brutality people were capable of.

Woo's sanctuaries from this grim world turned out to be the movies and religion. Through a sponsorship program in the Lutheran church his family attended, Woo was able to go to school, at one point even leading him to consider a career in the priesthood. While his day-to-day life was overwhelmed by so much ugliness and brutality, Woo would often recall, the church was always a place of stability, a place where qualities like honor, decency, and kindness existed in people. Although he would eventually earn a reputation as one of the most violent filmmakers in the world, this spiritual orientation would, arguably, always be a part of Woo's most personal works. No matter how chaos rages out of control in any John Woo action film, there is always a promise of a transcendent, better future, a promise of redemption. But Woo was ultimately counseled against joining the priesthood, told that his personality and temperament were too "artistic" for the structured, rigid regimentation of life in the clergy.[3] That artistic temperament, however, was perfectly suited to keep him dreaming about making films.

Woo's true education in films is quite similar to what accomplished filmmakers usually cite as their most useful curriculum in preparing for a film career: he went to the movies a lot. Although he continued his formal education until he was sixteen, finishing high school and enrolling in the Jesuit Matteo Ricci College, Woo had taught himself the most important fundamentals of the classic films by seeing as many as he could in Hong Kong's movie theaters.[4] He usually recalls in interviews that he was especially enchanted by musicals and his favorite film was *The Wizard of Oz*. The whimsical, exuberant energy and optimism of these films Woo always found to be the most welcome sort of escape from the grimy, harsh realities of everyday life among the poor and struggling of Hong Kong. While Woo had to leave school when he was sixteen and take a job at a newspaper to help support his family after his father's death, he remained committed to art and film. To his good fortune, the newspaper he worked for, *The Chinese Student Weekly*, had a film appreciation club where he could get together with other enthusiasts and discuss and analyze their favorite films. At the same time, he joined a couple of friends regularly involved in the Chinese Student Weekly Theater Company, broadening his artistic education by studying acting and performing in plays. "There were several people who had different artistic interests, and would form little groups within the newspaper," Woo recalls about his days at the newspaper and his informal education in film. "There was a poetry group, an art group, a philosophy group; I met up with the group of people who loved film. The newspaper rented art films for us to watch and afterwards we would discuss them. That was right around the time I started stealing theory books to study with."[5]

By the time he was twenty, Woo took the step to actually making films. Using 8mm and 16mm film equipment, he began writing and shooting his own short subject films. Once he felt his efforts were good enough to use as a résumé, he approached some of the production companies for a job in the film industry. To his luck, his timing for attempting the big break into the film business was just right. It was the '60s and the new wave of Hong Kong martial arts films were about to take off in the wake of Run Run Shaw's revamping of the genre into the type of hard-edged, hard-hitting masculine action/adventures King Hu and Chang Cheh were making.

After a brief stay at Cathay studios in an entry level position as a general apprentice and script assistant, Woo got the opportunity to make a move to Shaw Brothers in 1971. There, he eventually found the opportunity to advance another step closer to writing and directing. He also found a mentor who would impress upon him action-filmmaking techniques that laid the foundation for what would one day be recognized as the signature John Woo style.

At Shaw Brothers, Woo got a job as an assistant director to the prolific Chang Cheh. The two of them quickly forged a very effective working relationship and a close friendship. Chang became the perfect mentor to the young Woo, not just teaching him filmmaking techniques and how to negotiate the day-to-day workings of the film business, but also encouraging his interest in film as a vehicle for serious art. Moreover, in a film industry where the advance toward a directorial position was notoriously slow — most directors usually got their first chance to helm a picture when they were in their forties — Chang encouraged Woo to keep persevering until his talent was recognized and to believe that he would get a chance to make his own film sooner rather than later.[6]

But, more than anything, Woo admired Chang's films and he liked the unrestrained, energetic, chaotic action that usually propelled the old director's films. Even an adult John Woo believed that suffering had to be seen in its full, bloody, devastating totality to be understood. So did Chang, the "king of the stomach wounds." The seeds of Woo's theater of gunfire and hyperbolic destruction were planted as he worked for Chang. But aside from Chang's visuals and the unflinching look at violence his films always gave, Woo also admired the director's interest in themes of honor, redemption and the bonds between fighting men. Just like in Chang's films, a large number of Woo's action epics are underpinned by the theme of a bond between men in brutal, dangerous professions. Either bonds between gangsters or cops, or gangsters and cops locked into iron-clad obligations to destroy each other, are almost always a central theme in John Woo films.

Woo eventually got a chance to direct in 1973 when a friend of his wanted to enter the film business and, thanks to some well-rewarding business investments, had the money to spend on an independent production. He immediately turned to Woo and Woo, at twenty-eight, became one of the youngest men in the Hong Kong film business to get a chance to direct his own movie. The picture was a martial arts adventure called *The Young Dragons* and its fight choreographer was an up-and-coming stunt man named Jackie Chan. After Golden Harvest decided to release it, Woo had to leave his mentor behind at Shaw Brothers, but Woo was also on his way to working as a full-time director.[7]

The next phase of Woo's film career was not without its own share of frustrations, however. Like most accomplished directors who felt driven to make personal films, Woo always had very precise visions for what stories he wanted to tell. Directors like that do not like being trapped as journeymen turning out a studio's line of interchangeable, formulaic genre pictures. John Woo was no exception.

At Golden Harvest, he was tasked with making a series of martial arts films. However, none of them proved to be very successful. Nevertheless, as far as Golden Harvest was concerned, Woo was simply another member of their stable of kung fu directors.

When it didn't look like the studio was going to let him try his hand at anything else, Woo made the move to the newly established Cinema City studios. Founded by film comedians Karl Maka and Dean Shek, and writer/director Raymond Wong, Cinema City did not require Woo to keep making martial arts films. In fact, the Golden Harvest experience had so exhausted Woo with the martial arts that he would very pointedly refuse to even consider making another kung fu movie for years to come. Cinema City, instead, thrived on light comedies. For Woo, anxious to diversify and experiment with new genres — and hopefully get a taste of commercial success — comedies were worth trying. Woo's comedies, in fact, quickly became so successful that he cemented a reputation as one of the best comedy directors not just at Cinema City, but in the entire Hong Kong film business. Soon enough, however, Woo started developing some new ideas for films he wanted to make and they did not fit into the narrow categories his employers hoped he would keep working in. Basically, Maka, Shek and Wong wanted Woo to be Hong Kong's king of comedy. Woo, however, was interested in much, *much* darker themes, much more intense types of entertainment.

Woo, like moviegoers and up-and-coming directors the world over, had become enamored of the French New Wave directors. He was especially fond of their crime and gangster films. He became a big fan of Jean-Pierre Melville's *Le Samourai* (1967), starring Europe's new anti-hero superstar, Alain Delon. Tiring of his usual string of lightweight comedies, Woo desperately hoped to convince the Cinema City brass to let him try his own version of the European New Wave gangster film. He felt he could bring his own unique take to such films and he yearned for a chance to attempt a remake of *Le Samourai*. Light-years away from the typical comedies Woo was saddled with, Melville's film examined the psyche of professional killers. Woo, with his own background in a world riddled with crime and violence, a world ruled by professional gangsters and killers, was interested in a story about what life is like for a man who knows that violent death is an inevitable part of his profession. "*Le Samourai* is the closest thing to a perfect movie I have ever seen," Woo has said about the film and his deep admiration for it. "Melville understands that Jeff, played by Alain Delon, is doomed to be killed because he is a killer himself, that the way he is bound to die is built into the way he lives. When he chose his life, he was embracing his own death. He achieves redemption at the end by accepting his fate gracefully. To me, this is the most romantic attitude imaginable."[8]

Woo was given the chance to make his dream movie by director/producer Tsui Hark, an artist who had also made a profound impact on Hong Kong films in the 1980s. Hark specialized in a number of visual-effects-laden films that embraced the fantasy and supernatural roots of Chinese cinema. Dubbed the "Steven Spielberg of Hong Kong" for his fantasy and horror films and his love of special effects, Hark, by 1986, became a major movie power broker. Seeing similarly larger-than-life, surrealistic artistic inclinations in Woo, Hark agreed to produce Woo's gangster film, with Cinema City offering distribution.

Woo's career-changing film was called *A Better Tomorrow* (*Ying Hung Boon Sik*, 1986), and it is accurate to argue that the film's visual and stylistic flourishes changed the way the world would regard Hong Kong cinema and crime films. *A Better Tomorrow* laid down the basics of the themes, the look, the characters, and the depiction of action that Woo would go on to refine in both his subsequent Hong Kong films and his American films.

A Better Tomorrow is founded on the themes of brotherhood, bonds of honor between men, and the yearning for redemption by people who had given their lives to a world of violence and crime. The story involves brothers Ho (Ti Lung) and Kit (Leslie Cheung), the first being the supportive older sibling and the second a young student in the police academy, idolizing his big brother. Ho even makes sure that their ill, bed-ridden father is well cared for in a good hospital. Unbeknownst to Kit and their father, Ho can afford to take such good care of them because he is a high-ranking member of a local triad. Ho's closest and most loyal friend in the gang is Mark (Chow Yun Fat), a fast-living, suave hitman and a man of unbreakable codes of loyalty and friendship.

Soon enough, however, Ho's life of balance between

A Better Tomorrow (1986): John Woo and Chow Yun Fat shoot to international action stardom.

crime and family falls apart. He is betrayed during a business deal in Taiwan, captured by the police and jailed. Mark, in turn, tries to avenge his friend, going to Taiwan to kill the gangsters responsible for Ho's jailing. In the midst of a wild shootout, Mark is shot in the leg and left crippled.

By the time Ho is out of jail, much has changed in both the triad and his family. During a murder attempt on Kit, their father had been killed. Kit, already embittered by his discovery of his brother's true identity as a criminal, shuts Ho out of his life. Kit even promises his big brother that if they ever cross paths again and he has reason to believe that Ho is involved with a crime, he will gladly arrest him. The triad gang, in the meantime, has been taken over by Ho's betrayer. The crippled Mark has been reduced to a homeless vagrant washing cars' windows on the street.

When Ho and Mark reunite, they decide to seek revenge against the men who destroyed their lives. However, as Woo handles the third act of the film and the final showdown between the triad and Mark and Ho, *A Better Tomorrow* is lifted above the stylings of most rudimentary, by-the-book revenge melodramas. The ending of the film is not merely about vengeance, but about a couple of doomed, fallen criminals like Ho and Mark trying to find a way to atone for the lives they led. Even though both are too far gone for complete redemption, even though they are both as doomed as the criminals in Melville's *Le Samourai*, they still take the symbolic steps required towards atonement. Ho wants to gain some small measure of forgiveness from Kit and he thinks he can do that by helping Kit bring down the triad. Kit's career, it turns out, has stalled very badly since his brother's arrest. The police brass does not trust Kit because of his connection to the underworld. He has been repeatedly passed over for promotions and he is not allowed to work on major, career-making, organized crime cases. Mark, in turn, wants to help his friend in his honorable quest to right some of the wrongs with Kit. At the end of the film, not only are the triad members brought down, but Ho and Mark are forced to pay penance for their lives of evil by accepting harsh punishments. Mark is killed, whereas Ho surrenders to his brother. Although Kit must arrest him, the film suggests that Ho has earned some degree of forgiveness at last.

Not only did *A Better Tomorrow* finally grant John Woo a major commercial success, but it turned out to be an unqualified blockbuster hit. It was the most profitable film in the history of Hong Kong cinema until that time.

The careers of its principals were also immediately altered. Ti Lung had been going through a career slump since the downturn in the world-wide martial arts craze. Having been originally discovered by Chang Cheh and cast in Jimmy Wang Yu's *The Return of the One-Armed Swordsman*, Ti had spent much of the '70s as a kung fu cinema fixture. With the dwindling popularity of the genre, however, his career had been stalling very badly. Leslie Cheung, in turn, who was a successful pop singer working on establishing himself as a film actor, got a career boost that gave him the prestige of having attained superstardom in two major media. In the 1990s he would gain recognition outside of Hong Kong and outside of the action/crime genre. In 1993 he played one of the leads, the doomed homosexual Peking Opera star Dieyi, in Chen Kaige's Golden Globe–winning *Farewell My Concubine (Ba Wang Bie Ji)*.[9]

Chow Yun Fat, playing a mere supporting role as Mark, however, had his career energized even beyond the fame Ti Lung and Leslie Cheung enjoyed after *A Better Tomorrow*. John Woo had to lobby very hard to be able to cast this former TV actor in the film. With only a few films to his credit and usually in light-weight roles, with little indication that he had any true movie star potential, Chow was a gamble for Woo's producers and the Cinema City management. To let Woo have the last word, however, the Mark character emerged as the true star of the film in the eyes of audiences. Chow's youthful good looks, a cool, edgy demeanor that reminded audiences more than a little of Alain Delon in his roles of dangerous, darkly sexy anti-heroes, and his swaggering confidence captured Hong Kong moviegoers' imaginations immediately. Reportedly, after seeing the film, scores of young men took to imitating Mark's look. They sported dark sunglasses, chewed on toothpicks and wore dark trench coats. Department stores saw a sudden spike in the demand for dark overcoats, which they started calling "Mark coats." This rage over the coats continued all throughout the theatrical run of the film, even though dark trench coats are highly impractical in Hong's Kong's year-long warm and humid climate.[10] When Woo was pressed to make the inevitable sequel to the film, the studio and his financiers told him that he had to find a way of putting Chow Yun Fat back into the picture. Without Chow, they argued, *A Better Tomorrow* sequel would not be accepted by audiences. Since Mark is most definitely dead at the end of the first film, however, killed by an extremely bloody hole blown through his skull, Woo's only option was to borrow a plot twist straight out of soap operas. The sequel reveals that Mark had an identical twin brother.

The success of *A Better Tomorrow* not only made stars out of John Woo and Chow Yun Fat, it created a partnership that would soon be compared to the legendary John Ford/John Wayne, Kurosawa/Mifune, and Martin Scorsese/Robert DeNiro director/actor pairings. Not only did they make *A Better Tomorrow 2* (*Ying Hung Boon Sik 2*, 1987), but they also worked together on *The Killer* (*Dip Huet Seung Hung*, 1989), *Once a Thief* (*Zong Heng Si Hai*, 1991), and *Hard Boiled* (*Lat Sau San Taam*, 1992). While the two men — to date — actually produced fewer films together than Ford and Wayne or Scorsese and DeNiro, not to mention Kurosawa and Mifune, the ones they did make were such trend-setters that the two are inextricably linked in the minds of audiences. The Chow Yun Fat screen persona, the cool, laconic gunman who takes on hundreds of opponents while firing two guns, the image he would re-create over and over in a number of other directors' films, is basically a variation on Mark. Woo, in turn, often clearly said that he saw the Chow Yun Fat characters as his own alter ego.[11]

Aside from the themes of brotherhood, honor and redemption, an analysis of *A Better Tomorrow* is not complete without an examination of its look, its distinctive visual style, its tempo and the strikingly unique approach to its violence. Ultimately, it was the look of *A Better Tomorrow* and its stunning, dizzyingly chaotic violence that made the film an action/adventure benchmark. It was the film's distinctive visual style that Woo would continue repeating and refining until it got him the attention of the world. This visual style—soon known as the "John Woo style"—was what impressed Hollywood so much that the entire American action genre was soon overhauled after Woo made the move to Hollywood in 1992.

At the core of the John Woo style of filming action is a virtuoso control of events leading up to an explosion of extreme violence. A Woo action sequence always unfolds in a manner similar to a juggernaut starting to roll downhill. Once the first steps toward confrontation are taken, the violence becomes inevitable. Woo, in turn, puts the focus on all the little details that set in motion this downward plunge into chaos. The looks on people's faces, small movements of the hands, jackets parted to allow access to weapons, pistols cautiously fingered, are all a part of this chain of events. Once the move toward action begins, the violence can not be avoided. Woo, nevertheless, teases the audience along with his buildup, creating tension slowly and deliberately. The slow-motion camerawork, so much associated with Woo, begins during this buildup. The slowing of time allows the audience to be drawn into the moment, to contemplate the nature of the brutality that is about to come and is absolutely unavoidable. Finally, when a shootout starts in a John Woo film, the destruction wrought is total and complete. Many of his combatants, and most certainly his lead characters, will make sure to cause the maximum amount of damage by firing two guns at the same time. Each of the hundreds of bullets expended, in turn, will rain damage onto something. If the gunshots don't hit their intended targets, they shatter, splinter and demolish furniture, walls or windows all around. Each shot of a John Woo firefight is overwhelmed by movement, by wooden splinters, by jagged glass shards or sparks from ricocheting bullets whizzing and zigzagging across the screen. The characters that are hit are usually torn apart by gunfire, entry and exit wounds spurting voluminous gouts of blood and gore. A doomed, blood-soaked victim of a typical Woo gunshot will usually jerk and writhe in slow motion as the bullets exiting his body go on to reduce a piece of furniture behind him to kindling and/or blow a hole in a wall. Once the violence begins in a typical Woo film, nearly everything is destroyed.

An important aspect of each violent John Woo film is the balance maintained between the real and the surreal. This balance is a key factor usually missing from so many of the imitators trying to ape Woo films. Woo's films are, most often, both realistic and fantastic at once. He is the most concerned with reality when it comes to the creation of his characters. His protagonists and antagonists are always real people. They have layered, complex personalities and their motivations are understandable. Woo can usually be seen doing his best to lift all of his action films above the level of comic book spectacle. It is only once the action begins that the fantasy takes over. Since most of Woo's action sequences, especially in his films where he had the clout to get sizable budgets, are decidedly unrealistic, the outlandishness still remains anchored in reality because the audiences understand the combatants as real human beings.

The one notable critic of this technique, however, was actor Anthony Wong, who played Johnny, the main villain of Woo's last and most violent Hong Kong film, *Hard Boiled*. Since in *Hard Boiled* Woo seems to be attempting a synthesis of all of the visual styles and motifs he had worked with before, almost as a final, summary statement on his Hong Kong career before moving to Hollywood, the film is also his most violent. As far as Wong was concerned, though, the film's endless string of balletic shootouts and confrontations where the lone heroes outgunned *literally* hundreds of enemies completely reduced the film to a comic book movie.

After *A Better Tomorrow* and its inevitable sequel, Woo's second landmark film, the film that started garnering serious attention at all the major film festivals and made fans of American directors like Martin Scorsese and Oliver Stone, was *The Killer* (1989). Teaming again with Chow Yun Fat, Woo made another movie where stunning, ultra-kinetic bursts of stylized violence punctuate a story where brutal characters wrestle with their private codes of honor and obligation, and men who have made a living off of evil and violence are on a quest for redemption. The basic story involves a hitman named Jeff (Chow), doggedly pursued by maverick, loose-cannon cop Li (Danny Lee). In the course of carrying out an assassination, Jeff accidentally blinds Jenny (Sally Yeh), a nightclub singer. With his conscience tormenting him, Jeff decides to get out of the rackets, vowing only to take one last job that will pay him enough to take Jenny to America for an operation. Complicating matters, of course, is Li, hot on Jeff's trail, swearing to do whatever it takes to bring the gangster down.

The film does a remarkably creative job of contrasting the good and bad natures of both characters. Jeff, the criminal, for example, is a man who has led a largely corrupt, vicious life, yet he is still capable of remorse and he has a conscience. Li, on the other hand, is an enforcer of the law, yet he is a reckless, dangerous zealot. He had often put the safety of innocent bystanders at risk in shootouts and chases where his only concern was capturing his quarry. Amidst the mayhem, Woo shows the capacity for good in criminals and fringe outsiders, as well as the destructive, self-centered zealotry in those who have sworn to protect society.

With the increasing buzz around his films and career at the various international film festival circuits — boosted largely by *The Killer*— the early 1990s saw Woo considering a move to Hollywood. In 1990, when he formed a producing partnership with Terrence Chang, the impetus for the move gained momentum. For one, the 1990s would turn out to be a momentous decade for Hong Kong. In 1997, the British colony would revert to the control of the People's Republic of China. The prospect of the bastion of Asian free market capitalism being taken over by the world's biggest Communist power jangled nerves among Hong Kong's businessmen and filmmakers. In a film industry run by free-wheeling moneymen in a perpetual pursuit of blockbuster hits and blockbuster paydays, not to mention artists always sensitive to government interference in their creative work, 1997 looked ever more like a looming nightmare. Furthermore, the Tiananmen Square massacre of pro-democracy protestors in 1989 prompted many in Hong Kong to plan hasty exit strategies as the handover approached.[12] Woo's partnership with Chang looked like his own exit strategy. Chang, who had been educated at New York University's film school, used to work as a producer for Golden Harvest and as an executive specializing in international distribution for D & B Films. Chang was especially skilled in building alliances with Americans and moving Asian film stars into foreign film markets, and vice versa. He had been instrumental in Brandon Lee's first Hong Kong film deal as well as Cynthia Rothrock's. When Chang noticed Woo's growing reputation as a "director to watch" among the Hollywood community's Asian film fans and a good number of American critics who were aficionados of Hong Kong cinema, he realized that the buzz needed to be exploited right away. He put all of his energies into moving Woo across the Pacific as quickly as he could.[13]

Before making the move to Hollywood, Woo completed three films. Two of them were modest successes in Hong Kong and further helped spread his reputation at the film festivals. *Bullet in the Head* (*Die Xue Jie Tou*) and *Once a Thief*, both made in 1990, allowed Woo a chance to give his fans what they yearned to see, as well as an opportunity to bring some new angles to his action-packed body of work. In *Bullet in the Head*, he follows three friends (Tony Leung, Waise Lee, Jackie Cheung) from a childhood mired in the poverty of the slums to adult lives intersecting with the Vietnam War. Upon release, it was almost unanimously compared to *The Deer Hunter* (1978). In *Once a Thief*, the fast-paced action, as creative and visually arresting as ever, is softened by a comedic storyline of a group of art thieves (Chow Yun Fat, Leslie Cheung, Cherie Chung). Recalling his early career as a comedy director, Woo crafted *Once a Thief* as a light heist caper, putting the accent on fun over his usual angst-ridden struggles with honor and brotherhood. But Woo's farewell to Hong Kong, and ultimate signature piece as a master of bullet-riddled action, was *Hard Boiled*. The tone for this film became edgier once more. It examines the psyches of a pair of "hard boiled" cops, one (Chow Yun Fat) obsessed with destroying a gang of gunrunners and the other (Tony Leung) trying to retain some sense of his own identity as he slips further into his undercover role as a hitman working for the gang. Although the plot can be — and has been — accused of being a very standard rehashing of themes Woo has worked with before, the main objective of the film this time is not to study characters or mull over the existential issues of police work. In this film, Woo seems to declare that he can film action better than anyone in the world. From a teahouse shootout in the film's opening to two back-to-back warehouse gunfights in the midpoint and a hyper-violent mêlée where an entire hospital is turned into a war zone at the dénouement, the plot of *Hard Boiled* is merely an excuse to allow armies of gunmen to shoot everyone and everything in sight. As over-the-top and as numbing as the violence eventually gets in *Hard Boiled*— confirming Anthony Wong's criticism that it's basically a comic book film with no resemblance whatsoever to any sort of a real world — it became Woo's statement to Hollywood. *Hard Boiled* declared that John Woo could make action films every bit as rousing as anything the Americans turned out, if not infinitely more so.

Woo, however, did not have to worry about arriving in the U.S. without a fanfare. As a matter of fact, one of his loudest cheerleaders at the time was the newly-declared "genius" and "auteur" of the independent film world, who was expected to rewrite all the rules of Hollywood filmmaking himself. Quentin Tarantino had been a fan of Asian films and John Woo since his works premiered at the film festivals and he sang Woo's praises any chance he got.[14] For a time it was reported that the two directors would team up for the ultimate melding of American-style and Hong Kong–style action films. While the teaming has not happened yet, the rest of the 1990s quickly saw more of Hollywood's films looking more and more like those coming out of Hong Kong.

Despite the failure of a Woo/Tarantino project to materialize, the connection between the two filmmakers is an important one. Tarantino had proven to be one of the most effective gatekeepers a foreign filmmaker could ask for. Having been anointed as the new visionary of the film world, he became one of the most influential film stylists of the time with his two independent crime films, *Reservoir Dogs* (1992) and *Pulp Fiction* (1994). Almost immediately after these films were bombarded by critical adulation, scores of other filmmakers started turning out hip, violent crime films about articulate criminals discoursing on pop culture and the meaning of life while shooting each other with hundreds of rounds fired from two guns. Film schools in the '90s owed a lot of their enrollment to Tarantino. Just about everyone writing a screenplay and shooting a student film in these colleges used *Reservoir Dogs* and *Pulp Fiction* as their point of reference. Tarantino, in turn, had no problem explaining that so much of his signature style was actually a faithful homage to John Woo and the cinema of Hong Kong. *Reservoir Dogs*, he

Two-gun action. Quentin Tarantino's *Reservoir Dogs* (1992) borrows the John Woo Style (and Ringo Lam's plot from *City on Fire*, 1987).

readily admitted, was a very faithful remake of director Ringo Lam's film *City on Fire* (*Lung Fu Fong Wan*, 1987).[15] Lam's film also starred Chow Yun Fat. So, much of what other young filmmakers were copying from Tarantino, they were really indirectly taking from John Woo. Tarantino's admission to all this cribbing, on the one hand, helped turn more attention to Woo's work. On the other, it promoted the atmosphere of a "postmodern" approach to filmmaking as the '90s went on. This postmodernism — or, perhaps, the weighty-sounding, intellectual term for copying other people's works — helped give Woo's brand of stylized action a viral quality throughout the '90s and beyond.

In the eyes of American critics, filmmakers and cineastes, Woo's entire style could be interpreted as very postmodern in itself. His surreal, probing attention paid to the minutest details of violence was much like Sergio Leone's use of claustrophobic, tight close-ups of gunmen at the moments leading up to combat. Woo's slow-motion effects, his lingering appreciation of the buildup to violence, and the protracted scenes of destruction, flying bullets, shattering walls and furniture, and writhing, perforated bodies have a similar effect of deconstruction. These effects over-exaggerate the nature of such violence, almost making the viewer wonder if the true statement behind the film might be the director's acknowledgement of the absurdity, the artificiality of the entire action genre itself.

We can not be entirely sure of Woo's postmodernity, or whether or not he intends to critique his genre by accenting its artifice. He does always match the unreal spectacle with realistic, multifaceted characters, after all. As a matter of fact, he found it harder than he expected to get a suitable project into production upon arriving in Hollywood because he found so many of the scripts coming from the legions of eager agents, actors, and producers to be unacceptable for a very specific reason: almost all of them were little more than exercises in style. The stories were all full of action, showdowns, violence and the potential for high-tech spectacle, but had none of the character development and depth he was looking for. Reportedly, his partnership with Tarantino didn't materialize for the same reason. Tarantino had written a script — then rewrote and revised numerous drafts, trying to please Woo — of an action epic that would have taken place in the U.S. and Hong Kong. It even had a super-cool hero tailor-made for Chow Yun Fat. The coolness and spectacle, however, Woo felt, were ultimately hollow.[16] Tarantino — who would, once the critical infatuation had worn off, be dogged by accusations that he was little more than a talented filmic Xerox machine — just didn't seem to understand what Woo needed in an action film of substance.

A good comparison between the substance Woo was capable of fitting into his violence spectacles and the lesser efforts of his imitators can be found when placing Woo's first three American films beside a stylistic clone like *The Big Hit* (1998). And *The Big Hit* was even produced by Woo himself and directed by fellow Hong Kong expatriate Kirk Wong! Woo followed his American debut, *Hard Target*, with the John Travolta and Christian Slater thriller *Broken Arrow* (1996). Afterward, he reteamed with Travolta yet again and added Nicolas Cage to the cast of *Face/Off* (1997). In *Broken Arrow* and *Face/Off*, the relationships between the leading men propel the story much farther than the various high-priced stunts and visual effects. While his previous Hollywood effort, *Hard Target*, let Jean-Claude Van Damme dominate much of the spotlight and left costar Lance Henriksen to simmer and threaten in the background as the lead villain, Woo's two follow-up films pitted antagonists of equal strength and willpower against each other. *Hard Target* and *Face/Off* put its men in a series of skirmishes against each other, each sworn to destroy the other no matter the personal cost. The relationships that motivate the combatants, in turn, are well realized and the audience can feel that it's watching a pair of fully-formed human beings trying to best each other.

In *Broken Arrow*, the Travolta character is a disgruntled Air Force pilot who realizes that he can make a fortune by betraying a government he felt slighted by, a system that passed him over for promotions he felt he deserved. Slater, his earnest young partner, is fully-realized as the usual honor- and duty-bound John Woo protagonist.

But the most outlandish — and strangely compelling — characters go head to head in *Face/Off*. Based on a script Woo first rejected for being too much of a science fiction story, the film involves Travolta's earnest, honor- and duty-bound FBI agent, Sean Archer, trying the impossible: to stop Cage's psychopathic criminal, Castor Troy, from detonating a chemical weapon in Los Angeles. Once Troy is slammed into a coma by a jet engine in the film's high-octane opening shootout in an airplane hangar, Archer is left with a ticking time bomb somewhere in Los Angeles and no way to find it and defuse it. The only person who could give him the information is Troy's equally psychotic brother, Pollux (Alessandro Nivola). To get the information, Archer undergoes experimental surgery, having his face removed and replaced with Troy's face. While Archer infiltrates the top secret prison incarcerating Pollux, however, Troy comes out of his coma and forces the surgeons to implant Archer's face on his own skinless head. Once the two men have assumed each other's identities and lives, the film ups its ante by adding a couple of poignant family dramas to its strange mix. Soon after escaping from the prison, Archer takes up with Troy's former lover, Sasha (Gina Gershon), the mother of the young son Troy never knew he had. Troy, likewise, goes home to Archer's unsuspecting wife, Eve (Joan Allen), and daughter, Jamie (Dominique Swain). Only after spending time with the two impostors, however, do the two mothers get a chance to come to terms with the pained lives they are living. Eve is still suffering from the loss of their son years ago, murdered by Troy. Although the thirst for revenge is what has been driving Archer to keep up his unrelenting pursuit of Troy, his distance and his melancholy coldness have been slowly wrecking his family. Sasha, in turn, has been dreaming of a way to get her son away from the world of crime and violence. Once the climactic showdown at the end of the film reveals all the lies and masquerading, Archer reunites with his family, knowing that he has been healed of his pain and is now able to be the man his wife and daughter need. Although Sasha is killed in the crossfire, Archer promises to make sure her son does not grow up to be a criminal. The final scene of the film shows the Archers agreeing to adopt Troy's son.

In the case of *The Big Hit*, even Woo's involvement as an executive producer did little to infuse the story with anything resembling realistic behavior by real people. No matter that the film is intended as a comedy, there is nothing a viewer can relate to on any level whatsoever. Even Roger Ebert's review said that to laugh at anything here, "you would have to be seriously alienated from normal human values."[17] The film involves an early Mark Wahlberg performance as a hitman with the unlikely name of Melvin Smiley who falls in love with a Japanese businessman's daughter (China Chow) whom he has to kidnap, all the while juggling the attentions of his mistress (Lela Rochon), his fiancée (Christina Applegate), her parents (Elliott Gould and Lainie Kazan), and a rival hitman (Lou Diamond Phillips) out to kill him.

The film is a spectacular failure of an attempt to meld domestic comedy with the lives of organized crime figures. Had the film come a year later, TV's *The Sopranos* would have helped make *The Big Hit* look even more like an exercise in complete ineptitude. Although it does have several passable Hong Kong–style action sequences — characters diving through the air while shooting two guns, John Woo-esque Mexican standoffs, slow-motion action sequences — much of the film is actually a domestic farce with a harried Melvin trying to maneuver all of the people in his life so none of the parties stumbles onto the other. In one sequence a trash bag filled with dismembered body parts enters the fray.

One could almost call *The Big Hit* a "vapor movie," a term Ebert once used — it might have been for a 1980s Mark Harmon comedy called *Summer School*— to describe a film where one could sit through the entire picture and not feel he has really seen anything. The film is almost nonexistent. This is the sort of film where aliens could land in the middle of the story and they would not have any adverse effect on the narrative because nothing is, even in the slightest bit, realistic or relatable. None of the action is realistic, none of the characters are realistic, and their relationships are certainly not realistic. In the final analysis, *The Big Hit* is an almost perfectly-realized antithesis of anything John Woo ever made.

Although Hollywood could not quite recreate the substance of the quintessential John Woo action film, it immediately fell in love with the look of his films and the stylistic delivery of their violence. The slow-motion buildup to violence, the Mexican standoff where combatants stare each other down while holding pistols inches away from each others' eyes, the shooting of two pistols at once, and shooting while diving through the air in slow motion, have all turned into "must have" ingredients in the vast majority of Hollywood action/adventure films since the early 1990s. They are all adaptations of the Woo filmic style, and by today Woo himself has become a sort of shorthand term for directors and stunt and special effects coordinators when planning the look, the moves and the pacing of any action film. A "John Woo–style" shootout, or a "John Woo–style" camera angle, immediately conveys exactly how a sequence is supposed to look.

Legacy of the New Wave

Not only did John Woo become the most influential Asian filmmaker to come to Hollywood, his early career in Hong Kong had also been remarkable in another respect. His direction of *The Young Dragons* (*Tie Han Rou Qing*, 1974) at the age of twenty-eight was but a part of a watershed moment in Hong Kong filmmaking, something quite similar to the late '60s/early '70s "film school brat" generation's takeover of Hollywood. Woo's ascendancy as a star director signaled a similar generational shift in Hong Kong cinema. Woo is considered a part of the Hong Kong New Wave, a new generation of directors and writers that broke many of the rules of filmmaking and, most importantly, the rules of film production.[18] Woo's rise to power as a young director signaled that the old, slow, studio system–dominated career path of directors was coming to a close. The apprentice system, where filmmakers had to toil for years in lowly assistant positions until they were well into their forties, was being replaced by an edgier, more creative generation of independent filmmakers. The Asian artists discovered by Hollywood in the 1990s had also been revolutionary filmmakers in their homeland in the '70s and '80s.

The Hong Kong New Wave got its first impetus from television in the early 1970s and, much like in Hollywood, from film schools. Through the 1960s, the TVB channel ruled the airwaves and it did so through light, escapist fare. It specialized in soap operas, comedies and variety and game shows. It was TV programming to unwind with, to forget the world's problems, not material to be challenged by. The challenge would slowly take shape, however, with the launching of the government-subsidized Radio Television Hong Kong (RTHK) channel. It was programming intended to offer more issue-oriented material, programs that addressed the problems and social concerns of contemporary Hong Kong. A lot of the talent producing RTHK's programming, in turn, were young people. They were film school graduates who had learned their craft in colleges rather than through any "apprenticeships."[19] Many of these people had been educated in the U.S., then returned home, eager to break into and make their marks on the Hong Kong entertainment industry. They wanted to do what they had seen the American film school brats do in Hollywood. Tsui Hark, for example, a native of Vietnam who had grown up in Hong Kong, studied at the University of Texas and returned to Hong Kong in 1977 to start his directing career on television.[20]

Among the "realistic" and "issue-oriented" programming of RTHK, nothing had been more popular than their crime and police procedural shows. Much like American "reality" TV shows like *Unsolved Mysteries*, *Cops*, and *America's Most Wanted* that would do well over a decade later, these shows dramatized sensational crimes and police investigations. To what extent this type of entertainment is closer to exploitation than conscientious exposés of social problems is debatable. Even the turn-of-the-twentieth-century's sensationalistic school of American "yellow journalism" might have done some genuine good in putting a spotlight on the ills of life among the underclasses even as it sold millions of newspapers because all those social ills — in the form of murders, rapes, prostitution, gangs and organized crime enterprises — just made for really exciting and titillating reading. Almost a century later, this form of reality programming still boosted TV viewership and put a lot of aspiring young filmmakers to work. In fact, the programming was so successful that rival commercial stations TVB, TVC and Rediffusion/ATV stations followed suit and copied the format. A whole new generation of future crime and action film directors — as well as filmmakers who would turn out more experimental and highbrow art — were getting a chance to hone their craft for millions to see every week.

The TV boom was relatively short-lived, though. By the end of the '70s, ratings began to stagnate. Even the crime stories and sensationalism wasn't garnering audiences as well as it used to. But that was not so much a problem for TV's creative force. By the late '70s and early '80s, independent filmmaking was flourishing in Hong Kong. In 1977, the Hong Kong International Film Festival was launched, giving film fans and filmmakers a glimpse of the works of independent, visionary talent from around the world. With the establishment of more and more new, small film distribution companies to challenge the dominance of studios like Shaw Brothers and Golden Harvest, avenues were opening up for ambitious young filmmakers to bring their work to audiences.[21]

Not only was the new generation of movie makers more creative, driven and uncompromising in their quest to break into the film business fast, break in young and let their work be seen, but they brought new approaches and new sensibilities to old genres. This included the crime genres and even the venerable *wuxia* epics. When making crime and action films, many filmmakers and writers opted to approach the subject as the socially relevant television police procedurals had. Many were dark, bleak and cynical. When it came to the martial arts films, innovation, imagination, and even parody, mockery and subversion were often the rules of thumb for directors and writers.

The most influential martial artist since Bruce Lee would opt to go the route of mockery, parody and laughs. Even before the 1970s had come to an end, he was already recognized as the heir to the martial arts film throne that had been occupied for much too long by Bruce Lee clones.

10

Drunken Master in Hollywood's Eye: Jackie Chan Takes the West ... Twice

Although he has written, directed, worked as a stunt man, choreographed fights, coordinated stunt teams and even sung theme songs, Jackie Chan had originally been groomed to be an actor. He was to be a leading man in front of the cameras, a kung fu star who could help the production company of director Lo Wei — Bruce Lee's director and nemesis on *The Big Boss* and *Fist of Fury* — keep cashing in on the martial arts craze of the '70s. Unfortunately, when Chan was given his first chance to act and fulfill Lo Wei's desire to keep turning blockbuster profits from the martial arts, he was told that he was going to become the next Bruce Lee. To his chagrin, Jackie Chan was tasked with becoming one of the Bruce Lee clones. Much like the entire New Wave of the '70s, Chan too had been sensing that keeping in line with the rigid old formulas, with the codified conventions of traditional genres, was nothing but folly. He could see well enough how the Bruceploitation movement he had been forced into was quickly turning the martial arts genre into a farce, a worldwide punch line to jokes about the ridiculousness of Hong Kong cinema. Bruce Lee himself might have changed the look of martial arts movies when he shot to stardom in the early '70s, but the look, the style, the moves that Lee had once made seem so original had now become the established, inflexible dogma of the genre. In Chan's point of view, the only way the genre could be revitalized — and his own career kept from disintegrating — was through complete irreverence and subversion. Once given the opportunity to give his ideas a try, Jackie Chan rocketed to international fame. Less than two decades later he became the first Hong Kong actor since Bruce Lee to be accepted as a star in Hollywood.

Jackie Chan was born on April 7, 1954, to parents who had been among the incoming waves of refugees from the mainland, fleeing the Communist takeover. Charles and Lee-lee Chan named their son Chan Kong-sang to celebrate their arrival on the colony. Chan Kong-sang means "Born in Hong Kong Chan." But the new life the Chans found in Hong Kong was similar to the one John Woo and his family had to live. They were so poor that when Kong-sang was born, they seriously considered a doctor's offer to buy him for HK$500. It would have amounted to about $26 US.[1]

Although his parents decided to keep him, and even their fortunes improved soon afterward — Charles and Lee-lee both found jobs as servants to the French ambassador to Hong Kong — by the time Chan was seven years old, his life was about to take a very difficult turn. Much of it, by his own admission in his autobiography, was due to his own restless, aggressive temperament as a child. The young Chan didn't appear to be a good student and he had a penchant for finding ways to get into trouble. His parents had an ever more difficult time trying to keep him under control as he was getting older. Then, when Charles got a job offer as the head cook for the American embassy in Australia, he and Lee-lee were faced with a tough dilemma. Charles was going to go ahead to Australia alone and work until he had enough money saved to bring his family over. The one glitch in the plan was leaving his wife to contend with the unruly Kong-sang alone. Their son needed discipline and needed someone who could force structure and rules upon him every day. They eventually decided on Master Yu Jim-yuen's China Drama Academy to do the job.

Master Yu ran a Peking Opera school very much in the old-fashioned style of rigid discipline. They took in young children under contracts specifying various years of instruction, then drilled and trained them in all the skills of the traditional Opera performers. As Chan describes in his biography, the introduction most kids and their families got to the school was close to what could accurately be described as a con. The families were shown a school full of happy kids playing theater and make-believe all day. They were housed, clothed and fed well, basically given the things many of Hong Kong's poor families had to struggle for every day. But the subterfuge worked perfectly on the young Chan. He recalls that he could hardly wait for his parents to close the deal for his enrollment so he could join all the other kids for a life of endless play and good times. When his father asked him how long he wanted to stay there, Chan happily replied, "Forever!"

Later, in hindsight, he would recall his ten years at the Drama Academy as a living hell. The place was a brutally competitive environment run by an unyielding, authoritarian headmaster. The skills needed by future Opera stars were ingrained through violent discipline. Beatings were a regular, day-to-day part of life, administered by either Master Yu or elder students serving as "Big Brothers."

But, ultimately, Chan's upbringing at Master Yu's Academy was nearly an exercise in futility. By the late '60s and early '70s, the Peking Opera was dying. Even while Chan was enrolled, he and his fellow students were often loaned out to film companies for use as extras or stunt performers. The movies were the reigning art now. By the time Chan's ten-year contract was up, he found himself in a difficult position. He was basically without a formal education. He had no skills that would have provided any kind of a job other than a manual laborer. He had no choice but to pursue show business as a career, a new form of show business he hadn't exactly been trained for. But he didn't know how to do anything else.

Taking the name "Jackie" while enrolled in an English language course, Chan found work on and off in the film business as a stunt man. He had even been hired as a stunt double on Bruce Lee's *Fist of Fury* and *Enter the Dragon*. Ironically, Lee would soon enough turn out to be both a career blessing *and* a curse for Chan. After Lee's sudden death, the search was on for his replacement. In the Hong Kong film industry's mad dash to keep capitalizing on the worldwide Bruce-mania, they created a ridiculous spectacle of clones that could rival the Elvis impersonator phenomenon that emerged years later, after the rock 'n' roll icon's death. Lo Wei productions even wanted to remake *Fist of Fury*, calling the film *The New Fist of Fury* (*Xin Jing Wu Men*, 1976). In the wake of Lee's superstardom, Lo Wei had taken to calling himself Hong Kong's "Million Dollar Director," boasting that he had created Bruce Lee and he could turn any other actor into the next Bruce Lee as well.[2] One of Lo's executives, in turn, Willie Chan, was tasked with finding "The Next Bruce Lee." Having known and made friends with Jackie Chan earlier, Willie Chan now called him in to Lo Wei Productions to audition for the lead role in *The New Fist of Fury*. As it turned out, the scene of Jackie Chan's call to stardom itself could have come out of a movie. He had just given up on making a living in Hong Kong and joined his parents in Australia. He was working in a restaurant when Willie Chan gave him a call and told him they wanted him to star in a film.

Lo Wei, as Jackie Chan had already realized from the time he worked for him as a stuntman, was certainly no million-dollar director. The hack refugee from the Shaw Brothers merely got lucky when he was assigned to direct *The Big Boss*. Bruce Lee was responsible for that film's success and Lo Wei could certainly not duplicate it, especially when he attempted to do so by forcing Jackie Chan into the mold of a mediocre Bruce Lee impersonator. For Chan, however, it was a choice of either going along and doing his best to imitate Lee, or going back to Australia and working in a restaurant. So Chan did his best to carry Lo Wei's pictures, time after time after time. Unfortunately, just like most of the other faux Bruces in the overcrowded Bruce arena, Jackie Chan repeatedly struck out with each of his pictures. To fuel his frustration, he was hardly surprised by his films' failures. Imitators could never equal, much less surpass, an original like Bruce Lee. Chan knew that if he stood any chance of establishing a career for himself, the only way he could do it was by taking a *real* cue from Bruce Lee. He knew he had to do what Lee would have done: he needed to be original. Unfortunately, that was a concept beyond Lo Wei's comprehension. The director, to Chan's dismay, seemed resigned to the fact that he had made a spectacular mistake in bringing the ex–stunt man back from Australia. Lo was going to finish out Chan's contract then let him go.

Realizing he had no choice but to go for broke and beg his clueless director to let him try a different kind of martial arts film, Chan pushed as hard as he could, over and over again. He had, after all, nothing to lose. The martial arts genre had two major problems. It was taking itself too seriously, and fewer and fewer audiences were. If the serious kung fu movie was dying, the only thing left to do was to laugh at its demise. If all the heavy-handed seriousness was not working, Chan argued, why not make the genre funny? Jackie Chan knew that the only thing left to try was a comedy kung fu film. Eventually Lo Wei relented and the result was a film called *Half a Loaf of Kung Fu* (*Dian Zhi Gong Fu Gan Chian Chan*, 1978). But it wouldn't reach the movie screens quite as Chan had hoped.

With the film shot and edited, Lo Wei had the final word about Chan's ideas for comedy after all. He decreed the film unsellable and refused to release it. As for his star, whom no one in Hong Kong's theaters wanted to see, he could get rid of him by loaning him out to other producers until Chan's contract expired. This time, though, Lo did a real career-making favor for Chan.

Chan was loaned to the independent company Seasonal Films. The organization was run by Ng See-yuen, a producer with a reputation for discovering untried talent.[3] To Chan's luck, the company also employed another of Master Yu's China Drama Academy graduates: stunt coordinator Yuen Woo-ping. Although Yuen had left Master Yu's school before Chan came in, the two had worked together years before when Chan was a stunt man. Yuen himself was in a situation much like Chan. He, too, was looking for a chance to take his career to a new level. He was desperate for a chance to direct. Yuen was finally allowed to do so on a two-film deal Seasonal Films got through the loan arrangement with Lo Wei. Yuen, in turn, was completely of like mind with Jackie Chan on the issue of how they could best make an impression on jaded martial arts audiences. They both knew they had to take a radical departure from all the tired, overused clichés of the genre. Yuen, just like Chan, thought that humor was the best way to go. The films they planned to make were *Snake in the Eagle's Shadow* (*Se Ying Diu Sau*, 1978) and *Drunken*

Monkey in a Tiger's Eye (*Jui Juen*, 1978). The first film was a surprise success at the box office. In fact, it even outperformed *Way of the Dragon*, Bruce Lee's most successful Hong Kong movie. The second one, however, was a phenomenal blockbuster.

Snake in the Eagle's Shadow was approached according to Jackie Chan's theory that he needed to become the anti–Bruce Lee. He and Yuen Woo-ping decided that they would take Lee's image, his moves, his basic style and approach to martial arts films, and deconstruct it, turn it upside down and basically defy every Bruce Lee rule stagnating the genre. As Chan often said, "Instead of kicking high like Bruce Lee, I kick low. He plays the invincible hero, I'm the underdog. His movies are intense, mine are light."[4]

In *Snake in the Eagle's Shadow*, a martial arts school is saved not by its most talented and fearsome fighter, but by its lowliest misfit. Chan's character, Chien Fu, is an orphan adopted by the school and forced to live as their perpetually abused and disrespected janitor. But while Chien's martial arts skills might be lacking, the leadership of the school itself is not entirely fearsome either. Comedian Dean Shek, in fact, plays Master Li, one of the school's two unscrupulous and largely incompetent owners. The land, however, is besieged by clan warfare, and the Eagle Clan is the current victor in a series of battles intended to establish the reigning kung fu style. Through a series of complications, a fugitive Snake Style master (Yuen Siu Tien), a member of a rival clan, runs across Chien, takes pity on him after seeing all the abuse he's suffering at his school, and starts teaching him the Snake kung fu. Once the Eagle Clan realizes that one of its enemies is nearby and has passed his skills on to a new student, they attempt to hunt both down and wipe Snake kung fu out once and forever. Eventually, the bumbling Chien rises to the occasion, perfects his skill so well as to be able to expand and modify the Snake Style with his own Cat's Claw Style, and defeats the leader of the Eagle Clan.

Through this plot, the template had successfully been set for the unique, and spectacularly successful, new Jackie Chan style and film persona. He had, in effect, completely undermined the rigid Bruce Lee formulas that had been perpetuated ad nauseam by the Bruceploitation movement. In numerous Jackie Chan films to come, he would keep playing bumblers and clowns, lowly, semi-competent and/or immature characters who are suddenly facing an overwhelming and dangerous challenge. These characters quickly realize that they are hopelessly out of their league trying to take on an overwhelming foe, and that they must seek help or profoundly overhaul their entire approach to kung fu. As in *Snake in the Eagle's Shadow*, where the fugitive Snake Style master disguises himself as a bedraggled, drunken bum, the Chan character will often get help in perfecting his style by this sort of a comical trainer. Even in films where the student/mentor relationship is not used, Chan would still be the bumbler, comical and largely inept, bounced from fight to fight, beaten, thrown around and abused until he finally manages to overcome his opponents through sheer perseverance, willpower, and a great deal of luck.

Aside from functioning as a comical martial artist clown, Chan brings action to his films — the signature Jackie Chan style of fight choreography — a dizzying, hyper-paced series of acrobatic spectacles. The trademark Jackie Chan martial arts action scenes are a melding of acrobatics and martial arts. In most Chan action sequences, everything and everyone gets involved once a fight breaks out. Chairs, ladders, knives, clubs and (non-firearm) weapons of every sort are usually grabbed, spun, slashed, and tossed through the air in a seemingly chaotic spectacle of constant improvisation. As Chan often explained, his films don't merely set up fights as a means to an end. The fighting and martial arts in his films all serve as a spectacle in and of themselves, a way to dazzle audiences with the physical prowess and inventiveness of the stunt team and the choreographers. The legacy of the Peking Opera style is perhaps the most visible in Jackie Chan films where the superhuman acrobatic and martial arts skills of the performers need to dazzle and confound the audiences.

His second film with Yuen Woo-ping, *Drunken Monkey in the Tiger's Eye* (eventually given the more manageable title of *Drunken Master*), largely recognized as Chan's signature film, not only repeats much of the comical, acrobatic and irreverent approach of *Snake in the Eagle's Shadow*, but is downright subversive, if not heretical, in its handling of a martial arts legend. In this film, Chan plays none other than the martial arts demigod and Chinese folk hero Wong Fei Hung. However, this is not the noble, dignified hero played by Kwan Tak Hing. Chan's Wong is an immature, boastful, disobedient youth, a delinquent and a mediocre martial artist who is forced into perfecting his skills and character under the tutelage of Master Su Hua Chi. Yuen Siu Tien (director Yuen Woo-ping's father)[5] is back again as Wong Fei Hung's mentor in this film, as is Dean Shek in another comical performance as a Wong nemesis. Master Su, going under the name Beggar So, and mainly living as an itinerant, drunken vagrant, is also a supremely skilled fighter and the master of the Drunken Style of kung fu. When Wong's home town and family are threatened by the seemingly unbeatable leader of a fearsome clan, much as the Eagle Clan threatened in *Snake in the Eagle's Shadow*, Wong must go into intense training with Beggar So, perfect Drunken Style kung fu, and take on the threat. In this film, the absurdity is pushed even further than in the previous film. The very idea of becoming an effective fighter by not merely imitating the moves of a drunk but actually drinking large amounts of alcohol and literally getting drunk is preposterously unrealistic. However, Chan does the most thorough job of tearing up martial arts legends by his depiction of Wong Fei Hung. There is no more revered figure in martial arts legend and Chinese folklore than Wong, and turning him into a bumbling, incompetent young punk who can win a fight only by getting drunk would have been heretofore unthinkable in martial arts cinema. But in the late '70s and the blossoming of the Hong Kong New Wave, Chan's gamble on humor and irreverence paid off.

Proving again that in many respects Jackie Chan's life was quite cinematic in itself, his severing of professional ties to Lo Wei turned out to be frighteningly dramatic and intense — according to Chan's version of the events, at least. If his discovery and casting as a leading man is fitting for a feel-good, against-the-odds fantasy, his dealings with Lo Wei Productions could have come out of an organized crime thriller. According to Chan's autobiography, following the successes of *Snake* and *Drunken Master*, Golden Harvest offered

him a HK$4 million contract. This should have been more than enough to pay what Chan thought was a HK$100,000 fee for terminating Lo Wei's contract. However, the contract an unsophisticated and hungry Chan had first signed with Lo was a *blank* contract. The director/producer had told him the termination clause would come with a HK$100,000 fee, but that number had suddenly jumped to HK$10 million. As Chan details in his book, his allegation that Lo doctored the contract was met by a visit from local triad members hoping to "persuade" him not to leave Lo. The director's involvement in organized crime had been rumored for a long time,

The smiling subversive. Jackie Chan becomes a superstar by mocking kung fu cinema's most cherished traditions.

and the allegations lent themselves to the Bruce Lee death-conspiracy lore. Many Lee conspiracy theorists believe that Lo had Lee killed in 1973.[6] The negotiations that would eventually involve Golden Harvest's buying out Chan's contract, according to Chan, were brokered by actor Jimmy Wang Yu, also reputed to have been a powerful figure in Taiwan's organized crime circles.[7]

Once free of Lo, Jackie Chan's meteoric rise to Asian stardom continued at Golden Harvest. While Chan would ultimately make his move into the American market in the '90s, he had tried a number of times before, as early as 1980, as a matter of fact, then again in 1985. The failure of these efforts is a subject of much discussion and analysis among his fans. The reasons for the failure, though, can be tied to cultural trends in the U.S. They were trends affecting most of the martial arts action cinema at the time.

In 1980, Golden Harvest set up a co-production deal with Warner Bros. for Chan to make *Battle Creek Brawl* in the U.S. The project even had Robert Clouse signed on as director. Since his involvement in *Enter the Dragon*, Clouse had assumed the role of Hollywood's go-to director for martial arts films. To Chan's irritation, however, the *Battle Creek* project (eventually retitled *The Big Brawl*) became a replay of his early career. From Clouse's involvement in the film to the American press that relentlessly interrogated him about whether or not he had designs on becoming the next Bruce Lee, he found himself in the middle of a project he had almost no control over and one he immediately sensed was heading for failure.

Chan had meticulously created and controlled his onscreen image in Hong Kong after *Snake in the Eagle's Shadow* and *Drunken Master* and he was well aware of what his fans were expecting if they paid to see one of his movies. A Jackie Chan picture was supposed to be loaded with rapid-fire acrobatic stunts performed by martial arts experts and Chan was supposed to do all of his own stunts. A true Jackie Chan film had to be a martial arts version of the classic Hollywood musical, with breathtaking fight sequences taking the place of the elaborate dance numbers. As Chan often remarked, "I do with my fistfights what my old friend John Woo does with gun battles — make them into a thing of beauty, an intricately choreographed dance."[8] And, most of all, Jackie Chan films were supposed to be fun. He had carefully built an image as the Buster Keaton or Harold Lloyd or Charlie Chaplin of the martial arts cinema. In a number of films, in fact, he set up stunts that duplicated famous scenes from the films of those comedians. In *Project A*, for example, Chan hangs from the face of a giant clock. Unlike Harold Lloyd, Chan is really hanging over a three-story drop and eventually plunges to the ground, tearing through three awnings to break his fall. It was such a combination of acrobatics, death-defying stunts and a funny, irreverent approach to the martial arts that Jackie Chan audiences had come to expect.

Hollywood, unfortunately, understood only the fact that Chan was Asia's top-earning film star. They desperately wanted a piece of Chan's star power, yet they couldn't be bothered to understand exactly what he did to earn his fans' adulation. The usual Hollywood myopia had turned on Jackie Chan, just as it had on Akira Kurosawa and would one day almost stifle John Woo.

The Big Brawl turned out to be the unimaginative piece of hackwork Chan knew it would be. Something of an Old West version of *The Big Boss*, the story casts Chan as a Chinese-American youth who had promised his father never to fight, then has to save his brother's fiancée from a ruthless fight promoter. With a very sluggish, unimaginative approach to the action scenes, the film looks stale and tired, something that works neither as a straight action film nor as a comedy. Outside of hard core martial arts connoisseurs, no one in the U.S. bothered to see the film. The connoisseurs, in turn, had already seen Chan's Hong Kong work in the art house theaters and the theaters in the various Asian neighborhoods. They knew what a true Jackie Chan film was supposed to look like and the word quickly spread that *The Big Brawl* was not it.

While in the U.S. for *The Big Brawl* fiasco, Chan was also pressed into doing what would amount to a cameo appearance in a film that became a major hit, yet in a role that was both unsatisfying and insulting. Appearing alongside box office champ Burt Reynolds in the comedy *Cannonball Run* (1981) sounded like a good idea at first, until Chan was made to look like a fool in a small role as a racecar driver. Worst of all, he was cast as a *Japanese* driver. Clueless of the cultural sensitivities between the Chinese and the Japanese, the *Cannonball Run* team made the Chan character Japanese for no other reason than to pull off a cheap racial stereotype gag. Chan, partnered with fellow Hong Kong star Michael Hui, drives a computer-overloaded Mitsubishi, blinking and buzzing and beeping under a massive load of sensors and gadgets. The Japanese, after all, the joke went, were taking over the world with their computers and technology, and no Japanese could function without his massive load of computer banks and machines and databases.

To irk Chan even further, his *Cannonball Run* contract stipulated that he return to Hollywood three years later for a sequel. *Cannonball Run 2* turned out to be even more inane and unfunny than the first. But as unpleasant as the experience might have been for Chan, he still had stardom in Hong Kong to return to. *Cannonball 2*'s headliner, Burt Reynolds, would see his career and credibility in Hollywood sunk for over a decade as a result of his car chase comedies.

The one interesting impact *Cannonball Run* had on Chan's career, though, was an inspiration for the ending of all of his subsequent films. The comedies Burt Reynolds made with *Cannonball* director Hal Needham — the two having previously worked on two *Smokey and the Bandit* movies and *Hooper*—always included outtakes of flubbed lines, mistakes, and humorous miscues playing over the closing credits. Thinking this was the only amusing thing about *Cannonball Run*, Chan went on to imitate it in all of his own films. Chan's closing outtakes up the ante, however. They always include footage of stunts gone painfully wrong. Most of them include Chan himself.

Although *The Big Brawl* and the *Cannonball Run* films turned out to be excruciating experiences for Chan, he let Golden Harvest talk him into another try at American films in 1985. The results were even worse.

This time, he was teamed with Danny Aiello and director James Glickenhaus for the police thriller *The Protector*. In Chan's (pretty much accurate) analysis, Glickenhaus and company repeated the mistakes of *The Big Brawl*. They were either unable or just unwilling to let him use his established on-screen persona in the film. As much as *The Big Brawl* attempted to cast him as a cross between Bruce Lee and John Wayne, *The Protector* tried to turn him into Dirty Harry. In the best '80s tradition of grim, grimy police thrillers, the story is not only violent in a mean-spirited, realistic way, but matched with vulgar language and scenes of nudity as well. But as gritty as the film's violence might have been, it was also, ultimately, unimaginative and dull. Chan, in turn, received much the same treatment from *The Protector*'s creative team as he had on the set of *The Big Brawl*. As far as they were concerned, actors, especially foreign ones who could barely speak English, were expected to take direction, do as they were told, and get through their scenes as written on the page. Improvisation and suggestions from Chan were not welcome.[9] *The Protector* was another American-made Jackie Chan flop.

With Golden Harvest distributing the film in Asia, however, they did have the right to re-edit the film before it was their turn to move it into theaters. So in Hong Kong, Chan removed the profanities in the dubbing and re-shot the ending, incorporating his own acrobatic fighting style into the last moments of the film. Although the film was by no means a great success in Asia, it did outperform the American version.

As Jackie Chan fans usually explain, though, the one upside of the actor's American misadventures had always been a renewed eagerness to go back to Hong Kong and make several films that attempted to outdo any other picture he ever made before.[10] The aftermath of *The Big Brawl*, for example, produced hits like *Winners and Sinners* (*Wu Fu Xing*, 1983) and *Project A* (*'A' Gai Waak*, 1983). After *The Protector*'s failure, he made *Police Story* (*Ging Chaat Goo Si*, 1985), and *Armour of God* (*Long Xiong Hu Di*, 1987).

Ultimately, pinpointing the blame for Chan's 1980s failures in Hollywood is not as easy as it may appear. Certainly, it's a fact that he was badly mishandled by American producers and directors. He had been coaxed across the Pacific because of his phenomenal success in Asia, yet the style that made him a success in his Hong Kong films was never seriously considered for emulation. "I've seen a lot of Hong Kong cinema," James Glickenhaus had said. "I think it's very interesting, terrific stuff. It just doesn't have a chance in the United States."[11] As frustrating as that attitude might be to Chan's passionate core group of fans, Glickenhaus, to a degree, is also quite right. That core group of Hong Kong and martial arts purists made up a very small percentage of the American moviegoing audience. Furthermore, the rest of the 1980s action audience — as evidenced by the crop of homegrown action films of the decade — preferred their brawling and shooting and mayhem straight up. The Rambo, Dirty Harry and Chuck Norris fandom took its tough guys very seriously. American action cinema was in a period when tough, traditional, heroic masculinity was making a comeback. Jackie Chan's clowning, on the one hand, hardly fit this grim, post–Vietnam-allegory movement. On the other, if anything, Chan's films might have been an outright mockery of that sort of straight-faced, turgid, Reagan-era hyper-machismo. Chan, after all, had the temerity to ridicule China's most revered folk hero when he reduced Wong Fei Hung to an incompetent, drunken buffoon.

As Mark Gallagher's discussion of Chan's Hong Kong oeuvre suggests, a close enough analysis will always reveal the typical Jackie Chan film to be a lampooning of traditional, conservative constructions of masculinity.[12] Chan protagonists are, most often, bunglers who inadvertently find themselves in dangerous situations they are hardly equipped to handle. Comic interludes are always introduced where Chan will attempt to impress a woman with his display of traditional manliness and bravery, always to have the ruse blow up in his face. The end result is always Chan's humiliation. Even if his protagonists receive extra training, the benefits of a bedraggled, drunken master's secret kung fu techniques, their final fight with a chief villain is usually a comic parody of the generic macho showdown. In *Drunken Master*, for example, the moves of the Drunken Style kung fu are derived from a secret instruction booklet based on the moves of the mythic "Drunken Faeries." The Chan character's fight-winning moves are specifically the ones taken from the one female faerie. So Chan, essentially, fights and defeats his ultra-masculine opponent not by being more of a man, but by affecting exaggeratedly feminine moves. The secret technique could almost be called "drag fu."

Chan's 1980s action films might ultimately have failed because they were unimaginative, by-the-numbers B-grade hack work, yet it's hard to imagine that he could have made much more of a headway into American culture at that time had he faithfully re-created his irreverent, subversive brand of action from Hong Kong. In the Reagan era, America was reclaiming its damaged manhood, not trying to mock it.

By the 1990s, however, things had changed considerably. Just as the faltering of Jean-Claude Van Damme's and Steven Seagal's careers suggested, the era of turgid, angry machismo had come to an end. Even such hard-bodied action icons as Sylvester Stallone and Arnold Schwarzenegger either saw their careers hit roadblocks — as was the case with Stallone, who could never quite recover from the Cannon Group's *Cobra* and *Over the Top* debacles and soon saw his iconic Rambo character strike out with audiences in *Rambo III* (1988) — or just seemed to tire of the action/adventure tough guy posturing; Schwarzenegger tried to pursue more family-friendly comedies than his usual milieu of violent thrillers. As the decade went on, heading toward the millennium, the new generation of action heroes looked more like teen idols and heartthrobs than muscle men and tough guys. Actors like Tom Cruise, Keanu Reeves, Nicolas Cage, Brad Pitt, Ben Affleck, and Matt Damon had become the new faces of action. But, more than just tiring of the heavy handed machismo, audiences in the '90s wanted a change of scenery. They were interested in seeing new styles, approaches to filmmaking, to action, to comedy that were different from the predictable Hollywood fare. The recurring theme in all the commentaries and reviews of John Woo's and Jackie Chan's films is the rave about the "freshness," "originality," and "unpredictability." Whether because of the look, the pacing, the themes, or the re-imagining of the traditional role of the action hero, Asian filmmaking seemed to be the only antidote to the moribund staleness that gripped so much of Hollywood.

In 1996, when the Hollywood studios unrolled a lineup of their usual big budget, overblown spectacles like *The Rock*, *Mission: Impossible*, and — perhaps the biggest and most overblown (and over rated) film of all — *Independence Day*, Chan's Hong Kong import, *Rumble in the Bronx* (*Hung Faan Aau*), was the surprise action hit of the year. After John Woo's successful relocation to Hollywood, the interest in the Hong Kong style of action filmmaking was strong enough for New Line Cinema to gamble on yet another introduction of Jackie Chan to America. As Chan writes in his autobiography, he was resistant to the idea until he was told that the re-introduction was not another attempt at placing him in an American-made film. New Line, in fact, was so convinced that the cultural currents and audience tastes had changed by 1996 that they planned a nationwide release of *Rumble*. Unlike the usual appearances of Chan's films in art house theaters and Asian neighborhood movie houses, this authentic Hong Kong product, a *pure* Jackie Chan film, would be presented to the general moviegoing public. New Line's reading of the more open-minded — or hopelessly unsatisfied — American audience was accurate.

The success of *Rumble* led to the release of a line of Hong Kong–produced Jackie Chan films in the later half of the '90s, including *Operation*

Condor (*Fei Ying Gai Wak*, 1991), *Twin Dragons* (*Shuang Long Hui*, 1992), *Legend of the Drunken Master* (*Jui Kuen II*, 1994), and *Mr. Nice Guy* (*Yat Goh Hiu Yan*, 1997). Cable stations regularly ran most of his Hong Kong films. By 1998, Chan was convinced enough that Hollywood finally *got* the true essence of an authentic Jackie Chan film that he agreed to star in a series of three (to date) *Rush Hour* films. Chan co-starred with screeching, loud-mouth comic Chris Tucker as a Hong Kong detective coming to Los Angeles to pursue a kidnapper. Unlike *The Big Brawl* and *The Protector*, this time the film was a comedy and the action was more along the acrobatic lines of a true Jackie Chan film. By that time, Americans had opened up to foreign cinema enough to appreciate the tradition Chan was coming from and his approach to action, and they had enough of a sense of humor about their action heroes to enjoy seeing them as something other than grim, death-dealing avengers.

Of interesting note about Chan's late '90s and 2000s Hollywood action films is the fact that American filmmakers just seem so reluctant to let him be funny. Although the first *Rush Hour* is a slapstick comedy with Chan playing a hapless, fish-out-of-water character — something quite similar to what he plays in *Rumble in the Bronx*— the sequels found him more along the lines of a traditional, stoic tough cop. Set against Chris Tucker's spastic, hysterical screaming and tantrum-throwing shtick, Chan essentially becomes an ever-exasperated straight man. He once again fell into the straight-man role in *Shanghai Noon* and *Shanghai Knights*. There he played yet another noble, questing (although somewhat clumsy) Chinese hero out of his element in the Old West in the first film and in Victorian England in the second. In the *Shanghai* series, his comic foil is Owen Wilson, doing his usual laid back, "slacker dude" routine. Perhaps closest in flavor to his Hong Kong comedic roles were the special effects–laden *The Tuxedo* and *The Medallion*, which allowed him to do more broad physical comedy.

Although his later, American-produced films like *The Tuxedo* and *The Medallion* were box office disappointments, Chan had, by the early 2000s, established a solid fan following in the U.S. as well. He had, at one point, become a pitch man for products like computers, trash bags, and even Hanes underwear. He usually performed his acrobatic kung fu routines in commercials while trying to fight ninjas attempting to steal his laptop, handling unwieldy loads of trash that can't be contained by an ordinary trash bag, and struggling to remove the uncomfortable tags on inferior T-shirts that are impossible to tear off. From 2000 to 2005, his likeness even became the star of the *Jackie Chan Adventures* cartoon show on the WB network.

Some of the very direct influences Jackie Chan had on Hollywood included the comedic, absurdist approach to action and the martial arts — including the opening of the Hollywood door to one of his long-time collaborators from Hong Kong — as well as providing some of the most visually arresting scenes for American action films to "borrow."

By 2000, Hollywood had, at last, been able to appreciate the appeal of mixing chaotic, acrobatic, patently unrealistic yet visually captivating, martial arts sequences in comedy action films to start imitating the style. Although comedy and action have been mixed successfully for decades in Hollywood, from a genial Western adventure like *Butch Cassidy and the Sundance Kid* (1969) to Eddie Murphy's attitude and fast mouth in the gunfire-punctuated *Beverly Hills Cop* (1984, 1987, 1994) movies, these films still existed within a relatively realistic internal universe. American sensibilities have never been very open to the kind of broad burlesque, manic live-action cartoon films Hong Kong and Asian audiences enjoyed. In fact, even Chan's *Rush Hour* or *Shanghai* films will reveal a much tamer American product when seen next to the over-the-top outlandishness of his "authentic" films. But a look at a Hollywood film like 2000's *Charlie's Angels*, however, starts revealing that same kind of Hong Kong frenzy, the Jackie Chan–style exuberance and spectacle-at-all-costs approach to the action. In the film's sequel, that same sort of hyperbolic chaos/comedy was amped up even further.

In the 1998 to 2000 TV seasons, CBS presented its own version of a Jackie Chan police action comedy in the weekly series *Martial Law*. But since CBS couldn't get Chan for their weekly series, they got the next best thing: Chan's "Biggest Brother" from Yu Jim-yuen's China Drama Academy, actor/director Sammo Hung.

Sammo Hung's appearance in an American TV series is, in many ways, just as remarkable as if Jackie Chan himself had agreed to take the lead role. Hung (birth name Hung Kam-bo — Sammo was originally a nickname derived from his resemblance to a cartoon character named Sam-mo), the grandson of Chinese film pioneer and female martial artist Chen Zhi-gong, is one of Hong Kong's major martial arts/action stars, a former stunt choreographer, and one of the most sought-after directors of action films. Hung, in fact, directed Chan's *Winners and Sinners* (*Wu Fu Xing*, 1983), *Wheels on Meals* (*Kwai Tsan Tseh*, 1984), *My Lucky Stars* (*Fuk Sing Go Jiu*, 1985), *Twinkle, Twinkle, Lucky Stars* (*Xia Ri Fu Xing*, 1985), *Heart of Dragon* (*Long De Xin*, 1985), and *Dragons Forever* (*Fei Lung Maang Jeung*, 1987). When Chan had been struggling to make a living as a stunt man after leaving the Drama Academy, Hung had been the one to get many of his first jobs in film for him. Such, however, is the type of life-long relationships that should exist between the "brothers" of a typical Chinese school.

Sammo Hung's and Jackie Chan's personal and working relationship, however, has also been turbulent and contentious. Controversy, in fact, remains about the plot of one of Jet Li's films that Chan claims he originally conceived for himself and revealed only to Hung. Hung, however, went on to write and direct the Li film before Chan could make his own version of the story. Chan's *Shanghai Noon* became a revamped version of his original idea, involving a Chinese martial artist lost in the American Old West.[13] The two men's brotherhood, though, grew out of nearly ten years of intense personal loathing — on Chan's part at least — during their tutelage at Yu Jim-yuen's school. As Chan explains in his book, students were always expected to respect and obey their Biggest Brother. Biggest Brothers, in turn, always had to look out for and help their Little Brothers. The relationship was supposed to last a lifetime. However, Biggest Brothers also had as much right to discipline — i.e., beat — their Little Brothers as any of the instructors or Master Yu himself. According to Chan, Hung used to relish abusing this authority, acting as a tyrant, "a bully and a sadist." Nevertheless, once the two met a few years later and Hung was established as one of the top stuntmen in the field, he helped Chan get his foot in the door and earn a steady income in films. As Chan explains, though, it was more than just the Biggest Brother's obligation prompting Hung's magnanimity. He enjoyed being the "big shot" who gave others a handout. Their relationship became contentious again, according to Chan's version of events, once his career hit its superstar phase after *Drunken Master*. A Little Brother outshining his Biggest Brother apparently took a heavy toll on Hung's ego. Some of the strain in the two men's friendship was remarked upon by writer Bey Logan as well in the DVD commentary track of Hung's *Kill Zone* (*SPL: Sha Po Lang*, 2005). As Logan recalls, Hung had publicly commented several times that he hadn't been shown the proper respect a Biggest Brother is owed, once Chan's career had hit its highest gears. But whatever the extent of these frictions between the two filmmakers, they did work on numerous films together and they always appeared to make the best effort to help each other's careers and screen image.

When CBS introduced *Martial Law* in 1998, there was no mistaking the Hong Kong style all over the look, the tone and the pacing of the show. Sammo Hung led his team of American costars through weekly series of acrobatic, inventive and comic fights, chases, and showdowns. The film dealt with Chinese detective Sammo Law (Hung) getting transplanted to Los Angeles and trying to meld Eastern and Western police techniques. As outlandish as all the plots of *Martial Law* were in a TV-cop landscape dominated by a lot of gritty, realistic urban dramas and police procedurals like *Law and Order* and *Homicide: Life on the Street*, *Martial Law* did attract a surprising amount of critical praise. It also attracted a lot of critical amazement over Hung and his physical prowess. Hung is as good a martial artist and acrobat as Jackie Chan, and it is all the more amazing since he is — and has been since an injury at the China Drama Academy sidelined him for months[14] — quite portly. Even

Hong Kong audiences have always been stunned by how such a fat man could be so remarkably agile.

After *Martial Law* was cancelled in 2000, Hung returned to Hong Kong where he is still directing and acting. As he has gotten older, his career also has taken an interesting turn into more serious, dramatic action and police films. Unlike Chan, whose advancing age has recently made him appear to be less and less well-placed in his goofball clown roles, Hung appears to be comfortably easing into the dramatic films. His aging looks only seemed to help him establish this whole new phase in his career. As Hung always had a rather boyish-looking face, his size, coupled with a bowl haircut he usually sported, had for a long time made him look like an overgrown fat child. It was an appearance that always suited his comic performances well. As he got older, his face had started taking on a sort of lived-in, care-worn appearance. Hung had, in turn, been quite skilled at using this to grow and keep prospering as an actor. Should he ever return to the U.S., he would, most likely, find success in Hollywood as long as the interest in Asia and that particularly quirky, hyperbolic Hong Kong style of deadpan comic absurdity continues.

Finally, it is interesting to note how freely American action filmmakers have been given to borrowing from Jackie Chan's Hong Kong films, despite their long-standing reluctance to let him recreate his authentic films in Hollywood. For example, the 1989 Sylvester Stallone–Kurt Russell action comedy *Tango and Cash* faithfully recreates a bus stunt from *Police Story*. In the original, Chan stands in the path of an oncoming bus that had been hijacked by fleeing gangsters. As the bus barrels toward him, Chan starts firing at it until the vehicle comes to a skidding halt and two of the criminals are thrown through the windshield. In *Tango and Cash*, Stallone stares down a speeding semi truck smuggling cocaine. Just like Chan, he brings the truck to a sudden halt and deposits its driver and passenger on the asphalt in a shower of broken glass. Director Michael Bay also pilfered a memorable stunt from *Police Story*. In the opening of the Chan picture, a car goes careening down the side of a hill, smashing through the shacks of a sprawling shanty town. Bay's *Bad Boys II* likewise sends an out-of-control Hummer down the side of a hill in Cuba, smashing through a shanty town.

11

Jet Li: The Noble Warrior

The third major Hong Kong star to establish a mainstream career in Hollywood in the late 1990s nearly stole the last entry in the blockbuster *Lethal Weapon* series from heavyweights Mel Gibson and Danny Glover, and superstar comedian Chris Rock. When producer Joel Silver and director Richard Donner realized they needed to infuse fresh energy into their decade-old franchise manned by aging stars, they turned to Hong Kong martial arts action hero Jet Li. By the time *Lethal Weapon 4* hit theaters in the summer of 1998, Li himself had become the point of most of the "buzz" surrounding the film. Action fans, the word of mouth implored, *had* to see the incredible martial arts performance displayed by Jet Li.

Li does, indeed, make a spectacular impact on *Lethal Weapon 4* with his martial arts skills. His moves are so fast, his mastery of his body as a lethal weapon in itself is so impressive, as to make him look like a human special effect. But Li also impresses in this film not just with his martial arts skills, but with a very intense, very sinister performance as the lead villain's top assassin. Because of his poor command of English at the time, Li had been given few lines to recite, but his stony silence actually makes his presence all the more menacing and thoroughly effective. He comes across in the role as death personified: silent, unrelenting, and coldly, efficiently implacable.

Strong, serious performances, however, have been a Jet Li trademark since the start of his film career in mainland China in 1982. While Hong Kong martial arts stars like Jackie Chan and Sammo Hung brought comedy and irreverence to the genre to challenge the staleness, the self-important sameness the post–Bruce Lee kung fu films had been stuck in, Jet Li had emerged as the straight, solemn counterpoint to the Hong Kong burlesque. But as frightening as Li is in *Lethal Weapon 4*, the flawless image of psychopathic evil, that sort of villainous role had actually been a major career departure for him. The second Jet Li trademark had always been the playing of unshakably ethical and noble characters.

If Jackie Chan is the Buster Keaton of martial arts films and Bruce Lee is the genre's James Dean — or, perhaps, Clint Eastwood, in his more menacing and dangerous moments — Jet Li, as far as such Hollywood comparisons go, is more like a kung fu John Wayne. The typical Jet Li characters — the characters he had always *insisted* on playing — have always been larger than life, unbreakable, incorruptible figures of strength and integrity.[1] In his insistence on almost always playing heroes, in fact, he resembles Chuck Norris as well. But much like John Wayne in his countless roles as cowboys and frontiersmen, Jet Li likewise tallied a long résumé of period martial arts films. Like Wayne, who liked to fashion his characters as embodiments of Americans' romanticized vision of their past, the "code" of the West, Li has always been fond of characters who represent Chinese virtues and the ethics and values of the martial arts.

But by most accounts of Jet Li's life, much of what audiences see of the larger-than-life characters he plays is quite true to the real man.[2] The actor portraying supremely skilled martial artists was a world champion Wu Shu practitioner by the time he was 11. While he nearly always made his fearsome fighters men of integrity and spirituality, Jet Li has been a devout Tibetan Buddhist since the 1990s.[3] He has often said that he has never been in a fight outside of the competition ring. Above all, Li always claims, the values of the martial arts are about avoiding fights, not starting them in bellicose acts of machismo and posturing. Close friends and associates often talk about him in terms like those often used for Chuck Norris: he is a surprising contradiction of brutal fighting skills possessed by a truly gentle and kind man.

Jet Li was born Li Lian-jie in 1963 in Beijing, China. He was the fifth child in a family cared for by his mother alone after his father died when he was just two years old. Needing to struggle mightily to provide for her kids, Li's mother turned out to be obsessively protective of Lian-jie. But the future world-class action hero was also a small, weakly child. Driven by a gripping fear that something bad could easily happen to her smallest son at any time, Li's mother attempted for years to shield him from any possible threat, any hazard, *anything* that posed — no matter how remote a chance — a possibility of damage or injury. She didn't allow him to play outside too much, to partake in sports, even to ride a bicycle. Lian-jie, however, was also an obedient child in a culture that dictated respect for one's elders, for one's family, and for rules. Li himself would later remark that his preferences for heroes that are so supremely disciplined and duty- and honor-bound might be rooted in his early life structured and controlled by so many familial and social obligations.[4]

The social obligations, however, eventually got Li involved in the martial arts. In China's tightly-controlled Communist society, even an overprotective mother had no say-so when the state required her son to learn to fight. After their first year in elementary school, all Chinese students were required to attend a summer sports program. There, they were randomly placed into various sports training regimens. Lian-jie was placed in Wu Shu.

As it turned out, Li had a natural aptitude for the martial arts. His talent was also coupled with a personal drive and work ethic commanding him to push himself to excel, lest his failures bring disgrace to his family. Despite his mother's obsessively overprotective upbringing, Li had never been critical of her. As far as he was concerned, excelling in school and in his Wu Shu training was a way of repaying her for the immense effort and sacrifices she had made to keep her family together.

Li had quickly become so good at Wu Shu that he was one of the few top athletes recruited for the Beijing Sports and Exercise School. The athletes of this elite institution were polished and fine-tuned to be the best competitors the Chinese government sent to represent the country in foreign exhibitions and competitions. The highlight of Li's tutelage in the school came when he was selected to be a part of a goodwill exhibition tour to the U.S. in 1973. The group even performed their Wu Shu on the White House lawn for President Richard Nixon and the American and world media. After marveling at Li's Wu Shu skills, Nixon kidded with him by asking if Li wanted to be his bodyguard when he grew up. The 10 year old promptly replied, "No. I don't want to protect one person. When I grow up I want to protect billions of Chinese people."[5]

Li's patriotic response helped make him an instant celebrity in China and the subject of a long list of TV and newspaper stories and interviews.

Although being one of the Wu Shu stars of the Sports and Exercise School made a minor celebrity of the young Li, letting him partake in numerous other world tours and goodwill exhibitions, he did have enough foresight to ask himself some hard questions about what sort of a future Wu Shu could provide. Studying the martial arts, competing, and performing left him with a very minimal formal education. Most of the Sports and Exercise School's graduates could look forward to few adult prospects other than careers as coaches and Wu Shu instructors themselves.[6] Just as Li was contemplating whether or not it was worth devoting his life to only the martial arts, the opportunity that would lead to a film career presented itself.

In 1979, China hoped to enter the world's martial arts film market. Following Chairman Mao Zedong's death in 1976, power had been passed to Deng Xiaoping and the government embarked on a series of very limited, moderate political and economic reforms. The new regime also allowed a greater embrace of Chinese cultural history, a lot of which had been actively ignored, purged from history books, and repressed by Mao as being "counterrevolutionary."[7] Wu Shu training, as a matter of fact, was supported and subsidized by the government only as Mao's health began deteriorating and he withdrew into seclusion. In 1979, a more liberalized China chose to look to the past when it came to the production of its martial arts films. When looking for a star, it was natural to turn to the Beijing Sports and Exercise School and its most skilled and high-profile students.

Li was chosen to play the lead role in a film that was titled simply *The Shaolin Temple* (*Shaolin Si*). The story — which took two years to make it to screens, premiering in 1982 — involves a young man's rebellion against an evil seventeenth-century ruler named Wang (Qiang Hu-jiang). After seeing his father murdered, Jue Yuan (Li) escapes to a Shaolin monastery where he is trained by the monk Shi Fu (Hai Yu). Wang's minions, however, are not far behind and the monastery is attacked and burned. Shi Fu is killed, but Jue Yuan and Shi Fu's daughter, Bai Wu Xia (Din Laam), a feisty, beautiful shepherdess, escape the destruction. Jue soon regroups with a few of the monastery's survivors and a group of rebels trying to overthrow the despotic Wang. By the end of the film, of course, Jue and Wang face off in a battle to the death.

Despite its simple story and production values that look severely austere when compared to the more polished Hong Kong martial arts fare, *The Shaolin Temple* turned out to be a major hit. It even made more money than the Jackie Chan film, *Dragon Lord* (*Lung Sin Yau*), playing at the same time. It was nominated for a Best Action Choreography award at the 1983 Hong Kong Film Awards.[8]

With the unqualified success of his first film, Jet Li appeared poised to be the next major phenomenon in martial arts cinema. Soon, however, he would also learn about the unpredictable tastes of audiences and the fact that in a creative enterprise like filmmaking, there is no such thing as a sure thing.

The Shaolin Temple was followed by *The Kids from Shaolin* (*Shao Lin Xiao Zi*, 1984), a nominal sequel to Li's first hit. Playing more like a Wu Shu version of *Seven Brides for Seven Brothers*, the plot involves a family of brothers meeting a family of sisters, falling in love and melding their distinct martial arts styles. In the meantime, the families need to fight the forces of a rampaging warlord. Although not entirely a flop, the contrived, whimsical story did not see the sort of success *The Shaolin Temple* did.

From the middle of the 1980s until the end of the decade, Li's apparent overnight stardom seemed to be losing momentum from one film to the next. This period also saw his professional name change, adapting the American moniker "Jet" when his films were released in the Philippines. Needing a name that would be easier to pronounce and remember than Jian-lie — as is usually the case with many Chinese and Hong Kong performers adapting American screen names — a film distributor suggested billing him as "Jet Li." It was supposed to sound catchy and dramatic — if not gimmicky — an allusion to Li's preternaturally fast moves and the speed with which his career took off across Asia. Unfortunately, the problem was that rather than speeding up and soaring higher and higher, Li's career was stalling quickly. Even an attempt at moving to the U.S. in 1987 on a two-year exit visa to attempt a break into Hollywood did not turn out as well as hoped.[9] The unsteady martial arts cinema landscape in Hollywood in the 1980s would not even allow Li to try his hand at American stardom. With Jackie Chan's failures in *The Big Brawl* and *The Protector*, along with American audiences' new love for a traditionally macho, all–American, all–Caucasian roster of action heroes, not a single Hollywood producer was interested in Li. He managed to make only one Hong Kong–produced film in the U.S.: 1989's *Dragon Fight* (*Long Zai Tian Ya,* 1989). The shoddy, low-budget affair quickly and unceremoniously vanished from the few Chinese neighborhood movie theaters where it was shown.

Before returning to China, though, Li made one more Hong Kong film in Los Angeles. This one, titled *The Master* (*Long Xing Tian Xia*), was helmed by Hong Kong cinema's star director, Tsui Hark. Although it was hoped that

Tsui's pedigree as the "Spielberg of Hong Kong" would boost the film's profile if Li's waning stardom did not, *The Master* was yet another unceremonious failure. Tsui, however, still had faith in his star's potential. As he told the press at the time, he looked at *The Master* as a learning experience. He got to know and understand Li as an actor. Tsui had the chance to size up the strengths and limitations of the martial artist as a performer and star. Though *The Master* might have failed badly, Tsui was determined to work with Li again. Among the conclusions Tsui reached about Li's acting range was that he was just not very good at doing comedy. Tsui had conceived *The Master,* unfortunately, as more of an action comedy than a straight action picture. Li was effective in noble, stoic and intense per-

Former teenage Wu Shu champion Jet Li finds action stardom in Hollywood after his *Lethal Weapon 4* (1998) American debut.

formances, but he did not seem to know how to handle levity. Although Li was on his way back to China soon after finishing *The Master*, Tsui kept his observations in mind for future collaborations. They would, he sensed, happen soon.[10]

Returning to China in the early 1990s, Jet Li had not only a faltering career to contend with, but an even more turbulent country all around him. With the resignation of Communist Party Chairman Deng Xiaoping, the passage of new austerity programs to address economic problems, and the violent crackdown on pro-democracy movements, Li saw a future of uncertainty in his homeland. On the personal front, his marriage to Huang Qiuyan, one of his original costars in *Shaolin Kids*, had come to an end.[11] If he was to have a future as an actor, he decided, he had to go to Hong Kong.

Upon emigrating to the British colony, Li re-teamed with Tsui Hark. The filmmaker had a project in mind for Li. It was something tailored for the martial artist based on their experiences on *The Master* shoot. Tsui wanted Li to do what he did best, playing a virtuous hero. In fact, he wanted Li to play the greatest hero in Chinese folklore. After Jackie Chan's comedic deconstruction, Jet Li was going to rebuild Wong Fei Hung's legend as a larger-than-life champion of Chinese culture.

Simply titled *Wong Fei Hung* (and retitled *Once Upon a Time in China* for its American release), the Tsui Hark/Jet Li collaboration was a sprawling historical martial arts epic. Ultimately, not only would the film re-establish Wong Fei Hung as a noble hero, but it would take thematic elements, approaches to action choreography and character development, and synthesize them into a distinct Jet Li screen persona. This persona would stand throughout the 1990s and beyond. It is nothing less than Jet Li as the hero of Chinese pride, Chinese cultural unity, and the Chinese martial arts as the source of a nation's ethics and principles of bravery and honor.

The plot of *Once Upon a Time in China* presents Wong Fei Hung as the lynchpin in the struggle to keep Chinese society from falling apart under the destructive pressures of colonial incursion and internal disunity and corruption. In the 1870s, American and British colonial powers are trying their best to exploit China. At the same time, the Chinese are incapable of protecting their land and culture because they can never find a way to get along. In the beginning of the film, an official about to temporarily depart Canton asks Wong Fei Hung to form a militia to protect the locals. What the brave Wong finds himself contending with is an armada of American battleships anchored off China's coast, greedy Chinese government officials ready to sell their country's resources to the foreigners, thuggish triad gangs extorting the people, and rival marital arts clans and schools battling each other (and challenging Wong on occasion) to score reputations and settle old grudges. In particular,

Wong finds himself having to take on one of the triads, save himself from trumped-up charges blaming him for a disturbance, and stop a slavery ring from conning (and kidnapping) the Chinese into going to America to build the railroads.

In the midst of all this turbulence, Wong finds his own conservative, staunchly anti–Western attitudes challenged by the arrival of the beautiful Yee (Rosamund Kwan), his "Aunt 13," a relative by marriage and not, conveniently enough, by blood. Yee quickly becomes infatuated with Wong but, to her dismay, finds that the fearless, hard-fighting martial artist and pillar of the community is almost childishly inexperienced when it comes to the ways of women and romance. However, while Yee stirs romantic feelings in the awkward Wong, she has also been educated in the West, wears European clothing, wants to integrate Western customs into Chinese society, and has enthusiastically embraced Western technology in the form of a camera she always carries around.

The important elements in this film include the special nature of the Jet Li character as a hero, his relationship with women, and the hyperbolic fight and action choreography. Although, to some extent, all of these elements have appeared in Li's films already, Tsui Hark seems to put a sharper emphasis on them. *Once Upon a Time in China* can almost be seen as a self-conscious showcase of the quintessential Jet Li film. The film can also be interpreted as a template for much of what would follow in Li's Hong Kong and American films.

Aside from his nobility, his *seriousness*, Li's relationship to the Aunt Yee character is a point of interest and contemplation for his fans. Although Li has, in both Asia and America as well as the rest of the international markets where his films play, a sizable female audience, he has developed a very chaste, very old-fashioned on-screen persona. Although Wong Fei Hung and Aunt Yee eventually marry, Wong only pops the question in the third film in the series. Until then, their "courtship" is a series of gentle suggestions and hints of interest from Yee and embarrassed blushes from Wong. While some have praised this sort of conservative sexual restraint in Li's films, just as many, if not more, of his fans have been frustrated by it.[12] So far, romantic storylines in Jet Li films — even in the films to come after *Once Upon* — seem even more innocent than anything seen in an American TV sitcom in the 1950s. The most controversy this sort of chastity inspired came in Li's first American starring role following his guest role in *Lethal Weapon 4*. In *Romeo Must Die* (2000) — a martial arts adaptation of *Romeo and Juliet* (!), perhaps the most romantic story in Western literature — the Jet Li character and his sexy romantic interest, the late singer Aaliyah, don't share so much as a kiss on screen. The immediate reaction from American critics was to wonder if racism might have prompted this bizarre, asexual version of the Shakespeare classic. Might the producers have been too nervous over physical intimacy between the Asian Li and the African-American Aaliyah? One can't know for sure what must have been going on in the minds (or hearts, for the more melodramatically inclined) of the *Romeo* production team when they decided to keep the two characters' intimacy off screen (there was a scene of a single kiss filmed, but ultimately left out of the final cut). Their anemic explanation claimed that they were just trying to stay true to Jet Li's image and the behavior his fans were expecting to see.[13]

The other standards set in *Once Upon a Time in China* and the rest of the Tsui/Li Wong Fei Hung series involved the very elaborate and stylized wire-assisted martial arts sequences. Whereas Jackie Chan had already started defying the realist school of post–Bruce Lee fight choreography with his acrobatic slapstick, Tsui Hark took screen martial arts further back into the tradition of surrealistic fantasy spectacle. In a way, this kind of reintroduction of the unrealistic approach to combat — "wire fu," as film fans had dubbed the process — is a purely New Wave approach to filmmaking. The New Wave movement and Tsui Hark seemed to be declaring that their generation was taking on the filmmaking traditions, the pre-existing generic rules and conventions, and making them their own. One way they could do this, ironically, was by showing reverence for the ancient roots of martial arts cinema and fantasy and myth-inspired Chinese theater. Certainly, the Shaw brothers and Cheng Cheh and Bruce Lee might have brought stark, grim, bloody reality to the martial arts genre, but Tsui Hark and his New Wave cohorts were not interested in imitation. Tsui Hark did not want to be Bruce Lee or King Hu or Cheng Cheh. Bruce Lee, after all, had been an innovator. A slavish devotion to his style, the absurd rip-offs of his work, as Jackie Chan argued over a decade before, were in themselves an insult to Lee's memory. To Tsui, there was an entire history of imaginative Chinese fantasy and larger-than-life story-telling tradition that had been ignored by modern cinema. He wanted to use the latest special effects technology and the best martial arts choreographers to rediscover and celebrate these traditions.

In *Once Upon*, Jet Li seems to bend the laws of gravity to his will. From the opening of the film, where he leaps from one rope to another along a ship's sail and rigging lines, to a climactic fight all over ladders and towering scaffoldings, he floats and sails through the air, balances on the most precariously stacked objects and demolishes armies of villains like a Wu Shu superhero. The wire-aided fight scenes might not look realistic, but they make the film look like a big, epic, lavish, and gaudy martial arts fairy tale.

Although *Once Upon* and its sequels got only a limited American release in art house theaters, Tsui Hark's kung fu style would impact American filmmaking as hard as John Woo's two-pistoled shootouts did.

However, the wire fu has as many detractors as fans. The fact is that even Jet Li himself was resistant to the idea of getting lifted and propelled all over the studio, flying through the air on the end of a few lines and at the mercy of choreographer Yuen Woo-ping's stunt technicians. Li, a big Bruce Lee fan, was also eager to show his audiences what he could do without special effects trickery. Tsui Hark's retort was that as long as audiences could make an emotional connection with the characters, as long as they could identify with them, they would be willing to suspend disbelief and accept the most outlandish spectacle as being completely real and plausible. Although reluctant, Li went along with Tsui's plans. Essentially, he had no other choice.[14]

Once Upon's record-smashing success seemed to exonerate Tsui and wire fu, enough in fact for the director to continue the practice in the sequels. Jet Li, inadvertently, emerged as Hong Kong cinema's action star most associated with the wire technique. The criticism of the practice, however, has never gone away. Even among the legions of Jet Li fans, the argument that Li's true talents are being diminished by the absurdist wire fu routines are persistent. On *Once Upon*'s American DVD commentary track, martial arts film historian Ric Meyers repeatedly — and quite correctly — argues that Jet Li is so good a fighter that filmmakers need to free him from all the wires and special effects and let him dazzle audiences on his own.

Once Li made the move to Hollywood with *Lethal Weapon 4*, the wire fu became CGI fu. But although the computer manipulation of his fight scenes in *Weapon* are barely noticeable, his follow-up film more than made up for that subtlety. In *Romeo Must Die*, nearly every time he fights, the CGI effects quickly intrude into the sequence and have him suspended in mid-air or contorting in ways that clearly defy the laws of physics and body mechanics.

Despite the fact that, just like in his Chinese and Hong Kong films, Li aspired to play realistic characters in the U.S., films like *Romeo Must Die* made his name synonymous with wire fu and martial arts hyperbole. In Hong Kong, aside from five Wong Fei Hung films,[15] he made two films about Fong Sai Yuk, yet another real Chinese folk hero, and appeared in the Tsui Hark–produced period drama *Swordsman II* (*Siu Ngo Kong Woo Li*, 1992) as well as the period pictures *The Tai-Chi Master* (*Taai Gik Cheung Saam Fung*, 1993), *The Kung Fu Cult Master* (*Kei Tin Tiu Lung Gei Ji Moh Gaau Chu*, 1993), and *The New Legend of Shaolin* (*Hong Xi Guan Zhi Shao Lin Wu Zu*, 1994), plus a sort of Walter Mitty fantasy called *Dr. Wai in the Scripture with No Words* (*Mao Xian Wang*, 1996). He is a strong, noble hero in them all, yet the fantastic, wire and special effect–rendered martial arts seem to transport these tales into a kind of never-was fantasy world. A notable exception, however, is *Fist of Legend* (*Cheng Miu Ying Hung*, 1994), a remake of Bruce Lee's *Fist of Fury.* Here Li takes over the role of Chen Zhen, avenging the death of real martial arts master Huo Yunjia. With this film, Li adamantly insisted on keeping the kung fu real. With "wire fu" taking over films in the '90s, he argued that special effects can make just about anyone look like a martial arts master. Audiences, he said, needed to see what a true expert could do without the wires and camera effects.[16] The period pictures, near the end of his Hong Kong career, though, were mixed with contemporary crime and action thrillers like *The Bodyguard from Beijing* (*Chung Naam Hoi Biu Biu*, 1994), *My Father Is a Hero* (*Gei Ba Ba De Shen*, 1995), *High Risk* (*Sue Dam Lung Wai*, 1995), *Black Mask* (*Hei Xia*, 1996), and *Hitman* (*Saai Sau Ji Wong*, 1998). His post–*Lethal Weapon 4* work in the U.S., though, almost entirely consists of contemporary thrillers like *Rome Must Die, Kiss of the Dragon* (2001), the science fiction *The One* (2001), *Cradle 2 the Grave* (2003), *Unleashed* (2005), and *War* (2007). His U.S. body of work, as of this writing, has been diversified with films made by Chinese directors on only two occasions; once in the Zhang Yimou–helmed period epic *Hero* (*Ying Xiong*, 2002) and in Ronny Yu's *Fearless* (*Huo Yuan Jia*, 2006).[17] Many of the films with contemporary settings, though, still retain a great deal of the computer-enhanced effects. On occasion, as with *Kiss of the Dragon*, Li had been able to force more naturalistic fighting into his films, yet he is still fixed in moviegoers' minds as the chief purveyor of fantastic and surrealistic martial arts.

American audiences, however, still seem to like the special effects, the computerized hyperbole in their entertainment. What has been causing Li some problems, however, has been the larger-than-life, "strong, silent type" characters he is so fond of playing. In fact, most of his American films, so far, have been only moderate successes. While he has a solid fan base, none of his Hollywood films have been runaway blockbusters. As Li seems to have been consciously fashioning his characters to be the perfect renditions of classic, noble heroism, the postmodern American entertainment scene seems to have a difficult time taking these straight, old-fashioned macho men seriously. Hollywood, these days, wants to have its classical heroism undercut with irony. Much like Chuck Norris, Jet Li does not seem to be fond of doing this. As Tsui Hark observed during the filming of *The Master*, Jet Li does not do comedy well and he does not mock his heroes. Luckily for Li, one can guess that the outlandish computerized special effects might help American audiences, jaded with traditional heroism, position his stalwart heroes at an easily manageable distance, a sort of fantasy world they don't need to take entirely at face value.

12

At the Turn of the Millennium and Beyond: Magical Realism, Violence, and the Opening (and Closing) of the East

As the 1990s came to a close, action filmmaking in the U.S. took its cues from Asian cinema. Not only had a director like John Woo relocated to Hollywood, not only was he successful in retaining his own style of filmmaking (when not stymied by the illogical, absurd squeamishness of a schizophrenic organization like the Motion Picture Association of America), but his style of action direction had set the standard for American cop, action/adventure, and science fiction films where shootouts, chases and confrontations had to propel the plot forward. The action genre, where nearly every new hero had to fire two pistols at the same time, where Mexican standoffs punctuated anarchic gun battles and chaotic moments of destruction were seen through slow motion, could almost be renamed the John Woo genre.

Along with Woo, his favorite collaborator, actor Chow Yun Fat, had also made the move to Hollywood, starring in 1998's *The Replacement Killers* with Oscar-winning actress Mira Sorvino. Chow then re-created his cool, suave man-with-a-gun image yet again, costarring with Mark Wahlberg in *The Corruptor* in 1999. Chow's most interesting star turn in Hollywood, however, was the drama *Anna and the King* (1999) with Jodi Foster. The success of this film, a non-musical remake of *The King and I* (1956), is impressive since Chow was able to bring to America another side of his screen persona, something other than the cool, ultra-efficient gunman. Chow had become the first Asian ever to be cast as a romantic leading man in a Hollywood film. The fact that audiences accepted him was a clear enough sign that American moviegoers had, at last, been able to watch films through a more global perspective.

Following Chow Yun Fat's lead, Hong Kong star Michelle Yeoh was another successful transplant when in 1997 she costarred with Pierce Brosnan in the James Bond film *Tomorrow Never Dies*. Yeoh, a former Miss Malaysia beauty contestant, is also a popular martial arts and action star in Hong Kong. In fact, she had gotten Jackie Chan's highest praise for her action heroine proficiency after they worked together on *Supercop* (*Ging Chaat Goo Si 3: Chiu Kap Ging Chaat*, 1992).[1] Chan, who likes to encourage his costars to follow his lead and do as many of their own dangerous stunts as possible, was highly impressed by Yeoh's willingness to do one of the most dangerous stunts in the film. In a chase scene, she races a motorcycle onto a ramp and vaults it on top of a moving train.

Eventually, in 2000, Chow Yun Fat and Michelle Yeoh were paired in one of the most successful films to cement the connection between Hollywood and Asia.

One of the most influential films of the 1990s, however, premiered in March of 1999. It melded science fiction and action, but its approach to both was solidly rooted in the cinema and popular culture of the East. Not only did directors Andy and Larry Wachowski's science fiction epic, *The Matrix*, push every technical envelope in establishing the film's look, sound, feel and pacing as the new standard in action and futuristic spectacle, but it seemed to declare that Asian aesthetics had to be part of the new cutting edge.

The Matrix touched a profitable nerve in moviegoing audiences in 1999 because its dystopian future world exploited a concern that was much more immediate, much more relevant than the usual plots of generic dark-future science fiction films. *The Matrix* wasn't just the umpteenth version of a shadowy, or overcrowded, or post-apocalyptic world ruled by some standard-issue despot and opposed by a band of underground rebels. These elements were certainly in the film; *The Matrix*'s future is indeed dark, people are oppressed, a nuclear holocaust had, at one point, been unleashed, and a raggedy band of rebels (literally hiding underground) are trying to overthrow the system. But *The Matrix*'s vision of a controlling dictatorship is one where the control is exerted through the invisible manipulation of reality. This is not a world where people are kept in line by troops, secret police and open intimidation. Instead, they are brainwashed into seeing an entirely nonexistent world around them. In the Wachowskis' vision, the Matrix is an intelligent computer system into which all humans in the world are plugged. The Matrix runs off of the energies of these people — living batteries, in essence — and, in turn, it implants visions of a false world into their minds.

This concept turned out to be a boon for the Wachowski team because it was quickly interpreted as a metaphor for the way people live today. In a world of twenty-four-hour global media run by giant conglomerates that may or may not be manipulating information to suit their own nefarious purposes, multi-million-dollar public relations spin machines tasked with fabricating creative lies and distortions to exonerate political and corporate criminals, massive government and business bureaucracies that run every facet of people's lives, and an advertising industry that seems to have made a science out of manipulating people's desires, the idea of *The Matrix* seemed to be eerily relevant. In this world, when thousands are obsessed with ever-more-complex conspiracy theories — all basically arguing that what you see in the media, what you're told by the government, and what history books have been telling you is all a lie masking some dark, hidden truth — audiences seemed to find a representation of their anxieties in *The Matrix's* story. The most interesting phenomenon of the film, in fact, was how quickly it became a perfect ink-blot test for so many ideologies and philosophies. Everyone from post-modernists to social-constructionists, Marxists and even fundamentalist Christians saw their beliefs represented by *The Matrix*. In the modern world, everyone feels like they're being hoodwinked and oppressed by some massive global conspiracy.

But when the Wachowski brothers first proposed their film, they referred to Japanese anime and promised an action adventure narrative in the style of Hong Kong martial arts and crime films. The Wachowskis' first point of reference was the anime *Ghost in the Shell* (*Kokaku Kidotai*, 1995),[2] a story about computer-enhanced humans in the future having their memories, personalities, and very perceptions of the world manipulated by hackers who can access their minds just like a computer. In fact a major subgenre of Japanese animation involves dystopian visions of the future, most often warning about the mind-altering, subversive power of technology. Although that idea is not uniquely Japanese or Asian — an entire American genre of science fiction called cyberpunk had been dealing with these fears since the '80s — the Wachowskis borrowed the dark, dank urban look of *The Matrix* from the Japanese animated stories much as Ridley Scott borrowed the oppressively overcrowded future metropolis look of *Blade Runner* (1982) from the atmosphere of modern day Tokyo.

The action scenes of *The Matrix* could have been outsourced to John Woo to orchestrate and direct. From the slow-motion, juggernaut-about-to-tumble-out-of-control buildup of action scenes to shootouts spewing endless hails of gunfire, every frame of *The Matrix's* ballistic violence seemed to try to out–Woo John Woo.

But, aside from using a lot of guns and wearing a black overcoat and sunglasses he might have borrowed from Chow Yun Fat's Mark in *A Better Tomorrow*, Keanu Reeves' Neo character became as skilled a martial artist as Bruce Lee, Jackie Chan, and Jet Li rolled into one. In fact, Neo literally has all martial arts digitally combined and inserted into his brain. After being plugged into a computer, he becomes an expert in everything from kung fu to jujitsu to drunken boxing. One of his fighting moves, in fact, is directly taken from Jet Li's Wong Fei Hung films. The signature move Li gave Wong in the *Once Upon a Time in China* films has him sweeping one arm forward and the other backward and over his head. With the forward hand, he would nonchalantly wave for his opponents to make a move, to try their futile best to take him on. Keanu Reeves performs that exact move, down to the wave of the hand. But the fight choreographer for *The Matrix* is also the man who orchestrated the fights for Jet Li in the *Once Upon* films. Yuen Woo-ping was brought in by the Wachowskis to give *The Matrix*'s action scenes the same look he would give a quintessential Hong Kong martial arts film.

Ultimately, the 1990s had been a turning point in Hollywood action filmmaking because studios reacted to the growing staleness of the genre by revamping it in the image of a foreign cinema. But outside of making action films look fresh and exciting again, the arrival of John Woo and Jackie Chan and Jet Li is of importance because for the first time foreign filmmakers thrived in the American mainstream markets. These were not directors and actors who faded into the esoteric worlds of the art house theaters. They made their films for the mainstream, middle-American strip mall audiences and they changed the look and feel and tempo of one of Hollywood's biggest genres at the same time.

The 21st Century

The start of the new millennium was a good year for action films. Not only were two of the top films of 2000 action films, but both received the sort of critical adulation usually reserved for high-toned dramas, "personal" films and issue pictures. And one of these films was a martial arts epic that had fully embraced the fantasy roots of the genre. In the spring of 2001, while Ridley Scott's ancient Roman adventure *Gladiator* was given the Best Picture Oscar, Ang Lee's *Crouching Tiger, Hidden Dragon* (*Wo Hu Cang Long*) got the award for the Best Foreign Language Film.

Intended for a world martial arts market that had usually been open to foreign language films — and perhaps a run at the American art houses — *Crouching Tiger, Hidden Dragon* had been embraced by the mainstream American audience like few other foreign films had in a long time. While it's true that the film was co-produced by Sony Pictures Classics and given a generous U.S. marketing campaign, the film was, nevertheless, a foreign language picture. Americans had always been reluctant to read subtitles. Although Taiwanese director Ang Lee — trained in American schools like NYU's film program — had gotten previous exposure in the U.S., his work had largely been

Chow Yun Fat in *Crouching Tiger, Hidden Dragon* (2000). The martial arts film gets critical respect.

art house fare. His films like *Eat Drink Man Woman* (*Yin Shi Nan Nu*, 1994), *Sense and Sensibility* (1995), and *The Ice Storm* (1997) won critical praise and awards, but they were far from the usual multiplex material. *Crouching Tiger*, with subtitles and all, had played well in the strip malls and among the typical lineup of Hollywood films. As even New Line Cinema's releases of Hong Kong–produced Jackie Chan films never earned anywhere near what *Rush Hour* and *Shanghai Noon* brought in, *Crouching Tiger*'s blockbuster American take of $128 million was a foreign release phenomenon.[3]

The attitude shift among American moviegoers that had them embracing the influx of Asian talent throughout the '90s seemed to have been sustainable in a new decade. As the 2000s progressed, *Crouching Tiger* inspired the release of a series of similar films, all doing well in their wide releases far outside of the neighborhood fine arts theater. The same decade, however, also saw the increasing popularity of another Asian import. Japanese animation scored with an even larger segment of the U.S. population. This is significant because Japanese films had largely been ignored since Kurosawa. The distinct look of Japanese animation would also start to slowly diffuse into action cinema, capturing the imaginations of Hollywood directors much the same way the Wachowski brothers designed the look of *The Matrix* based on *Ghost in the Shell*. By the midpoint of the decade, however, an entirely new Asian cinema, that of Thailand, would promise to join Hong Kong and Japan as a source of imaginative action and adventure.

Crouching Tiger's success is noteworthy because it was able to convince audiences to embrace an entirely new model of story-telling. Labeled with the term "magical realism" from art, literary criticism, and the analysis of expressionistic filmmaking, *Crouching Tiger* makes no effort to offer explanations for why its characters are able to bounce weightlessly through the air, run up the side of a perfectly vertical wall and balance on the reedy ends of tree branches. The digitally-enhanced "wire fu" techniques used in films like the *Once Upon a Time in China* series now made the martial arts and acrobatics of *Crouching Tiger* look smoothly, ethereally flawless. The most important aspect of a film like this, again, is the fact that director Ang Lee offers no explanation for why all these fantastic things can happen. Even Americans accepted that the floating and flying and leaping of tall buildings just *can*. They had opened up to foreign story-telling practices and paradigms well enough to accept the fact that this film is a rendition of a Chinese fairy tale. In Chinese fairy tales, flying martial artists are as acceptable as dragons and ogres and witches are in European fairy tales. They just exist. For an American audience, however, explanations for the nature of fantastic things had always been a requirement. Superheroes always needed a well-fleshed-out "mythology," for example. They needed an origin story that gave an explanation for why they could fly or turn invisible, had superhuman strength or shot laser beams from their eyes. With *Crouching Tiger*, audiences were able to accept the stylistic re-creation of reality according to a foreign culture's model.

The film's impact on the careers of several principals was immediate. Ang Lee was propelled to the top of the Hollywood A-list of directors. His handling of the drama, the themes of personal passions clashing with obligations, the conflict between changing times and ancient traditions, all coupled with the action and special effects, quickly marked him as a serious popular director. In fact, Lee did say on various occasions that his approach to mainstream Hollywood projects would be one where he wanted to balance the entertainment with intelligent and personal themes.[4] He took that approach when asked to direct *The Hulk*, a big-budget, special effects–heavy feature adaptation of the comic book. Aside from the CGI mayhem, Lee anchored the fantasy with a grim story of a repressed man's tortured relationship with his father. Basically, Lee personalized the comic book film by fitting it well into one of his usual thematic concerns, into his oeuvre of conflicted family relationship stories.[5] The film's disappointing box office was unfortunate as Lee did a commendable job of humanizing a story that had quickly been taken over by one computer-drawn action set-piece after another. But Lee's major coup came after the underperforming *Hulk*. In 2006, he won the Oscar for *Brokeback Mountain*, becoming the first Asian director to be given the Best Director Academy Award.

While *Crouching Tiger* was headlined by Chow Yun Fat, Michelle Yeoh, and Shaw Brothers *wuxia* legend Cheng Pei Pei, the picture's breakout star was 21-year-old Zhang Ziyi (in the film's U.S. release, as in all her American films, she is credited as Ziyi Zhang). A graduate of the Beijing Dance Academy and the Central Academy of Drama, the petite, doll-like actress held her own against the seasoned action veterans. In fact, her youthful appearance and a disciplined bearing that hints at a much tougher, willful personality underneath was perfectly used for her role of Jen, a duplicitous daughter of an aristocrat, plotting to steal a legendary sword. With her career ignited by *Crouching Tiger*, Zhang went on to star in a series of films in both Asia and Hollywood. She usually appeared in similar roles of fragile-looking young women who turn out to be much stronger than they appear. However, her least-nuanced performance is in Jackie Chan's *Rush Hour 2*, her first Hollywood movie. In that film, she appears simply hard and dangerous, playing a homicidal henchwoman of a Hong Kong gangster. Her most notable Hollywood role came in 2005, reteaming with Michelle Yeoh for the adaptation of the best-selling novel *Memoirs of a Geisha*. Again displaying a talent for hard/soft characters, Zhang is a girl who had been sold into servitude by her destitute father and grows up to be one of the most celebrated geishas in prewar Japan.

The *Memoirs of a Geisha* publishing and film phenomenon yet again evidenced the ongoing melding of Asian culture into American popular entertainment. Both Arthur Golden's book and director Rob Marshall's film made great efforts to penetrate deep within the heart of a fabled and intricately detailed, rule- and ceremony-bound part of Japanese culture. It is remarkable that both the novel and the film found such mainstream success in the U.S.

Crouching Tiger, Hidden Dragon ultimately opened the door to a series of similar magical realism films. Chinese myth and fantasy had become the new Hollywood blockbusters in the 2000s. These films are all set in ancient China and they are all similarly stylized and fantastic in their staging of action scenes. Three major films following in *Crouching Tiger*'s wake were all made by Mainland China director Zhang Yimou (no relation to Zhang Ziyi).

Zhang, in fact, had said that Ang Lee's successful handling of *Crouch-*

ing Tiger, Hidden Dragon emboldened him to take on the *wuxia* fantasy drama. It is a genre that had interested and attracted the Chinese director for years. The martial arts film, like the Western for American directors, is a quintessential part of Chinese culture and the sort of genre many filmmakers almost feel obligated to work in at least once. As Lee himself said, "There's a real part of me that feels that unless you make a martial arts film then you are not a real filmmaker."[6]

Zhang Yimou had long been considered not just a real filmmaker, but one of the best Chinese directors of all time. Since his debut film, 1987's *Red Sorghum* (*Hong Gao Liang*), Zhang had won Best Picture and Best Director awards at every major international film festival, holding more film awards than any other Chinese director. With films like *Ju Dou* (1990) and *Raise the Red Lantern* (*Da Hong Deng Long Gao Gao Gua*, 1991), considered his signature works in both style and themes examining some of the stifling and tragic aspects of traditional Chinese customs and social structures, Zhang's preeminent reputation on the world film scene had been as an art-film director. Nonetheless, the draw of the martial arts film was just as strong on Zhang. In an interview for the DVD release of *Hero*, Quentin Tarantino—who had partnered on the American distribution of the film, endowing it with his name and a revamped title of "Quentin Tarantino Presents *Hero*"—even commented on how unusual it was to hear that the most esteemed of Chinese directors would be making a martial arts epic.

Zhang's magical realism *wuxia* films are *Hero* (*Ying Xiong*), *The House of Flying Daggers* (*Shi Mian Mai Fu*, 2004), and *Curse of the Golden Flower* (*Man Cheng Jin Dai Huang Jin Jia*, 2006). With *Hero*, he strengthened the appeal of his first *wuxia* epic by casting Jet Li in the starring role, joined by *Crouching Tiger* star Zhang Ziyi and Hong Kong action and martial arts stars Tony Leung and Donnie Yen. The film, however, did not complete its theatrical run without controversy. Objections to the film's theme were raised in both the U.S. and several foreign film festivals. *Hero*'s sympathetic treatment of a ruler who becomes a benevolent despot in order to unify Chinese lands was accused of promoting totalitarianism. Some saw it as thinly-veiled propaganda for the Chinese government, celebrating the reunification of Hong Kong with the Communist mainland, the takeover of Tibet, and a call for China to take back Taiwan. *Washington Post* critic Stephen Hunter, while mostly enjoying the film, did write about its reunification-through-strength theme that "that was the King of Qin's reasoning and it was all the other big bad ones' as well: Hitler and Stalin and most particularly that latter-day King of Qin named Mao, another great unifier who stopped the fighting and killed only between 38 and 67 million in the process."[7]

Although made in Communist China and, therefore, subject to government scrutiny, whether or not there are any intended pro-totalitarian and Chinese expansionist messages is still debatable. Zhang, as a matter of fact, had not had an easy relationship with the Chinese government for much of his life. As a youth, he had been banned from attending college, being forced instead to work as a farm laborer. His father had fought in the Kuomintang Army against Mao and the Communists during China's civil war, and Zhang, in turn, was deemed an unreliable counterrevolutionary and class enemy for years.[8] It is highly unlikely that he would purposefully make a propaganda picture celebrating Communist despotism and expansion. In the case of *Raise the Red Lantern*, the government had accused him of critiquing it and attacking Communist doctrine. That film was banned in China for several years. If anything, *Hero*'s romantic entanglements among rebels who may or may not be plotting to overthrow the despotic King of Qin propel much more of the plot than any political messages. In fact, in both *The House of Flying Daggers* and *Curse of the Golden Flower*, romantic intrigue, double-crosses, and lies are the prominent foci of the stories, effectively overpowering the subplots of rebellions and schemes to overthrow rulers.

It is more likely that for American audiences the most fascinating aspect of any of the Zhang Yimou pictures had been their spectacularly, sumptuously colorful visual images. As in many of Zhang's films, the use of vibrant colors dazzles the viewer in virtually every frame of the film. Much like in the case of *Crouching Tiger, Hidden Dragon*, audiences are overwhelmed by a completely original and vibrant film aesthetic they had never seen before. From the box office numbers of each of these films, it was clear that audiences very much liked being overwhelmed by Zhang's visions.

In the 1990s and 2000s one of Zhang's long-time collaborators also emerged as a performer to watch in both the art-house and the mainstream theaters in the West. The actress Li Gong (in her American films, just like Zhang Ziyi, she is usually billed as Gong Li), who had been cast in some of Zhang's most acclaimed films, including *Red Sorghum*, *Ju Dou*, and *Raise the Red Lantern*, gained international attention following her role in *Farewell My Concubine*. Her long collaboration with Zhang, producing nine films, was based on their romantic relationship. Controversy and scandal was the outcome of their romance, however, since Zhang happened to be married at the time he carried on the affair with Li. They parted ways professionally in 1995 when their relationship broke up.[9] They reteamed only once since then, making *Curse of the Golden Flower*. Li eventually made the move to Hollywood films in 2005 for an auspicious American debut opposite Zhang Ziyi and Michelle Yeoh in *Memoirs of a Geisha*. The casting of these three women, though, stirred some controversy around the film. The portrayal of three main Japanese characters by Chinese actresses drew protests from some Japanese audiences. Since *Geisha*, Li had moved on to playing Collin Farrell's love interest in Michael Mann's 2006 theatrical remake of his TV show, *Miami Vice*, and playing Lady Murasaki in *Hannibal Rising* (2007).

Crouching Tiger, Hidden Dragon was also responsible for Quentin Tarantino's lending his name to bringing another updated iteration of the Wong Fei Hung legend to American theaters in 2001. Much earthier than Zhang Yimou's explosions of color, the 1993 film *Iron Monkey* (*Siunin Wong Fei-hung Tsi Titmalau*), directed by Yuen Woo-ping, tells the story of a crossing of paths between a teenage Wong Fei Hung (13-year-old *female* performer and Wu Shu champion Tsang Sze-man) and a Chinese Robin Hood figure called the Iron Monkey. The story has Fei Hung's misguided father, Wong Kei Ying (Donnie Yen), offering to hunt down and capture the wanted masked criminal who calls himself Iron Monkey. Eventually, young Fei Hung helps his father realize that the real villain is not the Iron Monkey but the corrupt local governor. The Iron Monkey is none other than the kindly Dr. Yang (Yu Rongguang), who spends his time during the day treating sick peasants, then puts on his black mask and black outfit to battle injustice by night.

An Animated Future

Aside from the magical realism of China's fantasy *wuxia* films, a new Japanese export had, at last, made as much of an impact on American popular culture in the '90s and 2000s as the samurai sagas of Akira Kurosawa. This import came, however, from animation, not action cinema. The Japanese film industry, which had declined in the 1960s, could not, unfortunately, recover in the subsequent forty years. The budgets required to mount productions that would compete with the American blockbusters always so popular in Japan were simply not available to Japanese studios. Unless the Japanese film business turned sizable profits from the world and local markets, it did not have the resources to mount films on a scale that could compete in those same markets. This vicious circle had ravaged the country's film industry and any serious change in the status quo does not appear on the horizon.

Modern Japanese films are usually either of two varieties. There has been a strong new movement in personal, small-scale art films and highly stylized, mass-market genre films. On the one end of this spectrum, filmmakers in the '80s, '90s and 2000s have been emulating the introspective cinema of the post–World War II era. The examination of the nature of national identity and how this identity is constantly being negotiated between the modern world and the culture's ancient roots has been the subject of films by directors like Naomi Kawase, Fumiki Watanabe, Satoshi Isaka, and Hirokazu Kore'eda.[10]

Balancing the introspective school, however, has been a strong post-modernist movement in Japanese film as well. Since the early 1990s especially, absurdist, disjointed, often stunningly violent gangster, crime and horror films have assaulted viewers' senses with images of stylish nihilism, bleak visions of angst, anger, and alienation. As Donald Richie analyzes a traditionally Japanese approach to art and drama, this "cool," stylized approach to film-making is ultimately very Japanese. Japanese art has always sought to contain and re-create reality in such a way as to let the viewers know that what they are seeing is a carefully, yet not quite accurately, rendered reproduction. For example, the Japanese would not so much like to decorate their yard with a tree as have a stylized re-creation in the form of a little bonsai tree stand in for the real thing. Ironically, Richie argues, the look and feel of so much Japanese cinema today is influenced by the American cinema of Quentin Tarantino and his hip, knowing style of genre filmmaking that dwells on self-consciously re-creating and imitating past films. Quentin Tarantino, of course, has always been given to enthusiastically waxing about his love for Asian cinema.

Shortly after the turn of the millennium, Japan made a brief impression on the American horror genre. With Gore Verbinsk's 2002 adaptation of Hideo Nakata's 1998 film *Ringu* (*The Ring*) proving a major success, the door was briefly opened to several adaptations of Japanese horror films. In 2005, Nakata himself came to Hollywood to make *The Ring Two* (not an adaptation of his own sequel, *Ringu 2*). In 2004 Takashi Shimizu mounted a remake of his horror film *Ju-on* (2003) with an American cast. Retitled *The Grudge*, and featuring American horror regular and ex–Buffy the Vampire Slayer Sarah Michelle Gellar, this version of the film is notable because it did not change the location to the U.S. Although the cast is mainly American, the film was shot entirely in Japan. In 2006, Shimizu remade his sequel to *Ju-on* as well, as *Grudge 2*. In 2005, the far less successful adaptation of Hideo Nakata's *Honogurai Mizu No Soko Kara* (2002), *Dark Water*, seemed to have put a pause on the raiding of Japanese horror films. Nevertheless, Japanese horror does have an avid fan base in the U.S. and a large number of titles are available on DVD.

The brief success of these Japanese horror films, called "J-horror" by fans, can again be attributed to Hollywood's inability to keep a major genre fresh and innovative. After the teenage horror boom of the 1980s collapsed, 1996 saw a sudden rejuvenation of the form with the Wes Craven/Kevin Williamson hit *Scream*. Although the genre appeared to be making a comeback—*Scream* even birthed two sequels in the following years and inspired imitations like *I Know What You Did Last Summer* (1997) and the *Final Destination* films (2000, 2003, 2006)—the fact was that *Scream* was more of a parody of horror. The film's entire reason for being was to point out the artifice of the genre and its often illogical conventions. True horror fans were looking for real scares and films that took the genre seriously rather than demonstrating how Hollywood filmmakers, when left to their own devices, can do little else than imitate a narrow set of clichés over and over again. At least when Hollywood did some cribbing from Japan, it was able to offer up a few real scares and some interesting new ideas.

The "J-horror" movement, though, seems to have stalled not only because of *Dark Water*'s failure, but because the films were largely subtle psychological thrillers rather than explicit gore-fests. The American J-horror adaptations were all rated PG-13. The genre, though, along with American audiences, suddenly regained its blood lust around the 2003 remake of *The Texas Chainsaw Massacre* (1974). Of course, the spoof horror films like *Scream* and its imitators were PG-13 as well because of a wave of anti-media violence hysteria gripping the U.S. after a spate of school shootings in the late '90s. But with the advent of films like the *Saw* series (2004, 2005, 2006, 2007) and *Hostel* (2005), and the remake of Wes Craven's *The Hills Have Eyes* (2006), graphic shock-horror (dubbed "torture porn" by critics) became the entertainment of choice for horror fans.

The one area where the Japanese entertainment industry has been able to thrive, turn out products of unfettered creativity *and* function as a serious world trendsetter has been in animation. When it comes to the children's entertainment market, after all, Japan has long been very successful. Japanese toys and video games have been doing exceptional business around the world for decades. But the precise reason behind the runaway success of Japanese animation, or "anime" to its fans, is because the medium has always been so diverse. Anime is *not* just for kids. Especially as the fandom of comic books, cartoons, video games and what had traditionally been dismissed as kids' entertainment had been embraced by grownup baby boomers and "generation X-ers" in the '70s, '80s, and '90s, older audiences in the West have been devouring anime with obsessive, cultish voracity. The fan communities and collectors devoting themselves to anime in the U.S. today rival the fan cults of *Star Trek* and *Star Wars*. The aficionado will usually be able to differentiate between various subgenres, seeing both the obvious and subtle differences between the kid-friendly and the more mature anime. They will also often praise this art form, even the more juvenile ones, for the creativity and complex subject matter very rarely, if ever, seen in American cartoons.

Anime, if one keeps in mind Donald Richie's assessment of Japanese art as a hyper-stylized representation of the real world, is the perfect medium to manipulate and blur the boundaries between the realistic and fantastically, almost grotesquely, distorted renditions of the world. Anime, in other words, boldly addresses real-world concerns while, at the same time, peopling its stories with strange-looking caricatures of reality.

The features of many anime characters, for example, look like phantasmagorical, fun-house-mirror distortions of the human body. The standard and easily-recognizable anime-style characters usually have large, bulbous heads or domed foreheads expanding over pointy, pinched chins and small, wedge-like noses. Many characters, especially females, usually have abnormally large eyes. Body shapes can also vary between extremes. They might be either lanky, willowy-thin with long limbs, or densely compact and stocky. Anime hair may often come in rainbow-like multicolored hues, sprouting in all directions in a wild mane.

The significance of the appearance of anime characters, in fact, has long been a point of discussion and analysis among pop culture critics. The most obvious aspect of these characters is that they do not look Japanese or even faintly Asian. Hollywood cartoons with Asian characters, like Disney's *Mulan* (1998) or the human characters of *Lilo and Stitch* (2002), look much more Asian than anything drawn by anime artists. Some characters, especially in the space-war science fiction or military animes, might have a sort of bland, vaguely Caucasian appearance. In the fantasy, magical, or comedic anime features, the bulging heads and wide, saucer eyes seem to place the characters in some alternate universe's homo-anime species. But none of these anime denizens look even vaguely like the people of the culture that created them. The obvious question is why.

Anime historians usually explain that foreign export is not the reason. Anime has not been conceived as a global product and the themes and situations many anime stories deal with are very specific to Japanese culture.[11] Even since the global anime market exploded, Japanese artists do not seem to be motivated to tailor — or self-censor — their work for any specific foreign market. For example, anime's liberal use of sexual themes has not changed since Americans have discovered this art. Though its creators know how hyper-sensitive Americans can be to sexual content, especially themes of alternate sexualities, anime continues to be as risqué as ever. Homosexual characters and themes and homoerotic images abound in a lot of anime. Japanese animators seem to have a seller's-market attitude toward their art. They continue drawing their product for the Japanese audience and let the foreigners make of the stories what they will.

So the un–Japanese look of anime characters remains a point of interest and unresolved hypothesizing for popular culture analysts. For scholar Kenji Sato, the appearance of these characters might be rooted in the Meiji-era impulse for Japanese to divorce themselves from their Japaneseness and become more Western, more global. Since artists gained the ability to control their world, control reality through the tips of their pens, they seem to be redrawing it in such a way as to erase their marked Japaneseness.

American audiences, especially since the early 1990s, have devoured anime with a driven gusto. Many fans had been introduced to Japanese animation by the few occasional imports to show up on television in the 1960s and '70s, then with more regularity — and greater availability through video cassettes and specialty video stores in Asian neighborhoods — in the 1980s. Especially those who had seen anime as kids in the '80s fueled the demand for more mature and complex animation in the 1990s and after the turn of the millennium.

The American exposure to Japanese animation can be traced to the 1963 American debut of the anime series *Tetsuwan Atom*, retitled as *Astro Boy*. This was joined by Japanese imports like *Gigantor* and *Kimba*. *Speed Racer*, premiering in 1967, is the anime series that would have the longest American shelf life among this first wave of '60s imports. To this day, *Speed Racer* is a resilient pop culture icon, so much so that the production team behind *The Matrix* films, Larry and Andy Wachowski, along with producer Joel Silver, put all their special-effect resources into the making of the 2008 theatrical film version of the anime. The late 1970s saw the American premiere of *Star Blazers*, a dubbed and retitled version of the 1972 anime *Space Cruiser Yamato*. The most successful anime import of that decade, however, was the adaptation of *Kagaku Ninja Tai Gatchaman*, roughly translated as *Science Ninja Team Gatchaman* and retitled *Battle of the Planets*. This series, about a team of five young people piloting a high tech space ship and various personalized battle vehicles in an ongoing war with alien invaders bent on destroying Earth's environment, ran in American syndication well into the 1980s. In Japan, the series was so popular that it became a template for the team-of-mechanized-warriors-battling-aliens anime subgenre.[12] In this formula, alien invaders are challenged by a team that might have super powers (stemming from high technology), pilot a giant robot, or drive or fly super battle vehicles. Invariably, the team is made up of five members, consisting of a cool, competent leader, a big brawny sidekick, a beautiful woman, a young kid, and a surly, brooding loner.

But the most fruitful decade for exposing American kids to anime was the 1980s. In 1984, several Japanese cartoons and toys were used by American studios as inspirations for the *Voltron* (based on the *GoLion* and *Dairugger XV* animes) and *Transformers* (based on the Daclone and Microman line of Japanese toys) animated series.[13] In the case of *Voltron*, the lines of toys based on the story of futuristic, alien-battling warriors using a giant robot that had been joined from individual lion-shaped battle machines created a merchandising tie-in boon. In the case of the *Transformers*, the Hasbro company bought the remake rights to the Daclone and Microman toys, then commissioned the cartoons based on these toys. At one point, Marvel Comics debuted a line of *Transformers* comics. Their iconic Spider-Man and Nick Fury characters even made appearances in several of the *Transformers* stories.[14] But the most fondly recalled anime import of the '80s by the fans of the genre was *Robotech*. Cobbled together from three separate anime series (*Super Dimension Fortress Macross*, *Genesis Climber Mospeada* and *Cavalry Southern Cross*),[15] the Robotech story was — up to a point — slightly reminiscent of the *Battlestar Galactica* concept with its cast of characters marooned in space on a giant space fortress and battling alien invaders.

The legacies of the '80s anime series lived well into the 21st century. Robotech still has its legions of fans on the internet with countless tribute and discussion pages. *Transformers* was adapted into a critically and commercially successful 2007 film by action director Michael Bay. The film's warm critical reception was especially surprising as Bay is the Hollywood action director critics have long loved to hate. The director of the *Bad Boys* series, *The Rock*, *Armageddon* and *The Island*, Bay has been accused of being nothing more than a stylist, making empty films about car crashes, explosions and beautiful women occasionally moving about in the background as nothing more than eye-candy for male viewers. The consensus on *Transformers*, however, was that Bay had succeeded at last in making a film that was fun and engaging beyond the CGI–drawn visuals. Following the success of Bay's film, talks of a long-gestating *Voltron* film adaptation have also been revived.[16]

While people who watched *Robotech* and played with the *Transformers* and *Voltron* toys in the '80s matured into fans of darker, more challenging anime like *Akira* and *Ghost in the Shell*, the 1990s saw Japanese imports aimed at young viewers perform to record-setting ratings on television and amass vast fortunes in merchandise sales. Anime and anime based on Japanese toys like *Dragonball Z*, *Yu-Gi-Oh!*, *Pokemon*, *Digimon*, *Dual Masters* and *Sailor Moon* had captured American kids' imaginations like few genres of entertainment or toys had in years. With a lot of successful anime series originating in the popular Japanese *manga* comic books, virtually every American bookstore and comic book shop today carries an epic collection of *manga*. From 1993 until 1996, Saban Entertainment mixed action footage from three Japanese science fiction kids' shows, *Kyoryu Sentai*, *Gosei Sentai Dairanger*, and *Ninja Sentai Kakuranger*, with original footage of American actors for the blockbuster show *Mighty Morphin Power Rangers*. In 1995 and 1997, the success of the franchise led to the Twentieth Century–Fox theatrical films *Mighty Morphin Power Rangers: The Movie*, and *Turbo: A Power Rangers Movie*. In the 1990s, Japan had become the new merchant of cool to the world when it came to the youngest audiences. While American media had dominated most of the world markets since the end of World War II, in the 1990s Japan had replaced it as the new trend-setter of hipness.

The die-hard anime fan community usually explains that its devotion stems from the fact that this imported genre is so much more creative and challenging than most of what Hollywood turns out. For one thing, there really is no American equivalent for much of the imported anime. The original material usually runs for many hours since it was created for Japanese television. They are "mini series" in the true sense of the word. They were created as episodic TV entertainment, but they are self-contained with a limited story arc. They can tell a very complex, layered, ensemble-cast story over weeks or even months, yet the story is still finite. An anime series can focus on a limited set of questions and issues, explore them in detail, and eventually find a point of closure when the whole saga is wrapped up.[17]

Aside from the form, the depth and complexity of many anime series is usually what earns most of the fandom's respect. A lot of anime tackles weighty philosophical, moral, spiritual, political, and social issues. The futuristic anime, for example, the subgenre that has so many American fans, regularly deals with issues like war, environmental devastation, urban living conditions, crime, governmental corruption, and concerns over the impact of technology on the quality of everyday life, privacy, and security. An oft-examined issue in futuristic anime is the intrusive, stealthy threat of surveillance and cybernetic technology. In the best cyberpunk tradition, this type of anime shows a near-future where the daily reliance on technology, and the technological intrusion into the human body by way of computerized, robotic implants, nanotechnology, scanning and tracing devices, slowly lead one to question the very definition of humanity. Once again, there is almost no American equivalent to entertainment like this. Whether through animation or live action theatrical or TV entertainment, the American media has not been able to muster enough creativity and faith in the attention span or intelligence of its audiences to provide such cerebral entertainment. Of course, this is surprising, given the decades-long runaway success of a TV and film franchise like *Star Trek*. The Trekkies can usually be heard praising the "complexity," "issues," and "messages" of their favorite show and its spin-offs. The ongoing, evolving storylines of the *Harry Potter* novels and films — with their legions of adult fans — likewise demonstrate how audiences can remain loyal to characters that are complex and multi-faceted, and who grow and change in an interesting, fully-realized world of their own. Nevertheless, the American media can't seem to accept the fact that these films and TV shows might be more than flukes, aberrations, exceptions to the rule that aiming for the lowest IQ points can garner the biggest audiences. Especially when it comes to animation, thoughtful, philosophically-driven and issue-driven animation does not exist in the American market. The closest the U.S. entertainment industry is capable of getting to something that comments on, or at least acknowledges, current issues are the snarky one-liners on TV cartoons like *The Simpsons* and *Family Guy*. Big-screen versions are computer-animated comedies like the *Shrek* series, nominally intended for children but written with enough double entendres and in-jokes about pop culture to make adults tolerate the 90-minute show they need to sit through for the sake of the kids.

The New Thai Martial Arts Industry

A look at the most recent connection between the American action genre and Asian culture reveals the emergence of a new film industry as a possible major trend-setter. With two starring roles to his résumé as of this writing, Thai actor Tony Jaa is becoming the new martial arts star to watch for Asian-action fans. With the excellent production values of his films, *Ong-Bak, The Thai Warrior* (*Ong-Bak*, 2003) and *The Protector* (*Tom Yum Goong* [yes, named after the spicy Thai soup], 2005), and with a robust marketing campaign behind their American release, not only is Jaa quickly garnering fans, but he's also putting the focus on Thailand's growing film industry.

The charismatic Jaa, born Worawit Yeerum in 1976 in Surin, Thailand, had been so inspired by Bruce Lee, Jackie Chan and Jet Li films in his childhood that he embarked on an intensive martial arts and stunt training regimen to attempt to break into the film industry. Having seen the 1978 Thai action film *Born to Fight* (*Kerd Ma Lui*) and heard that its director, Panna Rittikrai, also trained athletes for stuntwork, Jaa sought him out and was accepted as an assistant/trainee for the filmmaker. After polishing his skills at the Maha Sarakham College of Physical Education, he worked as a stunt man and supporting player in several of Rittikrai's low budget films. He also did stunts for Sammo Hung in a commercial for an energy bar and for *Mortal Combat: Annihilation* stars Robin Shou and James Remar. Jaa vaulted to stardom when a demonstration reel of his skills — comprised of a formidable list of fighting arts, including Muay Thai kickboxing, Muay Boran, Aikido, Capoeira, Wu Shu, Krabi Krabong, Tae Kwon Do and gymnastics and sword-fighting techniques — impressed director/producer Prachya Pinkaew enough to write the lead role in *Ong-Bak* for him. After the film's initial Asian release, Pinkaew joined with French action director/producer Luc Besson to release the film in the U.S. As a result, Jaa was quickly named the most exciting new star in martial arts films by American critics.[18]

Jaa's moves, in fact, are highly impressive in both *Ong-Bak* and *The Protector*. Most importantly to martial arts fans, as *Ong-Bak*'s promotional materials loudly announced, Jaa does his very best to follow in Jackie Chan's footsteps and do all of his own stunts. There are no wires, no stuntmen and no CGI effects in a Tony Jaa film, taglines, posters, and interviews have all declared. In fact, much like Jackie Chan, or Jet Li when he is not flung through the air by wires or manipulated by computer effects, Jaa has lightning fast moves that often blur past the camera, especially when he uses his Muay Thai kicking techniques. Aiding his martial arts and gymnastic abilities, both of his films also gain from top-notch fight choreography and editing.

Both *Ong-Bak* and *The Protector* are also smartly made films, in the sense that they follow the simple plot formula for beginning actors. Director Pinkaew does his best to let his star dazzle primarily with his martial arts abilities, much like Brandon Lee in *Rapid Fire*. A largely untested actor, the reasoning must have been, needs to make himself familiar to audiences through his moves if he is to be established as a martial arts star. Since Jaa has very little acting experience, *Ong-Bak* and *The Protector* are content to let him kick and punch opponents for the better part of both films.

The plot of *Ong-Bak* involves the theft of head of a Buddha statue from a village by a gang of artifact smugglers. Believing that the statue protects the village's good fortunes, the locals send their best athlete, Ting (Jaa), to Bangkok to track down the thieves and retrieve the head. The gang just happens to make a side income from staging illegal fights as well, forcing Ting to get involved in several spectacular fights as he makes his way to the top echelon of the smuggling ring.

The Protector could almost have been a sequel to *Ong-Bak*. Its plot is almost identical, sending an elephant herder from a Thai village to Australia to find a pair of stolen elephants. The film's most exciting scene is Prachya Pinkaew's entry into the directorial contest of setting up the longest possible unbroken take. After Orson Welles' use of the device in *Touch of Evil*, setting up complex sequences where a scene goes on for minutes on end without a cut has been something directors like Brian DePalma and Martin Scorsese have been fond of attempting. Pinkaew's entry, though, is perhaps the most impressive because he uses the unbroken take to film a string of fights and very dangerous stunts. It involves Jaa's barging into a multistoried restaurant the animal smugglers use as a front, then taking on waves of thugs as he fights his way to the top level. The fight moves along a set of corridors that spiral upward and around an open central atrium. In a couple of instances, Jaa's opponents are hurled off the edge of the corridor, plunging to the bottom and smashing furniture on impact.

Although both films use Jaa very conservatively, protecting him from his own limited acting experience, what he is able to convey very well is a likable, charismatic presence. Although he does not act much, Jaa's presence exudes the "it" factor. With his good looks and boyish smile, he automatically gains an audience's sympathy. With his two films, Jaa was able to make enough of an impact on Hollywood heavyweights that Jackie Chan tried to cast him in *Rush Hour 3.* Reportedly, Jaa was unable to take up his idol's offer as it conflicted with the shooting schedule of *Ong-Bak 2.*[19]

With the international success of Tony Jaa's films, the companies that produced and released them, Baa-Ram-Ewe and Sahamongkolfilm, have followed up by attempting to establish another young graduate of Panna Rittikrai's stunt and fighting program as an up-and-coming action star. With his remake of *Born to Fight* in 2004, Rittikrai cast Dan Chupong as a cop who finds himself in the middle of a Die Hard–style takeover of a village by Burmese commandos in an attempt to free their jailed leader. Chupong then made *Dynamite Warrior*, about a silent, enigmatic loner in 1930s Thailand fighting to protect farmers from unscrupulous businessmen ... and occult practitioners.

Although neither *Born to Fight* nor *Dynamite Warrior* got the sort of theatrical releases Tony Jaa's films were afforded in the U.S., the establishment of Dan Chupong as a martial arts star in the West is still viable. The films got very thorough, extras-laden DVD releases by Dragon Dynasty, the company that has been releasing both new Hong Kong and Thai martial arts action films as well as classics from the Shaw Brothers and Golden Harvest collections.

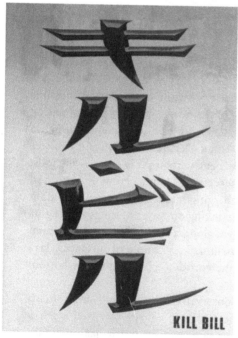

KILL BILL

Quentin Tarantino's *Kill Bill* (2003). A guided tour through the history of martial arts cinema.

New Directions?

The release of the classic films of the "kung fu craze" era shows the ongoing fascination with Asian cinema and the martial arts as the first decade of the twenty-first century draws to a close. The anime "craze" is more evidence that audiences yearn for the sort of creativity American producers can't seem to give them. Films like Quentin Tarantino's *Kill Bill* saga, referencing everything from the Shaw Brothers to Bruce Lee, Japanese *chambara* films and anime, prove that, indeed, the cinema of the East is the hippest art form Hollywood can imitate. The first of the *Kill Bill* films, in fact, can almost be viewed as a scene-by-scene checklist of homages to every major martial arts film. Uma Thurman's yellow jumpsuit, for instance, is the outfit worn by Bruce Lee in *Game of Death*. The Deadly Viper Assassination Squad and its eponymous leader, Bill, is a tip of the hat to Shaw Brothers' *Five Deadly Venoms*. The casting of Gordon Liu, the star of *Five Masters of Death* (*Shao Lin Wu Zu*, 1974), *Master Killer* (1978), *The 36th Chamber of Shaolin* (1978), and *8-Diagram Pole Fighter* (*Wu Lang Ba Gua Gun*, 1983), in the dual roles of Pai Mei and Johnny Mo is a literal move to put the legendary figures of "craze era" martial arts films into the most complete homage to the genre. The film's second such casting coup is using Sonny Chiba in the role of Hattari Honzo, the sword-maker. The Honzo character is directly lifted from Chiba's own Japanese *Hattari Honzo* films. As Tarantino said on the film's DVD release, there is no one else but Sonny Chiba who can possibly play a legendary sword-maker in a martial arts homage. The first film's climactic sword battle between Uma Thurman and Lucy Liu is a very accurate homage to *Lady Snowblood* (*Shurayukihime*, 1983), and a series of other scenes, fights, and lines of dialogue reference Hong Kong and Japanese martial arts films like *Chinese Boxer* (1966), *Black Lizard* (*Kurotokage*, 1968), *Goke, Bodysnatcher from Hell* (*Kyuketsuki Gokemidoro*, 1968), *Shaolin Executioner* (1977), *Fists of the White Lotus* (*Hong Wending San Po Bai Lian Jiao*, 1980), *Master of the Flying Guillotine* (*Du Bi Quan Wang Da Po Xue Di Zi*, 1975), *Battle Royale* (*Barou Rowairu*, 2000), and *Ichi the Killer* (*Koroshiya 1*, 2001).

With audiences eager for more martial arts, there are questions about the genre's future and how Hollywood will fulfill the fans in the upcoming years. There are several problems now standing in the way of providing a steady stream of authentic product to audiences.

While Jet Li can still make vigorous, action-packed martial arts thrillers, an older Jackie Chan's output is not as certain. There are two major obstacles Chan has been contending with for the past decade. The main one, of course, is his age and the limits of his body. While he made his name by boasting that he *always* does his own stunts, the fact is that Chan had been using stuntmen at least since starting to make films like the *Rush Hour* and *Shanghai* series in Hollywood. As martial arts and Asian-film experts Ric Meyers and Jeff Yang discuss in their DVD commentary for *Drunken Master*, Chan has been frustrated by the fact that he is getting ever-more-debilitating fractures and injuries doing stunts that never gave him more than minor bruises and scrapes in his youth. But the second major problem, according to Meyers and Yang, is subject matter. Chan has been equally frustrated by the fact that he seems to have made every possible variation on the comic martial arts film. The "Jackie Chan–style" film appears to be exhausted.

As far as Hong Kong cinema is concerned, the outlook is also uncertain.

Since the 1990s, very few major new personalities seem to have emerged. There appear to be only a small handful of new directors or stars that might be capable of making an impact on the world film scene. With the pre–1997 handover fears, investments in the Hong Kong film industry dwindled.

Plus, as business boomed in the '80s and the early '90s, the industry became contaminated by unsavory and dangerous elements. With huge sums of money to be made in films, the organized crime triads tried to muscle in on the movie-makers' racket. Usually the triad activity was very straightforward. Gangsters demanded that stars and directors hand over a cut of their salaries or face violent retribution. In 1992, for example, Jet Li's business manager, Jim Choi, was found shot to death. As Choi himself was alleged to have been a former heroin smuggler before going into the movie business, his killing was easily accepted as yet another instance of the real violence of real gangsters intruding into a movie business that had made millions from tales of make-believe triads.[20] Many believe that the exodus to Hollywood in the '90s was prompted by fear of the triads, in addition to the fear of the 1997 reunification.

Furthermore, the current generation of Hong Kong filmmakers seems to be more interested in entertainment that is very specifically local in its thematic concerns and less likely to fare well in foreign distribution.

But the future, of course, is not certain and the emergence of the next blockbuster martial arts or action/adventure director or star can never be accurately predicted. For example, in 2001 and 2004, American moviegoers were taken by surprise by the Hong Kong martial arts comedies *Shaolin Soccer (Siu Lam Juk Kau)* and *Kung Fu Hustle (Kung Fu)*. Both films — written, directed by, and starring comedian Stephen Chow — used an absurdist, live-action-cartoon approach (called Mo Lei Tau comedy)[21] to parody traditional martial arts clichés. The mainstream success of *Kung Fu Hustle* in the U.S. is especially remarkable since so many of its jokes are quite esoteric and intelligible to only a hard core martial arts cinema buff. But even in the ailing Hong Kong film economy, both *Shaolin Soccer* and *Kung Fu Hustle* have been enormous financial successes. *Hustle*, in fact, is the highest-grossing Hong Kong film to date. On the action/gangster front, *Infernal Affairs (Mou Gaan Dou*, 2002), the first film in a crime trilogy by co-directors Andrew Lau and Allan Mak, was the inspiration for Martin Scorsese's Oscar-winning *The Departed* (2006).

The 2000s even saw the return of the American martial artist. With its acrobatic, Hong Kong–style fight choreography (directed by Corey Yuen) and deadpan, morbid humor, *The Transporter* (2002) was a major hit and helped establish transplanted British actor Jason Statham as a new martial arts action hero.[22]

Statham, a champion-diver-turned-model-turned-actor made his first favorable impression on audiences and critics in director Guy Ritchie's crime films *Lock, Stock and Two Smoking Barrels* (1998) and *Snatch* (2000). After the move to Hollywood, he appeared in supporting roles in John Carpenter's science fiction *The Ghosts of Mars* (2001) and Jet Li's *The One*. *The Transporter*, however, made him the newest action hero in a Hollywood action market that had been devoid of actors specializing in action/adventure films.

The fascinating thing about Statham's action stardom is that it both faithfully relies on the hyperbolic Hong Kong stylings of the martial arts genre and, at the same time, puts the accent on the problems with the Eastern-style action genre. On the one hand, *The Transporter* films are remarkable in their demonstration that the Asian approach to staging and pacing an action film has become the default template in the genre. The slow-motion shootouts, the use of two guns, the markedly unrealistic, acrobatic moves, are all in place. But, on the other hand, the problems of the (over)stylized action choreography are highlighted by Statham himself. Basically, Statham makes a remarkably good action hero because he exudes a gritty, earthy reality that has been missing in action heroes since the late '80s. In the American action landscape that had been taken over by teen idols and Sexiest Men Alive like Matt Damon, Keanu Reeves, and Orlando Bloom, Statham is a man among boys.

He is certainly much harder, much more athletic and muscular, than any of his young colleagues, but not in a Stallone/Schwarzenegger, self-conscious bodybuilder way. If anything, Statham has more in common with men like Russell Crowe or Chuck Norris, or icons like Steve McQueen and Clint Eastwood. He is of the school of machismo that just telegraphs itself in the actor's bearing, in his face and eyes. This is the sort of macho that does not posture or brag, it just *is*. Actors with this quality seem to suggest that they could be more than competent in a real fight, taking care of violent business without the use of a stuntman or computerized special effects to make them look like tough guys. With Statham's often-stubbled face and his shaved head that

Jason Statham. The *Transporter* films (2002, 2005) made him the new generation American martial arts star.

shows the outline of male pattern baldness, there is an unpretentious, flawed reality about him. Of course, the drawback to using an actor like this in a cartoonish action film is that the special effects, the acrobatics, become distracting and annoying. When the audience sees as formidable a presence as Statham, they want to see him in fights, in action sequences as realistic as possible. Much like "wire fu" did for Jet Li in the eyes of martial arts purists, the burlesque, over-the-top fight choreography serves to diminish his presence, not enhance it.

This sort of cartoon action seems to be the course Statham settled on for now. The success of *The Transporter*, naturally, spawned *Transporter 2* (2005). More special effects and hyperbolic martial arts followed. His most outlandish film, however, was 2006's *Crank*, an incoherent stew of unfunny comedy, unrealistic action, and deafening heavy-metal music in an absurd plot about a hitman being poisoned by a substance that kills him unless he keeps his adrenaline pumping.

How long audiences will stay interested in such over-edited burlesque remains to be seen at this point. What people do want to see more of, one can certainly surmise these days, is more creative, more boundary-breaking popular entertainment. The steadily-declining box office numbers for Hollywood's films clearly indicate that moviegoers are not being satisfied by the home-grown product. In the past, Asian films have always been an antidote when American producers and studios lost their way. With the rising popularity of Thai star Tony Jaa, with the hope of a resurgent Hong Kong film industry in the wake of *Kung Fu Hustle* and the influential *Infernal Affairs*, this might stay the case in the near future.

Conclusions

The decades-long influence of Asian filmmaking on Hollywood carries social import that is worth considering. The implications for media analysts are certainly interesting and the implications for filmmakers and popular-culture purveyors are important.

The way global entertainment like the Hollywood action film industry has been challenged and fundamentally altered by artists in Hong Kong and Japan demonstrates the power of local audiences and local cultures as well as the importance of understanding how a global media culture must be approached by American filmmakers. Although Hollywood dominated world entertainment for years, this has been so because so many foreign film industries had been impoverished or under-developed. But once alternatives to the Hollywood product can be provided at a steady rate of output, the Hollywood flash and spectacle — unless it's backed by quality story-telling and intelligent, worthwhile plots — can just as easily fall to second-choice place for so many of the world's moviegoers. Simply put, Hollywood, no matter how much it might really want to (and no matter how much American media critics and intellectuals charge it does), can *not* brainwash audiences into uncritically accepting anything. Audiences are, and always have been, active, critical, and discerning consumers of information and entertainment.

Audience activity also brings up another issue when analyzing the *action* film industry. More than any other genre of film, action films have always been the most controversial. This is the only genre, after all, that exists for the express purpose of depicting aggression and violence. Nothing can rouse anti-media hatred, paranoia, and censorious hysteria more than the issue of violence in films and TV. In turn, various American media critics, "family advocates," and cultural commentators from all over the political spectrum are capable of stoking paranoia and censorious hysteria better than anyone in the world. The U.S., after all, is a country where a veritable axis of censorship, from the religious ultra right to the politically correct left, is always crusading for more government control over TV content and calling for boycotts of everything they personally dislike seeing, hearing, or reading. These are people who constantly attempt to link every conceivable social ill — from street crime to bullying, from children's over-eating to anorexics' under-eating, the devastation of the environment, a lack of "family values" and just a general cultural atmosphere of incivility — to "the media."

The fact that empirical research proving the truth of these apocalyptic fears is sketchy and inconclusive rarely deters these activists' zeal. Most who have taken a meta-analytical overview of all the published research on media effects and media violence usually declared in no uncertain terms that there is almost zero evidence to suggest a connection between crime, aggression, social disorder and the media. The media violence research, argues Jib Fowles, one of the most outspoken meta-analysts of violence scholarship, is not even as lengthy and rigorous as many have proclaimed. There are actually fewer than 200 studies that have been published between 1957 and today that directly tested the effects of violence. The findings of these studies, Fowles says, are all consistently inconclusive. In fact, an entire school of media research, called Cultural Studies, in England has been devoting itself to dispelling the myth of media-violence effects. As leading British Cultural Studies researcher David Gauntlett comments, "The search for 'effects' on behavior is over: every effort has been made, and they simply cannot be found."[23] If anything, most of the violence research is akin to the prophecies of Nostradamus: so vague and inconclusive that it could be used to justify any conclusion one wishes to reach.

The influx of all the Asian action, martial arts and anime films can be seen as a perfect example of the absurdity of all of the anti-media violence paranoia. Much of this entertainment is infinitely more violent — and sometimes sexual — than anything seen in American entertainment. Anime broadcast on American television is usually heavily edited. When originally broadcast on Japanese TV, it usually included very heavy doses of violence and sex. In fact, many people who have lived in Japan always comment on how much more violent and aggressive mainstream Japanese entertainment is than what Hollywood produces. Nevertheless, Japan has a microscopic rate of violent crime when compared to the U.S.

As far as the so-called "culture wars" are concerned, more importation of foreign media can help put the accent on the repressive, censorious impulses of a culture that purports to be the freest and most tolerant in the world. Bone-breaking martial artists, anarchic anime, and vengeance-seeking, sword-slashing ninjas and samurai prove that oftentimes a dose of violence can be quite good for a society.

Chapter Notes

Preface

1. David Bordwell, *Planet Hong Kong: Popular Cinema and the Art of Entertainment* (Cambridge, MA: Harvard University Press, 2000), 19.

Chapter 1

1. Richard Schickel, *Clint Eastwood* (New York: Knopf, 1996), 262. Schickel's exhaustive biography presents a very concise discussion of the hyperbolic and surrealistic nature of the violence of action films.

2. Christopher Heard, *Ten Thousand Bullets: The Cinematic Journey of John Woo* (Los Angeles: Lone Eagle Publishing, 2000), 210. Heard's biography includes a detailed interview with actor Chow Yun Fat. Their long-running collaboration has been compared to the Akira Kurosawa/Toshiro Mifune and John Ford/John Wayne partnerships.

3. Gina Marchetti, "Action-Adventure as Ideology," in *Cultural Politics in Contemporary America*, edited by Sut Jhally (London: Routledge, 1989), 46. Marchetti's article focuses in part on the various political interpretations that can be brought to the analysis of action films and the surreality of their depiction of violence.

4. Christopher Heard, *Ten Thousand Bullets: The Cinematic Journey of John Woo*, 127.

5. Ibid., 128.

6. Emanuel Levy, "Hard Target," review of *Hard Target* (*Variety*, 31 August 1993), 38.

7. Christopher Heard, *Ten Thousand Bullets: The Cinematic Journey of John Woo*, 126.

8. Georgia Brown, "Hard Target," review of *Hard Target* (*Village Voice*, 31 August 1993), 18.

9. Peter Cowie, *Revolution! The Explosion of World Cinema in the Sixties* (New York: Faber & Faber, 2005), 15. Cowie explores the cultural trends of the 1960s that not only saw a greater immigration of European talent to Hollywood, but the rise in visibility and popularity of local filmmaking talents around the world.

10. Nancy Griffin and Kim Masters, *Hit and Run: How Jon Peters and Peter Guber Took Sony for a Ride in Hollywood* (New York: Simon & Schuster, 1996), 85.

11. Thomas Schatz, *The Genius of the System: Hollywood Filmmaking in the Studio Era* (New York: Henry Holt, 1988).

12. Peter Biskind, *Easy Riders, Raging Bulls: How the Sex-Drugs-and-Rock 'n' Roll Generation Saved Hollywood* (New York: Simon & Schuster, 1999), 20.

13. Ibid.

14. Rock Brynner, *Yul: The Man Who Would Be King; A Memoir of Father and Son* (New York: Simon & Schuster, 1989), 154.

15. Richard Schickel, *Clint Eastwood*, 134–176.

16. Peter Biskind, *Easy Riders, Raging Bulls: How the Sex-Drugs-and-Rock 'n' Roll Generation Saved Hollywood*, 376–439.

17. Todd McCarthy, "Last Action Hero," review of *Last Action Hero* (*Variety*, 18 June 1993), 23.

18. Christopher Heard, *Ten Thousand Bullets: The Cinematic Journey of John Woo*, 61–96.

Chapter 2

1. Stephen Prince, *The Warrior's Camera: The Cinema of Akira Kurosawa* (Princeton, NJ: Princeton University Press, 1999), 14.

2. Ibid., 26.

3. Ibid., 341–342.

4. Martin Scorsese, "Milestones," *Time*, September 21, 1998.

5. NHK Japanese television newscast, September, 1988.

6. The TV show *The Simpsons* had a joke about *Rashomon*: Homer and Marge have different recollections of whether or not they enjoyed the film.

7. Roger Ebert has repeatedly given credit to Kurosawa as the inventor of the "team of specialists" action film.

8. Akira Kurosawa, *Something like an Autobiography* (New York: Vintage, 1983), 210.

9. Ibid., xi.

10. Ibid.

11. Stuart Galbraith, *The Emperor and the Wolf: The Lives and Films of Akira Kurosawa and Toshiro Mifune* (New York: Faber & Faber, 2001).

12. Donald Richie, *A Hundred Years of Japanese Film* (New York: Kodansha International, 2001), 17.

13. R. H. P. Mason and J. G. Caiger, *A History of Japan* (North Clarendon, VT: Tuttle Publishing, 1997), 227.

14. Joseph L. Anderson, *The Japanese Film: Art and Industry* (New York: Random House, 1960), 34.

15. Ibid., 35.

16. Donald Richie, *A Hundred Years of Japanese Film*, 22.

17. Donald Richie, *The Films of Akira Kurosawa* (Berkeley: University of California Press, 1996), 11.

18. Donald Richie, *A Hundred Years of Japanese Film*, 122–124.

19. Akira Kurosawa, *Something like an Autobiography*, 18.

20. Ibid., 25.

21. Stuart Galbraith, *The Emperor and the Wolf: The Lives and Films of Akira Kurosawa and Toshiro Mifune*, 26.

22. Donald Richie, *The Films of Akira Kurosawa*, 12.

23. Ibid., 13.

24. Ibid., 18.

25. Ibid., 14.

26. Ibid.

27. Ibid.

28. Stuart Galbraith, *The Emperor and the Wolf: The Lives and Films of Akira Kurosawa and Toshiro Mifune*, 56–57.

29. Donald Richie, *A Hundred Years of Japanese Film*, 104.

30. Akira Kurosawa, *Something like an Autobiography*, 120.

31. Donald Richie, *A Hundred Years of Japanese Film*, 113–114.

32. Ibid.

33. Donald Richie, *The Films of Akira Kurosawa*, 37.

34. Ibid., 36.

35. Ibid., 65.

36. Peter Biskind, *Easy Riders, Raging Bulls: How the Sex-Drugs-and-Rock 'n' Roll Generation Saved Hollywood*, 21.

37. Stephen Prince, *The Warrior's Camera: The Cinema of Akira Kurosawa*, 8.

38. Stuart Galbraith, *The Emperor and the Wolf: The Lives and Films of Akira Kurosawa and Toshiro Mifune*, 8.

39. Robert Warshow, "The Movie Chronicle: The Westerner," in *Film Theory and Criticism*, edited by Gerald Mast, Marshall Cohen & Leo Braudy (New York, Oxford University Press, 1992), 457.

40. Patrick Drazen, *Anime Explosion: The What? Why? & Wow! of Japanese Animation* (Berkeley, CA: Stone Bridge Press, 2003), 107.

41. John G. Cawelti, "Chinatown and Generic Transformation in Recent American Films," in *Film Theory and Criticism*, edited by Gerald Mast, Marshall Cohen and Leo Braudy (New York: Oxford University Press, 1992), 498–511. Cawelti argues that the most notable films of the 1970s are parodies and mockeries of such old-standard genres as the detective story and the Western.

42. As Stuart Galbraith's book *The Emperor and the Wolf* details, Kurosawa felt that Leone's film was too close to his own even to be acceptable as an "homage" or tribute. Kurosawa sued for plagiarism and won.

43. Donald Richie, *The Films of Akira Kurosawa*, 147.

44. Christopher Frayling, *Clint Eastwood* (London: Virgin Publishing, 1992), 81.

45. Ibid.

46. Richard Schickel, *Clint Eastwood* (New York: Knopf, 1996), 147.

47. Alan Arnold, *Once Upon a Galaxy: A Journal of the Making of "The Empire Strikes Back"* (New York: Del Rey, 1980), 111.

48. Stephen Prince, *The Warrior's Camera: The Cinema of Akira Kurosawa*, 6.

49. Ibid.

Chapter 3

1. Nathan Johnson, *Zen Shaolin Karate: The Complete Practice, Philosophy and History* (North Clarendon, VT: Tuttle Publishing, 1994), 15.

2. David Chow and Richard Spangler, *Kung Fu: History, Philosophy, and Technique* (Unique Publications, 1980), 4.

3. Jeff Yang, *Eastern Standard Time: A Guide to Asian Influence on American Culture, From Astro Boy to Zen Buddhism* (New York: Mariner Books, 1997), 260.

4. Jeff Yang, *Once Upon a Time in China: A Guide to Hong Kong, Taiwanese, and Mainland Chinese Cinema* (New York: Atria Books, 2003), 98.

5. Nathan Johnson, *Zen Shaolin Karate: The Complete Practice, Philosophy and History*, 39.

6. Jeff Yang, *Once Upon a Time in China: A Guide to Hong Kong, Taiwanese, and Mainland Chinese Cinema*, 5–7.

7. Ibid., 6.

8. Joshua Goldstein, *Drama Kings: Players and Publics in the Re-Creation of Peking Opera, 1870–1937* (Berkeley: University of California Press, 2007), 19.

9. David Bordwell, *Planet Hong Kong: Popular Cinema and the Art of Entertainment* (Cambridge, MA: Harvard University Press, 2000), 2.

10. Ibid., 8.

11. Ibid., 52.

12. Ibid., 51.

13. Jeff Yang, *Once Upon a Time in China: A Guide to Hong Kong, Taiwanese, and Mainland Chinese Cinema*, 38–40.

14. Ibid.

15. Ibid., 24.

16. *The Art of Action: Martial Arts in Motion Pictures* (Starz Entertainment Documentary).

17. Jeff Yang, *Once Upon a Time in China: A Guide to Hong Kong, Taiwanese, and Mainland Chinese Cinema*, 28–30.

18. Ibid.

19. Ibid.

20. Ibid.

21. David Bordwell, *Planet Hong Kong: Popular Cinema and the Art of Entertainment*, 35.

22. Ibid.

23. Jeff Yang, *Once Upon a Time in China: A Guide to Hong Kong, Taiwanese, and Mainland Chinese Cinema*, 46–48.

24. Poshek Fu and David Desser, *The Cinema of Hong Kong: History, Arts, Identity* (Cambridge University Press, 2002), 32.

25. David Schute and Andrew Klein, *The Master: Chang Cheh* (Documentary for *The One-Armed Swordsman* DVD).

Chapter 4

1. *Bruce Lee: A Warrior's Journey* (Starz Entertainment Documentary). This documentary was the first to present a new re-editing of Bruce Lee's *Game of Death* footage outside of what Robert Clouse used for his film.

2. Bruce Thomas, *Bruce Lee: Fighting Spirit* (Berkeley, CA: Frog, 1994), 4.

3. Ibid, 8.

4. Ibid., 9–11.

5. Ibid., 26.

6. Ibid., 31.

7. Ibid., 45.

8. Linda Lee, *The Bruce Lee Story* (Ohara Publications, 1989), 44. A personal history of Bruce Lee's life by his wife.

9. Bruce Lee, *The Tao of Jeet Kune Do* (Black Belt Communications, 1975), 23. Lee's approach to martial arts technique and philosophy in his own words.

10. *Bruce Lee: A Warrior's Journey* (Starz Entertainment Documentary).

11. Jack Hunter, *Intercepting Fist: The Films of Bruce Lee and the Golden Age of Kung Fu Cinema* (London: Glitter Books, 2005), 47.

12. Horace Newcomb and Robert S. Alley, *The Producer's Medium: Conversations with Creators of American TV* (Oxford University Press USA, 1985), 21.

13. Jack Hunter, *Intercepting Fist: The Films of Bruce Lee and the Golden Age of Kung Fu Cinema*, 55.

14. Ibid.

15. Ibid., 56.

16. Ibid., 60.

17. Ibid., 62.

18. David Bordwell, *Planet Hong Kong: Popular Cinema and the Art of Entertainment*, 53.

19. Peter X. Feng, *Screening Asian Americans* (New Brunswick, NJ: Rutgers University Press, 2002), 53–71.

20. Bruce Thomas, *Bruce Lee: Fighting Spirit*, 138.

21. Ibid., 136.

22. Jack Hunter, *Intercepting Fist: The Films of Bruce Lee and the Golden Age of Kung Fu Cinema*, 76.

23. Bruce Thomas, *Bruce Lee: Fighting Spirit*, 140–141.

24. Chuck Norris and Ken Abraham, *Against All Odds: My Story* (Nashville, TN: Broadman & Holman Publishers, 2004), 78–83.

25. *Bruce Lee: A Warrior's Journey* (Starz Entertainment Documentary).

26. Jeff Yang, *Eastern Standard Time: A Guide to Asian Influence on American Culture, From Astro Boy to Zen Buddhism* (New York: Mariner Books, 1997), 228.

27. The origins of the *Kung Fu* TV show are often in dispute. Various versions of its genesis are advanced. Parties close to Bruce Lee usually argue that the concept for the show came from Lee himself. Others maintain that it was CBS's idea and at one time they merely had discussions with Lee about possibly starring in the show.

28. Bob Wall, *Who's Who in the Martial Arts* (Los Angeles, CA: R. A. Wall Investments, 1985), 62.

29. Bruce Thomas, *Bruce Lee: Fighting Spirit*, 186–187.

30. Jack Hunter, *Intercepting Fist: The Films of Bruce Lee and the Golden Age of Kung Fu Cinema*, 45.

31. Bruce Thomas, *Bruce Lee: Fighting Spirit*, 189–191.

32. Ibid., 219–230.

33. Leon Hunt, "The Hong Kong/Hollywood Connection," in *Action and Adventure Cinema*, edited by Yvonne Tasker (New York: Routledge, 2004), 270–271.

34. Mikel J. Koven, *Blaxploitation Cinema* (Pocket Essentials, 2001), 40.

35. M. Ray Lott, *The American Martial Arts Film* (Jefferson, NC: McFarland, 2004), 59.

36. Donald Bogle, *Toms, Coons, Mulattoes, Mammies, and Bucks: An Interpretive History of Blacks in American Films* (Continuum International Publishing Group, 2003).

Chapter 5

1. Linda Lee, *The Bruce Lee Story* (Ohara Publications, 1989), 185.

2. Chuck Norris and Ken Abraham, *Against All Odds: My Story* (Nashville, TN: Broadman & Holman Publishers, 2004), 32.

3. Chuck Norris and Joe Hyams, *The Secret of Inner Strength* (Boston: Little, Brown, 1988). Norris' autobiography details the irony of how actively he rejected numerous suggestions to try an acting career for several years after an initial appearance in a 1968 Dean Martin spy spoof.

4. Ibid., 115.

5. Ibid., 123.

6. Frank Sanello, *Stallone: A Rocky Life* (Edinburgh: Mainstream Publishing, 1998), 61–79.

7. Chuck Norris and Ken Abraham, *Against All Odds: My Story*, 19.

8. Stephen King, *Danse Macabre* (New York: Berkley Books, 1980), 133.

9. Susan Jeffords, *Hard Bodies: Hollywood Masculinity in the Reagan Era* (New Brunswick, NJ: Rutgers University Press, 1994), brings the focus to the subtext of 1980s action adventure films, finding storylines functioning as narratives about masculine anxieties and the male fear of losing power and social prestige. In the same vein, Richard Schickel, *Clint Eastwood* (New York: Knopf, 1996), discusses the same themes of male anxiety, as approached by various Eastwood films. The theme of the masculinity crisis and popular culture is again visited by Susan Faludi in "The Masculine Mystique" (*Esquire*, October 1996), 88, and *Stiffed: The Betrayal of the American Man* (New York: William Morrow, 1999). Other writers exploring the theme are Helen Fisher, *The First Sex: The Natural Talent of Women and How They Are Changing the World* (New York: Random House, 1999); Neal King, *Heroes in Hard Times: Cop Action Movies in the U.S.* (Philadelphia: Temple University Press, 1999); Lionel Tiger, *The Decline of Males* (New York: St. Martin's Griffin, 1999); and Barna William Donovan, "The Essence of Action: Genre Theory and the Depiction of Values, Gender and Violence in the American Action Film," in *Communication Annual* (2005): 22–40.

10. Lionel Tiger, *The Decline of Males*, 2–11.

11. Neal King, *Heroes in Hard Times: Cop Action Movies in the U.S.*, 3.

12. Michael A. Anderegg, *Inventing Vietnam: The War in Film and Television* (Philadelphia: Temple University Press, 1991), provides a cultural history of the Vietnam War film, along with Linda Dittmar and Gene Michaud, *From Hanoi to Hollywood: The Vietnam War in American Film* (New Brunswick, NJ.: Rutgers University Press, 1991); Jeremy M. Devine, *Vietnam at 24 Frames a Second: A Critical and Thematic Analysis of Over 400 Films About the Vietnam War* (Jefferson, NC: McFarland, 1995; republished, Austin:

University of Texas Press, 1999); Lawrence H. Suid, *Guts and Glory: The Making of the American Military Image in Film* (University Press of Kentucky, 2002); and Mark P. Taylor, *The Vietnam War in History, Literature and Film* (University of Alabama Press, 2003).

13. Brian Thomas, *VideoHound's Dragon: Asian Action and Cult Flicks* (Detroit: Visible Ink Press, 2003).

Chapter 6

1. William Corr, *Adams the Pilot: The Life and Times of William Adams, 1564–1620* (New York: Routledge, 1995).

2. Eric Bercovici, *Shogun* (DVD documentary).

3. Will Murray, "The Executioner Phenomenon," in *Murder off the Rack: Critical Studies of Ten Paperback Masters*, edited by John L. Breen and Martin Harry Greenberg (Metuchen, NJ: Scarecrow Press, 1989), 135–144.

4. Dick Lochte, "Warren Murphy and his Heroic Oddballs," in *Murder off the Rack: Critical Studies of Ten Paperback Masters*, edited by John L. Breen and Martin Harry Greenberg, 155.

5. Jeff Yang, *Eastern Standard Time: A Guide to Asian Influence on American Culture, From Astro Boy to Zen Buddhism* (New York: Mariner Books, 1997), 110.

6. Ibid.

7. M. Ray Lott, *The American Martial Arts Film* (Jefferson, NC: McFarland, 2004) 86–87.

8. Marshall Julius, *Action! The Action Movie A–Z* (Bloomington, IN: Indiana University Press, 1996), 26–27.

9. Leon Hunt, *Kung Fu Cult Masters: From Bruce Lee to Crouching Tiger* (New York: Wallflower Press, 2003), 10.

10. Jeff Yang, *Eastern Standard Time: A Guide to Asian Influence on American Culture, From Astro Boy to Zen Buddhism*, 34–35.

Chapter 7

1. *E! True Hollywood Story*, "Jean-Claude Van Damme" (5/19/02)

2. Ibid.

3. Ibid.

4. Jean-Claude Van Damme (<www.imdb.com/name/nm0000241/bio>, accessed June 5, 2007).

5. Ibid.

6. The Van Damme films *Bloodsport* and *The Quest* have both given some degree of credit to Frank Dux, a California martial arts instructor — and in *Bloodsport* the Van Damme character is named Frank Dux — but Dux himself has attracted controversy in the martial arts community since several investigative journalists have questioned his claims to having been a world-class martial arts competitor and a government operative. Dux insists that the story of *Bloodsport* is about his real-life victory in the illegal Kumite tournament. Most martial artists claim that the tournament Dux is describing does not exist. Both the *Los Angeles Times* and *Soldier of Fortune* magazine have published investigative pieces alleging that Dux has falsified his military records and fabricated his own larger-than-life biography as a CIA operative. See also John Johnson, "NINJA: Hero or Master Fake? Others Kick Holes in Fabled Past of Woodland Hills Martial Arts Teacher," *Los Angeles Times*, May 1, 1988, Valley Edition, Metro, Part 2, page 4, as well as Larry Bailey, "Stolen Valor: Profiles of a Phony Hunter," *Soldier of Fortune*, November 1988, 58–61.

7. Frank Sanello, *Stallone: A Rocky Life* (Edinburgh: Mainstream Publishing, 1998), 156–160.

8. Jeff Yang, *Once Upon a Time in China: A Guide to Hong Kong, Taiwanese, and Mainland Chinese Cinema* (New York: Atria Books, 2003), 100.

9. *E! True Hollywood Story*, "Jean-Claude Van Damme" (5/19/02).

10. *E! True Hollywood Story*, "Steven Seagal" (12/22/02).

11. Ibid.

12. Steven Seagal Biography and Description (www.woofactor.com/celebrities/Steven_Seagal/biography>, accessed August 3, 2007).

13. Richard Corliss, "Seagal under Siege," *Time*, July 5, 1993 (<www.time.com>, accessed June 13, 2007).

14. David Halbfinger and Allison Hopeweiner, "Hollywood Waits to See Wiretapping Indictment," *New York Times*, October 19, 2005.

15. Steven Seagal, (<www.imdb.com/name/nm0000219/bio>, accessed August 3, 2007).

Chapter 8

1. *E! True Hollywood Story*, "Jean-Claude Van Damme" (5/19/02).

2. Brian Thomas, *VideoHound's Dragon:*

Asian Action and Cult Flicks (Detroit: Visible Ink Press, 2003), ix–xii.

3. Biography at (<www.cynthiarothrock. org>, accessed September 7, 2007).

4. Joshua Goldstein, *Drama Kings: Players and Publics in the Re-Creation of Peking Opera, 1870–1937* (Berkeley: University of California Press, 2007), 15.

5. Bruce Thomas, *Bruce Lee: Fighting Spirit* (Berkeley, CA: Frog, 1994), 237–239.

6. Jack Hunter, *Intercepting Fist: The Films of Bruce Lee and the Golden Age of Kung Fu Cinema* (London: Glitter Books, 2005), 50.

Chapter 9

1. Christopher Heard, *Ten Thousand Bullets: The Cinematic Journey of John Woo* (Los Angeles: Lone Eagle Publishing, 2000), 5.

2. Ibid., 3.

3. Ibid., 4.

4. Ibid., 5.

5. Ibid., 9.

6. Tony Williams, "John Woo," in *Fifty Contemporary Filmmakers*, edited by Yvonne Tasker (New York: Routledge, 2002), 404–405.

7. Christopher Heard, *Ten Thousand Bullets: The Cinematic Journey of John Woo*, 18.

8. Ibid., 41.

9. Leslie Cheung (<www.imdb.com/ name/nm0002000/>, accessed July 10, 2007).

10. Jeff Yang, *Once Upon a Time in China: A Guide to Hong Kong, Taiwanese, and Mainland Chinese Cinema* (New York: Atria Books, 2003), 86.

11. Bey Logan, *Hong Kong Action Cinema* (New York: Overlook Press, 1995), 110.

12. Ibid., 148.

13. Christopher Heard, *Ten Thousand Bullets: The Cinematic Journey of John Woo*, 111–112.

14. Ibid., 105–107.

15. Glyn White, "Quentin Tarantino," in *Fifty Contemporary Filmmakers*, edited by Yvonne Tasker (New York: Routledge, 2002), 440.

16. Christopher Heard, *Ten Thousand Bullets: The Cinematic Journey of John Woo*, 112.

17. Roger Ebert, "The Big Hit," review of *The Big Hit* (<http://rogerebert.suntimes. com>, April 24, 1998, accessed May 5, 2007).

18. Jeff Yang, *Once Upon a Time in China: A Guide to Hong Kong, Taiwanese, and Mainland Chinese Cinema*, 77–83.

19. Ibid.

20. Ibid.

21. Ibid.

Chapter 10

1. Jackie Chan and Jeff Yang, *I Am Jackie Chan: My Life in Action* (New York: Ballantine Books, 1998), 5.

2. Bey Logan, *Hong Kong Action Cinema* (New York: Overlook Press, 1995), 23.

3. Jackie Chan and Jeff Yang, *I Am Jackie Chan: My Life in Action*, 218–219.

4. Ibid.

5. Jeff Yang, *Once Upon a Time in China: A Guide to Hong Kong, Taiwanese, and Mainland Chinese Cinema* (New York: Atria Books, 2003), 65.

6. Fredrick Dannen and Barry Long, *Hong Kong Babylon* (New York: Hyperion, Miramax Books, 1997), 212.

7. Jackie Chan and Jeff Yang, *I Am Jackie Chan: My Life in Action*, 248.

8. Ibid., 302.

9. Ibid., 298.

10. Leon Hunt, "The Hong Kong/Hollywood Connection," in *Action and Adventure Cinema*, edited by Yvonne Tasker (New York: Routledge, 2004), 272–274.

11. Bey Logan, *Hong Kong Action Cinema*, 70.

12. Mark Gallagher, *Action Figures: Men, Action Films, and Contemporary Adventure Narratives* (New York: Palgrave MacMillan, 2006), 180–183.

13. Sammo Hung's involvement with Jet Li's *Once Upon a Time in China and America* is a subject of rumors and allegations, often by those wondering about the extent — or the tenuous state — of the friendship between Jackie Chan and Hung. Chan, after all, does not pull any punches in his recollections of having been tormented by Hung at the China Drama Academy and receiving abuse that went above and beyond regular discipline. He is likewise critical in several passages about the adult Hung and his character. But the point of the Jet Li issue is that Chan was alleged to have told only Hung about an idea for a comedy/martial arts/Western about a Chinese man losing his memory and wandering about in the Old West. Soon afterward, he was supposedly shocked to hear that Hung had signed on to direct Li's film and that the plot involved Li's losing his memory in the Old West. Later, Chan went on to make *Who*

Am I?, about an amnesiac, and *Shanghai Noon*.

14. As Chan writes in his autobiography, after a serious injury, Hung could not perform or exercise in any way for months. With a massive appetite, Hung quickly gained too much weight to be an effective stage performer and he left the Drama Academy.

Chapter 11

1. James Robert Parish, *Jet Li: A Biography* (New York: Thunder's Mouth Press, 2002), 85.
2. Ibid., 9.
3. Ibid., 160.
4. Ibid., 14.
5. Ibid., 25.
6. Ibid., 32.
7. Ibid., 12.
8. Ibid., 41.
9. Ibid., 60–65.
10. Lisa Morton, *The Cinema of Tsui Hark* (Jefferson, NC: McFarland, 2001), 195.
11. James Robert Parish, *Jet Li: A Biography*, 67.
12. Ibid., 153.
13. Ibid.
14. Lisa Morton, *The Cinema of Tsui Hark*, 198.
15. James Robert Parish, *Jet Li: A Biography*, 99. Li does not appear in the fourth Wong Fei Hung film made by Tsui Hark. After a falling out over his salary, Li left the franchise. He did take up the role for another director, however. Teaming up with Wong Jing, he played the noble martial artist in 1993's *Last Hero in China*. His co-star, Rosamund Kwan, also left Tsui's *Once Upon* series when Li did, although she did not appear with him in *Last Hero in China*. Once Li's differences with Tsui had been settled, he returned for *Once Upon a Time in China and America*, which Tsui produced and Sammo Hung directed. Rosamund Kwan joined him in that film.
16. Stefan Hammond, *Hollywood East: Hong Kong Movies and the People Who Make Them* (New York: McGraw Hill, 2000), 213.
17. In *Fearless*, Li plays the fabled, patriotic, early twentieth century Wu Shu instructor Huo Yuan Jia, the character Bruce Lee must avenge in *Fist of Fury*. Li, however, also appeared in a remake of *Fist of Fury*, called *Fist of Legend*, playing the Bruce Lee role — so, between the two films, Li plays both the murdered Wu Shu great and the student who avenges him.

Chapter 12

1. Jackie Chan's *Supercop* is sometimes titled *Police Story III: Supercop*. In Hong Kong films, sequels are not as tightly related as in Hollywood. Sometimes films are sold as sequels to something that had come before when, in fact, their plots have nothing to do with each other.
2. *Ghost in the Shell* is one of the landmark anime features of the 1990s, along with *Akira*, that helped ignite an enthusiastic American following of mature and philosophical anime. Most of the anime American adults showed particular interest in were the ones with cyberpunk-style, dystopian science fiction stories. Most of these films concerned themselves with the question of how we can still remain human once ever-more-advanced cybernetic technology starts taking over our bodies. This theme is especially close to the philosophical concern of French martial arts action specialist Olivier Gruner's *Nemesis*.
3. *Hung Faan Aau* (*Rumble in the Bronx*) (<www.imdb.com/title/tt0113326/fullcredits #cast>, accessed January 14, 2007).
4. Ian Haydn Smith, "Ang Lee," in *Fifty Contemporary Filmmakers*, edited by Yvonne Tasker (New York: Routledge, 2002), 234.
5. Ibid., 231.
6. Alan Morrison and Ron Wells, "Year of the Dragon," *Total Film*, 49: 60–6.
7. Stephen Hunter, "Hero: An Ending That Falls on its Own Sword," *Washington Post*, August 27, 2004, C01.
8. Jeff Yang, *Eastern Standard Time: A Guide to Asian Influence on American Culture, From Astro Boy to Zen Buddhism* (New York: Mariner Books, 1997), 104.
9. Ibid.
10. Donald Richie, *A Hundred Years of Japanese Film* (New York: Kodansha International, 2001), 236–241.
11. Patrick Drazen, *Anime Explosion: The What? Why? & Wow! of Japanese Animation* (Berkeley, CA: Stone Bridge Press), 3–15.
12. Ibid., 9.
13. Jeff Yang, *Eastern Standard Time: A Guide to Asian Influence on American Culture, From Astro Boy to Zen Buddhism*, 70.
14. Ibid.
15. Ibid., 60.

16. Voltron (<www.imdb.com/title/tt0472 429/>, accessed September 9, 2007).

17. Patrick Drazen, *Anime Explosion: The What? Why? & Wow! of Japanese Animation*, 3–15.

18. Ong-Bak (<www.imdb.com/title/tt03 68909/>, accessed July 15, 2007).

19. "Jackie Chan Says He Plugged Thai Tony Jaa for 'Rush Hour 3,' but He Didn't Sign On," *Associated Press*, September 20, 2006.

20. James Robert Parish, *Jet Li: A Biography* (New York: Thunder's Mouth Press, 2002), 91.

21. "Director Stephen Chow Talks Kung Fu Hustle" (<www.movieweb.com/news/68/ 7368.php, accessed April 9, 2007).

22. Jason Statham (<www.imdb.com/ name/nm0005458/>, accessed June 3, 2007).

23. David Gauntlett, *Moving Experiences: Understanding Television's Influences and Effects* (London: J. Libbey, 1995), 120.

Bibliography

Anderegg, Michael A. *Inventing Vietnam: The War in Film and Television.* Philadelphia: Temple University Press, 1991.

Anderson, Joseph L. *The Japanese Film: Art and Industry.* New York: Random House, 1960.

Arnold, Alan. *Once Upon a Galaxy: A Journal of the Making of "The Empire Strikes Back."* New York: Del Rey, 1980.

Bailey, Larry. "Stolen Valor: Profiles of a Phony Hunter." *Soldier of Fortune,* November 1988, 58–61.

Biskind, Peter. *Easy Riders, Raging Bulls: How the Sex-Drugs-and-Rock 'n' Roll Generation Saved Hollywood.* New York: Simon & Schuster, 1999.

Bogle, Donald. *Toms, Coons, Mulattoes, Mammies, and Bucks: An Interpretive History of Blacks in American Films.* New York: Continuum International Publishing Group, 2003.

Bordwell, David. *Planet Hong Kong: Popular Cinema and the Art of Entertainment.* Cambridge, MA: Harvard University Press, 2000.

Brown, Georgia. "Hard Target," review of *Hard Target* (Universal Pictures). *Village Voice,* 31 August 1993.

Brynner, Rock. *Yul: The Man Who Would Be King; A Memoir of Father and Son.* New York: Simon & Schuster, 1989.

Cawelti, John G. "Chinatown and Generic Transformation in Recent American Films." In *Film Theory and Criticism.* Edited by Gerald Mast, Marshall Cohen and Leo Braudy. New York: Oxford University Press, 1992.

Chan, Jackie, and Jeff Yang. *I Am Jackie Chan: My Life in Action.* New York: Ballantine Books, 1998.

Chow, David, and Richard Spangler. *Kung Fu: History, Philosophy, and Technique.* Hollywood, CA: Unique Publications, 1980.

Corr, William. *Adams the Pilot: The Life and Times of William Adams, 1564–1620.* New York: Routledge, 1995.

Cowie, Peter. *Revolution! The Explosion of World Cinema in the Sixties.* New York: Faber & Faber, 2005.

Dannen, Fredrick, and Barry Long. *Hong Kong Babylon.* New York: Hyperion, Miramax Books, 1997.

Devine, Jeremy M. *Vietnam at 24 Frames a Second: A Critical and Thematic Analysis of Over 400 Films About the Vietnam War.* Jefferson, NC: McFarland, 1995. Republished, Austin: University of Texas Press, 1999.

Dittmar, Linda, and Gene Michaud. *From Hanoi to Hollywood: The Vietnam War in American Film.* New Brunswick, NJ.: Rutgers University Press, 1991.

Donovan, Barna William. "The Essence of Action: Genre Theory and the Depiction of

Values, Gender and Violence in the American Action Film." *Communication Annual* (2005): 22–40.

Drazen, Patrick. *Anime Explosion: The What? Why? & Wow! of Japanese Animation*. Berkeley, CA: Stone Bridge Press, 2003.

Faludi, Susan. "The Masculine Mystique." *Esquire*, October 1996, 88.

_____. *Stiffed: The Betrayal of the American Man*. New York: William Morrow, 1999.

Feng, Peter X. *Screening Asian Americans*. New Brunswick, NJ: Rutgers University Press, 2002.

Fisher, Helen. *The First Sex: The Natural Talent of Women and How They Are Changing the World*. New York: Random House, 1999.

Fowles, Jib. *The Case for Television Violence*. Thousand Oaks, CA: Sage, 1999.

Frayling, Christopher. *Clint Eastwood*. London: Virgin Publishing, 1992.

Fu, Poshek, and David Desser. *The Cinema of Hong Kong: History, Arts, Identity*. New York: Cambridge University Press, 2002.

Galbraith, Stuart. *The Emperor and the Wolf: The Lives and Films of Akira Kurosawa and Toshiro Mifune*. New York: Faber & Faber, 2001.

Gallagher, Mark. *Action Figures: Men, Action Films, and Contemporary Adventure Narratives*. New York: Palgrave Macmillan, 2006.

Gauntlett, David. *Moving Experiences: Understanding Television's Influences and Effects*. London: J. Libbey, 1995.

Goldstein, Joshua. *Drama Kings: Players and Publics in the Re-Creation of Peking Opera, 1870–1937*. Berkeley: University of California Press, 2007.

Griffin, Nancy, and Kim Masters. *Hit and Run: How Jon Peters and Peter Guber Took Sony for a Ride in Hollywood*. New York: Simon & Schuster, 1996.

Halbfinger, David, and Allison Hopeweiner. "Hollywood Waits to See Wiretapping Indictment." *New York Times*, October 19, 2005.

Hammond, Stefan. *Hollywood East: Hong Kong Movies and the People Who Make Them*. New York: McGraw-Hill, 2000.

Heard, Christopher. *Ten Thousand Bullets: The Cinematic Journey of John Woo*. Los Angeles: Lone Eagle Publishing, 2000.

Hunt, Leon. *Kung Fu Cult Masters: From Bruce Lee to "Crouching Tiger."* New York: Wallflower Press, 2003.

_____. "The Hong Kong/Hollywood Connection." In *Action and Adventure Cinema*. Edited by Yvonne Tasker. New York: Routledge, 2004.

Hunter, Jack. *Intercepting Fist: The Films of Bruce Lee and the Golden Age of Kung Fu Cinema*. London: Glitter Books, 2005.

Hunter, Stephen. "Hero: An Ending That Falls on Its Own Sword." *Washington Post*, August 27, 2004, C01.

Jeffords, Susan. *Hard Bodies: Hollywood Masculinity in the Reagan Era*. New Brunswick, NJ: Rutgers University Press, 1994.

Johnson, John. "NINJA: Hero or Master Fake? Others Kick Holes in Fabled Past of Woodland Hills Martial Arts Teacher." *Los Angeles Times*, May 1, 1988, Valley Edition, Metro, Part 2, page 4.

Johnson, Nathan. *Zen Shaolin Karate: The Complete Practice, Philosophy and History*. North Clarendon, VT: Tuttle Publishing, 1994.

Julius, Marshall. *Action! The Action Movie A–Z*. Bloomington: Indiana University Press, 1996.

King, Neal. *Heroes in Hard Times: Cop Action Movies in the U.S.* Philadelphia: Temple University Press, 1999.

King, Stephen. *Danse Macabre*. New York: Berkley Books, 1980.

Koven, Mikel J. *Blaxploitation Films*. Harpenden: Pocket Essentials, 2001.

Kurosawa, Akira. *Something Like an Autobiography*. New York: Vintage, 1983.

Lee, Bruce. *The Tao of Jeet Kune Do.* Black Belt Communications, 1975.

Lee, Linda. *The Bruce Lee Story.* Ohara Publications, 1989.

Levy, Emanuel. "Hard Target," review of *Hard Target* (Universal Studios). *Variety*, 31 August 1993, 38.

Lochte, Dick. "Warren Murphy and His Heroic Oddballs." In *Murder off the Rack: Critical Studies of Ten Paperback Masters.* Edited by John L. Breen and Martin Harry Greenberg. Metuchen, NJ: Scarecrow Press, 1989.

Logan, Bey. *Hong Kong Action Cinema.* New York: Overlook Press, 1995.

Lott, M. Ray. *The American Martial Arts Film.* Jefferson, NC: McFarland, 2004.

Marchetti, Gina. "Action-Adventure as Ideology." In *Cultural Politics in Contemporary America.* Edited by Sut Jhally. London: Routledge, 1989.

Mason, R. H. P., and J. G. Caiger. *A History of Japan.* North Clarendon, VT: Tuttle Publishing, 1997.

McCarthy, Todd. "Last Action Hero," review of *Last Action Hero* (Columbia Pictures). *Variety*, 18 June 1993.

Meyers, Ric, Amy Harlib, Bill Palmer and Karen Palmer. *From Bruce Lee to the Ninjas: Martial Arts Movies.* New York: Citadel Press, 1986.

Morrison, Alan, and Ron Wells. "Year of the Dragon." *Total Film*, 49: 60–6.

Morton, Lisa. *The Cinema of Tsui Hark.* Jefferson, NC: McFarland, 2001.

Murray, Will. "The Executioner Phenomenon." In *Murder Off the Rack: Critical Studies of Ten Paperback Masters.* Edited by Jon L. Breen and Martin Harry Greenberg. Metuchen, NJ: Scarecrow Press, 1989.

Newcomb, Horace, and Robert S. Alley. *The Producer's Medium: Conversations with Creators of American TV.* New York: Oxford University Press, 1985.

Norris, Chuck, and Joe Hyams. *The Secret of Inner Strength.* Boston: Little, Brown, 1988.

Norris, Chuck, and Ken Abraham. *Against All Odds: My Story.* Nashville: Broadman & Holman Publishers, 2004.

Parish, James Robert. *Jet Li: A Biography.* New York: Thunder's Mouth Press, 2002.

Prince, Stephen. *The Warrior's Camera: The Cinema of Akira Kurosawa.* Princeton, NJ: Princeton University Press, 1999.

Richie, Donald. *The Films of Akira Kurosawa.* Berkeley: University of California Press, 1996.

_____. *A Hundred Years of Japanese Film.* New York: Kodansha International, 2001.

Sanello, Frank. *Stallone: A Rocky Life.* Edinburgh: Mainstream Publishing, 1998.

Schatz, Thomas. *The Genius of the System: Hollywood Filmmaking in the Studio Era.* New York: Henry Holt, 1988.

Schickel, Richard. *Clint Eastwood.* New York: Knopf, 1996.

Scorsese, Martin. "Milestones." *Time*, September 21, 1998.

Smith, Ian Haydn. "Ang Lee." In *Fifty Contemporary Filmmakers.* Edited by Yvonne Tasker. New York: Routledge, 2002.

Suid, Lawrence H. *Guts and Glory: The Making of the American Military Image in Film.* Lexington: University Press of Kentucky, 2002.

Taylor, Mark P. *The Vietnam War in History, Literature and Film.* Tuscaloosa: University of Alabama Press, 2003.

Thomas, Brian. *VideoHound's Dragon: Asian Action & Cult Flicks.* Detroit: Visible Ink Press, 2003.

Thomas, Bruce. *Bruce Lee: Fighting Spirit.* Berkeley, CA: Frog, 1994.

Tiger, Lionel. *The Decline of Males.* New York: St. Martin's Griffin, 1999.

Wall, Robert. *Who's Who in the Martial Arts.* Los Angeles: R. A. Wall Investments, 1985.

Wetmore, Kevin J. *The Empire Triumphant: Race, Religion and Rebellion in the Star Wars Films.* Jefferson, NC: McFarland, 2005.

White, Glyn. "Quentin Tarantino." In *Fifty Contemporary Filmmakers.* Edited by Yvonne Tasker. New York: Routledge, 2002.

Williams, Tony. "John Woo." In *Fifty Contemporary Filmmakers*. Edited by Yvonne Tasker. New York: Routledge, 2002.

Yang, Jeff. *Eastern Standard Time: A Guide to Asian Influence on American Culture, from Astro Boy to Zen Buddhism*. New York: Mariner Books, 1997.

_____. *Once Upon a Time in China: A Guide to Hong Kong, Taiwanese and Mainland Chinese Cinema*. New York: Atria Books, 2003.

Additional Resources — Documentaries

The Art of Action: Martial Arts in Motion Pictures. Starz Entertainment Documentary, 2002.

Bercovici, Eric. *Shogun* DVD documentary.

Bruce Lee: A Warrior's Journey. Starz Entertainment Documentary, 2000.

E! True Hollywood Story: "Jean-Claude Van Damme" (5/19/02).

E! True Hollywood Story: "Steven Seagal" (12/22/02).

The Master: Chang Cheh. Documentary for *The One-Armed Swordsman* DVD.

— Internet

Cheung, Leslie. <www.imdb.com/name/nm0002000/>.

Corliss, Richard. "Seagal under Siege." *Time*, July 5, 1993, <www.time.com>.

"Director Stephen Chow Talks Kung Fu Hustle." <www.movieweb.com/news/68/7368. php>, accessed April 9, 2007.

Ebert, Roger. "The Big Hit," review of *The Big Hit*. April 24, 1998, <http://rogerebert.sun times.com>, accessed May 5, 2007.

Hung Faan Aau (Rumble in the Bronx). <www.imdb.com/title/tt0113326/fullcredits#cast>, accessed January 14, 2007.

Ong-Bak. <www.imdb.com/title/tt0368909/>, accessed July 15, 2007.

Rothrock, Cynthia. <www.cynthiarothrock.org>.

Seagal, Steven. <www.imdb.com/name/nm0000219/bio>, accessed June 13, 1007.

Seagal, Steven. [Biography and Description]. <www.woofactor.com/celebrities/Steven_Sea gal/biography>.

Statham, Jason. <www.imdb.com/name/nm0005458/bio>, accessed June 3, 2007.

Van Damme, Jean-Claude. <www.imdb.com/name/nm0000241/bio>, accessed June 5, 2007.

Voltron. <www.imdb.com/title/tt0472429/>, accessed September 9, 2007.

Index